*Learn Active Directory Management
in a Month of Lunches*

Learn Active Directory Management in a Month of Lunches

RICHARD SIDDAWAY

MANNING

SHELTER ISLAND

For online information and ordering of this and other Manning books, please visit
www.manning.com. The publisher offers discounts on this book when ordered in quantity.
For more information, please contact

    Special Sales Department
    Manning Publications Co.
    20 Baldwin Road
    PO Box 261
    Shelter Island, NY 11964
    Email: orders@manning.com

Manning Publications Co.
20 Baldwin Road
PO Box 261
Shelter Island, NY 11964

Development editor:	Suzie Pitzen
Copyeditor:	Jodie Allen
Proofreader:	Melody Dolab
Typesetter:	Marija Tudor
Cover designer:	Leslie Haimes

ISBN: 9781617291197
Printed in the United States of America
1 2 3 4 5 6 7 8 9 10 – MAL – 19 18 17 16 15 14

To my children, Robert and Alexander
You make me so proud

brief contents

contents

preface

I've worked with many organizations over the last 10 years. In that time I've realized that Active Directory administration is a critical function for the continued health of a Windows environment. Unfortunately, many AD administrators aren't taught how to perform these tasks. An even worse scenario is when they are taught bad practices which have become ingrained in the organization. There are many administrators who find themselves responsible for administering an Active Directory without the skills and knowledge to do so.

This book looks at AD administration from a different viewpoint than most books on the subject. It concentrates on the day-to-day administration tasks *you* need to perform to get *your* job done. There's some theory, but just enough to explain why things are done the way they are. You can always learn the rest of the theory once you've put the fires out.

I've taken a pragmatic approach to the contents and kept a rigorous focus on the information you need to complete a task. Many of the administration tasks can be completed using GUI tools or through Windows PowerShell. I've tried to show both where possible—though some tasks only have a single possible way to complete them.

I've brought some of the experience I've had building Active Directories and troubleshooting AD in various organizations. Hopefully, this will help you avoid some of the pitfalls and problems I've seen.

The book is designed to be a tutorial, so work through the book, but also keep it close by as a reference for when you need it. My hope is that it will help you over some of the learning hurdles and help you become a skilled AD administrator.

Most of all, enjoy.

about this book

Most of what you'll need to know about this book is in chapter 1, but there are a few things that need to be mentioned up front.

First, this book is intended for the IT Pro that needs to learn about managing Active Directory. It's not a reference book. It won't teach you how to design a new Active Directory. It will teach you to manage your Active Directory and supply the theory you need to accomplish the management tasks. Most people learn best by using multiple techniques. I strongly recommend that you complete the exercises in each chapter and the lab section at the end of each chapter. You'll be "learning by reading" and "learning by doing."

Second, read the book from beginning to end. I've put the most common AD management tasks (user and group management) in the early chapters. This will enable you to become immediately effective as an Active Directory administrator. The later chapters build on this knowledge. Taking the chapters in a random order will provide a diminished learning experience.

Third, I'll show you how to complete the management tasks using a variety of tools. AD Administrative Center and AD Users and Computers are GUI tools that have been available through several versions of Active Directory. The other tool I'll show is Windows PowerShell which is Microsoft's scripting and automation language. Automation through Windows PowerShell is a topic that administrators are going to find increasingly important to their careers, and if you haven't learned how to use it, I recommend that you do. I concentrate on AD management in this book, so for the most part I just use PowerShell at the command line. You shouldn't have any difficulty following the commands, but if you want to learn more about PowerShell, I very strongly recommend *Learn Windows PowerShell 3 in a Month of Lunches* by Don Jones and Jeff Hicks (Manning, 2012).

Downloads

You will find the following available for download from the publisher's website at www.manning.com/siddaway3 or www.manning.com/LearnActiveDirectoryManage mentinaMonthofLunches:

- Code listings from the individual chapters
- Sample answers to the lab questions in each chapter

The book's web page at http://morelunches.com contains additional resources and information.

Author Online

Purchase of this book includes free access to a private web forum run by Manning Publications where you can make comments about the book, ask technical questions, and receive help from the author and other users. To access the forum and subscribe to it, visit www.manning.com/siddaway3. This page provides information on how to get on the forum once you're registered, what kind of help is available, and the rules of conduct on the forum.

Manning's commitment to readers is to provide a venue for meaningful dialogue between individual readers and between readers and the author. It is not a commitment to any specific amount of participation on the part of the authors, whose contribution to the forum remains voluntary (and unpaid). Let your voice be heard, and keep the author on their toes!

The Author Online forum and the archives of previous discussions will be accessible from the publisher's website as long as the book is in print.

about the author

Richard Siddaway is based in the U.K. and is currently working on automation projects for Kelway. With over 25 years of experience in various aspects of IT, Richard specializes in the Microsoft environment at an architectural level—especially around Active Directory (AD), Exchange, SQL Server, and infrastructure optimization.

Much of his recent experience has involved Active Directory migrations and optimizations, which often include Exchange. Richard has hands-on administration experience and is involved in implementation activity, in addition to filling architectural and design roles. He has extensive experience specifying, designing, and implementing high-availability solutions for a number of versions of the Windows platform, especially for Exchange and SQL Server.

Richard is always looking for the opportunity to automate a process, preferably with PowerShell. Automation has become the focus of Richard's recent work.

Microsoft has recognized his technical expertise and community activities by presenting a Microsoft Most Valued Professional award. Richard has presented to The PowerShell Summit in North America, The Technical Experts conference in the USA and Europe, the Directory Experts Conference, at various events at Microsoft in the UK and Europe, and for other user groups worldwide. Richard has a number of articles and technical publications to his credit including *PowerShell in Practice* (Manning, 2010) and *PowerShell and WMI* (Manning, 2012). He is a coauthor of *PowerShell in Depth: An administrator's guide* (Manning, 2013) and a coeditor and coauthor of *PowerShell Deep Dives* (Manning, 2013).

acknowledgments

I'm always surprised at the number of people it takes to actually produce a book like this. My name is on the cover, but there is a whole list of people who contributed behind the scenes. This is one of the best bits to write: where I get to thank them for the hard work they've put in on this book.

I have to start with Don Jones, who originally put the idea for the book into my head and has been a huge help in adapting to a very different writing style.

The Active Directory and PowerShell teams also need thanking because without their products I'd have nothing to write about.

The members of the team that Manning put together for this book have been superb, as usual. Their professionalism is second to none and they have consistently pushed me to produce the best book I can. I can't imagine what the book would have been like without them. Many thanks to Marjan Bace, Michael Stephens, Suzie Pitzen, Melody Dolab, Kevin Sullivan, Ozren Harlovic, Mary Piergies, Maureen Spencer, Christina Rudloff, Nermina Miller, Elizabeth Lexleigh, and Cynthia Kane.

There were a number of reviews of the manuscript during its development. The individual reviewers gave their time to read and comment on the book and I'm very grateful for the input. They helped improve the book by making me think about their comments, so many thanks to Allan Miller, Chad McAuley, James Arthur, James Berkenbile, Jason Helmick, Jeff Goldschrafe, Jeremiah Griswold, Joseph Moody, Ken Baker, Lincoln Bovee, Margriet Bruggeman, Mark Allen, Michael Bridge, Nikander Bruggeman, Saptarshi Kar, Tiru Srikantha, and Tom Geudens.

Aleksandar Nikolić provided the technical review and deserves a special mention and thanks for his attention to detail in testing all of the code.

During the MEAP process, a forum exists for readers to post comments about the early versions of the chapters and to ask questions. Thank you to everyone who took the time to post—your comments have been considered and added to the book where appropriate.

Notwithstanding the input of so many people, any errors of omission or commission are still mine.

A final thanks must go to my family, friends, and colleagues who've not only put up with me during the writing of the book but actively supported me.

Part 1

Managing Active Directory Data

This section of the book covers the fundamentals of managing your Active Directory data:

- Users
- Groups
- Computers
- Organizational Units

Chapter 1 starts the process by providing an overview of the book, along with required background information on Active Directory. Don't worry; this is a practical book, and the theory will be kept to a minimum.

Chapter 2 starts you on this process by showing how to create user accounts. Creating 1 user account is straightforward, but how do you create 100 in a batch? The answer is in chapter 2. When your user accounts have been created, you have to start managing them—modifying and even deleting properties. Chapter 3 provides the processes and information to perform these tasks.

Users are put into groups to make the management of permissions easier and more efficient. You'll learn how to create the different types of groups in chapter 4. This chapter also contains information on managing groups, especially group membership.

Chapter 5 discusses troubleshooting users and groups. What are the major problems you'll see when managing users and groups? How do you overcome them? This chapter has the answers.

Computer accounts usually create less work than users and groups, but you do need to know how to create them, as shown in chapter 6. There's also a section on troubleshooting computer account-related issues.

Part 1 closes in chapter 7 with a look at organizational units (OUs), which are used to subdivide Active Directory. The chapter also covers the creation and management of OUs, as well as how to protect the OU (and its contents) from accidentally being deleted. "Oops, I just deleted an OU with 500 user accounts in it" is not something you ever want to hear. Chapter 7 will show you how to prevent that from happening in your organization.

The topics in Part 1 cover the core areas of your day-to-day administration tasks when managing Active Directory. Let's start by seeing how to manage user accounts.

Before you begin

1

Imagine you work in a medium-size organization—about 3000 users, each with a PC, and 300 servers. Each user needs access to multiple servers. You wouldn't even want to think about the chaos, never mind the work, involved in trying to manage user logon accounts and permissions across all of those individual systems. And by the time you get to organizations with 10,000, 50,000, or even 100,000 users, it's impossible to manage each computer individually.

Active Directory (AD) provides a centralized service that links all of those machines and enables a user to log on and access any of them *provided they have been granted permission to do so.*

Imagine again that you arrive at work one Monday morning and are told "Congratulations, you're our new AD administrator!" You're now responsible for all those users, PCs, and servers. After taking a big gulp, you wonder where to start. You need to know how to administer Active Directory. You can live without the theory for now, but what do you need to do to keep things working? This book will show you. It's a straightforward guide to administering Active Directory delivered in lunch-size pieces, concentrating on what you need to do your job now.

Active Directory is a big subject, but to quote one of my favorite films, we'll "start out easy." This chapter is that start, where you discover just what Active Directory does for your organization and how the book will deliver on the promise to teach you how to administer Active Directory in a series of chapters that each fits into a lunch break. I've been working with Active Directory since the beta releases of Windows 2000. It's quite a shock to realize that this technology, which is fundamental to Windows environments, has been around for 14 years. Even after all that time, users frequently ask two questions:

- Why do I need Active Directory?
- What does it do for me?

Let's answer those questions so you know why you're doing all of this work.

1.1   *AD core deliverables*

Active Directory may seem like a big, scary technology that's difficult to understand. There are lots of different bits to Active Directory that don't seem to be related and all do different things.

> **NOTE**   Active Directory is part of the class of products known as Directory Services. Other products in this category include Novell's eDirectory and Red Hat's Directory Server. Some applications, such as Lotus (now IBM) Domino, have their own built-in Directory Service. In a Windows environment you'll use Active Directory even if other products are also in use.

It's not really scary, as you'll appreciate by the end of the book. Let's think about the past for a minute. When computers first came into big organizations, usually there was only one per organization and it was known as a mainframe. Many organizations still use this type of computer for big number-crunching operations. One computer meant it was relatively easy to give people identities so they could log on and work. And controlling who could access what was relatively easy to maintain on a single machine.

In a very small organization with one or only a few computers it'd still be possible to follow that model, but times have changed for most organizations.

Remember our definition: Active Directory provides a centralized service that links all machines in an organization and allows a user to log on and access any of them *they have been granted permission to do so*.

That last part is very, very important. Users must be granted permission to access things like file shares, databases, and even their mailboxes. Technically, we're talking about authentication and authorization. Authentication happens first, so we'll look at that next.

1.1.1   *Authentication*

Authentication, in AD terms, is the act of proving that you are who you say you are. This happens once when you first log on in the morning. You come in, boot up your machine, type in your logon name and password, and then you can get to your data.

There are other ways of proving who you are. Your organization could use smart cards or tokens sent to your phone, or you could have a machine that recognizes your fingerprints (biometric). You could even use a combination of these methods (known as multi-factor authentication) and passwords. Authentication comes down to three things:

- Something you know—login ID and password
- Something you have—smart card or soft token
- Something you are—fingerprint or other biometrics

I'm not going to cover the whole authentication process in detail, but there are a few things you need to know in the context of Active Directory:

- You're logging on to the domain, not an individual computer.
- Active Directory uses the Kerberos protocol for authentication. Kerberos is an industry standard protocol. Details are available from http://technet.microsoft .com/en-us/library/hh831553.aspx.
- Time synchronization within your Active Directory is important because the time stamp is used during the authentication process. If your PC's time is more than five minutes different from the domain controller, your authentication attempt will be rejected (time zones are managed automatically, so don't worry about them). The computer's clock will drift over time. I've seen cases where it's been wrong by hours. In those cases authentication wouldn't be possible. Time synchronization overcomes these problems.

Once you've authenticated to Active Directory, it's time to get to the data you need. But have you been authorized to access that data?

1.1.2 Authorization

Authorization is the act of granting users appropriate access to resources—such as file shares, databases, applications, and mailboxes—once they've authenticated themselves to Active Directory. The concept of authorization is simply one of proving you have permission to do something.

To simplify the process, when you log on a token is created on your local machine that contains your group memberships, privileges, and rights. This is presented to resources that you're trying to access. The system will check the token to see if your permissions allow you access to the file or other resource, and either grant or deny access based on the data presented in your token.

If you attempt to access a resource (for example, a file share, mailbox, or printer) on a remote machine, a local access token is created on that machine. The remote system's security system will use the token to determine if you're allowed to access the requested resource. This is an important point: *access tokens are never transmitted across the network from one machine to another.*

Authentication and authorization are combined into the concept of identity management. This identity management service is what Active Directory provides for your organization. To supply this service, it needs to store data and have a way of providing the service to the users.

You now know what Active Directory does for your organization. There are a few pieces of terminology and background information that you need to have before we move on.

1.1.3 AD definitions

This book isn't designed to be a full tutorial on AD theory, but there are some definitions and concepts that you need to be familiar with before you launch into administering Active Directory.

NOTE These definitions and concepts are only to get you started. Other AD components are defined in their appropriate chapters.

FOREST

The *forest* is the whole of your Active Directory. It can contain one or more domains arranged in trees (that's why it's called a forest). The forest is named after the first domain created in the forest (known as the root domain, which can't be changed).

All domains in a forest share a common Configuration container (for instance, they contain information on AD sites like services such as Exchange and AD partitions) and a common schema. The domains are linked together by transitive trusts that are automatically created when the domains are created.

NOTE *Transitive* means that if A trusts B and B trusts C, then A also trusts C.

The forest is the security boundary for Active Directory, which means you can't set permissions outside the forest, and objects outside the forest aren't granted permissions inside the forest. There are exceptions to those statements where you create trusts to other forests, but we'll get to that later.

Most organizations only need a single forest.

DOMAIN

A *domain* is a container for the objects you'll work with—users, computers, groups, and so on. The domain provides a number of boundaries within the organization:

- *It's an administration boundary.* Domain administrators don't have permissions in other domains.
- *It's a security administration boundary.* Permissions applied within the domain can't affect objects outside the domain.
- *It's a policy application boundary.* Best practice is to limit the application of Group Policy to a single domain. (See chapter 2. Group Policy is also covered in detail in chapters 8 and 9.) Applying policies across domains will slow processing and make administration much harder.

A domain has a fully qualified Domain Name System (DNS) name as its unique identifier.

Domains can be arranged in a hierarchy (trees) with parent-child relationships. These relationships don't have any administration connotation; an administrator in a parent domain doesn't automatically get administrator rights in any child domains. Most organizations only require a single domain.

ORGANIZATIONAL UNIT

An organizational unit (OU) is a container within a domain that can be used to hold user, computer, group, and other OU objects. There are two main reasons to create an OU:

1 To control the delegation of administrative privileges—that is, a certain group of administrators can only control the users, groups, and computers in a certain OU.

2 To control the application of Group Policy.

Domains are inflexible objects, and reorganizing the domains in a forest is a major undertaking. In contrast, reorganizing the OUs (and their contents) within a domain is a relatively straightforward matter.

> **TIP** If you think of OUs as being analogous to folders in the file system, you'll have a good idea of what they do.

OUs were stated to be containers for other objects. Just to complicate matters, you'll also find objects called containers in your Active Directory that are created with the domain. There are a number of these, but the ones you're most likely to come across are

- Built-in, which stores a number of the default groups.
- Users, which stores other default groups, especially the Domain Admins, Enterprise Admins, and Schema Admins. It's also the default location for the creation of new users if a specific OU isn't given.
- Computers, which is empty when the domain is created but is the default location for the creation of computer accounts when a new machine is joined to the domain.

The major differences between a container and an OU are that Group Policy cannot be applied to a container and child OUs can't be created within a container.

> **TIP** Think of the AD structures outlined in this section as analogous to a Russian nesting doll. Forests contain domains, which contain OUs, which contain users, groups, and computers.

1.2 Is this book for you?

Active Directory is a huge subject. It's a relatively easy matter to build up a library of AD books that span several feet of your bookshelf. In those books, you'll find a lot of theoretical background information, long discussions on designing Active Directory from scratch, and information on integrating other technologies, such as Exchange.

This isn't a lot of help to you as a new administrator. You need to know how to do your job now. In this book you'll find information on the day-to-day administration of Active Directory. It's not that I don't think the other information is important, but the book is designed for IT pros new to working with Active Directory—that is, someone in the situation described in the introduction to this chapter.

There will be occasional trips into theory, but only where it's absolutely necessary for your understanding. The goal is to enable you to administer your Active Directory. By the end of the book you'll be comfortable using the standard GUI tools to perform administrative tasks and you'll have been introduced to using command-line tools such as PowerShell. You'll be an effective and productive AD administrator in your environment.

1.3   *How to use this book*

This book is designed to be read sequentially, one chapter per day. It doesn't have to be read during your lunch break, but each chapter should only take 40 minutes or so to read, leaving 20 minutes to eat your sandwich and practice what you've learned.

MAIN CHAPTERS

Of the 22 chapters in this book, chapters 2 to 20 contain the main content:

- Part 1 (chapters 1 to 7) covers administering the data in your Active Directory—users, groups, computers, and organizational units.
- Part 2 (chapters 8 to 10) shows how to administer Group Policy and fine-grained password policies.
- Part 3 (chapters 11 to 18) discusses the AD service itself, covering domain controllers, DNS, trusts, replication, the AD topology, and protecting Active Directory.
- Part 4 (chapters 19 to 22) teaches how to troubleshoot, maintain, and monitor your Active Directory. Chapter 21 includes a final exam and some topics that you should investigate including technologies that rely on Active Directory. Cloud computing is growing in importance, and chapter 22 shows how your Active Directory can be extended into the cloud to enable your organization to take advantage of recent advancements, such as Infrastructure as a Service and Software as a Service.
- Two appendices are provided that cover searching Active Directory and give an overview of AD migrations and upgrades.

That's just about a month of lunches. Try to maintain that schedule as closely as you can. It's more important to your learning to complete the practice labs in each chapter than to cram another chapter's worth of reading into your break. Not every chapter will require a full hour, so sometimes you'll have time to enjoy your lunch before heading back to work.

HANDS-ON LABS

The main chapters contain some lab work. This is an essential part of your learning process. You'll get instructions and maybe even the odd hint, but the answers aren't printed in the book. You'll find sample answers in the download from the book's website, (http://morelunches.com), but it's better if you try to complete the lab yourself rather than relying on reading my answers.

The first task in any lab section will be to complete any "Try it now" sections in the chapter if you haven't already done so. There may be a hint or two thrown in to help you set off in the right direction. After that, you're on your own.

Everything you need to complete a lab is in the chapter in which it occurs or in earlier chapters (that might be where a hint comes into play). *There are no trick questions.*

The labs have been independently tested to ensure they'll work for you (unless your environment is really weird). I'll provide sample answers in the download from the book's website, but remember that I don't know your environment, so don't expect the answers to match exactly.

SUPPLEMENTARY MATERIALS

The book's website contains additional content, including

- Sample answers to the lab questions in each chapter.
- Code listings from the individual chapters so you don't need to type them in yourself.
- Links to further reference material.
- Links to my blog that contains many sample scripts for AD automation.
- A discussion forum for the book. I'll check this on a regular basis, but I can't guarantee the speed of response because I also have a day job.

You can contact me through the forum, or via my blog at http://msmvps.com/blogs/ RichardSiddaway/Default.aspx.

IDEAS FOR ON YOUR OWN

Many of the chapters conclude with ideas for further exploration on your own. Try to complete these as you can. The tasks aren't necessary, but they'll help to extend your AD knowledge.

GOING FURTHER

Chapter 21 is a final practical review of your AD skills. This chapter also outlines some more advanced topics to provide a framework for further study. Chapter 22 shows you how Active Directory extends into the cloud. Your organization can take advantage of cloud-based computing and still retain control of its Active Directory.

ABOVE AND BEYOND

As I mentioned earlier, Active Directory is a huge subject. As we progress through the book, there will be times when we go off path a bit to cover some interesting information that's useful but not essential. This will often be of the "Why does it work this way?" type of discussion. These sections will be short and can be skipped if you want, because this is a practical book, not a theoretical text. You can always come back and read them another day.

1.4　*Creating your lab environment*

This is a practical book. You'll be getting your hands dirty. That means you need somewhere to practice. Your first thought may be to create an area in your production Active Directory that you can use. *This is generally a bad idea.* I really can't emphasize enough that you shouldn't practice the things you'll learn in this book in your production environment. Just think of the consequences when you get to the section on deleting user accounts and you delete the boss's account rather than the test account you just created.

You need a lab environment to work through the practical examples in this book. My recommendation is that you create some virtual machines to work with. If you're lucky, your organization will have a test area in which you can create some virtual machines; otherwise you'll need to create your own lab. You'll need

- To get permission to create your test lab if you're doing this on your company's network.
- A machine to run your virtualization technology. I use Microsoft's Hyper-V, but you can use whatever you want. A spare desktop would be sufficient if you can get sufficient memory into it.
- Two virtual machines to act as domain controllers. You need two so that you can learn about replication. Instructions for promoting the systems to domain controllers are provided in chapter 11.
- Your virtual environment should have enough resources to enable you to create a couple of additional virtual machines as required.
- I recommend Windows Server 2012 or Windows Server 2012 R2 as the operating system for your virtual machines (a time-limited trial version can be downloaded from the Microsoft website at http://technet.microsoft.com/en-us/evalcenter/hh670538.aspx). You could use Windows Server 2008 R2, but you'll miss out on a few pieces of functionality. These differences will be covered in the appropriate chapters.
- Make sure that the fully qualified domain name (FQDN) of your forest doesn't conflict with anything in your environment. I would suggest using `ADLunches.test`. I would strongly recommend keeping the name simple. My test lab is named manticore.org, which I will use throughout the book.
- Use a NetBIOS name for your domain that matches your FQDN. If you use a FQDN of `ADLunches.test`, then use `ADLunches` for the NetBIOS name.

1.5   *Being immediately effective*

The primary goal of the book is for you to be immediately effective in your role as an AD administrator. The next chapter starts that process by showing you how to create new user accounts. Along with subsequent chapters, it's constructed around the tasks you need to perform in your environment. The chapters, with reinforcement from the labs, enable you to learn the skills needed to perform specific, everyday administrative tasks.

There may be a little bit of theory occasionally, but every chapter concentrates on the practical side. Given the choice, you'll get practical advice and information rather than theory. If there's theory information that I think you may need, I'll provide references for you to look it up yourself or cover it in the download material from the book's website.

That's enough background. I'm not going to provide a lab for this chapter. Enjoy your lunch, because tomorrow we look at creating user accounts.

Creating user accounts

2

Users are the main reason for your job, and according to some administrators, the greatest bane of their existence. You'll spend a lot of time administering user accounts during your career as an AD administrator.

User and computer accounts

Everyone logging on to a network requires a user account. These are the objects you'll work with the most because user accounts can be quite volatile with leavers, joiners, changes, and password resets. The volatility level relative to other AD objects is illustrated in figure 2.1.

> **NOTE** Computer accounts are a specialized form of user account, even though they're treated separately in this book. In most organizations they're put into separate organizational units (OUs) to make the Group Policy Object (GPO) application simpler. GPO is a way to centrally configure and manage the settings and security of computers and machine configuration made available to the user population. You'll learn about the details of GPOs in chapters 8 and 9.

As well as general user accounts, you may have accounts for

- Group or other specialized mailboxes
- Service accounts

Chapter 3 covers the anatomy of user account objects and the techniques you can use to modify them.

11

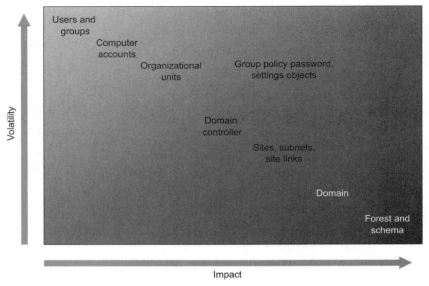

Figure 2.1   Volatility changes to AD objects and the impact of those changes

There are some management tasks involved; for example, setting permissions that are better performed on groups of users rather than on individual users. Groups are covered in chapters 4 and 5. User accounts are the most volatile of AD objects, and, with the exception of a few high-profile people in your organization, have the lowest impact if something goes wrong with them. Figure 2.1 illustrates and compares the subjective volatility and impact of the most common AD objects.

Figure 2.1 shows that modifications to users and groups occur frequently but have a low impact. Modifications to the forest or schema are very infrequent but potentially have a huge impact. Don't worry about this. Changing things like the forest, schema, or sites and subnets needs special permission—membership in the Enterprise Admins and Schema Admins groups. Membership in these groups should be under tight change control to protect the environment and the administrators. Without those permissions, you can't do anything to this part of AD—remember, you need to be authorized before you can do anything.

This is where you start to get your hands dirty and work with AD objects. In this chapter you'll learn how to create user accounts. You'll find that this is a common job in all but the smallest organizations. Active Directory has a few built-in accounts that are created when you install the first domain controller, but all other accounts have to be created by you, the administrator. You can't administer the accounts until you've created them, so this is an essential first step.

> **NOTE** Some specialized accounts and groups may be created by the installation of Microsoft products. The best advice for those accounts is to let the application create them and leave them alone.

The usual starting point is to create each new user account from scratch. This can be performed using GUI tools or PowerShell. One alternative, used in many organizations, is to use a template from which to create new user accounts. The template could be a standard user account or a specially created account that's used only as a template.

Large organizations with a significant amount of user turnover may need to look at performing the bulk creation of user accounts. This technique scales from one to many. A friend of mine works at a major British university and is responsible for creating over 7000 new accounts per year. He has only a few weeks to achieve this between the publication of entrance examination results and the start of the new academic year. He uses a highly automated bulk-creation system.

The final topic in this chapter is Managed Service accounts. These were introduced in Windows Server 2008 R2 and are intended for services such as Exchange or SQL Server. Resetting the password for service accounts can cause issues with the service. A Managed Service account can manage its own password, which can save you time, effort, and grief.

Your starting point for working with user accounts is creating new accounts, discussed next.

2.1 Creating new user accounts

You'll find there's a continual need to create new user accounts in Active Directory. All organizations have some rate of personnel turnover, with new joiners arriving periodically. The rate of change is dependent on the size of your organization and the stability of the user population.

> **TIP** Try to discover the personnel turnover rate in your organization. You may be able to use the information to plan your work better if you know the frequency of new users arriving, especially if the rate changes on a seasonal basis.

Whatever the turnover rate, at some point you'll need to create new users. A user account can be created using GUI tools or PowerShell.

AD management tools

Appendix A provides details on the tools you can use to manage Active Directory user accounts. If you're not familiar with the tools shown in this chapter, I recommend reading appendix A before proceeding.

The Active Directory Administrative Center (ADAC) was first introduced in Windows Server 2008 R2. It sits over the Active Directory PowerShell cmdlets (commands) and uses them in the background. An enhancement for Windows Server 2012 is that the PowerShell commands are now exposed as a learning tool. You can copy the PowerShell script and use it as the starting point of your own code. ADAC enables you to work with user and computer accounts, groups, and OUs. I recommend using ADAC if you have access to it.

(continued)

Active Directory Users and Computers (ADUC) is one of the tools from the initial version of Active Directory (Windows 2000). It serves a similar purpose to the ADAC in that you can manage user and computer accounts, groups, and OUs. There are still a few tasks that you can perform in ADUC that you can't perform in ADAC.

You'll also learn how to administer Active Directory using PowerShell. Starting in Windows Server 2008 R2, a PowerShell module (set of commands) is available for administering Active Directory. The functionality was enhanced in Windows Server 2012 and Windows Server 2012 R2. This functionality is also available as a separate download for Windows Server 2008.

The AD module is loaded into PowerShell using this command:

```
Import-Module ActiveDirectory
```

You need to run PowerShell with elevated privileges (Run as Administrator) to gain the maximum benefit from the AD module. The individual commands will be explained as you use them in this and subsequent chapters.

Do you know the information you require to create a new user? The minimum mandatory information required is similar in each case, as shown in table 2.1.

Table 2.1   **Minimum mandatory information required to create a new user account. The container is implicitly required when using GUI tools because you right-click on the container to initiate the process.**

Attribute	ADAC	ADUC	PowerShell	Must be unique
samAccountName	Yes	Yes	Yes	Yes, across the forest
Name	Yes	Yes, as full name	Yes	Yes, within the OU or container
Password		Yes, must comply with complexity settings		No
Container			Yes	

ADAC and PowerShell can create a user account without a password, but that account will not be enabled. A password must be supplied before the account can be used.

NOTE   PowerShell will create a user account when given just the name. It sets the samAccountName to be the same as the name and creates the account in the Users container.

Note the uniqueness constraints in the last column of table 2.1. The samAccountName must be unique across the forest because it's used to create the UPN (User Principal Name, which looks like an email address and can be used for logging in instead of a login ID). The name must be unique in the OU or container. The account won't be created if these criteria are failed.

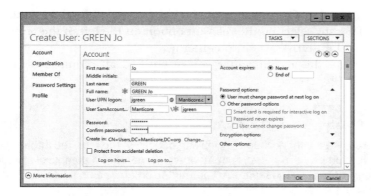

Figure 2.2 Creating a user account with ADAC

2.1.1 Creating a new user with ADAC

ADAC is the GUI tool of choice for managing user accounts in Windows Server 2012. To create a new user, follow these steps:

1 Open ADAC and navigate to the Users container.
2 Choose New from the Tasks pane.
3 Choose User.
4 Complete dialog box.

NOTE The Users container is used for this demonstration because it's always present in Active Directory. If you prefer to use another OU, feel free. You'll need to amend the instructions accordingly.

You'll see a version of the dialog box shown in figure 2.2, though without any data entered.

Enter the user name in the Full Name field and the samAccountName in the User samAccountNname field. The required fields are marked by red asterisks. The password can be entered at this time; double entry is required to confirm. Expiry dates, password options, and Protecting the Account from Accidental Deletion can all be entered or enabled on this screen.

Protect from accidental deletion

The Protect from Accidental Deletion (PAD) setting doesn't affect an AD attribute. It modifies the permissions on the user account or other objects. The permission to delete the object is denied to the Everyone group. Deny permissions take precedence over Allow permissions, meaning that no one can delete the object.

The PAD setting isn't infallible, because a rogue administrator can remove the settings, at which point the object can be deleted. This is a conscious act, though, rather than an accident.

PAD can be set on user and computer accounts, groups, and OUs. It's a simple action that can save you a lot of grief, so I recommend that you use it.

The Organization, Member Of (group membership), Password Settings, and Profile information can be set by selecting the relevant option on the left of the screen. The password is obscured by asterisks when you enter it.

Click OK to create the account after you've entered all required or available information.

TRY IT NOW: Create a user with ADAC

Open ADAC and create a user account. Try leaving out any of the required information, mistyping one version of the password, or ignoring the password complexity requirements, and observe the error messages. If you want to create the user shown in figure 2.2 use the following data:

- First name: Jo
- Last name: Green
- User samAccountName: jgreen
- Password: PasswOrd! (please don't use something like this for production accounts)

Feel free to add other data if you wish.

2.1.2 *Creating a new user with ADUC*

Creating a user account with ADUC is a similar process to that experienced with ADUC:

1 Open ADUC.
2 Right-click the required container—I used the Users container again.
3 Choose New > User from the context menus.
4 A screen similar to figure 2.3 will be displayed—complete the fields.

Figure 2.3 Creating a user account with ADUC

Entering data in the First name and Last name fields causes the Full name field to be populated. I always capitalize the last name, but you need to adopt your own convention.

User naming conventions

If your organization doesn't have a user naming convention, I recommend you create one. The convention should cover

- How the user name will be displayed
- How the samAccountName (logon ID) will be generated

In my test domain I've adopted the following convention:

- Capitalize last name
- Create name as <last name><space><first name>
- Create samAccountName as first letter of first name plus last name

I find this easy to work with. Look at what's done in your organization and decide if it needs changing.

Whatever you do, don't put a comma between the first and last names. It makes scripting much more difficult because a comma is the separator between the elements of the distinguished name.

To complete the dialog

1 The user logon name must be supplied (that is, the samAccountName attribute).
2 Click Next.
3 A password is supplied twice (for confirmation) and is obscured by asterisks.
4 Click Next and review the data.
5 Click Finish to create the account.

TRY IT NOW: Create a user with ADUC

Open ADUC and create a user account. Try leaving out any of the required information, mistyping one version of the password, or ignoring the password complexity requirements, and observe the error messages.

If you want to create the user shown in figure 2.3, use the following data:

- First name: Fred
- Last name: Green
- User Logon name: fgreen
- Password: Passw0rd! (please don't use something like this for production accounts)

Feel free to add other data if you wish.

2.1.3 *Creating a new user with PowerShell*

The final method you need to be aware of is using PowerShell. When you create a user in ADAC, you'll see the PowerShell commands that ADAC used in the PowerShell window at the bottom of the GUI.

> **NOTE** The commands you'll see here aren't exactly the same as those produced by ADAC. I've simplified and condensed the code. ADAC is more verbose because of the limitations of code generators that have cover all eventualities.

The following code can be used to create a new user:

```
$secpass = Read-Host "Password" -AsSecureString
New-ADUser -Name "GREEN Dave" -SamAccountName dgreen
➥ -UserPrincipalName "dgreen@manticore.org" -AccountPassword $secpass
➥ -Path "cn=Users,dc=Manticore,dc=org"  -Enabled:$true
```

The first line creates a password as a secure (encrypted) string. `Read-Host` prompts for the password, which is obscured by asterisks during entry. The `-AsSecureString` parameter ensures that the password is encrypted

`New-ADUser` is used to create the account. The parameters match with the data you've supplied when using ADAC or ADUC. In this case you have to explicitly supply all data to match the work done by the GUI; for example, ADUC creating the name from the First name and Last name fields as you enter the data. After typing the command, press Enter and the account will be created.

TRY IT NOW: Create a user with PowerShell

Try running this script. Use PasswOrd! as your password to be consistent with the previous examples:

```
$secpass = Read-Host "Password" -AsSecureString
New-ADUser -Name "GREEN Dave" -SamAccountName dgreen `
-UserPrincipalName "dgreen@manticore.org" -AccountPassword $secpass `
-Path "cn=Users,dc=Manticore,dc=org"  -Enabled:$true
```

Modify the `Path` and `UserPrincipalName` parameters to suit your environment. Try modifying the data and reusing it. *Hint:* you can reuse the same password.

The big question now is which of the three methods from this section you should use. As with so much in the IT industry, the answer is that it depends. In this case it depends on two things:

- What tools you actually have in your environment
- What you feel comfortable with using

My recommendations for creating a new single user are to use

- PowerShell by preference
- ADAC if you have Windows Server 2012 Active Directory or can install the Remote Server Administration Tools (RSAT) on a Windows 8 or Windows Server 2012 system
- ADUC on Windows Server 2008 R2 or earlier

Using PowerShell to create single users is a viable option. Compared to the GUI tools, it's a little more difficult to use when you're creating users from a template account, which is the next topic for your consideration.

2.2 *User creation from a template*

In the previous section you discovered how to create a single user account from scratch. The example showed account creation using the minimum amount of data. In reality, you need to add a lot more, such as

- Group membership
- Home-drive paths
- Logon script
- Organizational address information
- Manager
- Telephone numbers

This can be a lot of typing, which raises the probability of an error occurring. One way to reduce the amount of work you need to perform and reduce the chance of an error occurring is to use a template. This is a fully configured account that's copied to form a new account. The name, samAccountName, and other personalized information need to be entered for the new user.

You have two options when considering using a template:

- Use an existing account.
- Create an account to use as a template.

I recommend using an existing account. The creation of a template means that you have to keep it up-to-date. That won't be an onerous task if you have a relatively small organization with a few templates. An organization with thousands of users and hundreds of departments, each requiring its own template, will generate a significant amount of work.

> **TIP** If you use an existing account, be prepared to either convert it into a dedicated template or use another account if the user leaves. One organization I worked with would ask which user account to use as a template when a new user was requested.

Now that you've decided to use a template, how do you work with it to create a user account? Also, which tools should you use?

Figure 2.4
Copying a user account with ADUC

If you're creating a single account, the answer is simple: ADUC or PowerShell. It isn't possible to copy an account using ADAC. If you decide to use ADUC,

1 Open the tool.
2 Choose the account to use as a template.
3 Right-click it and choose Copy.
4 The dialog box shown in figure 2.4 appears.
5 Supply the name data in the First name and Last name fields.
6 The Full name field is automatically populated as you enter those names.
7 Enter the user logon name; the User logon name field (pre-Windows 2000) will be populated.
8 Click Next.
9 Enter and confirm the password.
10 Click Next.
11 Review the data you're shown and click Finish.

TRY IT NOW: Use ADUC to copy an account

Try copying one of the accounts you've already created.

Choose the Jo Green account you created earlier and follow the instructions. Use this data:

- First name: Mike
- Last name: Green
- User logon name: mgreen
- Password: PasswOrd! (please don't use something like this for production accounts)

Using PowerShell involves the -Instance parameter of New-ADUser, as follows:

```
$secpass = Read-Host "Password" -AsSecureString
$user = Get-ADUser -Identity jgreen -Properties memberof, office
New-ADUser -Name "GREEN Bill" -SamAccountName bgreen
➥ -UserPrincipalName "bgreen@manticore.org"
➥ -AccountPassword $secpass -Path "cn=Users,dc=Manticore,dc=org"
➥ -Enabled:$true -Instance $user
```

This is exactly the same as creating a single user, except you get a user to use as a template. The script starts by using Read-Host to create a password. An existing user account is accessed to create the template. You must specify the properties you want to copy when you create the $user variable by putting them in the -Properties parameter of Get-ADUser, which makes it painful to use if you fully populate the user attributes.

> **NOTE** You can't just use * to get all fields, as an error is thrown because you're trying to copy data that should be unique, such as the security identifier usually referred to as the SID.

The New-ADUser cmdlet is passed the information including the variable holding the template, which is put into the -Instance parameter.

> **TIP** This technique doesn't copy group memberships or other multivalue attributes. I recommend using ADUC for copying accounts.

So far you've seen how to create a single user. There are times when you need to create multiple accounts. What are you going to do when your boss says you have to create 50 new accounts at 4:55 p.m. on a Friday?

2.3 *User creation in bulk*

Creating users in bulk can be performed with GUI tools, but I promise you'll have sore fingers from clicking the mouse before you've finished. Any administrative action that has to be repeated should be automated.

> **TIP** Print out that last sentence and put it somewhere very visible by your desk. Every time you start to do something new, stop and think if you can automate the process instead of performing it manually.

The advantage to automating an action is that it becomes repeatable. You can create 1 user or 100 users and they'll be created in exactly the same way with exactly the same standards and conventions applied. I guarantee you can't create 100 users by hand and achieve that! Also, a scripted approach reduces errors. You know it's going to work because you've done it before.

The trick with automating user creation is to get your data organized. Create a comma-separated value (CSV) file to hold the data. Here are the contents of a sample file:

```
FirstName LastName SamAccountName
--------- -------- --------------
Dave      GREEN    dgreen
Fred      GREEN    fgreen
Jo        GREEN    jgreen
Mike      GREEN    mgreen
```

I've used names.csv as the filename. You can choose anything you want—just remember to modify the script. The file holds the FirstName, LastName, and the samAccountName fields you want to use. If you have a convention for samAccountName, you could get the script to create that value.

> **WARNING** The data in the CSV file will create the same accounts as seen earlier in the chapter. If you create a CSV file with this data, remember to delete the accounts you created earlier!

The following PowerShell script is used to automate the bulk creation of AD user accounts:

```
$secpass = Read-Host "Password" -AsSecureString
Import-Csv names.csv |
foreach {
  $name = "$($_.LastName) $($_.FirstName)"

 New-ADUser -GivenName $($_.FirstName) -Surname $($_.LastName) `
 -Name $name -SamAccountName $($_.SamAccountName) `
 -UserPrincipalName "$($_.SamAccountName)@manticore.org" `
 -AccountPassword $secpass -Path "cn=Users,dc=Manticore,dc=org" `
 -Enabled:$true
}
```

Use Read-Host to get the password as a secure string. The data file is read using Import-Csv. Each row in the data file is processed using foreach (short for ForEach-Object).

A variable, $name, is created from the FirstName and LastName fields. $_ refers to the object (the row of data being processed). Each field in the CSV file is a property of the object being processed. The New-ADUser cmdlet is used to create the user account. It's used in the same way as before, but the values are supplied as properties of the object being processed. This approach will create multiple accounts very quickly. You can add further steps to add additional information or even create an email account if required.

> **TIP** The CSV file and script are available in the book's download file.

The last topic you need to consider when creating user accounts is the accounts you use to run services.

2.4   *Creating managed service accounts*

Managed service accounts were introduced in Windows Server 2008 R2. They're used to run services such as SQL Server, Exchange, and IIS on systems within your domain. In this section we'll consider how to create them. Full details for using these accounts can be found on the Microsoft website at http://technet.microsoft.com/en-us/library/dd378925(WS.10).aspx.

The use of managed service accounts is outside the scope of this book, but you need to understand how to create them. ADAC doesn't supply an option to create these accounts. ADUC will show managed service accounts as an option when you choose New after right-clicking an OU. This isn't a recommended approach, as the GUI doesn't completely, or correctly, populate the object's attributes.

The recommended approach is to use the `New-ADServiceAccount` PowerShell cmdlet. An example for a Windows Server 2008 R2 environment is shown in the following code:

```
New-ADServiceAccount -Name TestMSA `
-Path "CN=Managed Service Accounts,DC=Manticore,DC=org"
```

The Managed Service Accounts container is the default location for these objects, but you can create them in any OU or container in your Active Directory by modifying the value given to the `-Path` parameter. The other property you must supply is the name of the account.

Windows Server 2012 slightly changes the way these accounts are created. A Microsoft Key Distribution Service root key must be created; otherwise, you'll get an error and you won't be able to create your managed service account. The root key can be created as follows:

```
Add-KdsRootKey -EffectiveImmediately
```

The key should be allowed to replicate through your environment before you attempt to use it—it's usual to allow 10 hours.

> **NOTE**   You can view the key using `Get-KdsRootkey`.

The Windows Server 2012 default approach to managed service accounts is to create a managed service group account that can be used on multiple machines. The PowerShell code to create a managed service account changes to the following:

```
New-ADServiceAccount
➥ -Path "CN=Managed Service Accounts,DC=Manticore,DC=org"
➥ -Name Test2012MSA
➥ -DNSHostName Test2012MSA.manticore.org -Enabled $true
```

The main difference is that a DNS host name must be supplied. In this instance the account is enabled. Alternatively, if the account is to be restricted to a single system, the following syntax is used:

```
New-ADServiceAccount
➥ -Path "CN=Managed Service Accounts,DC=Manticore,DC=org"
➥ -Name Test2022MSA -Enabled $true -RestrictToSingleComputer
```

You don't need to provide a `DNSHostname`, but you do need the `-RestrictToSingle-Computer` parameter.

This concludes your tour of the techniques used to create user accounts. You'll be able to use these directly in your environment, either directly or after a little modification for the PowerShell scripts. There's just the lab to complete before you return to your lunch.

2.5   Lab

The lab activities for this chapter involve practicing with the tools and determining how to create user accounts.

2.5.1   Complete the TRY IT NOW sections

If you haven't already done so, complete the TRY IT NOW exercises. The information is summarized in table 2.2.

Table 2.2   Data required to create test accounts

Property	ADAC	ADUC	ADUC (copying account)
First Name	Jo	Fred	Mike
Last Name	Green	Green	Green
SamAccountName / User Logon Name	jgreen	fgreen	mgreen
Password	PasswOrd!	PasswOrd!	PasswOrd!

To create a user account using PowerShell, run this script. Use PasswOrd! as your password to be consistent with the previous examples:

```
$secpass = Read-Host "Password" -AsSecureString
New-ADUser -Name "GREEN Dave" -SamAccountName dgreen `
-UserPrincipalName "dgreen@manticore.org" -AccountPassword $secpass `
-Path "cn=Users,dc=Manticore,dc=org"  -Enabled:$true
```

2.5.2   Create these accounts

Practice creating more accounts with your preferred creation method. The data in table 2.3 can be used.

Table 2.3   Data required to create additional accounts

Property	Account 1	Account 2	Account 3	Account 4
First Name	Bill	Dave	Tom	John
Last Name	Smith	Jones	Brown	James
SamAccountName User Logon Name	bsmith	djones	tbrown	jjames
Password	PasswOrd!	PasswOrd!	PasswOrd!	PasswOrd!

If you're going to create accounts from templates, determine a suitable account to use as a template and create the accounts using the template.

2.5.3   *PowerShell parameters*

The PowerShell cmdlet has many possible parameters. The following code shows the majority of the common options. Review the code to determine which ones you need. Modify the bulk creation script and add test data to the CSV file to test bulk creation:

```
$secpass = Read-Host "Password" -AsSecureString
New-ADUser -Name "KENT Bill" -SamAccountName bkent `
-GivenName "Bill" -Surname "Kent" `
-DisplayName "Bill Kent" -UserPrincipalName "bkent@manticore.org" `
-AccountPassword $secpass -ChangePasswordAtLogon:$true `
-Path "cn=Users,dc=Manticore,dc=org"  -Enabled:$true `
-Description "A test user with many standard options" `
-Manager mgreen -Organization  "ADML" `
-Company "ADML" -Department "IT" -Division "AD Admin" `
-Title "AD administrator" `
-Office "ADML House" -StreetAddress "1 ADML Road" `
-City "Peterborough" -State "Cambridgeshire" `
-Country "GB" -PostalCode "PE29 1HN" -POBox "1234" `
-OfficePhone "01789 600435" `
-HomePhone "0123 456789" -MobilePhone "0723 675689"  `
-HomeDrive "H:" -HomeDirectory "\\server1\Home\bkent" `
-ProfilePath "\\server2\profiles\wsc" -ScriptPath "logon.vbs"
```

> **NOTE**   The division and organization properties don't show in the GUI.

2.6   *Ideas for on your own*

User account creation is one of the fundamental activities you'll perform as an AD administrator. The information in this chapter will enable you to perform that activity more efficiently. One thing that hasn't been touched on is the overall process and how you interact with the business. Create the process documentation for account creation, or revise previously existing documentation. This should include the way the business requests an account and how the communication of information is performed.

In the next chapter you'll build on what you learned in this chapter by discovering how to manage the user accounts you've created.

Managing user accounts

User account management can be summed up as CRUD, or create, read, update, delete. I originally came across this acronym in terms of dealing with data and databases during software development, but it can be applied to any data store. Ultimately, Active Directory is just a data store.

You learned how to create user accounts in the previous chapter. In this chapter you'll learn how to update and delete user accounts.

NOTE I'll use attributes and properties interchangeably throughout the book. Technically, the AD schema class used to create the object has attributes and the object itself has properties. Common usage is to use the two words interchangeably when working with AD objects.

The process of updating user accounts can be divided into two areas. First, you need to be able to update the data that forms the user account. The data is held in the user account properties, and you'll learn how to use GUI tools and PowerShell to modify those properties. Second, the status of the account can be updated by disabling or enabling it. A disabled account can't be accessed, and you'll see why you may want to disable an account, as well as how to perform the task.

Everything in IT has a lifecycle, and user accounts are no different. Eventually an account will no longer be required because the user has left the organization for one reason or another. Leaving accounts that aren't needed in your Active Directory is inefficient because you don't need to manage that data and it could potentially be a security risk. This is when you need to consider deleting the account—once you're satisfied the user really has left the organization!

Working with user accounts as just outlined will form a large part of your work with Active Directory. Many senior administrators still get involved with administering user accounts. It's a requirement and skill that never goes away.

The place to start is modifying accounts, because that lays the foundation for the other two activities you'll discover in this chapter.

3.1 Modifying user account properties

Why do you need to modify user accounts? You received all of the information needed to create the account, but things change. Some of the properties that may need to be changed include

- Names—changing because of marriage
- Address—changing office or department
- Phone numbers—changing location
- Group membership—covered in chapter 4

Active Directory needs to be updated to enable the organization to get the maximum benefit from it. It's your job to keep it up-to-date.

> **TRY IT NOW: Review AD account properties**
>
> Open up an account in your favorite GUI tool and scan through the available properties. Which are most likely to need modification?
>
> Some items to consider are
>
> - Last name. If you change it in the GUI, are the name and display name properties automatically updated? What about if you change the name using PowerShell?
> - Address information. Compare the labels in the GUI with the attribute names in the Attribute Editor. Do they match? *Hint:* check City and Office attributes.
> - Telephone numbers. How many do your users need? Check the "Other" buttons in the GUI to see if multiples are set or required.
> - Enable Advanced features on the View menu in ADUC to gain access to the Attribute Editor.

The AD attributes you'll need to modify fall into two broad groups—single value and multiple value—as illustrated in figure 3.1. There can be hundreds of properties on a single user account when Exchange is installed. The telephone number properties will be used as an example of single-value and multivalue properties. The techniques you learn for those are directly applicable to other properties.

Figure 3.1   Attribute listing for a user account showing single-and multivalue attributes. In a multivalue attribute the values are separated by semi-colons.

Attributes can be modified using GUI tools or PowerShell. It's very important that you modify the correct account. Getting it wrong could have consequences that range from embarrassing to career-threatening.

Imagine you need to modify the telephone numbers that are stored in Active Directory for a user. Figure 3.1 shows that there's an attribute called homePhone that takes a single value, and an attribute imaginatively named otherHomePhone that takes multiple values. The multiple values are shown in Attribute Editor separated by a semicolon. You don't need to supply a semicolon.

Let's see how you can modify these attributes in GUI tools.

3.1.1   *Using GUI tools to modify user accounts*

User accounts can be modified by following these steps:

1 Using ADAC, find the account you need to modify.
2 Right-click on the user account and choose Properties.
3 A dialog similar to figure 3.2 will be displayed. In this case you're modifying the office (main) phone number. All of the phone number properties work in the same way.
4 Scroll down to the properties you want to modify.

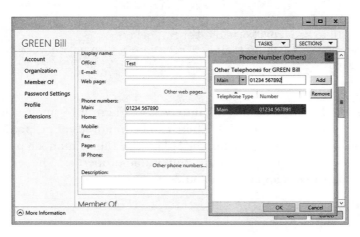

Figure 3.2   Modifying user account properties in ADAC. Single-value attributes are modified directly in the dialog. A popup is supplied to modify multivalue attributes.

TIP   If you know the subsection in which the properties are found, click the link to the left of the dialog to jump directly to them.

A single-value attribute can be modified by typing directly into the field in the dialog. Remember to clear the field if you're changing the value, rather than adding a value into an empty field.

If you want to modify the other phone numbers

1   Click Other Phone Numbers... in the dialog to see the popup.
2   The type of phone you want to modify the properties of can be chosen from the drop-down menu.
3   Type the number in the box and click the Add button to add it to the user account.
4   If you want to remove a value, choose it and click the Remove button.
5   Click OK to close the popup.
6   Click OK on the main dialog to close the dialog and save the changes you've made.

The process for ADUC is similar, as shown in figure 3.3.

In ADUC there's a separate tab for telephones. To perform modifications to the property

1   Click the Telephone tab.
2   Modify the numbers showing in the tab as required.
3   If you need to modify the other numbers, click the appropriate "Other" button to see a popup similar to that shown.
4   Use the box to enter values.
5   Click the Add button to accept.
6   Highlight an existing number to edit or remove using the appropriate button.
7   Click OK to close the popup.
8   Click OK to close the dialog and accept the changes.

Figure 3.3   Modifying phone numbers with ADUC

TRY IT NOW: Amend a test account

Open up an account in your favorite GUI tool and modify.

- Find the Bill Green user account.
- Set the Home Phone Number to 01234 567890.
- Add these other numbers: 01234 567891, 01234 567892.

3.1.2 *Using PowerShell to modify user accounts*

The version of ADAC in Windows Server 2012 kindly shows the PowerShell code it's generating. ADAC produces verbose code that can be simplified. If you compare the code in the book with that produced by ADAC, you'll be able to determine what's been removed. The code you get here works just as well, but is simpler and quicker to type.

Modifying a single value is a simple matter of replacing the value that's currently present with a value that you supply:

```
Set-ADUser -Identity "CN=GREEN Bill,CN=Users,DC=Manticore,DC=org" `
-OfficePhone "01234 567895"
```

Using `Set-ADUser`, the user is identified by the distinguished name of the AD object. The PowerShell naming convention is verb-noun. `Set` is the verb used when you want to change something. The `-OfficePhone` parameter is used to supply the phone number you want to change. Many of the common user properties are available as parameters on the `Set-ADUser` cmdlet.

Modifying the additional phone numbers uses a slightly different approach. Use `Set -ADUser` again, but instead of the named parameter, use one of the generic parameters:

- `Add`—adds one or more values to a property
- `Clear`—clears all values of a property
- `Remove`—removes one or more values from a property
- `Replace`—replaces the values of a property with the values you supply

When you use the `Add`, `Remove`, `Replace`, and `Clear` parameters together, the operations will be performed in the following order:

1 `Remove`
2 `Add`
3 `Replace`
4 `Clear`

In this case you don't have any existing values, so you could use `-Add` or `-Replace`:

```
Set-ADUser -Identity "CN=GREEN Bill,CN=Users,DC=Manticore,DC=org" `
-Replace @{otherTelephone="01234 567896","01234 567897"}
```

You supply a hash table—the `@{}` part—with the name of the property and the new value separated by an equals sign.

TRY IT NOW: Amend a test account with PowerShell

Use this code to modify a test user account:

```
Set-ADUser -Identity "CN=GREEN Bill,CN=Users,DC=Manticore,DC=org" `
-OfficePhone "01234 567895"

Set-ADUser -Identity "CN=GREEN Bill,CN=Users,DC=Manticore,DC=org" `
-Replace @{otherTelephone="01234 567896","01234 567897"}
```

View the account in the GUI to determine that the changes have been made.

The examples in this section have assumed that you're supplied the information you require to modify the user account. What happens when you're told to get the information from another user?

3.1.3 Copying attributes from another account

A common administrative scenario involves modifying the properties of one account based on the value or values of the same property in another account. In GUI tools this involves performing the following actions:

1 Open the GUI tool.
2 Find the user you're copying from.
3 Find the property.
4 Read or copy the value.
5 Close the property dialog (best practice to avoid accidents).
6 Find the user you're modifying.
7 Find the property.
8 Type or paste the value.
9 Click OK to save.
10 Close the tool.

This is a bit long-winded, and you'll soon get bored if you have to do this for a number of users.

A little bit of PowerShell can make your life much easier:

```
$source =
➥ Get-ADUser -Identity bgreen -Properties OfficePhone, otherTelephone

Set-ADUser -Identity "CN=GREEN Dave,CN=Users,DC=Manticore,DC=org"
➥ -OfficePhone $($source.OfficePhone)
➥ -Replace @{otherTelephone = $($source.otherTelephone)}
```

Use `Get-ADUser` to create a variable representing the user account from which you'll copy data. The properties you need to copy are explicitly retrieved by putting their names in the `-Properties` parameter. `Get-ADUser` returns a very small number of properties by default.

> **TIP** Notice that the samAccountName is used in Get-ADUser, but the distinguished name is used in Set-ADUser. Either can be used with the identity parameter (you'll see both used throughout the book). Details of other attributes that can be used with the -Identity parameter are given in appendix A.

`Set-ADUser` is used to modify the user account you need to change. You can combine both techniques shown in earlier PowerShell scripts in this section and use the `-Office-Phone` and `-Replace` parameters together. The use of a subexpression—for example, `$($source.OfficePhone)`—ensures that you get the value correctly substituted.

You should now feel comfortable modifying the properties of a user account. What about changing its status?

3.2   *Enabling or disabling user accounts*

Enabling or disabling an account is a straightforward action, but why would you want to disable an account?

An enabled AD account is a potential security vulnerability for your organization. If the user's logon details are compromised, an attacker could access company data. Accounts that aren't being used but that are still required should be disabled so that they can't be used to log on. Disabling is preferred for short-term prevention of access, because enabling the account is less work than recreating an account with the same name and ensuring the properties and group memberships are set correctly.

> **TIP**   If you create new user accounts in advance of them being required, leave them disabled until the users actually need them.

Disabling an account with GUI tools involves finding the account, right-clicking it, and choosing Disable in ADAC or Disable Account in ADUC. You'll see a popup message stating that the user account has been disabled in ADUC, but ADAC doesn't supply a message. In both cases the icon representing the user will change to show a downward-pointing arrow at the bottom right of the icon.

PowerShell supplies a cmdlet to disable the account:

```
Disable-ADAccount -Identity dgreen
```

The identity can be supplied as the samAccountName, as in the example, or the distinguished name can be used. A quick way to test if accounts are disabled (you shouldn't have too many in your Active Directory) is to run this code:

```
Search-ADAccount -AccountDisabled |
Format-Table Name, DistinguishedName –AutoSize
```

Enabling accounts follows the reverse process. In GUI tools right-click the account and choose Enable in ADAC or Enable Account in ADUC. You'll get a popup message with ADUC.

PowerShell supplies a cmdlet to enable accounts:

```
Enable-ADAccount -Identity dgreen
```

As a safety net when using PowerShell, there's an alternative syntax. Use `Get-ADUser` to confirm you're working with the correct object, and then modify the code by piping into `Disable-ADAccount`. This involves running the following code:

```
Get-ADUser -Identity dgreen
Get-ADUser -Identity dgreen | Disable-ADAccount
```

A similar approach can be used for enabling accounts.

Disabling accounts should be a temporary measure. How do you remove accounts completely?

3.3   *Deleting user accounts*

When an account is deleted, it doesn't vanish from your Active Directory immediately. You'll learn more about this in chapter 13, but the short version is that

- In Windows Server 2008 and earlier, the object is tombstoned.
- In Windows Server 2008 R2 or Windows Server 2012 without the AD Recycle Bin enabled, the object is tombstoned.
- In Windows Server 2008 R2 or Windows Server 2012 with the AD Recycle Bin enabled, the object goes into the AD Recycle Bin.

A tombstoned object has most of the properties removed. It can be made live again, but the properties have to be recreated. An object in the recycle bin is complete and can be restored with all properties intact.

Objects remain in the tombstone area or AD Recycle Bin for the tombstone period. This is either 60 days or 180 days, depending on the version of Windows used to originally create your Active Directory. You can modify this period upwards if required. After the tombstone period has expired, the object is finally removed from Active Directory automatically by the system.

Deleting an object using GUI tools is performed as follows:

1 Find the object.
2 Right-click to show the Context menu.
3 Click Delete.
4 Confirm the action in the popup message box.

If you have Protect from Accidental Deletion enabled, you won't be able to delete the object. A popup like figure 3.4 will be displayed if this feature is set.

The protection must be removed before the deletion can occur. There's a checkbox in the Account section of the user properties in ADAC and on the Object tab in ADUC—uncheck the box to remove the protection.

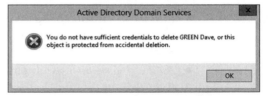

Figure 3.4   Popup displayed by ADAC and ADUC when attempting to delete a user account that's protected against accidental deletion. The protection must be removed before the account can be deleted.

> **TIP**　The Object tab isn't visible by default in ADUC. You need to select View > Advanced features from the ADUC menu bar.

When you try to delete an account with PowerShell, you'll get an Access Denied message if the account is protected from deletion, which doesn't tell you the cause of the problem. You can check if the object is protected as follows:

```
Get-ADUser -Identity dgreen -Properties ProtectedFromAccidentalDeletion
```

The property will have a value of `True` if protection is turned on. Setting and removing Protect from Accidental Deletion is covered in more detail in chapter 10, but for now the protection is removed as follows:

```
Get-ADObject -LDAPFilter "(Name=green dave)" |
Set-ADObject -ProtectedFromAccidentalDeletion:$false
```

You have to search for the object and pipe it into `Set-ADObject`. The search uses an LDAP filter, which is covered in detail in appendix A. The `Set-ADUser` cmdlet doesn't have the facility to remove the protection—you have to use `Set-ADObject`.

You'd then use this syntax to perform the deletion:

```
Remove-ADUser -Identity dgreen -Confirm:$false
```

Leave off the `-Confirm:$false` if you want a message to force you to confirm the action. Not a bad idea with deletes!

This completes your initial look at modifying user accounts. You'll see the techniques presented in this chapter used throughout the rest of the book.

3.4 Lab

The lab for this chapter consists of more practice of the user modification techniques you've learned.

3.4.1 Complete the TRY IT NOW sections

If you haven't already done so, complete the TRY IT NOW exercises.

REVIEW AD ACCOUNT PROPERTIES

Open up an account in your favorite GUI tool and scan through the available properties. Which are most likely to need modification? Some items to consider are

- *Last name*—If you change it in the GUI, are the name and display name properties automatically updated? What about if you change the name using PowerShell?
- *Address information*—Compare the labels in the GUI with the attribute names in the Attribute Editor. Do they match? *Hint:* check City and Office attributes.
- *Telephone numbers*—How many do your users need? Check the "Other" buttons in the GUI to see if multiples are set or required.

AMEND A TEST ACCOUNT

Open up an account in your favorite GUI tool and modify it as follows:

- Find the Bill Green user account.
- Set the Home Telephone Number to 01234 567890
- Add these other numbers: 01234 567891, 01234 567892.

AMEND A TEST ACCOUNT WITH POWERSHELL

Use this code to modify a test user account:

```
Set-ADUser -Identity "CN=GREEN Bill,CN=Users,DC=Manticore,DC=org" `
-OfficePhone "01234 567895"

Set-ADUser -Identity "CN=GREEN Bill,CN=Users,DC=Manticore,DC=org" `
-Replace @{otherTelephone="01234 567896","01234 567897"}
```

View the account in the GUI to determine whether the changes have been made.

3.4.2 *Modify one value out of a multivalue attribute?*

Multivalue attributes may appear awkward to work with, especially if you just want to modify one of the values of the attribute.

If you're using GUI tools, you can use the techniques shown in section 3.1.1. Use those techniques to change the otherTelephone attribute on the bgreen test account to have these values:

- 01234 568816
- 01234 568826
- 01234 568836

Once you've added a value, is there a way to edit it?

Using PowerShell, you can work with multivalue attributes. Work through this code as you read it. You can view the values held in multivalue attributes like this:

```
Get-ADUser -Identity bgreen -Properties * |
select -ExpandProperty otherHomePhone
```

To remove a single entry from the list, enter the following code:

```
Set-ADUser -Identity bgreen -Remove @{otherHomePhone = "01234 568826"}
```

To add an extra value, enter this code:

```
Set-ADUser -Identity bgreen -Add @{otherHomePhone = "01234 568856"}
```

Use `Get-ADUser` to verify the changes.

3.4.3 *Bulk modification of user accounts*

Imagine that your organization has just opened two new offices. A number of staff have been transferred into each office and you need to change the information held in Active Directory. GUI tools do support multi-object selection and editing for some, but not all, attributes. If you need to change the nonsupported attributes using the GUI, it'll be painful (literally, if there are a lot of users), but by modifying the technique you used for bulk user creation, it becomes much less stressful and allows you to work across multiple OUs simultaneously, which GUI tools can't do.

Create a CSV file with the following information:

```
SamAccountName,Office,StreetAddress,POBox,City,State,Zip,Country
mgreen,"North East","1 West Street",PO567,Boston,Massachusetts,567890,US
dgreen,"North West","1 New Street",PO123,Seattle,Washington,123456,US
jgreen,"North East","1 West Street",PO567,Boston,Massachusetts,567890,US
bgreen,"North West","1 New Street",PO123,Seattle,Washington,123456,US
```

Then run this code:

```
Import-Csv -Path C:\Scripts\officechange.csv |
foreach {
 Set-ADUser -Identity $_.SamAccountName -Office $_.Office `
 -StreetAddress $_.StreetAddress -POBox $_.POBox -City $_.City `
  -State $_.State -PostalCode $_.Zip  -Country $_.Country
}
```

If you check this in the GUI, be aware that POBox isn't shown in ADAC—you have to use the Attribute Editor to see the value. POBox does appear on the address tab in ADUC.

3.4.4   *Renaming an account*

Renaming an account isn't a common activity, but it does occur. Follow this procedure in your GUI environment:

1 Right-click the bgreen (GREEN Bill) account.
2 Choose Rename.
3 Change the name to GREEN William.
4 Press Enter.
5 Complete the dialog with this information:
   - Full Name: GREEN William
   - First Name: William
   - Last Name: GREEN
   - Display Name: GREEN William
   - User Logon Name: wgreen
6 Click OK.

Renaming an account in PowerShell is slightly more complicated. Try running this code:

```
Get-ADUser -Identity wgreen |
Rename-ADObject -NewName "GREEN Bill"

Get-ADUser -Identity wgreen -Properties * |
Set-ADUser -DisplayName "GREEN Bill" -SamAccountName bgreen `
-GivenName "Bill"
```

The rename process has been split into two to make the code more straightforward.

3.5   *Ideas for on your own*

Modifying user accounts will be a large part of your daily work. How can you make this task easier for yourself? Spend a little time discovering the most common changes you're being asked to make. Turn those into PowerShell scripts and you'll have a greatly reduced workload compared to performing all changes in GUI tools.

> **NOTE** Moving objects between OUs is a task you'll need to perform on a frequent basis. It's covered in chapter 7, where you'll learn about managing the OUs in your domain.

If you work in GUI tools, save a number of changes and perform them together. It's quicker than having to keep opening the tools.

You now have a good handle on how to create and modify user accounts. In chapter 4 you'll learn about working with groups.

Managing groups

4

AD groups provide a way to make your day-to-day work more efficient. You allocate permissions to a group, and all of the users in the group get those permissions. You do the task once for the group instead of individually for the tens or hundreds of users in the group. This chapter shows how to manage groups in your Active Directory so that you can get these efficiency benefits. You'll discover how to create and delete groups, as well as how to manage a group's membership.

AD groups

AD groups are objects that act as containers for users, computers, and other groups. Groups are used to make the management of users easier, especially when it comes to granting permissions to access resources. There are a number of different types of groups, as you'll discover in the next section. For now, just remember that you should apply permissions to groups, not users.

There are two categories of groups: security and distribution. These categories can span a number of scopes: Domain Local, Global, and Universal. The categories and scopes will be explained in this chapter, with suggested best practices for using the different types of groups in your environment.

NOTE Groups can contain computer accounts. Don't mix computers and users in the same group. Keeping them separate enables more granular and efficient assignment of permissions and easier filtering for the application of Group Policy. If your organization has mixed users and computers in groups, then analyze where it's causing problems and recommend splitting the groups.

Groups have a simple lifecycle:

1 Creation
2 Use and modification of membership
3 Deletion

You'll learn how to create the different group types. The primary modification to a group is to change its membership. You can achieve this using GUI tools or PowerShell. First, though, you need to understand the different group types.

4.1   *Group types*

Groups can be split into two categories:

- *Security groups*—The subject of this chapter; primarily used to assign permissions
- *Distribution lists*—Used in Exchange to send emails to multiple recipients

AD administrators usually manage security groups. Distribution lists are managed by Exchange administrators. In many organizations these may be the same people, but we'll assume they're separate sets of administrators.

An AD group can have one of three scopes. The scope controls where the group membership can come from and where the group can be used, as shown in table 4.1.

Table 4.1   Group scope, membership restrictions, application restrictions, and nesting rules

Group scope	Membership from	Apply in	Nestable in
Domain Local	Any domain in the forest	Domain in which the group was created	Domain Local groups from same domain
Global	Domain in which the group was created	Any domain in the forest	Global groups from same domain Any Domain Local or Universal group
Universal	Any domain in the forest	Any domain in the forest	Any Domain Local or Universal group

The membership of a group can be user accounts, computer accounts, or nested groups, as long as the nesting rules shown in table 4.1 are followed. Universal groups don't add much if you only have a forest with a single domain, though Exchange requires the Universal scope for its distribution lists.

The official Microsoft way to use groups is shown in figure 4.1. User accounts (or computers or other allowed groups) are added to a Global group. Global groups are added to Domain Local groups, which are then added to Access Control Lists (ACLs). The ACLs control access and rights to resources such as shares, folders, files, and printers.

As an example, consider this scenario: you have a file share that's accessed by three departments—sales, marketing, and engineering. Each department needs the same access level. Use figure 4.1 to follow these steps:

1 Create three Global groups containing the members of the sales, marketing, and engineering departments, respectively.
2 Create the share—for example, SMEdata.
3 Create a Domain Local group; you could use SMEdata_access as a name that also describes its purpose.
4 Add the three Global groups to the Domain Local group.
5 Assign the correct permission on the share and the underlying folders to the Domain Local group.

Access to other systems, such as SQL Server, can also be controlled through the use of AD groups.

Is this the best way to perform this task? I think it is for a number of reasons:

- You have a set of granular groups that you can reuse; for instance, sales and marketing may need access to another shared data area, but engineering doesn't. All you do is create another Domain Local group to which you assign permissions and add the existing sales and marketing groups to it.
- You reduce your overall work; for instance, in the preceding scenarios, adding a user to the sales group automatically grants them access to the two shares.
- It's easier to keep track of the purpose of individual groups and remove groups that are no longer required.

In multi-domain forests, Universal groups may be used to gather Global groups from many domains into a single group that can be added to the appropriate Domain Local group.

In practice, many single-domain organizations don't bother with Domain Local groups and instead assign permissions via Global groups to reduce the administrative overhead. This is especially true for organizations that used Windows 2000 where Domain Local groups didn't exist. Examples of this type of approach could include

- Putting all of the Sales department users into a Sales Global group and assigning permissions to the file shares used by sales to that group
- Creating a Global group of users who are allowed to access a color printer and assigning the appropriate print permission to the group

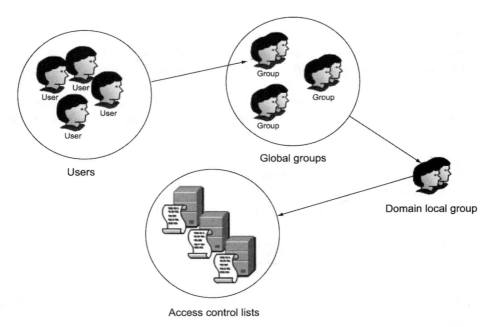

Figure 4.1   Using groups. Put user accounts into Global groups. The Global groups are added to Domain Local groups. Domain Local groups are added to ACLs to give permissions to resources such as file shares.

In reality it makes little difference in a single-domain forest, but in a multi-domain forest it's best to follow the scheme in figure 4.1.

Now that you understand the different types of groups and what they're used for, let's look at creating some.

4.2   Group lifecycle

As stated at the start of the chapter, AD groups have a very simple lifecycle:

1   Creation
2   Use and modification of membership
3   Deletion

In this section you'll discover how to create and delete groups. Modifying their membership will be postponed until later in the chapter. One other activity that you may need to perform is changing the group's scope—you'll learn that as well. First, let's see how to create AD groups.

4.2.1   Creating groups

A group's lifecycle starts when you create it. Group creation is a much simpler process than creating a user. In fact, the good news is that you already have all the skills you need to create a group.

You can create a group using the GUI tools or with PowerShell. You need the following information to create a group:

1 Container or OU where you're creating the group
2 Group name
3 Group samAccountName

When you're creating a group through the GUI tools, the samAccountName (called Group Name pre-Windows 2000) is automatically populated when you type in the name. If you use the Microsoft PowerShell AD cmdlets, you only need to supply the name, because it uses the same information for the samAccountName.

> **TIP** Ensure you supply the samAccountName with non-Microsoft cmdlets or scripts, because Active Directory will create one for you if you don't. The samAccountName will be random characters of the form `$K46000-PFVI6U20JC9D`, which isn't easy to remember!

The practicalities of creating a group are similar no matter what GUI tool you use.

CREATING A GROUP WITH ADAC

ADAC can be used to create a group by following these steps:

1 Open ADAC.
2 Navigate to the OU or container in which the group will be created.
3 Right-click the container or OU.
4 Choose New (can also select New from the Task pane).
5 Choose Group.
6 Complete the dialog in figure 4.2.
7 Click OK to finish.

A new group defaults to a global security group as shown in figure 4.2. These settings can be modified by choosing the appropriate radio buttons. The required information is marked by red asterisks.

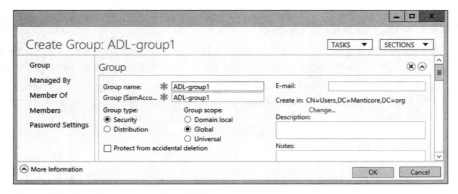

Figure 4.2   Creating a group with ADAC

The group manager, group members, groups of which this new group is a member, and any password settings (see chapter 10) can also be applied using this dialog. Protection from accidental deletion can also be applied at this stage (which is highly recommended) by checking the checkbox immediately below the group types and scopes.

TRY IT NOW: Create a group with ADAC

Following the instructions supplied, create a group in ADAC with the following information:

- *OU*—Users
- *Name*—ADACtest
- *samAccountName*—ADACtest

Using ADUC is a similar experience.

CREATING A GROUP WITH ADUC

ADUC is the original tool for working with AD data. A group is created by following this procedure:

1 Open ADUC.
2 Navigate to the OU or container in which the group will be created.
3 Right-click the container or OU.
4 Choose New.
5 Choose Group.
6 Complete the dialog in figure 4.3.
7 Click OK.

The default group is a global security group, as shown in figure 4.3. The radio buttons can be used to modify this choice. In the dialog the SamAccountName is labeled as Group name (pre-Windows 2000).

Group description

Should you add a description to a group? I recommend you do, because six months from now it will make understanding the group's purpose much easier.

If you use ADAC or PowerShell, you can add the description during the creation process; with ADUC, you have to create the group and then right-click it and modify the properties.

Figure 4.3   Creating a group with ADUC

The ADUC is a simpler dialog than ADAC, but it still gets the job done.

TRY IT NOW: Create a group with ADUC

Following the instructions supplied, create a group in ADUC with the following information:

- *OU*—Users
- *Name*—ADUCtest
- *samAccountName*—ADUCtest

If you need to automate or script your group creation, PowerShell is the tool to use.

CREATING A GROUP WITH POWERSHELL

You've had enough exposure to PowerShell to guess the name of the cmdlet you'll use to create a group. If you answered New-ADGroup, well done. The PowerShell verb New is always used in cmdlets where you're creating a new object.

The New-ADGroup cmdlet is used like this:

```
New-ADGroup -Name PStest -Path "CN=Users,DC=Manticore,DC=org"
    -GroupCategory Security -GroupScope Global
    -Description "Test group for AD Lunches"
```

TRY IT NOW: Create a group with PowerShell

Try running this code:

```
New-ADGroup -Name PStest -Path "CN=Users,DC=Manticore,DC=org" `
-GroupCategory Security -GroupScope Global `
-Description "Test group for AD Lunches"
```

(continued)

You'll need to ensure that you're running PowerShell with elevated privileges and that you've imported the AD module. PowerShell 3.0 and later automatically load modules for you, but it's a good habit to force the loading yourself, especially when using PowerShell remoting.

The name of the group is required. It's automatically used for the samAccountName. The `-Path` parameter is used to define the OU or container in which the group will be created. After defining the scope and category for the group (see section 4.1), a description is supplied.

There are two sets of cmdlets for working with groups, as shown in table 4.2.

Table 4.2   Group and group membership PowerShell cmdlets

Group cmdlets	Group membership cmdlets
New-ADGroup	n/a
Set-ADGroup	Add-ADGroupMember
Remove-ADGroup	Remove-ADGroupMember
Get-ADGroup	Get-ADGroupMember

The group cmdlets are used to manage the group lifecycle:

- `New-ADGroup`—creates a group
- `Set-ADGroup`—modifies group properties
- `Remove-ADgroup`—deletes a group
- `Get-ADGroup`—searches for groups

A similar set of cmdlets is used to modify group membership:

- `Add-ADGroupMember`—Adds a member to a group
- `Remove-ADGroupMember`—Deletes a member from a group
- `Get-ADGroup`—Lists the members of a group

You'll meet these cmdlets in the following sections of this chapter, starting with changing a group's scope.

4.2.2   *Changing group scope*

Don't worry if you get a group scope or category wrong when you create it—you can change it. Changing the category is a rare occurrence because you'll usually be creating security groups (distribution lists are best created with the Exchange tools).

NOTE You can change a distribution group to a security group if you need the ability to assign permissions and target emails. Personally, I prefer to keep the two groups completely separate. Many organizations have separate Exchange and AD management teams, which means the two types have to be kept separate.

The usual reason for changing a category, in my experience, is because the wrong category was assigned originally.

Scope change and nested groups

There's a very important point to remember when changing scope: any nested groups must be allowed to be nested in the new scope; however, the new group scope must still abide by the nesting rules in table 4.1.

Changing a group's scope is slightly more complicated because there are a number of restrictions on the possible changes, as shown in table 4.3.

Table 4.3 Allowed group scope changes

	Domain Local	Global	Universal
Domain Local	n/a	No	Yes
Global	No	n/a	Yes
Universal	Yes	Yes	n/a

A Universal group can be changed to a Global or Domain Local group, as shown in table 4.3. A Global group can't be changed into a Domain Local group directly—it has to first be made into a Universal group. Changing from a Domain Local to a Global group also has to be via a Universal group.

Performing a change using ADAC is illustrated in figure 4.4.

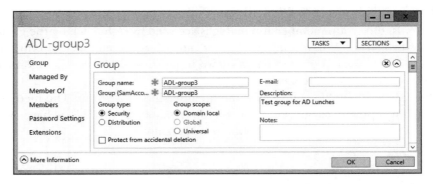

Figure 4.4 Group properties, in ADAC, showing that nonapplicable scopes are made not available (grayed out)

Find the group in ADAC or ADUC. Right-click and choose properties. Choose the new scope. Only allowed scopes will be available; for instance, the group would have to be converted to a Universal group before it could be converted to a Global group.

Using PowerShell to change scope is performed like this:

```
Set-ADGroup -Identity ADL-group1 -GroupScope Universal
Set-ADGroup -Identity ADL-group3 -GroupScope Universal
Set-ADGroup -Identity ADL-group3 -GroupScope DomainLocal
```

ADL-group1 and ADL-group3 were both created as Global groups. ADL-group1 can be converted directly to a Universal group, but ADL-group3 can't be converted directly to a Domain Local group; it has to first be converted to a Universal group.

One last operation to consider on groups is deletion.

4.2.3   Deleting a group

Deleting a group is a task you need to perform when the group is no longer required. In GUI tools, right-click the group and choose Delete. With PowerShell, use this code:

```
Remove-ADGroup -Identity ADL-Test3 -Confirm:$false
```

> **NOTE** Protect from Accidental Deletion will prevent deletion if it's enabled. Remember to remove the protection before deletion.

This completes our look at the group object lifecycle. The other important task associated with groups is managing their members.

4.3   *Managing group membership*

You'll need to perform three actions on group membership:

- View current membership
- Add new members
- Remove members from the group

As usual, these tasks can be performed using GUI tools or PowerShell.

4.3.1   Using GUI tools to manage group membership

In GUI tools, the group membership dialog is accessed by right-clicking the group and choosing Properties. When using ADAC, you can access the membership through the Members link to the left of the GUI, as shown in figure 4.5. The corresponding dialog for ADUC is shown in figure 4.6.

These displays enable you to view the membership of a group. The members are arranged in alphabetical order based on their name. Both dialogs have Add and Remove buttons for modifying the group membership.

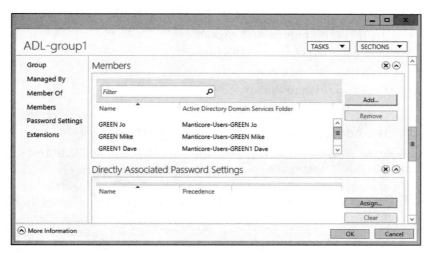

Figure 4.5   Viewing group membership with ADAC. Use the Add and Remove buttons to modify membership.

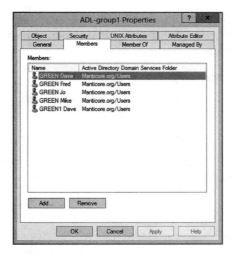

Figure 4.6   Viewing group membership with ADUC. Choose the Members tab of the Properties dialog. Use the Add and Remove buttons to modify membership.

Add a user to a group by performing the following steps:

1 Click the Add button shown in either dialog. You'll then see the dialog shown in figure 4.7.

2 Type the name, or part name, into the lower box.

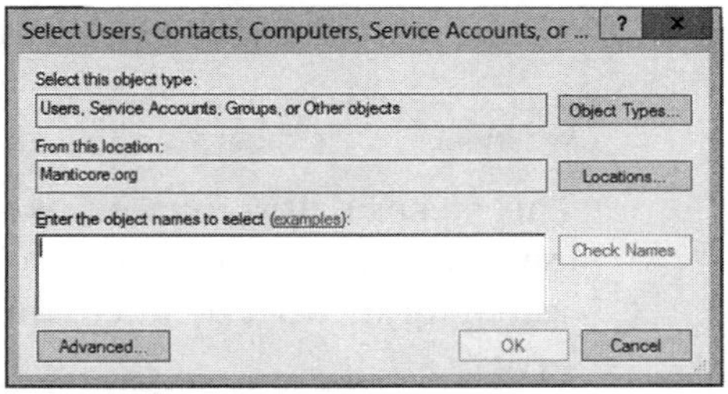

Figure 4.7   Dialog to add one or more users to a group

   3 Click Check Names.

   4 Select the users you require and click OK.

   5 The names will then change to this format:

```
GREEN Bill (bgreen@manticore.org)
```

   6 Click OK to add them to the group.

TRY IT NOW: Add members to a group using GUI tools

Using the supplied instructions, add members to the ADACtest and ADUCtest groups. Use ADAC and ADUC, respectively.

When searching for the user, enter GREEN as the name. This will find the users you created in chapter 2. You can select multiple users in the dialog so that they're all added to the group in one go.

Removing users from a group is achieved by highlighting the user or users and clicking the Remove button.

> **WARNING** ADUC will prompt to confirm that you want to remove a user when you click the Remove button. ADAC doesn't, but it'll ask if you want to save the changes when you close the dialog shown in figure 4.5.

4.3.2 *Using PowerShell to manage group membership*

PowerShell has three cmdlets with the noun ADGroupMember, as listed in table 4.2. To view the members of a group, use the Get-ADGroupMember cmdlet:

```
Get-ADGroupMember -Identity ADL-group1 | select Name, DistinguishedName
```

> **TIP** I always select the Name and DistinguishedName, because those are the properties that I need for other processing. It also reduces the display and makes it more readable.

Get-ADGroupMember is limited by default to returning a maximum of 5000 objects. This limit is set in the AD Web Service. You can modify the AD Web Service config file to increase this limit if you need to. Most organizations won't have groups with over 5000 members. Instructions for modifying the config file are available in the book's download material.

   Adding a member to a group is performed using the Add-ADGroupMember cmdlet:

```
Add-ADGroupMember -Identity ADL-group1
 -Members "CN=GREEN Bill,CN=Users,DC=Manticore,DC=org"
```

This means that you have to know the distinguished name (samAccountName works as well). Usually, you're told "add Bill Green to the ADL-group1." Remember, you can search for the user to add to the group:

```
Add-ADGroupMember -Identity ADL-group1
 -Members (Get-ADUser -LDAPFilter "(Name=Green Bill)")
```

This uses a neat PowerShell trick that lets you put parentheses around a piece of PowerShell and use that as input. Remember that `Get-ADUser` will return the `distinguishedName`, which is the property you want. You could also use (`Get-ADUser -Identity bgreen`) if you know the samAccountName. It's easier to filter on the name as shown, unless you belong to a very small organization where you can remember the samAccountNames of all users.

> **TRY IT NOW: Add members to a group using PowerShell**
>
> Try running this code:
>
> ```
> Add-ADGroupMember -Identity PStest `
> -Members (Get-ADUser -LDAPFilter "(sn=Green)")
> ```
>
> The LDAP (Lightweight Directory Access Protocol) name for the attribute holding a user's last name is `sn`. All users with a last name of "Green" are returned and added to the group.

One common scenario is that your boss tells you to add one user to all of the groups to which another user belongs. You'll learn how to do this in the next chapter in section 5.5.

Removing a member from a group requires—yes, you've guessed it—`Remove-ADGroupMember`:

```
Remove-ADGroupMember -Identity ADL-group1 -Members bgreen -Confirm:$false
```

Alternatively, you could use the distinguished name or the following:

```
Remove-ADGroupMember -Identity ADL-group1
➡ -Members (Get-ADUser -LDAPFilter "(Name=Green Bill)") -Confirm:$false
```

This concludes working with groups. It's time for a lab, I think.

4.4 Lab

After working through chapters 2 through 4, you'll have a good appreciation of working with the AD tools. This lab will build on that by providing practice with groups.

4.4.1 Complete the TRY IT NOW sections

If you haven't done them already, complete the TRY IT NOW exercises. The information for these exercises is summarized as follows.

CREATE A GROUP WITH ADAC

Following the instructions supplied, create a group in ADAC. Use the following information:

- *OU*—Users
- *Name*—ADACtest
- *samAccountName*—ADACtest

CREATE A GROUP WITH ADUC

Following the instructions supplied, create a group in ADUC. Use the following information:

- *OU*—Users
- *Name*—ADUCtest
- *samAccountName*—ADUCtest

CREATE A GROUP WITH POWERSHELL

Try running this code:

```
New-ADGroup -Name PStest -Path "CN=Users,DC=Manticore,DC=org" `
-GroupCategory Security -GroupScope Global `
-Description "Test group for AD Lunches"
```

You'll need to ensure that you're running PowerShell with elevated privileges and that you've imported the AD module.

ADD MEMBERS TO A GROUP USING GUI TOOLS

Using the supplied instructions, add members to the ADACtest and ADUCtest groups. Use ADAC and ADUC, respectively.

When searching for the user, enter GREEN as the name. This will find the users you created in chapter 2. You can select multiple users in the dialog so that they're all added to the group in one go.

ADD MEMBERS TO A GROUP USING POWERSHELL

Try running this code:

```
Add-ADGroupMember -Identity PStest `
-Members (Get-ADUser -LDAPFilter "(sn=Green)")
```

The LDAP name for the attribute holding a user's last name is sn. All users with a last name of "Green" are returned and added to the group.

4.4.2   *Create six new groups*

Create six new groups using your preferred tool. Create the groups in the Users container based on the information in table 4.4. Ignore the text of the description and create all of the groups as global security groups.

Table 4.4   Data for group creation exercise

Name and samAccountName	Description
ADLgroup1	ADL Global group 1
ADLgroup2	ADL Global group 2
ADLgroup3	ADL Domain Local group 1
ADLgroup4	ADL Domain Local group 2
ADLgroup5	ADL Universal group 1
ADLgroup6	ADL Universal group 2

If you want to use PowerShell to create groups in bulk, create a CSV file from table 4.4 (use Name and Description as the headers) and run this code:

```
Import-Csv -Path .\groups.csv |
foreach {
  New-ADGroup -Name $_.Name -Path "CN=Users,DC=Manticore,DC=org" `
  -GroupCategory Security -GroupScope Global `
  -Description $_.Description
}
```

A sample CSV file is supplied in the book's download file.

4.4.3 Change group scope

Change the scope of four of the groups: two to Universal and two to Domain Local. Use GUI tools and PowerShell. Change the groups to the scope given in table 4.5.

Table 4.5   Data for group creation exercise

Group	New Scope
ADLgroup3	Domain Local group
ADLgroup4	Domain Local group
ADLgroup5	Universal group
ADLgroup6	Universal group

4.4.4 Add group members

Add all of the test accounts you created in chapter 2 to each group you created in section 4.4.2. Use ADAC for ADLgroup1 and ADLgroup2, ADUC for ADLgroup3 and ADLgroup4, and PowerShell for ADLgroup5 and ADLgroup6.

4.4.5 Remove a user from group

Remove the user GREEN Mike from each of the six groups you created in section 4.4.2. Use ADAC for ADLgroup1 and ADLgroup2, ADUC for ADLgroup3 and ADLgroup4, and PowerShell for ADLgroup5 and ADLgroup6.

4.4.6 Nest groups

Attempt to nest groups as shown in table 4.6. You add a group in exactly the same way as a user, except that with PowerShell you use Get-ADGroup instead of Get-ADUser. Some of these may not be allowed—which won't work?

Table 4.6   Data for group nesting exercise

Group	Add groups
ADLgroup1	ADLgroup2, ADLgroup3
ADLgroup2	ADLgroup6

Table 4.6   Data for group nesting exercise *(continued)*

Group	Add groups
ADLgroup3	ADLgroup1, ADLgroup2, ADLgroup5
ADLgroup4	ADLgroup3, ADLgroup6
ADLgroup5	ADLgroup1, ADLgroup2, ADLgroup6
ADLgroup6	ADLgroup3, ADLgroup4

4.4.7   Delete user account

Add the user GREEN Mike into all groups created in section 4.4.2

Delete the account GREEN Mike. What happens to the group membership?

4.4.8   Add computer account to group

Computers can be added to groups using the following steps:

1   Create a new group called ADLcomputers in the Computers container.
2   Add the computer accounts ADLComp1 and ADLComp2 to the group.

Creating computer accounts is covered in chapter 6. For now, run this code to create the computer accounts:

```
"ADLComp1", "ADLComp2" |
foreach {
 New-ADComputer -Name $_ -Path "cn=Computers,dc=Manticore,dc=org"
}
```

4.5   Ideas for on your own

In many organizations there isn't a naming convention for groups—think about establishing one if your organization doesn't have one. If your groups don't have descriptions, think about adding them as you're working with individual groups. Don't sit and do all groups in one pass. Add them as you manage them.

An activity that comes up from time to time is copying the group membership from one user to another. How could you do that?

In the next chapter, you'll learn about troubleshooting issues with user accounts and groups.

Troubleshooting users and groups

5

Troubleshooting—every administrator's favorite activity. It's late in the afternoon, you want to go home, and the phone rings. It's the boss. A VIP can't log on to the network—and it's your fault (we know you didn't do it, but administrators are always blamed). How are you going to fix the problem?

That's where this chapter will help you: by teaching you how to troubleshoot the common AD-related problems for users and groups.

User- and group-related issues usually manifest as the user being unable to log on or access resources such as email, a file share, an application, or a printer. The most common problems are

- The user's password has expired.
- The user has forgotten the password and it needs resetting.
- The user has locked the account, usually because they used the wrong password too many times.
- The user isn't a member of the correct group to access the resources.

Have you noticed a pattern emerging? It's not quite a standard progression but makes a great framework around which to structure your troubleshooting activities. This chapter will walk you through these activities, so that by the end of the chapter you'll have a solid grasp of these techniques.

> **TIP** A lot of the problems that the AD administrator needs to resolve are password-related issues.

How are you going to find out about these problems? If you're lucky, the user will report them through whatever help desk mechanism your organization runs. If you're unlucky, you'll get a phone call as in the preceding scenario. Once the problem reaches you, you're the one in the hot seat, so how are you going to troubleshoot the problem? What troubleshooting methods are available to you?

5.1   *Troubleshooting first steps*

Having a method of troubleshooting problems will save you a lot of time. Over the years, I've seen administrators spend a lot of time clicking around various tools until they stumble across something that may help them resolve the problem. Stop! Think about what you need to do and then do it. After thinking about the problems listed in the introduction, your first steps should be

1. Check to see if the account is disabled.
2. Check to see if the account has expired.
3. Check to see if the account is locked out (see section 5.4).

Assume that a help desk call has been raised for a user. You're going to use the Dave Green account that was created in chapter 2. AD-related problems for users usually come down to two things:

- They can't log on.
- They can't access a resource.

The user has reported that he can't log on. Being an educated user, he's has tried logging on from another machine, so you can rule out a problem with his normal workstation. Also, all of his colleagues are still working, so it's not a general networking problem.

Your working assumption is that there's a problem with his account. You need to investigate his account. You could do that in a number of ways:

- Searches using the GUI tools
- Manual inspection using the GUI tools
- PowerShell scripts

Searching via the GUI tools is a possible route, but the types of filters you need to write to perform these tasks aren't very nice—for instance, to find disabled accounts you'd write this:

```
(useraccountcontrol:1.2.840.113556.1.4.803:=2)
```

This is a filter that you would use with the –LDAPFilter parameter of Get-ADUser. It's checking the useraccountcontrol attribute to determine if the bit with a value of 2 is set. There are much easier ways to discover disabled accounts, and I don't recommend using this approach— searching in these cases is much easier in PowerShell.

TIP It's possible to create a set of standard search scripts that have the required filters hardcoded. Filters for finding disabled accounts and other situations covered in this chapter can be found in the download on the book's website.

Searching from the command line using PowerShell is a much easier proposition.

You have the advantage of knowing that there's a problem with a particular user's account. Using the GUI tools to discover problems makes sense in this case, because you can go straight to the user's account and examine its properties.

5.1.1 Step 1: Is the account disabled?

Your first step is to see if the account is disabled. This is indicated by a small downward-pointing arrow superimposed on the bottom right of the icon representing the user. The context menu displayed by right-clicking the account will show the option Enable, rather than the normal Disable. If the account is disabled and it should be enabled, enable the account by choosing Enable from the context menu.

Alternatively, use PowerShell:

```
Search-ADAccount -AccountDisabled | select Name, samAccountName
```

This code will display a list of disabled accounts. If your user is in the list, enable the account like this:

```
Get-ADUser -Identity dgreen | Enable-ADAccount
```

Assuming the account is enabled, where do you look next?

5.1.2 Step 2: Check account status

Let's start with ADAC to stay consistent with the earlier chapters. Open the account properties by double-clicking the account. You'll see a display similar to figure 5.1.

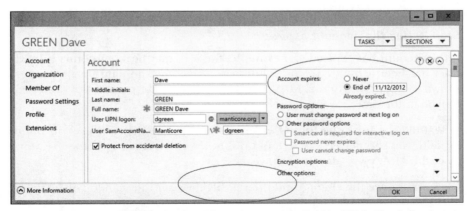

Figure 5.1 Areas to view for account expiry and account lockout in ADAC. Check the ringed areas at top-right to see if the account has expired and bottom-center to determine if the account is locked out (compare with figure 5.5.).

Figure 5.2   Areas to view for account expiry and account lockout in ADUC. Check the ringed areas at bottom-left to determine if the account has expired and center-left for a locked-out account. This figure shows the normal display (compare with figure 5.6, which shows a locked-out account).

If ADUC is your tool of choice, you'll see a display similar to figure 5.2.

> **TRY IT NOW: View user properties**
>
> Open one of the user accounts you created in chapter 2 in ADAC and ADUC and com-pare the results to figures 5.1 and 5.2.
>
> If you're familiar with the normal look of an AD account, the changes that occur when in the scenarios covered in this chapter will be more obvious to you.

Has the account expired?

5.1.3   *Step 3: Has the account expired?*

If the account has expired (for example, the user may be a temporary hire whose con-tract has been extended), the solution is to change the date in the property dialog shown in figures 5.1 or 5.2. ADUC supplies a date picker popup, but ADAC expects you to type in the date.

WARNING   Check the format expected by ADAC. When you click in the date field, you should see a little tool tip showing the format. I get the U.K. format of dd/MM/yyyy—day/month/year..

Click OK to save the change and then notify the user they can log on again.

TIP   If the user is in a remote site, you may need to allow the change to repli-cate. Alternatively, connect the tool to a domain controller in their site to make the change.

If the account is locked, jump to section 5.4 to remedy it.

PowerShell can be used to search for expired accounts, as follows:

```
Search-ADAccount -AccountExpired |
Format-Table Name, SamAccountName, DistinguishedName,
AccountExpirationDate -AutoSize
```

Once you've identified the expired account, a new date can be set like this:

```
Get-ADUser -Identity dgreen |
Set-ADAccountExpiration -DateTime (Get-Date).AddDays(30)
```

Using the samAccountName to identify the user in Get-ADUser, the user object is piped to Set-ADAccountExpiration, which will set the expiry date to 30 days from now. Alternatively, you could set a specific date using code like this:

```
Get-ADUser -Identity dgreen |
Set-ADAccountExpiration -DateTime ([datetime]'11/25/2013')
```

The date you supply is the date the account expired, so the GUI will report that expiry will occur at the end of the previous day.

> **WARNING** If you use this technique, the date must be presented as month/day/year. This is due to the way that .NET works and can't be changed.

You could decide to remove the expiry date entirely, in which case choose the Never button shown in figures 5.1 or 5.2. The PowerShell equivalent is

```
Get-ADUser -Identity dgreen | Clear-ADAccountExpiration
```

This uses the Clear-ADAccountExpiration cmdlet to remove the expiry date and set the account to never expire.

If the account isn't disabled or expired, the next place to look is the password.

5.2 *Password expiry*

AD passwords need to be changed every 42 days by default. Most organizations modify this value so the users need to change their password more frequently—I normally recommend 30 days.

You and your users will be prompted to change the password as the expiry date approaches. It for any reason the password isn't changed (such as the user being ill or away on vacation), it will expire. The user will not be allowed to log on if they can't remember the old password and the password will need resetting. If they do remember the old password, they can perform the reset themselves following the prompts they'll receive.

Neither of the GUI tools supply a direct way to see if the password has expired. You could work it out from the password reset date, but there's an easier way.

The Search-ADAccount cmdlet can provide information on accounts with expired passwords:

```
Search-ADAccount -PasswordExpired
```

If the password has expired, the solution is to reset the password.

5.3   *Password reset*

You've just seen that passwords may need resetting because they've expired. The other common reason for a password reset is that the user has been away from work and has forgotten their password. If you're lucky, they call you before attempting to log on; otherwise you'll be unlocking their account (see section 5.4).

Resetting a password should be a user activity. There are a number of situations when an administrative reset of a password can cause problems; for instance, if you're using Encrypted File System (EFS), a forced password change can lock users out of their own files. You can force the users to change their password after they've entered the temporary one you gave them. This is the recommended approach.

The password reset options are easily found in the GUI tools:

1   Open your GUI tool: ADAC or ADUC.
2   Find the user of interest.
3   Right-click the user account.
4   Choose Reset Password on the context menu. A dialog box, as shown in figure 5.3 (ADAC), or figure 5.4 (ADUC), will be displayed.
5   Enter the password in the two text boxes. Ensure they match; otherwise the reset will be rejected.
6   Leave the *User must change password at next log on* checkbox selected.
7   Click OK.

Figure 5.3   Resetting a password using ADAC. The password is entered twice. Ensure the *User must change password at next log on* box is checked and click OK.

Figure 5.4   Resetting a password using ADUC. The password is entered twice. Ensure the *User must change password at next log on* box is checked and click OK.

TRY IT NOW: Reset a password

Open one of the user accounts you created in chapter 2 in ADAC and then in ADUC and follow the instructions to reset a password.

Compare the dialog boxes presented in the different tools.

Performing a password reset in PowerShell is a bit more difficult:

```
$password = Read-Host -Prompt "Password" -AsSecureString

$id = "dgreen"
Set-ADAccountPassword -Identity $id -NewPassword $password -Reset
Set-ADUser -Identity $id -ChangePasswordAtLogon:$true
```

Create a new password as a secure string. The system will prompt for the information and mask what you type in. The `Set-ADAccountPassword` cmdlet is used to reset the password. The `-Reset` parameter negates the need for the old password. `Set-ADUser` is then used to force the user to change the password at the next log on.

   Password problems can lead to a user being locked out.

5.4 *Unlocking a user account*

An account lockout occurs when a user enters the wrong password too many times in a short time period. The number of errors and the time period are defined in the default domain policy—common settings are three errors in 30 minutes, though many organizations use a shorter period. Once an account is locked, it'll remain locked for a time period defined in the policy (often 30 minutes), or in the worst case until an administrator (you) unlocks it.

Forcing a lockout

It's impossible to force an account to be locked out directly using PowerShell (or any other scripting/programming approach) or the GUI tools. This means you have to fall back onto my all-time favorite technique: brute force.

If you need to lock an account for experimental purposes, try this code:

```
$cred = Get-Credential
1..30 | foreach {
Get-WmiObject win32_ComputerSystem -ComputerName win7 -Credential $cred
}
```

`Get-Credential` will display a dialog box that looks very much like the logon prompt. Supply the user account (in the form domain\logon ID) and a phony password.

Then run the second line of code. It attempts to access the machine (I've used a machine called Win7, but you need to use a machine in your domain) using those credentials. The attempts fail and you have a locked-out account.

The standard lockout policies in your domain will apply—if you don't lock accounts, of course, this approach (like all others) will fail.

When a user enters the wrong password too many times, the account will lock and they'll be informed that it has locked. At that point, you're the lucky individual who'll get a help desk call. If you open ADAC and look at the properties of the user, you'll see the padlock symbol as ringed in figure 5.5.

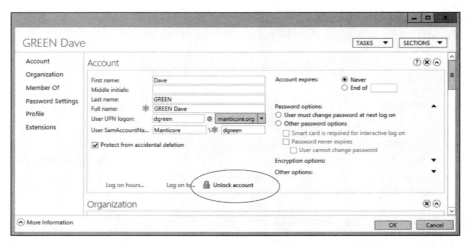

Figure 5.5   Locked account viewed in ADAC. Click the padlock symbol to unlock. Clicking OK will save the change.

ADUC shows a different view, as shown in figure 5.6.

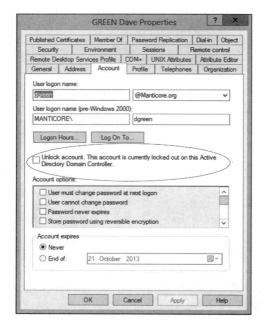

Figure 5.6   Locked account viewed in ADUC. Click the *Unlock account* box and click OK to unlock.

Finding a locked account with PowerShell can be accomplished using the `Search-ADAccount` cmdlet:

```
PS> Search-ADAccount -LockedOut

AccountExpirationDate :
DistinguishedName     : CN=GREEN Dave,CN=Users,DC=Manticore,DC=org
Enabled               : True
LastLogonDate         : 03/10/2012 20:58:16
LockedOut             : True
Name                  : GREEN Dave
ObjectClass           : user
ObjectGUID            : 28f0c168-d142-417f-a223-333488cdaa77
PasswordExpired       : False
PasswordNeverExpires  : False
SamAccountName        : dgreen
SID                   : S-1-5-21-3881460461-1879668979-35955009-6270
UserPrincipalName     : dgreen@manticore.org
```

The `Unlock-ADAccount` cmdlet can be used to perform the unlocking:

```
Unlock-ADAccount -Identity dgreen
```

> **NOTE** There's no `Lock-ADAccount` cmdlet.

The task can be accomplished in one pass by combining the two cmdlets like this:

```
Search-ADAccount -LockedOut | Unlock-ADAccount
```

Once you've unlocked the account, the change needs to replicate. Alternatively, make the change on a domain controller in the same AD site as the user. AD accounts shouldn't be locked out under normal operational conditions, so this should be a safe operation. If you find you're getting a lot of locked accounts, either your users need some education, or you may be seeing the results of an attempt to attack your environment. In either case you need to escalate the situation to your management.

That completes your tour of user issues. The issue of access to resources still remains.

5.5 *Group membership*

As you saw in chapter 4, groups are used to give access to resources such as file shares and applications. You'll get calls such as "I can't access file share X." That usually means the user isn't in the right group.

You saw how to view group membership in section 4.3. Review that section if you need a refresher. After testing if the user is in the correct group, you can add them using the techniques from section 4.3.

You may find that a user changes roles and isn't a member of any of the groups they need to be for their new role. Let's say you have a user, mgreen, who is a member of one group. You can view his group membership like this:

```
PS> Get-ADUser -Identity mgreen -Properties memberof |
select -ExpandProperty memberof

CN=ADL-group3,CN=Users,DC=Manticore,DC=org
```

The result is the AD distinguished name of the group, in this case "CN=ADL-group3,CN=Users,DC=Manticore,DC=org".

You want him to have the same group membership as dgreen, whose group membership you can check like this:

```
PS> Get-ADUser -Identity dgreen -Properties memberof |
select -ExpandProperty memberof

CN=ADL-group2,CN=Users,DC=Manticore,DC=org
CN=ADL-group1,CN=Users,DC=Manticore,DC=org
```

One method would be to open GUI tools, look at the membership of dgreen, and write down all the groups of which he's a member. You can then open up the properties for mgreen and change his group membership to match dgreen. Too much work. A much simpler way that will save you time, effort, and mistakes is to run a script like this:

```
$target = Get-ADUser -Identity mgreen -Properties memberof
foreach ($member in $target.memberof){
 Remove-ADGroupMember -Identity $member -Members $target -Confirm:$false
}

$source = Get-ADUser -Identity dgreen -Properties memberof
foreach ($member in $source.memberof){
 Add-ADGroupMember -Identity $member -Members $target -Confirm:$false
}
```

The properties for mgreen are retrieved from Active Directory, including the group membership (`memberof` property). The groups are cycled through using `foreach` and mgreen is removed as a member. You then get the properties of dgreen, including the group membership. Cycle through those groups and add mgreen as a member. The job is done quicker than you can read this section.

> **TRY IT NOW: Copy group membership**
>
> Run the preceding code in your test environment. If you completed the lab from chapter 4, the user mgreen would have been deleted. Recreate the user and add him to `ADLgroup3` before running the code.

That covers the common troubleshooting activities for users and groups. The techniques in this chapter provide a basis for developing further troubleshooting techniques of your own.

5.6   Lab

It's time to complete this lunchtime activity with a quick lab.

5.6.1   Complete any TRY IT NOW sections

If you didn't complete the TRY IT NOW exercises, do so now. The information is summarized here.

VIEW USER PROPERTIES

Open one of the user accounts you created in chapter 2 in ADAC and then in ADUC and compare the results to figures 5.1 and 5.2.

If you're familiar with the normal look of an AD account, the changes that occur in the scenarios covered in this chapter will be more obvious to you.

RESET A PASSWORD

Open one of the user accounts you created in chapter 2 in ADAC and then in ADUC and follow the instructions to reset a password.

Compare the dialog boxes presented in the different tools and try resetting the password with PowerShell. How can you tell that a password has been reset?

COPY GROUP MEMBERSHIP

Run the last code block shown in section 5.5 in your test environment. If you completed the lab from chapter 4, the user mgreen would have been deleted. Recreate the user and add him to `ADLgroup3` before running the code.

5.6.2 *Account expiry*

Perform the techniques in section 5.1 to change an account that has expired. An account can be forced to expire by changing the expiry date like this:

```
Set-ADAccountExpiration -Identity dgreen -DateTime (get-date).AddDays(-5)
```

Repeat the exercise of resetting the account expiry date using ADAC, ADUC, and PowerShell. Try setting the account to never expire.

5.6.3 *Account lockout*

Determine your organization's account lockout policy. How does that affect what you learned in section 5.4? Lockout an account using the technique in section 5.4.

> **WARNING** Only perform this action in a test domain.

Unlock the account.

5.6.4 *Disable an account*

Deliberately disable an account like this:

```
Disable-ADAccount -Identity dgreen
```

Repeat the exercise of enabling the account expiry date using ADAC, ADUC, and PowerShell.

5.7 *Ideas for on your own*

Determine if there are any other common troubleshooting needs in your organization and how you're going to deal with them. This may mean looking ahead through the table of contents to find the section dealing with those issues.

In the next chapter you'll learn about computer accounts.

Managing computer accounts

If you were asked "What's in your Active Directory?" your instinctive answer would most likely be users and groups. It's what everyone thinks of because that's where the bulk of the work lies. The other big data set is computers.

Every computer that's part of your Active Directory has an account that has to be managed. This chapter will show you how to manage all the computers in your domain with minimal effort—that's not zero effort, just minimizing the effort.

Why do you need computer accounts in Active Directory? Imagine an organization with thousands of users, each with their own desktop computer. This organization also has 2000 to 3000 servers. Now, you could manage the settings on all of those machines manually—good luck. A better and easier approach is to use Group Policy, which we'll cover in chapters 8 and 9. Using Group Policy requires the machines to be in your Active Directory. Applications like Exchange require that the server is in the AD domain.

You already know a lot about managing computers because you learned how to manage users in chapter 2. Computer accounts in Active Directory are specialized variants of user accounts, which means you can apply a lot of your existing knowledge (re-read chapter 2 to refresh your memory if required). Everything else will be covered in this chapter.

Every object in your Active Directory has a lifecycle. I've mentioned this concept a few times, and make no apologies for the fact that I'm going to keep on mentioning it. Working with the lifecycle of AD objects enables you to keep on top of managing the objects, as well as applying some best practices.

Computer objects have a more limited lifecycle than user objects. The creation and deletion of the object are the obvious endpoints, but you won't perform as many updates to the computer accounts as you do to user accounts. The computer needs to join the domain, which may happen with a preexisting account, or the account can be created as the machine joins the domain.

Each computer has a secure channel to the domain controller it authenticates—yes, computers authenticate as well as users. It happens in the background so you don't see it. This channel may, very occasionally, develop problems and need resetting.

As with any object in your Active Directory, the final act is to delete it. Occasionally you may decide to disable a computer account, but it's not an action that I've used very much; however, you'll learn how to do this for completeness.

The first thing is to create some computer accounts.

There are two main ways to deal with creating computer accounts:

- Create the account and then join the computer to the domain.
- Create the account as you join the computer to the domain.

Which way is best? It depends on how you create your computers. If you use an automated system such as Windows Deployment Services, it expects a computer account to exist. On the other hand, if you build your machines from an image or template, then you'll create the account as you join the machine to the domain.

Another advantage to creating the account in Active Directory, known as prestaging, is that the account is in the correct OU, so the machine will receive the correct GPOs as soon as it joins the domain. Also, you can control who can join the machine to the domain.

Let's see how to create a computer account.

6.1　*Creating an AD computer account*

Creating a computer account in Active Directory is a much simpler proposition than creating a user account, primarily because you don't need to supply as much information. As usual, you'll start by creating a computer account using GUI tools.

6.1.1　*Creating a computer account using ADAC*

In the examples in this chapter you're going to create the accounts in the Computers container. This is the default location for computer accounts, but you can create an account in any OU.

> **TIP**　It's best practice to keep your computer and user accounts in separate OUs to make the application of GPOs easier.

You can create an account using ADAC by following these steps:

1　Open ADAC.
2　Select the container or OU in which you'll create the computer account (in this case the Computers container).

Figure 6.1   Creating a computer account with ADAC. The only mandatory information is the computer name, which auto-populates the NetBIOS field as you enter it. This dialog also provides options for setting Protect from Accidental Deletion, the administrator(s) who will manage the computer, and the groups to which it'll belong.

3   Choose New from the Tasks menu.

4   Choose Computer.

5   The dialog box in figure 6.1 will be displayed.

6   Add the computer name (the NetBIOS field auto-populates as you type).

7   Check Protect from accidental deletion.

8   Click Change to select the users or groups that can join the machine to the domain.

9   Add the computer manager if required.

10   Add the computer to one or more groups if required.

11   Click OK to create the account.

Creating a computer account with ADUC is a similar process.

6.1.2   Creating a computer account using ADUC

ADUC has a slightly different approach to creating computer accounts, and in one important point has an advantage over ADAC in that you can add the computer GUID used by automated deployment systems. You create a computer account in ADUC by following these steps:

1   Open ADUC.

2   Select the container or OU in which you'll create the computer account (in this case the Computers container).

3 Right-click the container name and choose New from the context menu.

4 Choose Computer.

5 The dialog shown in figure 6.2 will be displayed.

6 Add the computer name (the pre-Windows 2000 name will auto-populate).

7 Click Change to modify the user or group that can add the machine to the domain.

8 Click Next.

9 The dialog in figure 6.3 will be displayed.

10 Choose "This is a managed computer" and add the computer GUID as required (only if using automated build systems such as Windows Deployment Services).

11 Click Next.

12 View the summary.

13 Click Finish to complete the creation of the computer object.

Figure 6.2 Creating a computer account with ADUC. Add the computer name (the pre-Windows 2000 name will auto-populate). Click Next.

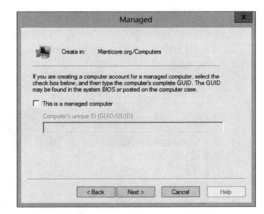

Figure 6.3 Adding a computer's GUID in ADUC. Click Next to continue.

Pre-Windows 2000 computers

In the dialogs for both ADAC and ADUC you'll notice the option to assign this computer account as a pre-Windows 2000 computer.

Ignore it!

This option exists to allow AD to be aware of pre-Windows 2000 systems and interact with the client software that allowed the user (but not the computer) to authenticate against Active Directory. Because those operating systems are all out of support, it's unlikely you'll see them in your environment.

Creating computer accounts with GUI tools is great for the once-in-a-while activity, but if you need to create lots of computer accounts, you need to use PowerShell.

6.1.3 *Creating a computer account using PowerShell*

One of the great advantages of ADAC is that it's built on top of PowerShell. The version released with Windows Server 2012 shows you the PowerShell commands it used to perform the actions you've initiated in the GUI. This is illustrated in figure 6.4, which shows the PowerShell generated when you created the computer account in figure 6.1.

The code that ADAC generates can be overly verbose. A simplified version would be

```
New-ADComputer -Enabled $true -Name ADLComp3 `
-Path "CN=Computers,DC=Manticore,DC=org" `
-SamAccountName ADLCOMP3
```

You can also set a number of other properties, such as who manages the computer account and the operating system information (completed automatically when the machine joins the domain). PowerShell really comes into its own when you need to create multiple accounts, which you'll see in the lab.

The other way to generate a computer account is to create one as the system joins the domain.

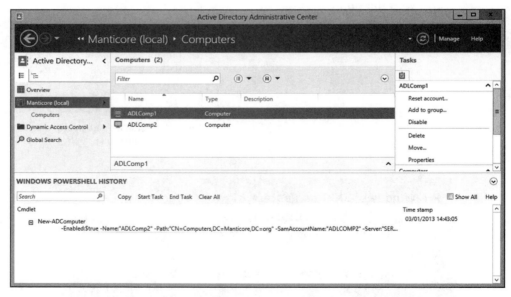

Figure 6.4   PowerShell command to create a computer account. The Windows PowerShell History window is normally minimized. You open it by clicking on the upward-pointing arrow at the bottom-right corner of the ADAC GUI.

6.2   Joining a computer to the domain

By default, any user can join 10 computers to the domain. This is normally thought to be a bad idea, and most organizations use Group Policy to limit who can join a computer to the domain.

A number of prerequisites needs to be in place before you can join the computer to the domain:

- The machine should be configured with the address of at least one DNS server that manages the DNS zone for your Active Directory.
- You need local administrator permissions on the machine.
- You need the account name and password of a user account that has permissions to join the machine to the domain.
- Ideally, the machine should have been renamed to the name you want it to have in Active Directory.

You can join a computer to the domain using a GUI tool or through PowerShell.

6.2.1   Using GUI tools to join a machine to the domain

Using GUI tools is the traditional method of joining a machine to the domain. The procedure involves the following steps:

1   Open Control Panel.
2   Choose System.
3   Choose Advanced System Settings.
4   Choose Computer Name.
5   Choose Change.
6   The dialog shown in figure 6.5 will be displayed.
7   Choose the Domain button and supply a domain name.
8   Click OK.

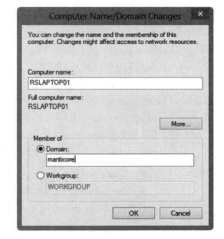

Figure 6.5   Dialog to add a computer to the domain

You'll be prompted for the name and password of an account with permissions to add the computer to the domain. Supply the data and click OK. You'll see a message welcoming you to the domain and prompting you to reboot. The reboot is required. The machine will not function as part of the domain until the reboot has occurred. The computer account will be created in the default location, usually the Computers container.

> **TIP**   If you're running a system with PowerShell v3, you can display the Control Panel System applet using this PowerShell command:

```
Show-ControlPanelItem -Name System
```

The alternative approach is to use a PowerShell cmdlet.

6.2.2 *Using PowerShell to join a machine to the domain*

The following code can be used to join a machine to the domain:

```
$cred = Get-Credential
Add-Computer -Credential $cred -DomainName Manticore `
-OUPath "OU=Security Servers,OU=Servers,DC=Manticore,DC=org" -Force
Restart-Computer
```

The `Get-Credential` cmdlet displays a dialog box for you to enter a user ID and password. Make sure that you enter the user ID in the domain/user format. The password will be masked as you enter it. The `Add-Computer` cmdlet needs the name of the domain and the credential. The `OUPath` is optional but useful, because it controls where the account is created and saves the work of moving it later. The `-Force` parameter suppresses the conformation prompt, which is the best way to proceed in a script. The final command, `Restart-Computer`, performs the reboot.

Once your machine has been added to the domain, it communicates across a secure channel with the domain controller. That channel may need to be tested if you're having issues with the machine.

6.3 *Managing the secure channel*

All computers (Windows 2000 and later) in an AD domain communicate with a domain controller. They authenticate over that channel every time the machine is restarted.

A password is used to authenticate the machine. This password is automatically reset every 30 days—you don't have to do anything, it just happens. The secure channel is a robust mechanism and usually doesn't go wrong.

This doesn't mean that it can't go wrong. Sometimes you'll see problems that manifest when you try to log on:

- You receive a message that states no logon servers are available.
- You receive a message that Windows cannot connect to the domain because a domain controller isn't available.
- You receive a message that your computer account wasn't found.

The exact wording will depend on your version of Windows. All of these messages mean that the secure channel between the computer and the domain has become corrupted. This can happen in a number of scenarios:

- A desktop machine has been switched off for more than 30 days, which is common in classroom scenarios.
- A user has had extended leave and their machine hasn't been switched on.
- A spare laptop has been kept in a cupboard and not used.
- A preconfigured server was started for the first time more than 30 days after configuration.
- A virtual machine hasn't been started for an extended period, which is very common in lab environments.

These scenarios all have one thing in common: the machine hasn't been connected to the domain for more than 30 days, so the password on its secure channel has expired. The domain controller doesn't recognize the password and therefore won't authenticate the machine.

There are a few ways to fix this problem:

- Remove the machine from the domain and rejoin it to the domain.
- Choose the computer object in ADAC. Choose Reset Account from the Task menu. A confirmation request will be displayed and the reset will occur.
- Right-click the computer object in ADUC and choose Reset Account. A confirmation request will be displayed and the reset will occur.

Using ADAC or ADUC to reset the account results in you having to remove the machine from the domain and rejoin it back to the domain. This requires a number of reboots and is very time-consuming.

None of these options provide a way to test that the secure channel is the cause of the problem. A simpler approach is to use the PowerShell `Test-ComputerSecureChannel` cmdlet, as shown in figure 6.6.

The command `Test-ComputerSecureChannel` performs the test. Use the `-Verbose` parameter for more output. A value of `False` is returned if the secure channel is corrupted (a return value of `True` indicates the channel is good). The cmdlet can be rerun with the `-Repair` switch to reset the password and repair the secure channel. These options are shown in figure 6.6.

Alternatively, you can test and fix in one go:

```
if (-not(Test-ComputerSecureChannel)){
 Test-ComputerSecureChannel -Repair -Verbose
}
```

The only drawback here is that you don't get any feedback if the channel is good.

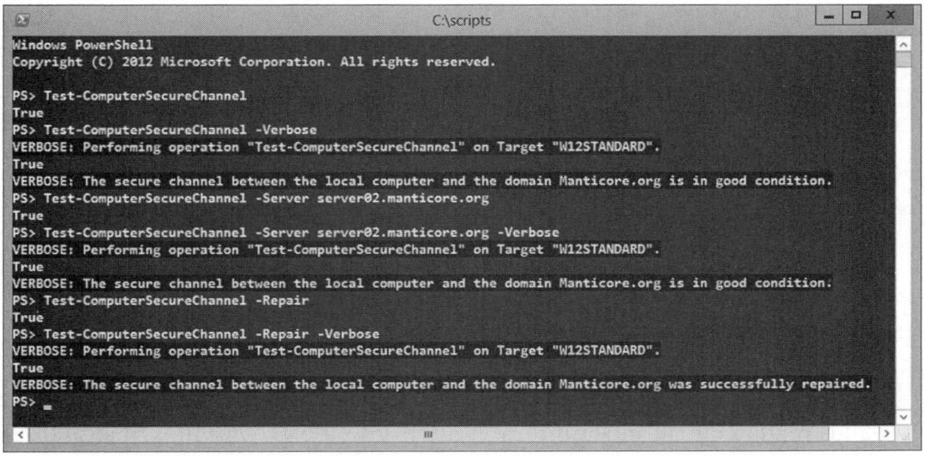

Figure 6.6 Using `Test-ComputerSecureChannel`

Testing and repairing the secure channel with PowerShell has one great advantage: you don't have to remove the machine from the domain and then rejoin it, which is a huge timesaver.

There isn't much more you can do for a computer account. It's worth setting a description on your servers—use the techniques you leaned in chapter 3, but use `Set-ADComputer`'s `-Description` parameter. Computer objects in Active Directory are low-maintenance, but they do have a finite lifecycle and eventually need to be deleted.

6.4   *Deleting a computer account*

Deleting a computer account is the last step in the object's lifecycle. There are a few reasons for deleting an account:

- The computer is no longer required.
- The computer has been rebuilt with a new name.
- The computer has been removed from the domain and the account wasn't deleted automatically.

Discovering computer accounts to delete usually happens in one of two ways. Either you know you need (or are told that you need) to delete the account because of other activities taking place, or you run a regular test to discover computer accounts that may need deleting.

You can run the following PowerShell snippet to discover inactive (haven't logged on to the domain) computer accounts:

```
Search-ADAccount -AccountInactive  -ComputersOnly |
Format-Table Name, DistinguishedName, LastLogonDate, ObjectClass  -Autosize
```

There are some drawbacks to this:

- The time period after which the account is deemed to be inactive isn't defined.
- It takes no account of which domain controller is contacted.
- In my testing it also returns managed service accounts.

The last point needs a bit more clarification. Using `Search-ADAccount -Account-Inactive` returns user and computer accounts. Adding the `-UsersOnly` switch returns just users, excluding managed service accounts. I suspect that the `-ComputersOnly` switch tells the cmdlet to return all accounts that aren't users; unfortunately, this also includes managed service accounts.

You can fix all of the issues by defining an explicit timespan that accounts for AD replication and also filtering out managed service accounts:

```
Search-ADAccount -AccountInactive -ComputersOnly -TimeSpan "90:00:00"|
where ObjectClass -eq "Computer" |
Format-Table Name, DistinguishedName, LastLogonDate, ObjectClass -Autosize
```

This will search for computer accounts that have been inactive for 90 days—the time-span is read as days:hours:minutes. A filter only allows computer objects through:

```
where ObjectClass -eq "Computer"
```

The code completes by displaying the selected properties in a table. Now that you know which computers have inactive accounts, how do you delete them?

> **TIP** If for some reason a domain controller appears on your list, investigate carefully before deleting it. GUI tools in Windows Server 2008 R2 and Windows Server 2012 remove the other references in Active Directory to the domain controller if you delete the computer object, but in earlier versions of Windows you need to clean up the domain controller references (see chapter 11).

If you only have one or two computer accounts to delete, you can find them in Active Directory (using either ADAC or ADUC); right-click the object and choose Delete. You'll get a message box asking you to confirm the deletion. Click Yes to delete and No to cancel the action.

In a situation where you have many objects to delete, this can be achieved using a PowerShell script:

```
Import-Csv -Path C:\Scripts\ADLunches\computersTodelete.txt |
foreach {
 Remove-ADComputer -Identity $_.Name -Confirm:$false
}
```

The computer names are in a file. The names are passed to `Remove-ADComputer`, which performs the deletion. This technique is covered further in the lab section. `Remove-ADComputer` can also be used to delete individual accounts.

This concludes your lesson on computer accounts—time for some lab work.

6.5 *Lab*

This lab contains exercises based on the computer object lifecycle. You'll practice creating, managing, and deleting computer accounts.

6.5.1 *Create computer accounts*

Try creating the computer accounts shown in the figures and code snippets in section 6.1, using the instructions provided. The accounts are all created in the Computers container. The names are

- ADLComp1
- ADLComp2
- ADLComp3

The computer name and pre-Windows 2000 (samAccountName) should be identical. It's possible for them to be different, but there's no good reason to do so. The accounts should be created in an enabled state. Do you have to do anything in the GUI to achieve this?

6.5.2 *Create computer accounts in bulk*

Creating accounts in bulk is required if you have a large number of servers coming online or if you're performing a desktop refresh. This task is easiest performed using

PowerShell. Create a CSV file with the computer name and the description. An example would be

```
Name,Description
ADLComp10, "Test Machine for AD Lunches"
ADLComp11, "Test Machine for AD Lunches"
ADLComp12, "Test Machine for AD Lunches"
```

The file can have a CSV or TXT extension. You can use code like this to create the computer accounts:

```
Import-Csv -Path C:\Scripts\ADLunches\computers.txt |
foreach {
 New-ADComputer -Enabled $true -Name $_.Name `
-Path "CN=Computers,DC=Manticore,DC=org" `
-SamAccountName $_.Name         `
-Description $_.Description -PassThru
}
```

Try creating a file and running the code. How could you alter the code so that accounts were created in different OUs?

6.5.3   *Searching for computer accounts*

There's some useful information stored in the computer account object. You can search on this information. Try these searches and view the results. *Hint:* you'll need to modify the computer names for your environment.

FIND ALL COMPUTERS

This will display all computers in your Active Directory:

```
Get-ADComputer -Filter * | select Name, DistinguishedName
```

FIND A SPECIFIC COMPUTER

Use this snippet to view all the properties of a specific computer:

```
Get-ADComputer -Identity dc02 -Properties *
```

FIND A SPECIFIC OPERATING SYSTEM

This displays all computers with a Windows Server 2012 operating system:

```
Get-ADComputer -Properties *   `
-Filter "OperatingSystem -like '*Server 2012*'" |
select Name, DistinguishedName
```

How could you modify this for other operating systems? *Hint:* try using this to see the OS versions present in your AD.

```
Get-ADComputer -Properties * -Filter * | select OperatingSystem -Unique
```

Examine the full list of properties for a computer object. How can you filter on the service pack as well as on the operating system?

FIND EXPIRED ACCOUNTS

```
Search-ADAccount -AccountInactive -ComputersOnly -TimeSpan "90:00:00"|
where ObjectClass -eq "Computer" |
Format-Table Name, DistinguishedName, LastLogonDate, ObjectClass -Autosize
```

Modify the timespan to determine the optimum for your environment. Could you change this to find disabled computer accounts?

6.5.4 *Managing the secure channel*

Pick a computer (noncritical) from your environment and log on to it. Use the Power-Shell commands from section 6.3 to test and reset the secure channel.

Reset the account from GUI tools. What happens to the computer account? Rejoin the computer to the domain.

6.5.5 *Deleting computer accounts*

You created three computer accounts in section 6.5.1. Delete those three accounts:

- ADLComp1—delete with ADAC
- ADLComp2—delete with ADUC
- ADLComp3—delete with PowerShell

Take some of the computer names you used for bulk creation in section 6.5.2 and create a CSV file like this:

```
Name
ADLComp21
ADLComp22
ADLComp23
ADLComp24
```

Use the bulk deletion code to remove those accounts:

```
Import-Csv -Path C:\Scripts\ADLunches\computersTodelete.txt |
foreach {
 Remove-ADComputer -Identity $_.Name -Confirm:$false
}
```

Is there a way to make this any safer? How would you change the code so you confirmed each deletion?

6.6 *Ideas for on your own*

Managing computer accounts is not as big a task as managing user accounts, but you can make your life more efficient by adopting some automation. Here are some ideas to build into your administration work cycles:

- Use the scripts in this chapter to create a mechanism for removing expired accounts. *Hint:* make it a two-stage process to find the expired accounts and examine them to determine which to delete. Then perform the deletion.
- Create a process for the bulk creation of computer accounts.
- Create a script that tests the service-pack level of your computers. You can then proactively start reporting which machines need to be service packed.

This concludes our examination of computer accounts. Next, we'll look at organizational units.

7
Managing organizational units

Imagine you have a domain with 6000 users, 6000 workstations, 700 groups, and 500 servers. If all of those objects are in a single container, you'll have a hard time delegating administrative permissions and applying Group Policy. Organizational units (OUs) are used to give structure to your domain. You can put objects that are related by the rules you define, such as all the users in a specific business unit or location, into specific OUs and use those OUs to control the delegation of administrative permissions and the application of Group Policy. In a nutshell, OUs break the mass of objects in your domain into manageable sets.

In the preceding example, an OU may contain a few hundred users or computers, which is a more manageable proposition. OUs contain the objects you've read about in chapters 2 through 6. This chapter covers the OU lifecycle.

You might assume that managing OUs begins with creating them, but in this case you need to know why you're creating them and for what you intend to use them. After a little bit of background, which explains the whys, you'll learn how to create OUs.

One nightmare scenario for AD administrators is "I've just deleted an OU with hundreds of user accounts in it." There's a simple technique to protect your OUs and their contents from accidental deletion. It'll be second nature to use it after you've finished this chapter.

Once you've created an OU, there isn't much to do to it. You can set a description and who manages it, but there aren't many other properties to change. An activity you'll find yourself performing is moving objects between OUs. You can do this with GUI tools or PowerShell. The final part of the OU lifecycle is deleting them.

First up, though, you need to understand why OUs are important and what they do for you.

7.1   *OU concepts*

An OU is a container within a domain that can be used to hold user, computer, group, and other OU objects. There are two main reasons to create an OU:

- To control the delegation of administrative privileges—that is, a certain group of administrators can only control the users, groups, and computers in a certain OU
- To control the application of Group Policy

OUs can't be assigned permissions, so you can't use them in place of groups.

Domains are inflexible objects, and reorganizing the domains in a forest is a major undertaking. In contrast, reorganizing the OUs (and their contents) within a domain is a relatively straightforward matter.

> **TIP**   If you think of OUs as being analogous to folders in the file system, you'll have a good idea of what they do and how they operate.

OUs were stated to be containers for other objects. Just to complicate matters, in your Active Directory you'll also find objects called containers that are created with the domain. There are a number of these, but the ones you're most likely to come across are

- Built-in, which stores a number of the default groups.
- Users, which stores other default groups, especially the Domain Admins, Enterprise Admins, and Schema Admins. It's also the default location for the creation of new users if a specific OU isn't given.
- Computers, which is empty when the domain is created, but is the default location for the creation of computer accounts when a new machine is joined to the domain.

The major differences between a container and an OU are that Group Policy cannot be applied to a container and that child OUs can't be created within a container.

There are a number of patterns available to you when creating the OUs in your domain:

- Map the organization structure—create OUs to represent the major business units and possibly create child OUs for subteams.
- Map the geographic locations—create OUs for the major locations in your organization. Depending on the size of the organization, this could be at the building, town, or country level.
- Create separate OUs (or OU structures) for users and workstations, which ease the application of Group Policy.
- Separate servers into their own OU structure for Group Policy application.

OU depth

You'll see numerous references to not creating a deep OU path—that is, OUs with child OUs that have child OUs, and so on. But how deep is too deep?

It's not so much the depth of the OU tree that matters, but how many GPOs that are linked to that structure. GPOs are processed from the domain level down the OU tree until the OU containing the object is reached. The more GPOs that have to be processed, the slower the logon process and the more likely that you'll get complaints from the users. So how deep is too deep?

A depth of three with a single GPO linked to each level is unlikely to cause problems. A depth of two dozen OUs, each with one or more GPOs linked, will definitely cause problems. Sensibly, if you keep the maximum depth under six or so and keep the number of GPOs to a minimum, you shouldn't see any problems under normal operations.

These patterns aren't mutually exclusive; for instance, you could create OUs based on the location, each of which had separate child OUs for computers and users. There's no specific right answer that will suit all organizations. You need to consider the granularity of administration delegation, your Group Policy strategy, and what gives the optimum model for your organization. The good news is that OUs are flexible and can be reorganized relatively easily.

It's time for you to investigate the OU lifecycle, starting with how you can create them.

7.2   *Creating an OU with the GUI tools*

The OU lifecycle starts with creation of the OU; actually, it starts with determining the requirements and need for a new OU, but we'll take that as a given for the purposes of this discussion. You can use GUI tools or PowerShell to create OUs.

> **WARNING**   OU names don't have to be unique across the domain. They do have to be unique at the same level. You can't create two OUs called Workstations in the root of the domain, but you can create OUs called Seattle and Boston and then create an OU called Workstations inside each of them.

Building on what you know about creating users, groups, and computers, creating OUs shouldn't hold any surprises. ADAC is considered first, followed by ADUC. PowerShell is covered in the next section.

7.2.1   *Creating an OU with ADAC*

You can use the ADAC tool in Windows Server 2012 or later to create an OU by following these steps:

1   Choose a parent OU or the domain.
2   Choose New from the Tasks window.

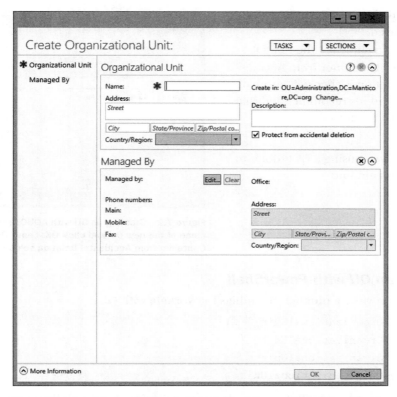

Figure 7.1   Creating a new OU using ADAC. The only mandatory information is the name of the new OU. Click OK to create the OU.

3 Choose Organizational Unit.
4 The dialog in figure 7.1 will be displayed.
5 Supply the name of the new OU.
6 Supply other information as required.
7 Protect from Accidental Deletion is checked automatically, and it's recommended that this is left selected.
8 Click OK.

Using ADUC is a similar proposition.

7.2.2   Creating an OU with ADUC

The dialog for OU creation in ADUC doesn't supply as many options as ADAC. Follow these steps to create a new OU:

1 Right-click the parent OU or the domain.
2 Choose New from the context menu.
3 Choose Organizational Unit.

4 The dialog in figure 7.2 will be displayed.
5 Supply a name for the new OU.
6 Protect Container from Accidental Deletion is checked automatically, and it's recommended that this is left selected.
7 Click OK.

The alternative to using a GUI tool is to use the command line.

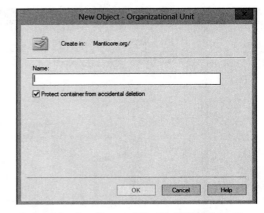

Figure 7.2   Creating an OU with ADUC. Enter the name of the new OU and click OK. Leave Protect Container from Accidental Deletion selected.

7.3   *Creating an OU with PowerShell*

PowerShell provides a number of cmdlets for working with OUs:

- New-ADOrganizationalUnit
- Get-ADOrganizationalUnit
- Set-ADOrganizationalUnit
- Remove-ADOrganizationalUnit

This list is arranged to match the lifecycle of these objects. As with all PowerShell cmdlets, the verb describes the action and the noun provides the object type to which the verb applies. An example of creating an OU is provided in this code:

```
PS> New-ADOrganizationalUnit -Name ADML3 -Path "DC=manticore,DC=org" `
-ProtectedFromAccidentalDeletion:$true -PassThru

City                      :
Country                   :
DistinguishedName         : OU=ADML3,DC=manticore,DC=org
LinkedGroupPolicyObjects  : {}
ManagedBy                 :
Name                      : ADML3
ObjectClass               : organizationalUnit
ObjectGUID                : e0988aaa-951b-42dd-9b59-12ccd7c1f1bc
PostalCode                :
State                     :
StreetAddress             :
```

This cmdlet doesn't produce any output normally, so it's difficult to know if your command succeeded or not. If you use the -Passthru parameter as shown in the code, you'll get a display of the OU's core properties, as in the previous output. The other parameters supply the path to where you want to create the OU—in this case the root of the domain, the name of the new OU, and that you want to check Protect from Accidental Deletion. I can't stress enough how good an idea that is.

Creating an OU that's a child of an existing OU is achieved by modifying the value passed to the -Path parameter:

```
New-ADOrganizationalUnit -Name Chapter7 `
-Path "OU=ADML3,DC=manticore,DC=org" `
-ProtectedFromAccidentalDeletion:$true `
-PassThru
```

The other parameters supply the name and set Protect from Accidental Deletion to on. The parent must exist. If it doesn't, you'll get an error:

```
New-ADOrganizationalUnit -Name Chapter7 `
-Path "OU=ADML4,DC=manticore,DC=org" `
-ProtectedFromAccidentalDeletion:$true `
-PassThru

New-ADOrganizationalUnit : Directory object not found
At line:1 char:1
+ New-ADOrganizationalUnit -Name Chapter7 -Path
      "OU=ADML4,DC=manticore,DC=org" -Pr ...
+ ~~~~~~~~~~~~~~~~~~~~~~~~~~~~~~~~~~~~~~~~~~~~~~~~~~~~~~~~~~~~~~~~~~~~~~~~
    + CategoryInfo          : ObjectNotFound:
    (OU=Chapter7,OU=ADML4,DC=manticore,DC=org:String)
[New-ADOrganizationalUnit], ADIdentityNotFoundException
    + FullyQualifiedErrorId : ActiveDirectoryCmdlet:
Microsoft.ActiveDirectory.Management.ADIdentityNotFoundException,
Microsoft.ActiveDirectory.Management.Commands.NewADOrganizationalUnit
```

Do you need to create OUs in bulk? I suspect not in your day-to-day administration tasks. If you're restructuring your domain or you have a standard structure that you create for each new location, you may need to create a number of OUs quickly, but this is unlikely to be a common activity.

This can be achieved using a similar pattern for creating other objects in bulk—put the data that defines the object into a CSV file and pipe its contents into the working part of your script. Create the file with two fields: Name (the name of the new OU) and Path (the location in which you want to create the OU). The file will look something like this:

```
Name,Path
ADML4,"DC=Manticore,DC=org"
Computers,"OU=ADML4,DC=Manticore,DC=org"
Users,"OU=ADML4,DC=Manticore,DC=org"
Desktops,"OU=Computers,OU=ADML4,DC=Manticore,DC=org"
Laptops,"OU=Computers,OU=ADML4,DC=Manticore,DC=org"
Staff,"OU=Users,OU=ADML4,DC=Manticore,DC=org"
Contractors,"OU=Users,OU=ADML4,DC=Manticore,DC=org"
Managers,"OU=Users,OU=ADML4,DC=Manticore,DC=org"
```

The script to create the OUs is a modification of the code used to create a single OU:

```
Import-Csv C:\Scripts\ADLunches\ous.txt |
foreach {
New-ADOrganizationalUnit -Name $_.Name -Path $_.Path `
-ProtectedFromAccidentalDeletion $true -PassThru
}
```

The file is read, and for each row in the file the `New-ADOrganizationalUnit` cmdlet is used to create the OU using the Name and Path fields. Make sure that the file is ordered correctly to ensure that the parent OU is created before a child OU. It takes very little time to create the file if you use cut-and-paste to create the rows.

In all of the examples for creating OUs you've been advised to enable Protect from Accidental Deletion. It's time to take a closer look at this option and what it means to you.

7.4   *Protecting OUs from accidental deletion*

Imagine you're in the office quite happily working through your tasks for today. One of your colleagues suddenly says, "Oh no!" When asked what's happened, he informs you that he has just accidentally deleted an OU containing 200 to 300 user accounts. Active Directory replicates changes through the domain. You now have nearly 300 users who can't log on and access their applications or data.

This isn't a far-fetched scenario. I've seen it happen. At this stage, your only remedy is to restore the OU and the accounts. That takes care of your evening and possibly a large part of the night as well.

Imagine how worse this scenario gets if you delete the OU with the Finance users when they're on a tight deadline to process the end-of-year finances, or you delete the OU containing the accounts of the senior managers!

If you work on the principle that prevention is better than a cure, how can you prevent yourself from getting into a situation like this? There's nothing that will guarantee you can't make a mistake, but you can enable Protect from Accidental Deletion on the OU and its contents. This will stop you deleting objects by mistake, but because it can be removed, it doesn't stop a rogue administrator from removing it and then deleting the OU.

Protect from Accidental Deletion appears as a checkbox on the dialogs in the GUI tools or as a parameter on the PowerShell cmdlets. It's important that you realize it isn't an AD property. What happens is that when you apply the protection, the Delete permission is denied to the Everyone group. This is a group maintained by Active Directory and does include everyone—no exceptions. If you attempt to delete an object that's protected from accidental deletion, you'll receive a dialog asking you to confirm the deletion and then you'll be shown a message similar to figure 7.3.

There are two scenarios where you need to remove the protection:

- You need to delete the object because it has come to the end of its lifecycle.
- You need to move the object to another OU.

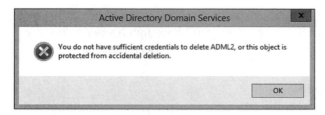

Figure 7.3   Message received when attempting to delete an object protected from accidental deletion. This is an improvement on earlier versions of Windows, where you were just told you didn't have permission to perform the deletion. If you get a message like this, check if Protect from Accidental Deletion is enabled.

To remove the protection using GUI tools

1   Choose the object.
2   Right-click the object.
3   Choose Properties from the context menu.
4   Choose Object in ADUC (the checkbox is on the main properties dialog in ADAC).
5   In both tools, clear the Protect from Accidental Deletion checkbox.
6   Click OK.

Before you dive into removing the protection with PowerShell, do you know how to test if an object is protected? If not, try this:

```
Get-ADObject -Filter {Name -eq "ADML1"} `
-Properties ProtectedFromAccidentalDeletion
```

In this case ADML1 is an OU. You can substitute a user, group, or computer name and this code will still work. To remove the protection

```
Get-ADObject -Filter {Name -eq "ADML1"} |
Set-ADObject -ProtectedFromAccidentalDeletion $false -PassThru
```

Get the object and pipe it into `Set-ADObject`. The `-ProtectedFromAccidental-Deletion` parameter is given a value of false. Turning protection back on involves reversing the setting by giving the `-ProtectedFromAccidentalDeletion` parameter a value of `true`:

```
Get-ADObject -Filter {Name -eq "ADML1"} |
Set-ADObject -ProtectedFromAccidentalDeletion $true -PassThru
```

If you remove the protection from the OU object, the objects within the OU still retain protection if it's set. You can force deletion of the OU and the objects it contains. If you're moving the object, remember to restore the protection after the move by reversing the instructions.

There are a small number of administration activities related to the OUs themselves that you'll see next.

7.5 Managing OUs

Once your OU framework is created, you won't have much work to do to maintain it. There are a few tasks that you may need to perform occasionally:

- Renaming the OU
- Setting the description
- Changing who manages the OU
- Deleting an OU

7.5.1 Renaming an OU

Renaming an OU isn't a task that you'll perform often. In my experience, the usual reason for renaming is that you mistyped the name when creating it, but didn't notice until after you had added other objects. The easiest thing to at this stage is rename.

Renaming in ADAC involves

1 Select the OU in ADAC.
2 Right-click the OU.
3 Choose Properties from the context menu.
4 Type the new name in the dialog.
5 Click OK.

By contrast, ADUC has a more obvious way of accomplishing this task:

1 Select the OU in ADUC.
2 Right-click the OU.
3 Choose Rename from the context menu.
4 Type the new name.
5 Press Enter.

The ADUC renaming method is more like renaming a file in Windows File Explorer.

You've seen the `Rename-ADObject` cmdlet in use for renaming other objects. It works on OUs as well:

```
Get-ADObject -Filter {Name -eq "ADML12"} |
Rename-ADObject -NewName ADML1
```

The object is found with `Get-ADObject` and piped into `Rename-ADObject`. The `-New-Name` parameter is used to supply the string containing the new name. Put the new name in quotes if it contains spaces.

Depending on the structure of your OUs and any naming conventions in place in your organization, it may be helpful to put a description on the OU.

7.5.2 Adding a description to the OU

If you give an OU a name such as "All Groups," you probably have a good idea what it contains. A name such as "ADML1" is more enigmatic and is a good candidate for a description so that you can see the OU's purpose at a glance.

Adding a description with GUI tools can be achieved by following these steps:

1. Right-click the object in ADAC or ADUC.
2. Choose Properties from the context menu.
3. In ADUC, ensure you're on the General tab.
4. In ADAC or ADUC, enter the description into the appropriate textbox.
5. Click OK to save the change.

Adding a description in PowerShell follows the Get | Set pattern you've seen in previous chapters:

```
Get-ADOrganizationalUnit -Filter {Name -eq 'ADML1'} |
Set-ADOrganizationalUnit -Description "AD Month of Lunches Test OU"
```

The Set-ADOrganizationalUnit cmdlet doesn't have a -Filter parameter, so either provide the full distinguished name of the OU to the Identity parameter or use the Get | Set pattern. I prefer using Get | Set because it's less typing and I can always refine the search by using the Get cmdlet and then add the Set cmdlet once I've correctly identified the OU.

> **TIP** Set-ADOrganizationalUnit can also be used to add or remove protection from accidental deletion.

You can use the techniques in this section to set the address information for the OU if your organization populates those attributes.

The final modification you can make on an OU is to the Managed By attribute.

7.5.3 *Changing the Managed By setting*

The important point to note about the Managed By setting is that the user account entered doesn't get any extra permissions on the OU or its contents. If you want to control who can administer the OU's contents, you need to delegate those permissions (you'll learn how to do this in chapter 14). The ManagedBy property can be best described as a label that tells you the business owner of the OU and its objects.

Setting this property in GUI tools can be accomplished by

1. Choosing the OU in ADAC or ADUC.
2. Right-clicking the OU.
3. Choosing Properties from the context menu.
4. If you're using ADUC, choose Managed By.
5. In ADAC, click on Edit (see figure 7.1).
6. In ADUC, click on Change.
7. Choose the user through the dialog.
8. Click OK to save the setting.

You should be able to guess how to do this with PowerShell—yep, you use the Get | Set pattern, though this time I'll show you a little trick to make things quicker:

```
Get-ADOrganizationalUnit -Filter {Name -eq 'ADML1'} |
Set-ADOrganizationalUnit `
-ManagedBy (Get-ADUser -Filter {Name -eq "Green Jo"})
```

Use `Get-ADOrganizationalUnit` to identify the OU. Pipe that object to `Set-ADOrganizationalUnit` and use the –ManagedBy parameter. The value for the parameter is

```
(Get-ADUser -Filter {Name -eq "Green Jo"})
```

This means use `Get-ADUser` to find the user whose identity you want to set as manager of this OU. Any PowerShell parameter can be passed as an expression in parentheses () and it'll evaluate that expression to discover the value it needs.

When you choose to set the `ManagedBy` property, any address or telephone information set for the user is used to populate the corresponding attributes on the OU.

7.5.4 *Deleting an OU*

All good things come to an end, and eventually you have to say goodbye to an OU. You may be deleting the OU, or you may be removing its contents as well. To delete an OU in GUI tools

1   Choose the OU.
2   Right-click the OU.
3   Choose Delete from the context menu.
4   You'll receive a confirmation message.
5   Click OK.
6   You'll see the message stating Protect from Accidental Deletion is in place.
7   Remove the protection.
8   Repeat steps 1–5.
9   If child objects exist, you'll see a dialog box similar to figure 7.4.
10   Click the checkbox and click Yes to delete the OU and all of its contents.

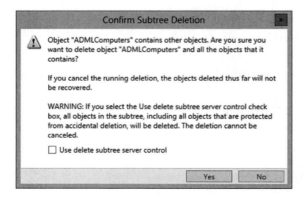

Figure 7.4   **Confirming a subtree deletion. Click the checkbox and click Yes to delete the OU and all of its contents.**

Deleting an OU through PowerShell can be achieved like this:

```
PS> Get-ADOrganizationalUnit -Filter {Name -eq "ADML5"} |
Remove-ADOrganizationalUnit -Recursive

Are you sure you want to remove the item and all its children?
Performing recursive remove on Target: 'OU=ADML5,DC=Manticore,DC=org'.
[Y] Yes  [A] Yes to All  [N] No  [L] No to All  [S] Suspend  [?] Help
     (default is "Y"): Y
```

If you want to avoid the confirmation message, add `-Confirm:$false` to the code after `-Recursive`. The `-Recursive` switch is used to force PowerShell to remove any child items in the OU.

The last action for you to consider is moving objects between OUs.

7.6 *Moving objects between OUs*

Why would you want to move objects between OUs? There are a number of reasons:

- New objects are created in the default containers (Computers and Users) and must be moved to their correct location. This is most likely for computer accounts created by joining a machine to the domain.
- You're reorganizing your domain.
- A user has moved into another role and requires a different set of GPOs.
- Your OU structure is designed to mimic the organizational structure, and when users move between departments their user accounts and computers need to be moved to the new OU.

There are a couple of implications inherent in moving an object between OUs:

- The GPOs applied to the object will change.
- The administrator may change if you have a delegated administration model.

You can move any object—users, computers, groups, and OUs. If you move an OU, you also move its contents. The movement between OUs can be accomplished by

- Using ADUC drag-and-drop mode
- Using the Move command in GUI tools
- Using PowerShell

A drag-and-drop move is performed exactly as it sounds. Find the object in ADUC, click it, and drag it to the new OU. If you can move files around by performing a drag-and-drop in File Explorer, you can do the same in the AD GUI tools.

There's a slight drawback to the drag-and-drop mechanism. If you drop it in the wrong place, the object may have a Group Policy applied that isn't optimum, or potentially could be harmful.

The alternative when using the GUI is to use the Move option:

1 Choose the object in ADAC or ADUC.
2 Right-click the object.

3 Choose Move from the context menu.

4 A dialog is displayed showing the OUs and containers within the domain.

5 Choose the destination—you can navigate through any OU trees in the dialog.

6 Click OK to perform the move.

PowerShell offers a simple command-line option for moving objects:

```
Get-ADObject -Filter {Name -eq "ADLComp10"} |
Move-ADObject -TargetPath "OU=ADML1,DC=Manticore,DC=org"
```

Find the object using its name as a filter. Pipe the object to `Move-ADObject`. You need to provide the distinguished name of the OU to which you want to move the object.

> **WARNING** If you have Protect from Accidental Deletion enabled on an object, you won't be able to move it. This is because you're effectively performing a copy and delete, and you can't delete the source object! The answer is to remove the protection, perform the move, and then reapply the protection.

That completes your look at OUs, which means it's time for a lab session.

7.7   Lab

In this lab you'll work through the OU lifecycle. You can use GUI tools, PowerShell, or a mixture to complete the tasks. I recommend that you split the tasks between one of the GUI tools and PowerShell to ensure you understand both approaches.

7.7.1   Creating OUs

Create five OUs in the root of your domain. Use these names:

1 ADML1
2 ADML2
3 ADML3
4 ADML4
5 ADML5

In each case, ensure that Protect from Accidental Deletion is enabled.

7.7.2   Renaming OUs

Change the names of the OUs you've created as shown in table 7.1.

Table 7.1   Information for renaming the OUs in the lab

Old name	New name
ADML1	ADMLComputers
ADML2	ADMLUsers
ADML3	ADMLGroups
ADML4	ADLunches

7.7.3 Setting descriptions and Managed By

Set the descriptions in table 7.2 on the OUs you created in section 7.7.2.

Table 7.2 Information for setting the description on OUs in the lab

OU	Description
ADMLComputers	Contains computer accounts for the AD Lunches labs
ADMLUsers	Contains user accounts for the AD Lunches labs
ADMLGroups	Contains groups for the AD Lunches labs
ADLunches	Contains all objects for the AD Lunches labs

Set the OUs to be managed by the users in table 7.3. The table assumes that you created the accounts in the lab in chapter 2. If you don't have these accounts available, substitute the accounts you did create in the lab.

Table 7.3 Information for setting the ManagedBy property on OUs in the lab

OU	Managed By
ADMLComputers	Dave Green
ADMLUsers	Dave Green
ADMLGroups	Dave Green
ADLunches	Jo Green

Hint: can you perform both tasks simultaneously?

7.7.4 Moving objects between OUs

Perform these moves:

- Move ADMLComputers, ADMLUsers, and ADMLGroups into ADLunches.
- Move the user accounts you created in chapter 2 into ADMLUsers.
- Move the group accounts you created in chapter 4 into ADMLGroups.
- Move the computer accounts you created in chapter 6 into ADMLComputers.

Hints:

- Can you select multiple objects in the GUI and move them simultaneously?
- Will anything stop you from performing the move?
- You can move multiple objects with PowerShell as follows:

```
Get-ADObject -Filter {Name -like "ADLgroup*"} |
Move-ADObject `
-TargetPath "OU=ADMLGroups,OU=ADMLunches,DC=Manticore,DC=org"
```

7.7.5   *Deleting an OU*

The ADML5 OU that you created in section 7.6.1 hasn't been touched yet. If you have time, create a child OU inside it along with some user or computer accounts.

Try deleting with and without Protection from Accidental Deletion enabled. What happens if you have child objects and don't use the `-Recursive` parameter on `Remove-ADOrganizationalUnit`?

7.8   *Ideas for on your own*

Organizational units are the framework for your administration activities. Are your OUs designed to help you administer AD? How would you change them? You know how to manage all of the common data objects in Active Directory; therefore, it's time to start thinking about how your Active Directory is organized and if a different OU structure would make life easier for you.

This chapter concludes part 1. In the next part you'll learn about Group Policy.

Part 2

Managing Group Policy

In chapter 1 you saw that Active Directory is used to control access to resources in your environment. Active Directory can also be used to manage the security and configuration of computers (servers and workstations) in your domain. This is accomplished through Group Policy, which is the subject of the first two chapters in this part.

Chapter 8 introduces Group Policy and teaches you how to create these objects. You'll also learn how to modify Group Policies. Logon scripts have been a feature of networked environments for many years. Group Policy preferences offer an alternative that can simplify your environment.

Chapter 9 examines how to apply these polices to the users and computers in your domain. As you'll see, Group Policy can be applied to the domain or to an OU tree. The application of the policy can be controlled by blocking inheritance of the policy from OUs higher in the tree. The blocking can be overridden, which can potentially lead to a bewildering set of conflicting settings. Best practice for dealing with this will be presented.

Part 2 closes with chapter 10, where Fine Grained Password policies (PSOs) are discussed. PSOs, which were introduced with Windows Server 2008, enable you to overcome the restriction of only having a single password policy in a domain. You'll learn how to create and manage these objects, along with practical advice for when to use them.

Administrators face the challenge of supporting an ever-increasing number of users, computers, and applications. Group Policy supplies a mechanism to centralize the management of the environment and move a large part of the configuration processing on to the computers. Before you can do that, you need to create your policies.

Creating Group Policies

Group Policy is a method of managing the configuration and security of the computers in your environment. The policies can be applied to user or computer settings and enable centralized efficient management of the environment.

This chapter starts by explaining the concepts you need to be effective with Group Policy. In this chapter you'll discover how to create new policies and manage their settings. The application of Group Policy is left until chapter 9.

8.1 Group Policy basic concepts

Group Policy has nothing to do with groups. A Group Policy Object (GPO) defines a number of settings—for example, the screensaver to be used, the control panel options that are available to a user, and the features available on the Start menu or in Internet Explorer. These settings can then be applied to sets of users or computers by linking them to OUs or the domain.

Group Policy is immensely powerful. A GPO contains thousands of settings to manage your environment. You can use GPOs to manage many things, including

- Rights to log on to particular machines
- User settings, such as logon scripts, printers, and mapped drives, and organizational standards such as wallpaper, event log configuration, and rights to access the file system
- Control of Windows components like Windows Update, and applications like Microsoft Office
- Software availability, settings, and distribution

Some administrators think that Group Policy is too powerful and damages your environment. The last part of that statement is true when mistakes are made. I was on a customer site many years ago and sat watching servers dropping off the network at an alarming rate. This problem spread across the world faster than we could work out what was happening. It turned out that an unauthorized change had been made to a Group Policy, which stopped these machines from communicating. Once we corrected the change we could get the machines back on the network. The moral of the story is that Group Policy doesn't cause problems—unauthorized and unchecked changes cause problems.

> **TIP**   Always get your Group Policy changes checked and approved.

Many, if not most, organizations don't get the best out of GPOs because they don't take the time to investigate the settings and discover how to manage their environments using Group Policy.

> **NOTE**   Password Setting Objects may appear to be related to Group Policy but are a totally different concept. You'll learn about them in chapter 10.

Supplying best-practice recommendations on Group Policy for your environment is difficult without knowing the environment. However, there are a few accepted guidelines you should take into consideration:

- Keep user and computer settings in separate GPOs.
- Apply the smallest number of GPOs to solve the problem.
- Try to avoid duplicating settings between GPOs.
- Use Starter GPOs as templates when you have to apply the same suite of settings in multiple policies or export the GPO to multiple domains.

Two GPOs are created by default when you first install Active Directory:

- Default Domain Policy
- Default Domain Controllers Policy

The Default Domain Policy sets the password policy for the domain (password length, age complexity, and so on), while the Default Domain Controllers Policy sets the default security on the domain controllers. Many organizations leave these policies at the default settings and make modifications to the password policy or domain controller security through additional policies. This approach allows you to remove the additional policies and still have basic security in place in the event of an issue with the additional policies.

The starting point of your Group Policy's lifecycle is creation.

8.2   *Creating a Group Policy*

You can't create GPOs using any of the GUI tools you've met so far.

GPO settings and links

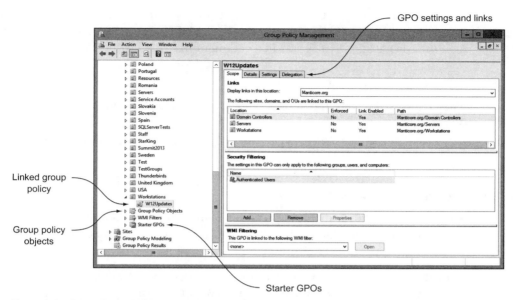

Linked group policy

Group policy objects

Starter GPOs

Figure 8.1   Group Policy Management Console (GPMC). The left pane shows a tree view of the domain's OUs with lined GPOs. The Group Policy Objects container stores all GPOs. The Starter GPOs container is used to store Starter GPOs. If a GPO is selected, the details, including links and settings, are shown in the right panel.

TIP It's a good practice to create GPOs in the GPO container. That way they're easy to find and you don't run the risk of them being applied to an OU before you're ready (which can happen if you create them directly attached to an OU).

You need to use the Group Policy Management Console (GPMC) shown in figure 8.1.

You'll see how to use the full functionality of the GPMC in this chapter and the next. For now, let's concentrate on how to create a GPO.

8.2.1   Creating a GPO with the GPMC

Creating a single GPO with the GPMC can be accomplished by following these steps:

1 Open GPMC.
2 Choose the Group Policy Objects folder (or a specific OU).
3 Right-click the selected container.
4 Choose New.
5 Supply the GPO name (figure 8.2).
6 Choose the Starter GPO (if needed).
7 Click OK.

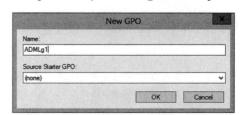

Figure 8.2   GPMC dialog to create a GPO. Enter a name and select a Starter GPO (if required). Click OK to create the GPO.

One issue with the GPMC is that you can't add a comment or description during the creation process. You can use PowerShell to add the description. Assuming you've created the GPO `ADMLg1`, you can add a comment like this:

```
$gpo = Get-GPO -Name ADMLg1
$gpo.Description = "AD Lunches GPO"
```

The change will take effect immediately. You can check in the GPMC or use the `Get-GPO` cmdlet:

```
Get-GPO -All | where DisplayName -like "ADML*"
```

You can also use PowerShell to create GPOs.

8.2.2 *Creating a GPO with PowerShell*

Windows Server 2012, including R2 (and Windows Server 2008 R2), provides Power-Shell cmdlets for working with GPOs. You can perform all GPO management tasks except modifying a GPO's settings with these cmdlets.

> **NOTE** There are commercial offerings of PowerShell cmdlets for working with GPO settings, most notably from SDM Software Inc.

The Microsoft GPO cmdlets are found in the `GroupPolicy` module. You can load them, if required, using `Import-Module`:

```
PS> Import-Module GroupPolicy
```

The cmdlets in the module can be investigated using `Get-Command -Module Group-Policy`. Once they're loaded (PowerShell v3 will automatically load them for you), you can create a new GPO using this code snippet:

```
PS> New-GPO -Name ADMLp1 -Comment "AD Lunches GPO"


DisplayName      : ADMLp1
DomainName       : Manticore.org
Owner            : MANTICORE\Domain Admins
Id               : 4ebaea13-59f6-4c65-a0d2-87f2a5b2045d
GpoStatus        : AllSettingsEnabled
Description      : AD Lunches GPO
CreationTime     : 30/01/2013 21:08:18
ModificationTime : 30/01/2013 21:08:19
UserVersion      : AD Version: 0, SysVol Version: 0
ComputerVersion  : AD Version: 0, SysVol Version: 0
WmiFilter        :
```

This cmdlet provides output showing the new GPO by default.

To use a Starter GPO when creating a new GPO, supply its name like this:

```
New-GPO -Name ADMLp2 -Comment "AD Lunches GPO from starter GPO" `
-StarterGpoName ADMLstarterGPO2
```

TRY IT NOW: Creating GPOs

Create two GPOs:

- Use the GPMC to create the first GPO. Call it `ADMLgpo1`.
- Use PowerShell to create the second GPO. Call it `ADMLgpo2`. Add a comment during the creation process of "GPO for ADM Lunches."
- Use PowerShell to add a comment to `ADMLgpo1`.

You've seen Starter GPOs being used several times. How do you go about creating one?

8.2.3 Creating Starter GPOs

Imagine the following scenario:

- You have 10 locations in the organization.
- Each needs a GPO to perform a number of configuration items.
- The GPOs will share a significant number of settings.
- A few settings will be location specific.

The ideal solution would be to create a template with the common settings and clone it to produce the required GPOs. This is the purpose of Starter GPOs. They function as a template for creating new GPOs, but you need to remember that only Administrative Template settings can be used in a Starter GPO.

In a complex environment with many domains, you can create and test a GPO in one domain and then export the settings to a Starter GPO that can be imported into the remaining domains. If you're lucky enough to have a test domain, the creating and testing can be performed in that environment and then transferred to your production environment.

Finding the Starter GPOs

The first time you access the Starter GPOs container, you'll be prompted to create a SYSVOL folder to store your Starter GPOs. Eight Starter GPOs will also be created. Two are for configuring and reporting on firewall settings. The other six are for configuring Windows Vista and Windows XP clients.

If you download and install the Microsoft Security Compliance Manager (SCM) from http://www.microsoft.com/en-us/download/details.aspx?id=16776 on a Windows 7 or Windows 8 machine, you'll get baseline configurations for later operating systems.

The baseline settings can be exported from SCM as GPO backups and then imported into GPMC:

1 Open SCM.
2 The Microsoft security baselines will be created the first time you use SCM.
3 Select the baseline you wish to export.
4 Choose Export > GPO Backup (folder) from the right pane.

(continued)

5   Select the folder in which to create a backup.
6   A backup will be created in a subfolder with the name of the form {94017276-5fb6-4ca0-97fe-fa94bca2c81f}.
7   Copy that folder to the system used for GPO administration, if needed.
8   Open GPMC.
9   Right-click GPO Objects and choose New.
10   Supply the name. Click OK.
11   Right-click the new GPO.
12   Choose Import Settings.
13   Use the wizard to navigate to the backup (step 6).
14   Click Next. Click Next. Click Next.
15   Click Finish.
16   Click OK to close the dialog.

There's no method to import these settings directly into a Starter GPO, because the GPMC appears to manage the "normal" and Starter GPOs as two separate groups. If you want to use SCM settings in a Starter GPO, you'll have to manually copy the settings into the new Starter GPO.

Starter GPOs can be created in the GPMC:

1   Open GPMC.
2   Choose the Starter GPO container.
3   Right-click the Starter GPO container.
4   Choose New.
5   Supply the GPO name (figure 8.3).
6   Supply the comment.
7   Click OK.

The Starter GPO will be given a type of Custom, rather than System, that's applied to the out-of-the-box Starter GPOs.

Figure 8.3   Creating a Starter GPO with GPMC. A name is required; however, the comment is optional but recommended.

Alternatively, you can use PowerShell to create the Starter GPO:

```
PS> New-GPStarterGPO -Name ADMLstarterGPO2 `
-Comment "ADM Lunches starter GPO 2"


DisplayName         : ADMLstarterGPO2
Id                  : 388a01bf-e63d-4ce7-8c89-30a50ee074ea
Owner               : BUILTIN\Administrators
CreationTime        : 30/01/2013 21:52:24
ModificationTime    : 30/01/2013 21:52:24
UserVersion         : 0
ComputerVersion     : 0
StarterGpoVersion   :
StarterGpoType      : Custom
Author              :
Description         : ADM Lunches starter GPO 2
```

> **NOTE** Starter GPOs are created with `New-GPStarterGPO`, not `New-GPO` as used for normal GPOs.

Once you've created your Starter GPO, you can use it to create standard GPOs as described in the earlier sections. You can also use it directly to create a new GPO, as follows:

1 Open GPMC.
2 Choose the Starter GPO container.
3 Right-click the Starter GPO to be used as a template.
4 Choose New GPO from Starter GPO.
5 Supply the GPO name (figure 8.2).
6 The Starter GPO is selected but not changeable.
7 Click OK.

Creating an empty GPO is the starting point, but you need to modify the settings in the GPO for it to be useful.

TRY IT NOW: Creating Starter GPOs

Create two Starter GPOs:

- Use the GPMC to create the first GPO; call it `ADMLStartergpo1`.
- Use PowerShell to create the second GPO; call it `ADMLStartergpo2`. Add a comment during the creation process of "StarterGPO for ADM Lunches."
- Use PowerShell to add a comment to `ADMLStartergpo1`.

8.3   Modifying GPOs

A new GPO doesn't have any settings configured. You need to configure the GPO to apply to users or computers (not both) and configure the individual settings in the policy.

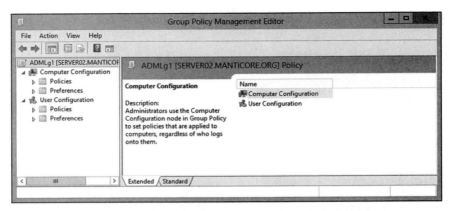

Figure 8.4   Anatomy of a GPO. Best practice is to configure a GPO with either user or computer settings.

8.3.1   *Computer versus user configuration*

A GPO has two broad groups of settings, as shown in figure 8.4:

- Computer configuration—applied to a computer irrespective of the user who logged on
- User configuration—applied to a user irrespective of the computer they're using

TIP   Once a GPO no longer applies to a user or computer, the settings imposed by that GPO are automatically removed by the system.

Each of the configurations has Policies and Preferences settings available.

POLICIES

Policies are the settings that have been available since GPOs were introduced with Windows 2000. The thousands of Policy settings are grouped into

- Software delivery
- Windows settings, including security
- Administrative templates used to manage the configuration of Windows components, such as Internet Explorer or the event logs, the Control Panel, and networking

PREFERENCES

Preferences were introduced in Windows Server 2008 and can replace many of the configuration items that have been applied via logon scripts, such as

- Drive and printer mappings
- Power scheme management
- File and folder management, including creation and deletion
- Applications, including Microsoft Office
- Network Share management

Preferences, in contrast to Policies, aren't enforced, meaning that the user can override the settings. In addition, Preferences

- Are more flexible
- Aren't removed when a GPO no longer applies
- Support item-level filtering
- Are processed during every Group Policy refresh (every 90 minutes by default)

8.3.2 Designating a GPO for users or computers

GPMC can be used to manage whether a GPO applies to users or computers:

1. Open GPMC.
2. Select the GPO to be modified.
3. Right-click the GPO.
4. Choose GPO Status.
5. Choose one:
   - Enabled—both User and Computer configurations are enabled (default for a newly created GPO)
   - User Configuration Settings Disabled
   - Computer Configuration Settings Disabled
   - All Settings Disabled

You can also perform this task from a PowerShell prompt:

```
$gpo = Get-GPO -Name ADMLg1
$gpo.GpoStatus = "UserSettingsDisabled"
```

You have these four options, which match the GPMC options:

- `AllSettingsEnabled`
- `UserSettingsDisabled`
- `ComputerSettingsDisabled`
- `AllSettingsDisabled`

The next step in making your GPO usable is to configure the settings it'll apply.

8.3.3 Configuring GPO settings

Configuring the settings to be applied by your GPOs is a balancing act. You need to keep the numbers of GPOs being applied to a sensible level and make the GPOs themselves granular enough that you're not duplicating settings across multiple GPOs. The result of this balancing is dependent on the exact circumstances within your organization.

NOTE You can't change settings with the native PowerShell cmdlets.

The GPMC is where you modify settings you want the GPO to apply:

1. Open GPMC.
2. Select the GPO to be modified.

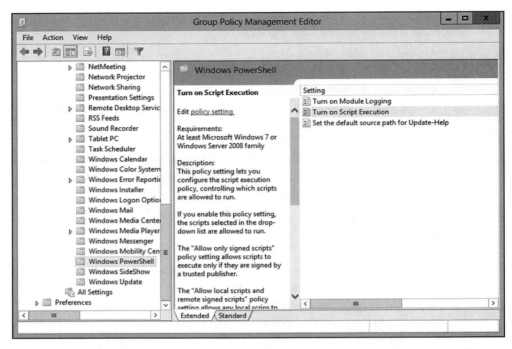

Figure 8.5   A GPO being edited. In this example the User Configuration > Policies > Administrative Templates > Windows Components > Windows PowerShell settings are being modified. Double-click on a setting to open the editing dialog.

3 Right-click the GPO.

4 Choose Edit.

5 The Group Policy Management Editor (figure 8.5) opens.

6 Select the policy you need to change.

7 If the Extended tab (recommended) is used, you'll see a description of the policy and the meaning of the available settings.

8 Double-click on the setting you wish to edit.

9 A dialog similar to figure 8.6 will be displayed.

In the policy dialog (figure 8.6), change Not Configured to Enabled using the radio button. Select the required execution policy from the dropdown menu. Allow Local Scripts and Remote Signed Scripts is equivalent to the PowerShell `RemoteSigned` execution policy. Click OK for the change to be saved.

> **WARNING** There's no confirmation dialog when editing Group Policies. When you click OK, the change is saved and will start replicating. Double-check before saving!

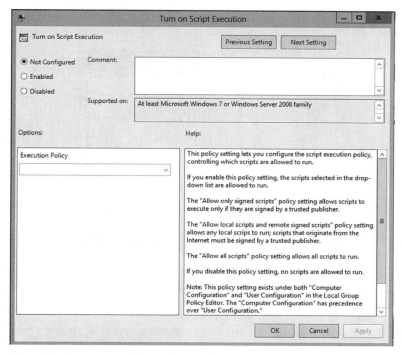

Figure 8.6 The dialog to modify a GPO setting. Choose Enabled and then use the dropdown menu to set the execution policy. Notice the Supported On data—this indicates which versions of Windows support this policy.

TRY IT NOW: Modify a GPO

- Modify `ADMLgpo1`.
- Disable the computer settings.
- Configure PowerShell execution policy. Navigate to User Configuration > Policies > Administrative Templates > Windows Components > Windows PowerShell. Enable the policy and choose Allow Local Scripts and Remote Signed Scripts.

Group Policy preferences are modified in a slightly different manner.

8.4   Setting Group Policy preferences

Preferences can be used to replace much of the work traditionally performed by logon scripts; for instance, to set drive mappings. An item-specific dialog is presented when you need to make modifications:

1 Open GPMC.
2 Select the required GPO.

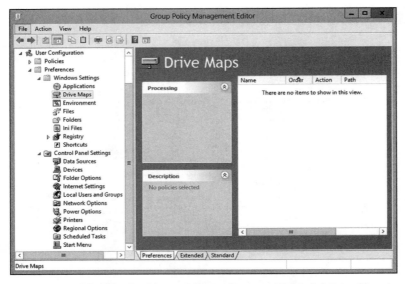

Figure 8.7   Configuring the drive-mapping preferences. Right-click Drive Maps in the left pane and choose New.

3   Open the GPO for editing.

4   Navigate to the desired preference setting (figure 8.7 shows the drive-mapping preference).

5   Right-click the preference.

6   Choose New.

7   Complete the dialog (figure 8.8 shows the drive-mapping dialog).

8   Click OK to save the setting.

Figure 8.8   Configuring a drive-mapping preference. Configure the location and drive letter. Choose Reconnect to ensure the drive mappings aren't lost if the user logs off.

TRY IT NOW: Add a GPO preference

- Modify `ADMLgpo1`.
- Configure a drive mapping.
- Navigate to User Configuration > Preferences > Windows Settings > Drive Maps, and create a drive mapping.

8.5   *LAB*

In this lab you'll have a chance to practice creating and configuring GPOs.

8.5.1   *Complete the TRY IT NOW sections*

If you haven't already done so, complete the TRY IT NOW exercises from this chapter.

CREATING GPOS

Create two GPOs:

- Use the GPMC to create the first GPO; call it `ADMLgpo1`.
- Use PowerShell to create the second GPO; call it `ADMLgpo2`. Add a comment during the creation process of "GPO for ADM Lunches."
- Use PowerShell to add a comment to `ADMLgpo1`.

CREATING STARTER GPOS

Create two Starter GPOs:

- Use the GPMC to create the first GPO; call it `ADMLStartergpo1`.
- Use PowerShell to create the second GPO; call it `ADMLStartergpo2`. Add a comment during the creation process of "StarterGPO for ADM Lunches."
- Use PowerShell to add a comment to `ADMLStartergpo1`.

MODIFYING A GPO

Modify `ADMLgpo1`:

- Disable the computer settings.
- Configure the PowerShell execution policy. Navigate to User Configuration > Policies > Administrative Templates > Windows Components > Windows Power-Shell. Enable the policy and choose Allow Local Scripts and Remote Signed Scripts.

ADDING A GPO PREFERENCE

Modify `ADMLgpo1`:

- Configure a drive mapping.
- Navigate to User Configuration > Preferences > Windows Settings > Drive Maps and create a drive mapping.

8.5.2   *Configuring a Starter GPO*

Configure `ADMLstartergpo1`. Enable the following:

- Computer Configuration > Administrative Templates > Control Panel > User Accounts > Apply the Default Account Picture to All Accounts
- Computer Configuration > Administrative Templates > Windows Components > Desktop Gadgets > Turn Off Desktop Gadgets
- Computer Configuration > Administrative Templates > Windows Components > Presentation Settings > Turn Off Presentation Settings
- Computer Configuration > Administrative Templates > Windows Components > Windows Calendar > Turn Off Windows Calendar

8.5.3 *Creating a GPO from a Starter GPO*

Create a new GPO from the `ADMLstartergpo1`; call it `ADM Lunches Computer Settings`. Disable the user settings on the new GPO. Check that the settings have been copied properly from the Starter GPO.

8.6 *Ideas for on your own*

GPOs are a very powerful tool. You should ensure that you understand the GPOs that are being applied to your environment before you start making any changes. Documenting the settings in your GPOs and understanding what each is supposed to do will pay back the investment by reducing the potential for mistakes.

In chapter 9 you'll learn how to apply GPOs and their interactions, as well as how to test GPOs by modeling the results of your proposed changes.

Managing Group Policies

In chapter 8 you saw how to create Group Policy Objects (GPOs). In this chapter you'll learn how to apply them to your environment to centrally manage user and computer configurations.

> **TIP** This chapter follows directly from chapter 8. If there's a time gap between your reading the two chapters, review chapter 8 before starting this chapter.

In the first section of this chapter you'll learn how to link GPOs to AD sites, domains, and OUs. No one can ever remember which GPOs are linked where, so you'll then learn how to discover the linkages. GPOs need to be removed once they're no longer required. You can modify the way GPOs are processed by modifying the inheritance rules.

Modeling the policies that are applied to your users and computers when the multiple GPOs you've applied combine is a useful technique for troubleshooting and experimentation. The last section of the chapter shows you how to force the refresh of the application of GPOs to ensure the changes are active in your environment.

The chapter closes with a lab section that enables you to practice the skills you've learned in this chapter and chapter 8.

9.1   *Applying or removing a GPO*

The act of applying a GPO is known technically as linking. You can link, or apply, GPOs to three types of places in your Active Directory:

1. The domain—the GPO is applied to all OUs in the domain
2. An OU—the GPO is applied to all child OUs
3. An AD site—the GPO is applied to all users or computers that are located in that site

Applying a GPO to a site is usually not recommended because it can affect a wider audience than you intended in a multi-domain environment. GPOs applied at the site level can be overridden by GPOs applied at the domain or OU, which can easily negate the effect you require. Save site GPOs for multi-domain usage or where a specific setting such as a proxy server needs to be set for everyone in the site.

GPO application is a very flexible process:

- You can apply a GPO as it's created.
- You can apply an existing GPO to an OU or to the domain.
- You can block the inheritance of GPOs.
- You can override the blocking process.

Later in the chapter, figure 9.5 illustrates some of these concepts, and you'll also learn more about them in section 9.2. Multiple approaches to GPO creation and application can lead to a very chaotic situation in which conflicting polices are applied, blocked, or override-blocked. This can make troubleshooting very difficult. The best advice I can give is to keep your GPO application as simple as possible and avoid the complication of blocking and override blocking as much as possible. A GPO link has a lifecycle: it's created, discovered for further modification, and eventually removed. As with all lifecycle activities, the act of creating the link is your starting point.

9.1.1   *Creating a link*

CREATING A LINK USING THE GPMC

The Group Policy Management Console (GPMC) you used in chapter 8 to create GPOs is also used to apply them. Section 8.2 showed how to link a policy as you create it. To link an existing policy

1. Open GPMC.
2. Navigate to where the GPO is linked—the domain, OU, or site.
3. Right-click.
4. Choose Link an Existing GPO….
5. Select the GPO.
6. Click OK.

The linked policies are shown under the OU name and in the right pane of the GPMC, as illustrated in figure 9.1.

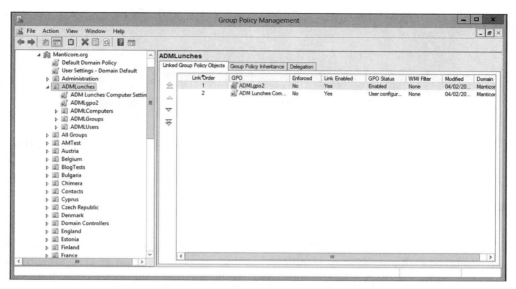

Figure 9.1   The GPMC opened at the ADMLunches OU showing the linked GPOs.

CREATING A LINK USING POWERSHELL

You can also link an existing GPO using the PowerShell GPO cmdlets:

```
Get-GPO -Name ADMlgpo2 |
New-GPLink -Target "OU=ADMLunches,DC=manticore,DC=org"
```

The GPO is retrieved by name using `Get-GPO`, and is then piped to `New-GPLink` with the `Target` parameter used to indicate the OU to which the GPO is to be linked.

TIP   Scripting GPO links can be useful if you frequently add new groups of people to the organization and use a standard OU structure together with a consistent set of GPOs.

TRY IT NOW: Linking GPOs

Apply the GPOs you created in chapter 8 as follows:

- Link `ADMLgpo1` to the ADMLUsers OU.
- Link `ADMLgpo2` to the ADMLUsers OU.

Use GPMC or PowerShell to perform the linkage.

Modify the settings in `ADMLgpo1`:

- Disable Computer Configuration.
- Enable User Configuration > Policies > Administrative Templates > Control Panel > Prohibit Access to Control Panel and PC Settings.

(continued)

Modify the settings in `ADMLgpo2`:

- Disable Computer Configuration.
- Enable User Configuration > Policies > Administrative Templates > Windows Components > Desktop Gadgets > Turn Off Desktop Gadgets.

To properly understand your environment, you need to understand how the GPOs in that environment are affecting your users and computers. The first step is to discover the GPO linkage pattern.

9.1.2 *Discovering links*

Do you know which GPOs affect the computers or users in a particular OU? Do you know how a particular GPO is linked to your environment? If you have a large environment with a significant number of GPOs, you can't be expected to carry this information in your head, so the questions are better cast as "Do you know how to find out how the GPOs are linked in your domain?"

DISCOVERING LINKS USING THE GPMC

One way of discovering links is to browse through the GPMC, as shown in figure 9.1. The left pane shows the domain's OU structure. The GPOs that are linked to a particular OU are displayed under that OU.

 If you want to see the links for an individual GPO, click on that GPO in the GPO Objects folder of the GPMC. The right pane will show where the GPO is linked, as illustrated in figure 9.2.

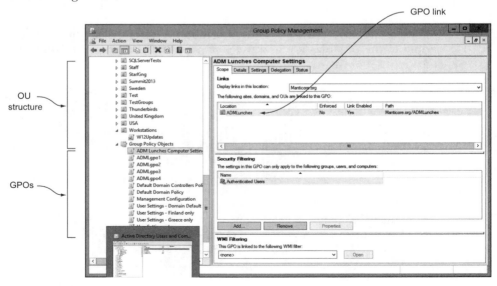

Figure 9.2   GPMC showing links for an individual GPO

DISCOVERING LINKS USING POWERSHELL

With PowerShell, you can discover GPO linkage information by using the Get-GPInheritance cmdlet. You need to provide the OU to be investigated as follows:

```
PS> Get-GPInheritance -Target "OU=ADMLunches,DC=manticore,DC=org"

Name                    : admlunches
ContainerType           : OU
Path                    : ou=admlunches,dc=manticore,dc=org
GpoInheritanceBlocked   : No
GpoLinks                : {ADMLgpo2, ADM Lunches Computer Settings}
InheritedGpoLinks       : {ADMLgpo2, ADM Lunches Computer Settings,
                           User Settings - Domain Default,
                           Default Domain Policy}
```

There are two properties supplying information on GPO links: GpoLinks and InheritedGpoLinks.

GPOLINKS PROPERTY

The GpoLinks property indicates the GPOs that are directly linked to the OU. Those GPOs that are inherited from the domain or higher-level OUs are shown in the InheritedGpoLinks property (just to be confusing, it also includes the directly linked GPOs). PowerShell can wrap text in multivalued properties (called collections), and by default only shows the first four members (as set by the FormatEnumerationLimit variable that can be viewed through the variable drive as $variable:FormatEnumerationLimit. It isn't recommended to modify the value of this variable).

You can create a more readable display by expanding the two collections:

```
$gpos = Get-GPInheritance -Target "OU=ADMLunches,DC=manticore,DC=org"
$linked = $gpos.GpoLinks | select -ExpandProperty DisplayName
$gpos | select -ExpandProperty GpoLinks
$gpos | select -ExpandProperty InheritedGpoLinks |
where DisplayName -NotIn $linked
```

A variable $gpos is created that holds the information from Get-GPInheritance. The DisplayName of the GPOs directly linked to the OU are stored in $linked. The $gpos variable is expanded to show the GPOs directly linked (GpoLinks) and inherited (InheritedGpoLinks). The directly linked GPOs are filtered out of the inherited list.

INHERITEDGPOLINKS PROPERTY

Alternatively, you can use the InheritedGpoLinks property and display the information as follows:

```
PS> Get-GPInheritance -Target "OU=ADMLunches,DC=manticore,DC=org" |
select -ExpandProperty InheritedGpoLinks |
Format-Table DisplayName, Order, Target -AutoSize

DisplayName                      Order Target
-----------                      ----- ------
ADMLgpo2                             1 OU=ADMLunches,DC=Manticore,DC=org
ADM Lunches Computer Settings        2 OU=ADMLunches,DC=Manticore,DC=org
User Settings - Domain Default       1 DC=Manticore,DC=org
Default Domain Policy                2 DC=Manticore,DC=org
```

The advantage to this approach is that you see where the individual GPOs are linked and the order of their processing.

TRY IT NOW: Discover GPO links

Discover the GPOs linked to the ADMLUsers OU. Which GPOs are applied directly and which are inherited?

If you want to see a listing of all OUs that have GPOs linked and the GPO names, or you need to see a list of GPOs and where they're linked, use the code in the following listing.

Listing 9.1 Generating a list of GPO links

```
$gpolinks = Get-ADOrganizationalUnit -Filter * |                    Generate
where LinkedGroupPolicyObjects |               Filter OUs with  ❶ list of OUs
foreach {                                   ❷ linked GPOs
  $ou = $_.DistinguishedName
  $_.LinkedGroupPolicyObjects |                    Iterate contents of
  foreach {                                      ❸ LinkedGroupPolicyObjects
    $x = $_.ToUpper() -split ",", 2
    $id = $x[0].Replace("CN={","").Replace("}","")
    $props = [ordered]@{
      OU = $ou
      GPO = Get-GPO -Guid $id | select -ExpandProperty DisplayName
    }
    New-Object -TypeName PSObject -Property $props    Retrieve GPO
  }                                                   display name ❹
}
$gpolinks | sort OU | Format-Table OU, GPO -AutoSize
$gpolinks | sort GPO | Format-Table GPO, OU -AutoSize
```

A variable $gpolinks is created that stores a set of objects that contain an OU name and the linked GPO. This is the most complicated script you've seen in the book, so I'll walk you through it. The cmdlet Get-AdOrganizationalUnit is used to generate a list of OUs in the domain ❶. The –Filter * parameter is used to ensure that all OUs are returned. A further filter is applied by Where-Object (aliased to where ❷) to only accept OUs that have linked GPOs.

The script iterates over the contents of the LinkedGroupPolicyObjects property ❸. The GPO's GUID is used in Get-GPO ❹ to retrieve the GPO's DisplayName property. An object is created containing the display name and the OU.

The last two lines of the script display the data sorted by OU or GPO, respectively.

WARNING This won't show any GPOs that have no links.

The sample output (truncated) when sorted by the OU name is as follows:

```
OU                                   GPO
--                                   ---
OU=ADMLunches,DC=Manticore,DC=org    ADM Lunches Computer Settings
```

```
OU=ADMLunches,DC=Manticore,DC=org        ADMLgpo2
OU=Austria,DC=Manticore,DC=org           User Settings - restricted
```

When you sort by GPO, the output (truncated) looks like this:

```
GPO                                  OU
---                                  --
ADM Lunches Computer Settings        OU=ADMLunches,DC=Manticore,DC=org
ADMLgpo2                             OU=ADMLunches,DC=Manticore,DC=org
Default Domain Controllers Policy    OU=Domain Controllers,DC=Manticore,DC=org
```

The last step in managing the GPO linkages is to remove a link.

9.1.3 Removing links

You can remove a GPO link in two ways. First, you could delete the GPO, in which case you'll remove all of its links in your domain. The second method is to unlink the GPO from one or more OUs.

DELETING A GPO USING THE GPMC

Deleting a GPO is a simple matter with the GPMC:

1 Open GPMC.
2 Select the Group Policy Objects container.
3 Right-click the GPO.
4 Click Delete.
5 A message box appears asking "Do you want to delete this GPO and all links to it in this domain? This will not delete links in other domains." (See figure 9.3.)
6 Click Yes to perform the deletion.

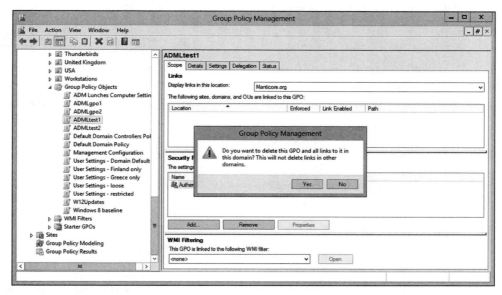

Figure 9.3 Deleting a GPO

The GPO will be deleted as soon as you click Yes. The settings won't be removed from the target users or computers until the GPOs are refreshed, which could take an hour or two.

DELETING A GPO USING POWERSHELL
Using PowerShell to delete a GPO is a one-step process:

```
Remove-GPO -Name ADMLtest2
```

It's possible to use the `-KeepLinks` parameter to keep the GPO links, but I don't recommend that action, as it leaves orphaned links that you'll have to clean up at a later time.

UNLINKING A GPO USING THE GPMC
Rather than deleting the GPO, you may just need to unlink it from an OU. This is often the case where a GPO isn't relevant to the users in that OU but is still needed for other sets of users.

> **TIP**   Unlinking a GPO doesn't delete the GPO.

Unlinking a GPO using the GPMC is similar to the deletion actions you've already seen:

1 Open GPMC.
2 Navigate to where the GPO is linked—the domain, OU, or site.
3 Right-click the GPO.
4 Click Delete.
5 A message box appears asking "Do you want to delete this link? This will not delete the GPO itself."
6 Click OK.

UNLINKING A GPO USING POWERSHELL
The PowerShell alternative involves using `Remove-GPOLink`:

```
Remove-GPLink -Name ADMLgpo2 -Target "OU=ADMLunches,DC=Manticore,DC=org"
```

You need to supply the OU from which you want to remove the link.

Now that you know how to manage the way a GPO is linked to your OUs, it's time to discover how to modify the way GPOs are applied to your users and computers.

9.2   *Modifying GPO application*

What happens when you have multiple GPOs applied to an object? Remember that you can apply GPOs to the domain, anywhere in the OU tree, and to AD sites. How are these potentially conflicting policies resolved to determine the settings applied to the computer or user configuration?

9.2.1   *GPO application order*

Active Directory applies GPOs in a predetermined order when a computer is started or a user logs onto the domain:

1 Any local policies defined on the computer (not GPOs but included for completeness).

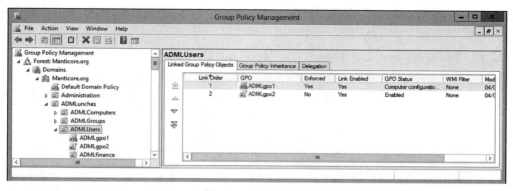

Figure 9.4 GPO links to an OU showing the processing order

    2 GPOs applied at the site level.

    3 GPOs applied at the domain level.

    4 GPOs applied to the OU tree containing the object. This starts at the topmost GPO in the tree and works down to each child OU applying any GPOs that are linked. This continues until the OU containing the objects is reached where any GPOs linked at that level are applied.

If multiple GPOs are applied to an OU, they're processed in order of precedence, as shown in figure 9.4.

The GPOs are applied in the order shown in the right pane of figure 9.4. In this case, ADMLgpo1 is applied first, followed by ADMLgpo2. Any settings that conflict between the two GPOs would be resolved in ADMLgpo2's favor—the last applied GPO wins. Any nonconflicting settings are merged. The order of GPO application can be modified in the GPMC by selecting the GPO and using the arrows to move the GPO up or down in the precedence order.

The policies that finally configure the object represent the cumulative impact of all the GPOs affecting that object. As an example, consider the Run command that's available in the Start menu. GPOs can be used to control whether this is available to the user. Assume a number of GPOs that either enable or disable this setting:

    1 A policy that disables the setting and is applied to the domain

    2 A policy that enables the setting and is applied to the parent OU

    3 A policy that disables the setting and is applied to the child OU

Users in the parent OU have the Run command available because the last GPO applied enabled the setting, but users in the child OU don't see the Run command because the last GPO applied to them disabled the setting.

> **TIP** Try to control settings in the minimum number of GPOs, preferably one. If a GPO has the setting configured as Not Configured, it'll leave the setting unchanged.

Working through these linkages will take time, and too many GPOs will slow down user logon or machine startup, as discussed in chapter 7.

9.2.2   *Blocking and overriding*

Imagine a situation where you need to prevent a GPO applying to a part of the OU tree, but you have to apply it to multiple OUs with the tree. This is illustrated in figure 9.5. You need to apply GPOs to the users in the ADMLunches OU tree:

- ADMLgpo1 has to be applied to all users.
- ADMLgpo2 has to be applied to all users except VIP users (in the ADMLvip).

From the layout in figure 9.5, you may be tempted to apply ADMLgpo1 four times (once to each of the OUs) and ADMLgpo2 three times (to all OUs except ADMLvip). This is inefficient because you need to repeat the same action a number of times. One way to perform this task is to

- Apply ADMLgpo1 to the ADMLusers OU. Each OU below that will inherit the application of the GPO.
- Apply ADMLgpo2 to the ADMLusers OU. Each OU below that will inherit the application of the GPO.
- Prevent the application of the GPO to the ADMLvip OU by blocking inheritance.

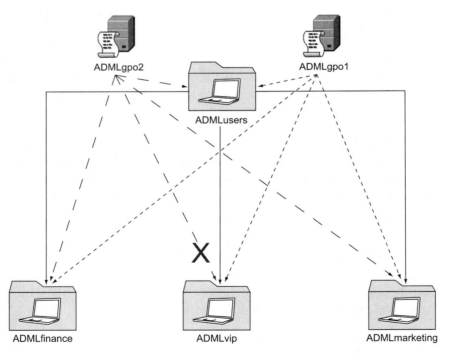

Figure 9.5   Application of GPOs—ADMLgpo1 **is applied to all OUs, but** ADMLgpo2 **is blocked from being applied to ADMLvip**

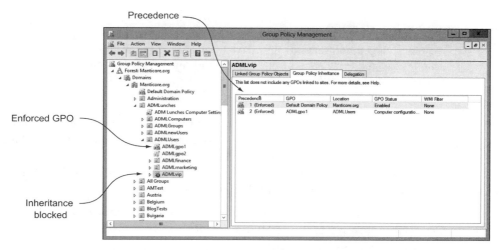

Figure 9.6 Application of GPOs showing Block Inheritance and Enforcement

Blocking inheritance is an all-or-nothing proposition. It blocks the inheritance of all GPOs when it's applied. If you want some GPOs to be inherited by the OU where you've blocked inheritance, you need to set them to be Enforced (this is also referred to as the No Override setting). This can lead to the situation in figure 9.6.

The ADMLvip OU is decorated with a blue circle containing a white exclamation mark. The GPOs `ADMLgpo1` and `Default Domain Policy` are decorated with a padlock to indicate they're enforced (and to override the inheritance blocking). The Group Policy Inheritance tab in the right pane of the GPMC (see figure 9.6) also shows that the GPOs are enforced.

Enabling the Block Inheritance setting is accomplished in the GPMC:

1 Open the GPMC and select the OU of interest.
2 Right-click the OU.
3 Choose Block Inheritance.

The Enforce setting is applied to a GPO:

1 Open the GPMC and select the GPO of interest.
2 Right-click the GPO.
3 Choose Enforced.

Either of the settings can be removed following the preceding steps and deselecting Enforced or Block Inheritance as appropriate.

NOTE The `Set-GPInheritance` PowerShell cmdlet can be used to set or remove Block Inheritance on an OU. `Set-GPLink` can be used to add or remove the Enforced setting on a GPO.

TRY IT NOW: Block inheritance

To block GPO inheritance to the ADMLUsers OU, first get the list of applied GPOs. Has it changed from section 9.1? If so, how and why has it changed? Remove the Block Inheritance setting.

Using the Block Inheritance and Enforced settings has started to get complicated with just a few GPOs involved. Imagine what it would be like with many OUs blocking inheritance and needing to have GPOs set to be enforced.

In situations like this, try and reorganize the OU structure to avoid using block inheritance and enforcement. In this instance you could

1 Move the ADMLvip OU to be a direct child of the ADMLunches OU.
2 Apply ADMLgpo1 to the ADMLunches OU.
3 Apply ADMLgpo2 to the ADMLUsers OU as at present.

9.2.3 *Filtering options*

You have other filtering options available to you when applying Group Policy. These are filtering by groups, WMI Filtering, and loopback processing.

FILTERING BY GROUPS

Filtering by groups (security filtering) is applied through the security filtering pane (see the middle of figure 9.7):

1 Open GPMC.
2 Select the GPO at its point of linking.

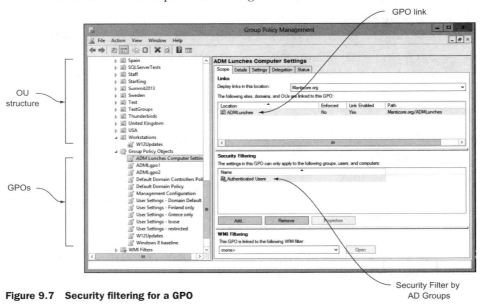

Figure 9.7 Security filtering for a GPO

3 In the Security Filtering pane click Add.

4 Select the group, or groups, in the standard AD search dialog.

5 Click OK.

This creates a filter so that the GPO is only applied to the users or computers in groups listed in the Security Filtering pane. The default is Authenticated Users (all users and computers that have successfully authenticated to the domain).

It's also possible to prevent a group from receiving a GPO:

1 Open GPMC.

2 Select the GPO at its point of linking.

3 Choose the Delegation tab.

4 Select the group to deny.

5 Click Advanced.

6 Choose Deny Read Permission.

7 Click OK.

WMI FILTERING

You can restrict the application of the GPO based on the value of a machine property that can be determined through WMI, such as a specific operating system version, memory installed in the machine, or free disk space. The value is checked by a WMI Filter. WMI Filters are created in the GPMC:

1 Open GPMC.

2 Navigate to the WMI Filters container.

3 Right-click the WMI Filters container and choose New.

4 Supply a Name and Description.

5 Create a WMI query. Click Add. Select the WMI namespace (most classes will be in the default root\cimv2 namespace). Enter a WMI Query Language (WQL)-based query such as `"SELECT * FROM Win32_OperatingSystem WHERE Caption LIKE '%Windows 7%'"`.

6 Click Save.

7 Select the GPO (at the point of linkage).

8 At the bottom of the Scope tab (see figure 9.3), select the filter from the WMI Filtering dropdown menu.

9 You'll be asked to confirm the filter change—choose Yes.

TIP For more information on WMI and WQL with many examples of WMI queries, see *PowerShell and WMI* by Richard Siddaway (Manning, 2012). You can't create a WMI Filter with PowerShell, but you can use PowerShell to test the filter before applying it.

LOOPBACK PROCESSING

In some instances, such as public-facing kiosk machines or machines in meeting rooms, you may want to lock down the machine so every user gets the same settings. You can do this through loopback processing. In GPO you want to apply the following:

1 Navigate to the Computer Configuration > Policies > Administrative Templates > System > Group Policy folder.
2 Choose Configure User Group Policy Loopback Processing Mode.
3 Choose Enabled.
4 Choose Replace Mode to replace all user settings with this policy, or Merge to combine the computer settings with the user settings (the computer's settings take priority).

You've seen how to apply GPOs and modify the way they're applied, but how do you know which settings have actually been applied to a user or a computer?

9.3   *Modeling GPO results*

There are two main groups of scenarios you may consider when determining the actual GPO settings applied to a user. First, you may be troubleshooting a problem and need to determine the results of the GPOs applied to the user or computer. The second group of scenarios covers the situation where you're making changes and want to test the results of those changes before you apply them. In both cases, you want to determine the settings produced by the cumulative application of all relevant GPOs. This is achieved by using the Group Policy Modeling wizard:

1 Choose Group Policy Modeling in the GPMC.
2 Right-click and choose Group Policy Modeling Wizard.
3 Click Next.
4 Select the domain and domain controller. Click Next.
5 Select the container (OU) or specific example for user and computer information. Click Next.
6 Select to simulate slow network connections, loopback processing, or a specific AD site if required. Click Next.
7 Add or remove User Security Groups to achieve the desired model. Click Next.
8 Add or remove Computer Security Groups to achieve the desired model. Click Next.
9 Add or remove User WMI Filters to achieve the desired model. Click Next.
10 Add or remove Computer WMI Filters to achieve the desired model. Click Next.
11 On the Summary of Selections page, click Next (see figure 9.8).
12 Click Finish.

The Summary tab shows any GPOs that generate special alerts, such as being Enforced. The Details tab shows which settings have been applied from which GPO. Drill down into the settings to see the policy, setting, and winning GPO.

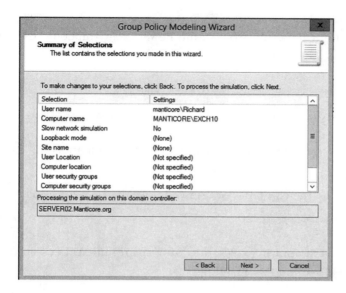

Figure 9.8   Summary of Selections page of Group Policy Modeling Wizard

TIP   This is a superb troubleshooting technique if you suspect problems due to misapplied GPOs. If you do include a specific user and computer, ensure that the user account has logged onto the machine.

GPOs are applied when a machine is started and when a user logs on. The GPOs are periodically reapplied. If you've made changes to one or more GPOs, you may want to force those changes to be applied rather than waiting for the next refresh.

9.4   *Customizing GPO Refresh settings*

The default Group Policy refresh processing interval is every 90 minutes with up to a 30-minute offset. Domain controllers are the exception with a 5-minute refresh interval. Security settings are reapplied every 16 hours (5 minutes for domain controllers) even if the GPOs are set not to reapply unless they're updated.

These timing periods can be modified. How? By changing some Group Policy settings! The settings are contained in the Group Policy node at `Computer Configuration - Policies - Administrative Templates - System - Group Policy`. The two settings are

- Group Policy Refresh Interval for Computers
- Group Policy Refresh Interval for Domain Controllers

Enable the settings and set the appropriate time.

TIP   Unless you want to have mismatched GPO refresh periods that could become an administrative headache, you should apply these settings at the domain level.

You can manually force a GPO refresh by using the `gpupdate` command. This isn't a PowerShell cmdlet, but it can be run from within PowerShell (you could use Invoke-GPUpdate if you prefer). The syntax for the command is

```
PS> gpupdate /?
Description:  Updates multiple Group Policy settings.

Syntax:  Gpupdate [/Target:{Computer | User}] [/Force] [/Wait:<value>]
    [/Logoff] [/Boot] [/Sync]
```

To update both computer and user GPOs, use the following command:

```
PS> gpupdate
```

If you only want to update the computer or user GPO, use the relevant switch:

```
PS> gpupdate /Target:Computer
PS> gpupdate /Target:User
```

That concludes our look at applying GPOs into your environment. Let's move on to the lab where you can practice these techniques.

9.5   *LAB*

Before you start this lab, you should have completed the labs from earlier chapters, especially chapters 7 and 8. This should give you an OU structure of

- ADMLunches
- ADMLComputers—contains the computer accounts you created in chapter 6
- ADMLGroups—contains the groups you created in chapter 4
- ADMLUsers—contains the user accounts you created in chapter 2

You should also have two GPOs that were created in chapter 8:

- ADMLgpo1—Computer Configuration disabled. GPO preferences used to set a drive mapping.
- ADMLgpo2—no settings enabled.

If you don't have this in place, perform the labs from earlier chapters to produce this structure. The alternative is to map the following exercises onto the OU structure in your lab environment.

9.5.1   *Complete the TRY IT NOW sections*

If you haven't done so already, complete the TRY IT NOW exercises from the chapter. The exercises are summarized here for your convenience.

LINKING GPOS
Apply the GPOs you created in chapter 8 as follows:

- Link ADMLgpo1 to the ADMLUsers OU
- Link ADMLgpo2 to the ADMLUsers OU

Use GPMC or PowerShell to perform the linkage.

Modify the settings in `ADMLgpo1`:

- Disable Computer Configuration.
- Enable User Configuration > Policies > Administrative Templates > Control Panel > Prohibit Access to Control Panel and PC Settings.

Modify the settings in `ADMLgpo2`:

- Disable Computer Configuration.
- Enable User Configuration > Policies > Administrative Templates > Windows Components > Desktop Gadgets > Turn Off Desktop Gadgets.

DISCOVER GPO LINKS

Discover the GPOs linked to the ADMLUsers OU. Which GPOs are applied directly and which are inherited?

BLOCK INHERITANCE

Block GPO inheritance to the ADMLUsers OU. Get the list of applied GPOs. Has it changed from section 9.1? If so, how and why has it changed? Remove the Block Inheritance setting.

9.5.2 *Create additional OUs and GPOs*

Create the following three OUs as children of the ADMLUsers OU:

- ADMLfinance
- ADMLmarketing
- ADMLvip

HINT   Review chapter 7 if you need a refresher on how to perform this task.

Create two more GPOs called

- `ADMLgpo3`
- `ADMLgpo4`

Disable the Computer Configuration in each GPO. Apply both GPOs to the ADML-Users OU. Block inheritance to the ADMLvip OU. Compare the GPOs applied to the ADMLvip and the ADMLfinance OUs.

9.5.3 *Resultant set of policies*

Model the resultant set of policies for the dgreen user in the ADMLUsers OU. Ignore the computer aspect. Move the dgreen user account into the ADMLfinance OU and generate the resultant set of policies. Move the dgreen user account into the ADMLvip OU and generate the resultant set of policies. Compare the three sets of results. What are the differences and how are they derived? Pick a real computer and user in your environment and model the resultant set of policies.

9.6   *Ideas for on your own*

GPOs are a very powerful tool for managing your environment. You can use them to produce a centrally managed and consistent desktop experience for your users. Examine the GPOs in your environment and determine how they're applied. Is it optimum? What could you change to improve the user's experience and make your life easier?

This concludes our look at GPOs. In the next chapter you'll learn about fine-grained password policies.

Fine-grained
password policies

Now that you've learned how to administer your environment using Group Policies, it's time to look at customizing the password settings in your domain. You'll perform this task using fine-grained password policies, which are also known as Password Settings Objects (PSOs). The two terms are used interchangeably in this chapter. They enable you to have multiple password policies in the domain, which means your organization saves the cost of having multiple domains. PSOs make security more granular and enable you to apply stricter password requirements to sensitive groups such as your administrators.

The chapter starts with an overview of the concepts surrounding PSOs. After this short theory section, we'll get back to the practical nature of administering Active Directory by showing you how to create, apply, and test fine-grained password policies.

Once the policies have been created, you need to be able to apply them to your users and groups. There are times when you need to determine the password policy that applies to a particular user. This technique is covered in the last section of the chapter. A number of practical exercises are supplied throughout the chapter, culminating in a lab section to close the chapter.

Before you can learn to manage these objects, you need to understand what they are and what they can do for your environment.

10.1 Fine-grained password policy concepts

When Active Directory was first introduced, it was only possible to have a single password policy (password length, complexity, frequency of change, and so on) in a domain. This was applied through a GPO linked at the domain level.

125

TIP   It's possible to apply GPOs that modify the password policy at the OU level but whose settings are ignored during GPO processing.

If an organization needed to have multiple password policies—for instance, to give administrators a longer password—another domain would have to be created, which increases cost (more domain controllers) and complexity.

Windows Server 2008 introduced fine-grained password policies. A PSO enables you to define an extra password policy; for example, administrators are required to use a password of 12 characters instead of the standard 8. Multiple PSOs can be defined in a domain. They're linked to groups rather than organizational units. This concept is illustrated in figure 10.1.

WARNING   Never give in to the urge to set a weaker password policy for a group of users. You may compromise your environment!

In figure 10.1 the default password policy is applied at the domain level and is therefore applied to the two OUs shown on the left. All users in the OUs have the default policy applied.

The group of users on the right has a policy applied that forces them to have a password that's at least 12 characters long. This group can be situated in one of the OUs on the left or in another OU. The PSO that's applied to them overrides the default policy.

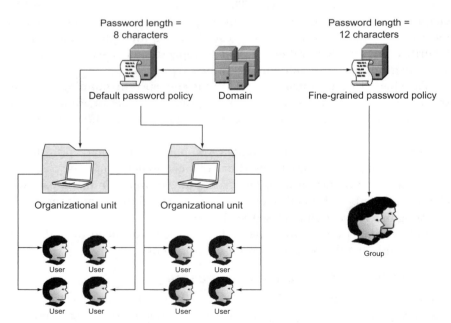

Figure 10.1   Default password policy of 8 characters applied to the users in the OUs on the left. A harsher password policy demanding a 12-character password is applied to the users in the group on the right.

> **Tools for managing fine-grained password policies**
>
> In Windows Server 2008 the only tool available to manage fine-grained password policies was ADSI Edit. This wasn't a pleasant experience, and, being a kindly soul, I won't inflict it on you. There are much better tools available now. Windows Server 2008 R2 added some PowerShell cmdlets (also available in Windows Server 2012), and a GUI tool became available in Windows Server 2012.

Password policies can be applied to AD groups or to AD users, but applying these policies to groups is the best practice because it reduces the administration overhead. When a user logs on to the domain, the following tests are applied:

1 If PSOs are linked directly to the user, then the PSO with the lowest precedence wins and is applied. Precedence is set when a policy is created. Each policy should have a unique precedence number.

2 If no PSOs are linked to the user but PSOs are linked to groups of which the user is a member, the group PSOs are compared and the PSO with the lowest precedence is applied.

3 If no PSOs are linked to the user or any groups of which the user is a member, the default password policy is applied by the GPO.

That's enough theory for now. Let's see how to create these policies.

10.2 *Creating fine-grained password policies*

You have a choice of two tools for creating fine-grained password polices: the GUI tool available through ADAC, or PowerShell. The choice is yours, but I prefer PowerShell for its automation capabilities. In either case there's a set of information you need available before you create the policy:

- Name you'll give the policy
- Precedence number to assign to the policy (lower-numbered policies take precedence)
- Minimum password length
- Number of passwords to remember
- Whether password must meet complexity requirements
- Minimum password age
- Maximum password age
- Account lockout policy (optional)
- Number of failed logon attempts allowed
- Reset failed logon count after n minutes
- Account will be locked out for n minutes or until administrator unlocks the account
- Description (strongly recommended)

Once you have that information available, you can start creating your policy.

10.2.1 *Creating a PSO using ADAC*

ADAC is the only GUI tool available. You can't create password setting objects using ADUC. The creation task is performed in a similar manner to other objects: open the tool, choose New and the object type, and complete the dialog. The steps required to complete these tasks are as follows:

1 Open ADAC.
2 Select the System folder.
3 Select the Password Settings Folder (the current PSOs will be visible).
4 Choose New.
5 Choose Password Settings.
6 Complete the dialog shown in figure 10.2.
7 Name and precedence are mandatory.
8 The Directly Applies To section can be used to set groups or users to whom the policy applies.
9 Click OK.

When you create a new policy in the GUI tool, the settings are set to the same values as the default domain policy when the tool opens. You can modify them as required to create a stronger policy. Don't be tempted to create weaker policies—I've said this before, and I'll keep repeating it!

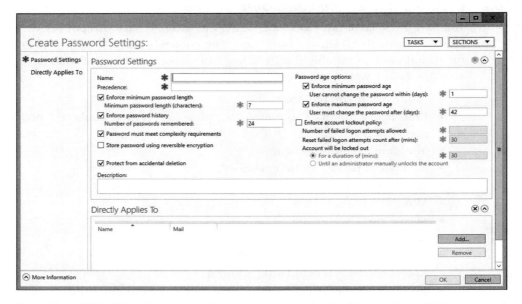

Figure 10.2   **ADAC dialog for creating a fine-grained password policy. The mandatory fields are marked with an asterisk. Default values based on the default password policy prepopulate the fields, such as password length or minimum password age.**

TRY IT NOW: Create a PSO with ADAC

Create a PSO using ADAC following the instructions is section 10.2.1. The following values can be used:

- Name: `ADMLpso1`
- Precedence: 100
- Minimum password length: 12
- Maximum password age: 10
- Password history count: 25

Leave all other values as the default but ensure that the checkboxes to use those values are selected.

10.2.2 Creating a PSO using PowerShell

If you need to create a policy in multiple domains, using PowerShell is more effective because you can save the code into a script and rerun it as required. Windows Server 2008 R2 (also available in Windows Server 2012) introduced PowerShell cmdlets for working with PSOs. You're creating an object, so you need a cmdlet with a verb of `New`. The `New-ADFineGrainedPasswordPolicy` cmdlet may have a long name, but it's simple to use. As an example, try this code:

```
New-ADFineGrainedPasswordPolicy -Name ADMLpso2 -Precedence 200 `
-MinPasswordLength 12 -MaxPasswordAge "21" -MinPasswordAge "2" `
-PasswordHistoryCount 50 -ComplexityEnabled:$true `
-Description "ADML policy 2" -LockoutDuration "4:00" `
-LockoutObservationWindow "4:00" -LockoutThreshold 3 `
-ReversibleEncryptionEnabled:$false
```

The time periods for parameters, like the `-LockoutDuration` or `-MinPasswordAge`, is supplied as a Timespan object (it's input as a string just to be confusing). PowerShell can interpret the string to use the data as a Timespan. The format is DD.HH:MM:SS.FF, where

DD = days (0–1,0675,199, which is nearly 29,250 years!)

HH = hours (0–23)

MM= minutes (0–59)

SS = seconds (0–59)

FF = fractions of a second (0–9,999,999)

TIP I always prefer to fully define all values when creating PSOs with PowerShell. This ensures I don't forget anything and that the values will be what I want rather than blindly accepting defaults. In the GUI you can see the suggested values, so set a reminder to change them if required.

Using PowerShell may seem to involve a lot of typing, but tab completion (type a partial cmdlet name or parameter name and press the Tab key to complete the name) will reduce the effort of using the cmdlet.

> ## TRY IT NOW: Create a PSO with PowerShell
>
> Try creating a policy using this PowerShell code:
>
> ```
> New-ADFineGrainedPasswordPolicy -Name ADMLpso2 -Precedence 200 `
> -MinPasswordLength 12 -MaxPasswordAge "21" -MinPasswordAge "2" `
> -PasswordHistoryCount 50 -ComplexityEnabled:$true `
> -Description "ADML policy 2" -LockoutDuration "4:00" `
> -LockoutObservationWindow "4:00" -LockoutThreshold 3 `
> -ReversibleEncryptionEnabled:$false
> ```
>
> How is this different from the policy you created with ADAC?

You can now create fine-grained password policies, but do you know which policies are available in your domain?

10.3 *Determining policies that exist in the domain*

Discovering the fine-grained password policies that have been created in your domain can be accomplished through ADAC or PowerShell. Of the two methods, PowerShell supplies the most flexibility and the best way of comparing settings between policies.

10.3.1 *Determining policies using ADAC*

Using ADAC involves navigating to the Password Settings Container:

1 Open ADAC.
2 Select the System folder.
3 Select the Password Settings folder (the current PSOs will be visible as shown in figure 10.3).

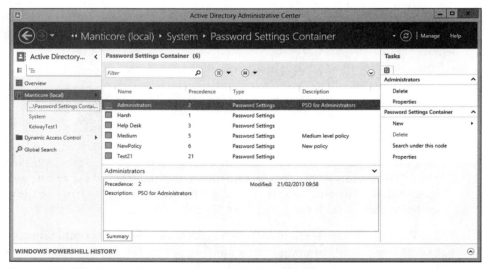

Figure 10.3 Viewing the fine-grained password policies in ADAC

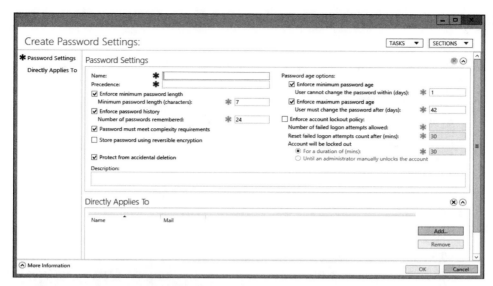

Figure 10.4   Dialog to view the PSO properties

The current password policies that are available in my domain are visible in figure 10.3. When viewing the Password Settings Container, you can double-click on any of the policies to view the settings within that policy. A dialog similar to that shown in figure 10.4 is made available.

The settings can be modified if required.

10.3.2 Determining policies using PowerShell

PowerShell displays the whole set of policy information by default using this code:

```
Get-ADFineGrainedPasswordPolicy -Filter *
```

A display similar to the following is obtained for each policy:

```
AppliesTo                 :
    {CN=AdminStaff,OU=Administration,DC=Manticore,DC=org}
ComplexityEnabled         : True
DistinguishedName         : CN=Administrators,CN=Password Settings
    Container,CN=System,DC=Manticore,DC=org
LockoutDuration           : 00:30:00
LockoutObservationWindow  : 00:30:00
LockoutThreshold          : 1
MaxPasswordAge            : 20.00:00:00
MinPasswordAge            : 1.00:00:00
MinPasswordLength         : 11
Name                      : Administrators
ObjectClass               : msDS-PasswordSettings
ObjectGUID                : 3f7369e7-a6ab-4294-b2de-1d674e6a079a
PasswordHistoryCount      : 20
Precedence                : 2
ReversibleEncryptionEnabled : False
```

You can view an individual policy by using its name; for example

```
Get-ADFineGrainedPasswordPolicy -Identity Administrators
```

You can view the groups and users to which the various policies are applied:

```
Get-ADFineGrainedPasswordPolicy -Filter * |
Format-Table Name, AppliesTo -AutoSize
```

The lockout policy settings can be compared:

```
Get-ADFineGrainedPasswordPolicy -Filter * | sort Precedence |
Format-Table Name, Precedence, ComplexityEnabled, Lockout*  -AutoSize
```

The password policy settings can be compared:

```
Get-ADFineGrainedPasswordPolicy -Filter * | sort Precedence |
Format-Table Name, Precedence, ComplexityEnabled, *Password*  -AutoSize
```

TRY IT NOW: View the policies

Open ADAC and view the policies available in your domain. Double-click on a policy to view the settings.

View the same policy with PowerShell. Use the code examples in section 10.2.3 to compare the policies in your domain.

You can create policies and view the existing policies. Now it's time to see how to apply them to your users.

10.4 Applying PSOs to users and groups

Fine-grained password policies only become useful when you apply them. You can apply a policy to a security principal, such as a user account or an AD group. The application of PSOs to groups will minimize the administration effort for you.

> **WARNING** GPOs are applied to OUs. PSOs are applied directly to users and groups. This is a common source of confusion. If you need to apply a PSO to all users in an OU, you'll need to create a group for those users and apply the PSO to the group.

You can use ADAC or PowerShell to apply a PSO. I think that PowerShell is quicker and easier to use, though if you're creating the PSO in ADAC and can set the application at that time, then use ADAC.

10.4.1 Applying a PSO using ADAC

Applying a PSO using ADAC can be accomplished during the creation of the policy by adding the user or group to the Directly Applies To box shown at the bottom of figure 10.5.

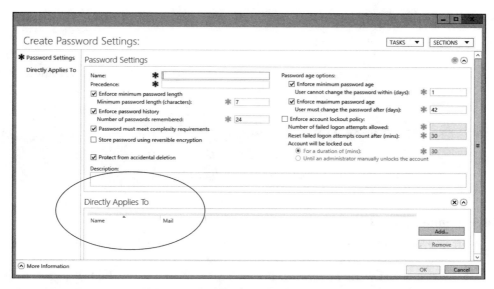

Figure 10.5   The Directly Applies To area of the PSO creation screen in ADAC. Use this to apply the PSO to preexisting AD groups as you create the policy.

If you need to apply a policy to a group (or user) after creation, follow these steps:

1. Open ADAC.
2. Select the System folder.
3. Select the Password Settings folder.
4. Double-click on the policy to open the settings dialog.
5. Click Add.
6. Select the groups and/or users using the standard AD users and groups selection dialog.
7. Click OK.
8. Click OK.

You can stop the application of a policy for a group or user by removing it from the Directly Applies To box. Open the PSO settings dialog, select the group (or user), click Remove, and then click OK.

10.4.2   *Applying a PSO using PowerShell*

The PowerShell cmdlets for managing the application of PSOs are

- `Add-ADFineGrainedPasswordPolicySubject`
- `Get-ADFineGrainedPasswordPolicySubject`
- `Remove-ADFineGrainedPasswordPolicySubject`

You can apply a policy to a group like this:

```
Add-ADFineGrainedPasswordPolicySubject -Identity ADMLpso2 `
-Subjects ADLgroup1
```

The `-Identity` parameter relates to the PSO and the `-Subjects` parameter supplies the group to which the policy will be applied.

> **TRY IT NOW: Apply the policies**
>
> Open ADAC and apply `ADMLpso1` (created earlier) to group ADLgroup1.
>
> Use PowerShell to apply `ADMLpso2` to group ADLgroup1.

10.4.3 Removing a PSO

If you need to remove a policy from a group, change the cmdlet name you use to `Remove-ADFineGrainedPasswordPolicySubject`.

If you just want to remove the policy from one individual in a group of users, remove them from the group and the policy won't apply anymore.

One last question relating to fine-grained password policies needs to be answered: which policies apply to a particular user or group?

10.5 *Testing the results of a policy applied to a user using PowerShell*

As you saw in section 10.4.1, ADAC can show you the users and groups to which a particular policy applies, but it can't show the policy that's actually applied to a user. That's a job for PowerShell.

> **TIP** The `Get-ADFineGrainedPasswordPolicySubject` cmdlet shows the users and groups to which a particular policy applies, not the resultant policy.

The resultant policy is determined only at the user level. It's determined from the policies applied directly to a user, policies applied to the groups the user is a member of, and the default domain password policy. One policy is selected as the winner according to the rules in section 10.1, which can be summarized as follows:

- The PSO with the lowest precedence that's directly linked to a user wins.
- If no PSOs are directly linked to the user, the PSO with the lowest precedence that's linked to a group of which the user is a member wins.
- If no PSOs are linked to the user or any groups of which the user is a member, the default password policy is applied by the GPO.

Password policies aren't merged in the same way as GPOs. GPOs are applied in a hierarchical manner from the domain, down the OU tree to the OU storing the user or computer. A setting that's set at the domain level or a high-level OU can be overridden by a GPO applied at a lower level. The last change wins. Nonconflicting settings are merged. PSOs are winner-takes-all—that is, all of the settings of whichever PSO is selected are applied.

The resultant policy is determined and displayed by running the following cmdlet:

```
Get-ADUserResultantPasswordPolicy -Identity dgreen
```

The -Identity parameter supplies the user to test. The resultant policy will be displayed.

TRY IT NOW: Test the policy application

Using PowerShell, pick a member of group ADLgroup1 and test the resultant policy. Which policy is applied? Why?

This concludes your work with fine-grained password policies. It's time for a quick lab before lunch is over.

10.6 *LAB*

This lab is concerned with managing fine-grained password policies.

10.6.1 *Complete the TRY IT NOW sections*

If you haven't done so already, complete the TRY IT NOW exercises. They're repeated here for your convenience.

CREATE A PSO WITH ADAC

Create a PSO using ADAC following the instructions in section 10.2.1. The following values can be used:

- Name: ADMLpso1
- Precedence: 100
- Minimum password length: 12
- Maximum password age: 10
- Password history count: 25

Leave all other values as the default, but ensure that the checkboxes to use those values are selected.

CREATE A PSO WITH POWERSHELL

Try creating a policy using this PowerShell code:

```
New-ADFineGrainedPasswordPolicy -Name ADMLpso2 -Precedence 200 `
-MinPasswordLength 12 -MaxPasswordAge "21" -MinPasswordAge "2" `
-PasswordHistoryCount 50 -ComplexityEnabled:$true `
-Description "ADML policy 2" -LockoutDuration "4:00" `
-LockoutObservationWindow "4:00" -LockoutThreshold 3 `
-ReversibleEncryptionEnabled:$false
```

How is this different from the policy you created with ADAC?

VIEW THE POLICIES IN THE DOMAIN

Open ADAC and view the policies in your domain. Double-click on a policy to view the settings. View the same policy with PowerShell. Use the code examples in section 10.2.3 to compare the policies in your domain.

APPLY THE POLICIES

Open ADAC and apply `ADMLpso1` (created earlier) to group ADLgroup1. Use PowerShell to apply `ADMLpso2` to group ADLgroup1.

TEST THE POLICY APPLICATION

Using PowerShell, pick a member of group ADLgroup1 and test the resultant policy. Which policy is applied? Why?

10.6.2 *Create a PSO*

Create three new PSOs. The following values can be used for the first policy:

- Name: `ADMLpso3`
- Precedence: 100
- Minimum password length: 12
- Maximum password age: 20
- Password history count: 25

These values can be used for the second policy:

- Name: `ADMLpso4`
- Precedence: 200
- Minimum password length: 10
- Maximum password age: 20
- Password history count: 25

The third policy can be given these values:

- Name: `ADMLpso5`
- Precedence: 50
- Minimum password length: 6
- Maximum password age: 20
- Password history count: 25

You can use ADAC or PowerShell to create these policies. I recommend using both.

10.6.3 *Apply fine-grained password policies*

Apply all three new policies (`ADMLpso3`, `ADMLpso4`, and `ADMLpso5`) to the user dgreen that you created in chapter 2.

10.6.4 *Determine a resultant policy*

Determine the resultant policy applied to user dgreen. Why is this policy applied to this user? Check another user in ADLgroup1, such as jgreen. Compare the results. Do they get the same policy? Why is the policy the same or different?

10.6.5 *Delete a policy*

Delete the policy ADMLpso5 using ADAC or PowerShell. Determine the resultant policy for user dgreen. Has anything changed?

10.7 *Ideas for on your own*

Fine-grained password polices supply a method of increasing the security for important groups in your environment, such as administrators and finance users. Consider the groups in your environment for which you may need to tighten the password policy and design a set of polices to apply to them.

This chapter concludes the section on policies (both Group Policies and fine-grained password polices). In the next chapter you'll learn about managing the AD service when we look at creating domain controllers.

Part 3

Managing the Active Directory service

So far you've learned to manage the data in your Active Directory (users, groups, computers, and OUs) as well as the policies you apply to those objects (Group Policy and Fine-Grained Password Policies). In this section you'll discover how to manage the underlying Active Directory service.

Domain controllers are essential to your Active Directory. They're the machines that store a copy of the AD database and handle the authentication and authorization requests from your users. In chapter 11 you'll learn how to create domain controllers. This information is extended in chapter 12 when you learn to manage your domain controllers.

The data stored in your Active Directory is vital to the wellbeing of your organization. The methods you can utilize to protect that data are described in chapter 13. The way that data is accessed and managed is an important aspect of protecting the data. Chapter 14 shows how to use Active Directory's default groups and delegation techniques to control who can do what to your precious data.

A correctly configured DNS is essential for Active Directory. Chapter 15 teaches you how DNS works with AD and how you can manage your DNS implementation.

Active Directory replicates data between domain controllers. The replication topology is defined by AD Sites and Site Links. These, together with AD subnets, are the topic of chapter 16. Replication itself, and how to monitor it, are the subjects of chapter 17.

Sometimes you'll need to create links to other ADs. These links are known as trusts and form the subject of chapter 18.

Let's begin our discussion of managing your Active Directory service by looking at how to create domain controllers.

Creating domain controllers

11

Domain controllers (DCs) are the essential part of your Active Directory. This chapter shows you how to create them. There are a number of reasons for creating a new domain controller; one of the most common in a stable environment is if an existing domain controller has to be replaced due to hardware failure.

A domain controller is a server within the domain that has AD Domain Services installed. It hosts a copy of the AD database (ntds.dit) and the SYSVOL share (containing logon scripts and Group Policy data files). Domain controllers respond to authentication attempts by users and computers. They also store the data that controls access to resources like email systems and file stores.

> **NOTE** It's strongly recommended that your domain controllers don't have any services installed on them beyond those necessary to control Active Directory. They shouldn't be used as a web server or file server, for instance.

A domain controller is situated in an AD site. You'll learn more about AD sites in chapter 16. A common question is "How many domain controllers do I need in my domain?" As with so much in IT, the answer is that it depends. A production domain should have at least two domain controllers. The state of your network connections between locations helps determine any further domain controllers that are needed. If you have fast, reliable, network links, you can centralize your domain controllers. If your network links are slow or unreliable, put domain controllers on remote sites with more than 60 or 70 users.

WARNING Only put a full, writable, domain controller, not a Read Only Domain Controller, in a location that has sufficient physical security, such as a lockable, restricted-access server room.

In an AD environment, all domain controllers can read and write to the database. Changes are replicated between domain controllers. This is known as a *multimaster* environment. In this respect all domain controllers are equal, but there are some caveats to that statement concerning Read-Only Domain Controllers (RODCs) and Flexible Single Master Operations (FSMO) roles. You'll learn about RODCs in the last section of this chapter, and FSMO roles are covered in chapter 12. AD replication is covered in detail in chapter 17.

NOTE You may see online references to primary and backup or primary and secondary domain controllers. This terminology is a remnant of Windows NT and should be ignored.

This chapter opens with a quick look at some of the basic concepts of domain controllers—what they are and what they do for you. Once you've digested that, it's straight into learning how to create a writable domain controller in your environment.

The last section of the chapter shows you how to create and manage an RODC. RODCs were introduced in Windows Server 2008. They provide a way to give authentication services to remote offices that don't offer secure server rooms. The chapter concludes with a lab section.

You now understand what a domain controller does—it controls the authentication and authorization operations within your domain. However, before you can work with them, you need to create them.

11.1 *Creating writable domain controllers*

There are a number of common situations in which you may need to create a new domain controller, including the following:

- The organization is expanding and you need to provide services to a new location.
- A domain controller has failed, or its hardware needs replacing.
- You're creating a new domain in your forest.
- You're creating a new forest.

In all cases, you need to ensure that the prerequisites are met before you create the domain controller. Techniques for performing these actions are presented in two of my other books, *PowerShell in Practice* (Manning, 2010) and *PowerShell and WMI* (Manning, 2012). The requirements are explained in table 11.1.

Table 11.1 Prerequisites for creating a domain controller

Order	Prerequisite	Commentary
1	Install operating system, service pack, and patches.	Ensure that the patching is up to date and that any service packs have been applied. This should be a part of your normal build process. Ensure Windows is activated by your organization's standard mechanism.
2	Rename the machine.	Windows provides a machine-generated name when you first perform the installation. Change the name before making the system a domain controller.
3	Configure the machine with a static IP address.	Domain controllers can be configured to obtain an IP address from DHCP, but it's best practice to configure a static IP address.
4	Configure the machine to use a DNS server.	If you're creating a new domain or forest, you may not need this step if the system will become a DNS server as well as a domain controller.
5	Join the machine to the domain.	You can't do this if you're creating a new domain or a new forest.
6	Permissions.	In all cases you need to have administrator access to the system. You need to be a member of the Domain Admins group to create a domain controller in an existing domain. To add a domain to an existing forest you need to be a member of the Enterprise Admins group (in the root domain).

Assuming that you've configured your machine as described in table 11.1, you need to add the AD Domain Services role.

11.1.1 *Installing AD Domain Services role*

Once you've installed the base Windows operating system, you can configure additional functionality by installing one or more roles and features. Windows Server can be installed with a full GUI interface or as a Server Core installation, in which case you only get the command line.

INSTALLING WITH A FULL GUI INTERFACE

With a full GUI installation, one way to install AD Domain Services is to use Server Manager:

1 Open Server Manager (it normally opens by default when you log on to the server).
2 Click Manage.
3 Choose Add Roles and Features.

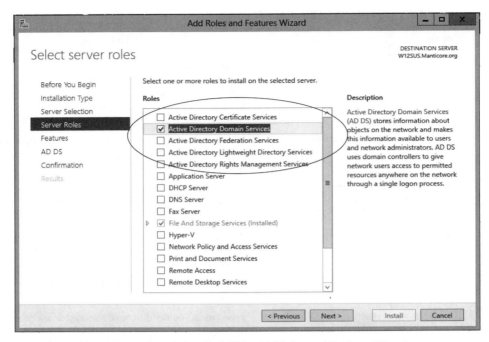

Figure 11.1   Selecting AD Domain Services in the Add Roles and Features Wizard

4   Read the introductory screen if you haven't seen it before. Click Next.

5   Choose the role-based or feature-based installation radio button. Click Next.

6   Select the server. The local server will be highlighted. You can perform the installation on a remote server, including a Server Core instance, if required. Click Next.

7   Select the server role or roles to be installed—in this case, AD Domain Services, as shown in figure 11.1. Currently installed roles are shown as ticked or shaded in the case of a partial installation. Click Next.

8   Select any required features—none are needed for AD Domain Services. Click Next.

9   Read the AD Domain Services information page. Click Next.

10 Choose Restart the Destination Server Automatically if required. Click Install.

11 You'll see progress information as the installation proceeds.

12 When the installation is complete, you'll see a message informing you that additional steps are required to make the machine a domain controller.

INSTALLING WITH POWERSHELL

The alternative is to use the Server Manager PowerShell cmdlets:

```
Install-WindowsFeature -Name AD-Domain-Services -Confirm:$false
```

If you're working locally on a Server Core machine, you'll need to use PowerShell. On any version of Windows, you'll need to run PowerShell with elevated privileges to perform the role installation. This is so easy that I wouldn't dream of using the GUI to perform the task. Once you have the role installed, you can create the domain controller.

> **TRY IT NOW: Discover the installed roles**
>
> Use Server Manager to discover the installed roles and features on a number of servers in your domain. Repeat using PowerShell cmdlets.

11.1.2 Performing the domain controller promotion

The act of turning a machine into a domain controller is often referred to as *promotion*. In earlier versions of Windows, you'd use a command called dcpromo. In Windows Server 2012 and later, you start the promotion from Server Manager.

The steps involved are

1 Open Server Manager.
2 Choose the Notifications icon (the flag in figure 11.2). You'll see a post-deployment dialog that includes the Promote This Server to a Domain Controller link (ringed in figure 11.2).

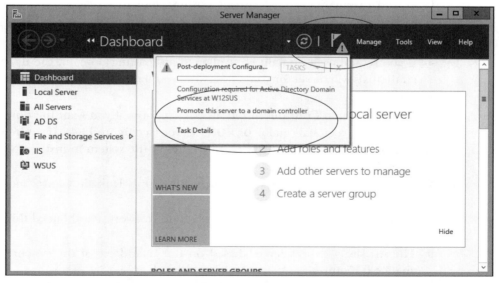

Figure 11.2 Start the domain controller promotion by selecting the Notifications icon and then Promote This Server to a Domain Controller link.

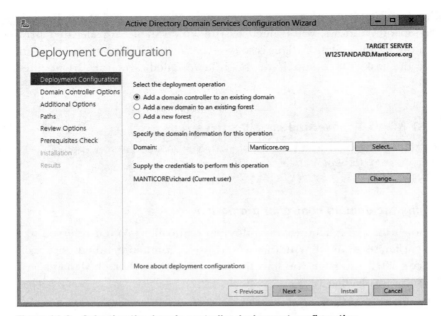

Figure 11.3   Selecting the domain controller deployment configuration

3   On the Deployment Configuration page choose one of the following as the deployment operation (figure 11.3):
   ▪ Add a Domain Controller to an Existing Domain
   ▪ Add a New Domain to an Existing Forest
   ▪ Add a New Forest

4   If you're adding a domain controller to an existing domain, the domain and credentials will be set for you. Otherwise, you'll need to supply the information.

5   Click Next.

6   On the Domain Controller Options page, choose if you want the domain controller to be a global catalog or a DNS server (see figure 11.4). If you're running an AD-integrated DNS (see chapter 15), allow the system to install DNS for you from this wizard.

7   Choose if you want the system to be a Read-Only Domain Controller (see section 11.3).

8   Supply the Directory Services Restore Mode Password (you'll need this in chapter 13).

9   The AD site will be selected based on the IP address of the system. You can change if required.

10   Click Next.

11   Click Next to skip the DNS delegation page.

12   Choose the Install from Media Option if required.

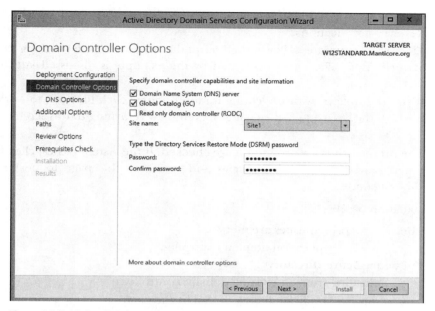

Figure 11.4   Selecting the domain controller options

13 Select the domain controller to replicate from if required.

14 Click Next.

15 Set the paths for the AD database, logs, and SYSVOL folder (figure 11.5). In most cases, the defaults will be more than adequate.

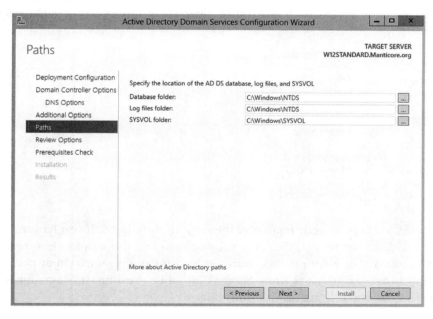

**Figure 11.5
Selecting the
database,
logs, and
SYSVOL paths**

16 Click Next.

17 Review your selections.

18 The wizard generates a PowerShell script that you can view by clicking the View Script button. The script generated by the example is discussed later in this section.

19 If you're unhappy with the configuration options, click Previous to work back through the wizard to make changes, eventually returning to this screen.

20 Click Next.

21 The prerequisites for promotion are checked. If the system passes, click Install; otherwise, correct the deficiencies and return to this page to perform the check again.

The installation process will

- Confirm the prerequisites are met.
- Determine the replication domain controller.
- Configure Active Directory.
- Start replicating from an existing domain controller.
- The schema will replicate first, followed by the data.
- DNS will be configured.
- Kerberos policy will be configured.
- The server will reboot.

When the server restarts, you'll have a working domain controller. The computer account will have been moved into the Domain Controllers OU.

The domain controller promotion wizard gives you the option to view the Power-Shell script it's going to use. The script produced from the example in this chapter is as follows:

```
Import-Module ADDSDeployment
Install-ADDSDomainController `
-NoGlobalCatalog:$false `
-CreateDnsDelegation:$false `
-CriticalReplicationOnly:$false `
-DatabasePath "C:\Windows\NTDS" `
-DomainName "Manticore.org" `
-InstallDns:$true `
-LogPath "C:\Windows\NTDS" `
-NoRebootOnCompletion:$false `
-SiteName "Site1" `
-SysvolPath "C:\Windows\SYSVOL" `
-Force:$true
```

The parameters are directly related to the steps in the wizard. If you have to create a number of new domain controllers in your domain, use the script to ensure a consistent and repeatable build process. Windows Server Core is an excellent platform for domain controllers. If you're using Server Core, then creating the domain controller using the PowerShell cmdlet is your only option.

In some situations—for instance, where the physical security of the location isn't sufficient—you won't want to deploy a full domain controller, but a RODC may solve the problem.

11.2 Read-Only Domain Controllers

RODCs were introduced with Windows Server 2008. They don't have a copy of the database and must relay an authentication attempt or object change to a domain controller with a writable copy of the database. The primary usage scenario for an RODC is in a branch office. Branch offices can't usually provide the correct level of physical security for a domain controller, and often have slow or unreliable WAN links that could adversely impact replication between domain controllers. In the event of the server being stolen, an RODC doesn't give an attacker a copy of the AD database to work with.

An RODC can be allowed to cache passwords locally, but any changes still need to be relayed to a full domain controller. All replication is one-way on to the RODC. All data, including passwords, is stored in memory. Nothing is held on disk. If the RODC is rebooted, the password information is replicated again from a full domain controller.

11.2.1 Creating an RODC

There are two ways to create an RODC. The first option is to create a computer account for the RODC and then promote the system to a domain controller—this is known as a staged deployment. Alternatively, you can join the computer to the domain and promote the machine to a domain controller using `Install-ADDS-DomainController` with the `-ReadOnlyReplica:$true` parameter. I prefer the staged approach because it removes one reboot from the creation process. You saw the single-step process when you created a full domain controller. You'll use the staged install for creating in this section.

In either case, you need to perform the usual activities involved in creating a new machine, including the following:

- Install and patch the operating system.
- Rename the machine.
- Configure networking.

A staged install for an RODC is a two-step process:

1. Create a computer account and set the accounts whose passwords can be replicated to the RODC.
2. Attach the RODC to that account and promote it to be a domain controller.

The creation of the computer account can be performed through the GUI, but I recommend using PowerShell because you can save the command into a script and you only need to change a few values to create another RODC. The number of RODCs your organization requires depends on the size—that is, the number of users at each location, together with the speed and reliability of your network connections. If you use RODCs, use at least two per location to provide resiliency.

TIP   Using a script promotes consistency, which is difficult to achieve using the GUI.

The computer account is created with the `Add-ADDSReadOnlyDomainController-Account` cmdlet. The parameters for this cmdlet are explained in table 11.2.

Table 11.2   Parameters for the `Add-ADDSReadOnlyDomainControllerAccount` cmdlet used to stage an RODC computer account

Parameter	Purpose
`-SkipPreChecks`	Specifies that only a base set of validations will be performed when this cmdlet is executed.
`-DomainControllerAccountName`	Specifies the name of the RODC account that you're creating.
`-DomainName`	Specifies the domain name for the user name (account credentials) for the operation.
`-SiteName`	Specifies the name of an existing site where you can place the new domain controller.
`-AllowPasswordReplicationAccountName`	Specifies the names of user accounts, group accounts, and computer accounts whose passwords can be replicated to this RODC.
`-Credential`	Specifies the user name and password that correspond to the account used to install the domain controller. This account has to be a member of the Domain Admins group.
`-DelegatedAdministratorAccountName`	Specifies the name of the user or group that will install and administer the RODC.
`-DenyPasswordReplicationAccountName`	Specifies the names of user accounts, group accounts, and computer accounts whose passwords aren't to be replicated to this RODC.
`-NoGlobalCatalog`	Specifies that the RODC will not be a global catalog server.
`-InstallDNS`	Specifies whether the DNS server service should be installed.
`-ReplicationSourceDC`	Specifies the name of the domain controller to be used as the source for replicating to this RODC.

An example of this cmdlet in action would be

```
Add-ADDSReadOnlyDomainControllerAccount `
-SkipPreChecks `
-DomainControllerAccountName RODC1 `
-Credential (Get-Credential) `
-DomainName Manticore.org `
-SiteName Site1 `
-AllowPasswordReplicationAccountName ADMLrodc1 `
```

```
-DelegatedAdministratorAccountName dgreen `
-InstallDNS `
-ReplicationSourceDC server02.manticore.org `
-Force
```

A number of parameters from table 11.2 deliberately haven't been used in the example. You can test the values you want to use by swapping `Test-ADDSReadOnlyDomain-ControllerAccountCreation` for `Add-ADDSReadOnlyDomainControllerAccount` in the preceding code.

Once you've created the account and the machine is in its correct physical location configured with the correct IP address, you can promote it to an RODC. Attaching an RODC requires membership in the Domain Admins group in Windows Server 2012. This can be performed through the GUI tools (from Server Manger) for full versions of Windows. It's recommended that you use Server Core installations for RODC systems, so PowerShell is the way to perform the task:

```
Import-Module ServerManager
Install-WindowsFeature -Name  AD-Domain-Services

Import-Module ADDSDeployment

Install-ADDSDomainController -Credential (Get-Credential) `
-CriticalReplicationOnly:$false `
-DatabasePath "c:\windows\NTDS" -DomainName "manticore.org" `
-LogPath "C:\windows\NTDS" -SysvolPath "c:\windows\SYSVOL" `
-UseExistingAccount:$true -NoRebootOnCompletion:$false -Force
```

You need to install the AD services before promotion to an RODC. This is performed with the `Install-Windowsfeature` cmdlet from the `ServerManager` module. When the install has finished, you can import the `ADDSDeployment` module and run `Install-ADDSDomainController` as shown.

You'll be prompted for the credential and the safe password. The credential is for an account that can join the machine to the domain and perform the promotion—it must be a member of the Domain Admins group. The `-UseExistingAccount:$true` parameter forces the RODC to attach to the account you created earlier.

After replication occurs and the RODC reboots, it's ready for your users to use.

11.2.2 Managing an RODC

When an RODC is created, no passwords are cached on the machine by default. If you want that to happen, you have to administer those changes. The examples in the previous section used `-AllowPasswordReplicationAccountName ADMLrodc1` in `Add-ADDSReadOnlyDomainControllerAccount` to enable the members of the ADMLrodc1 group to have their passwords replicated and cached. This enables users in the site to be authenticated by the RODC instead of relaying the request to a writable domain controller.

> **WARNING** Users can't change their password at an RODC. The request has to be relayed to a writable domain controller and the changed password replicated back to the RODC.

Each RODC has an independent Password Replication Policy as illustrated in figure 11.6. When the RODC is first created, a number of Deny entries are made in the policy. These are groups containing accounts that have greater levels of permissions in the domain and are therefore more sensitive. These groups are marked with an arrow in figure 11.6. More details on the permissions conferred by these groups are available in chapter 14. One of the main reasons for using an RODC is because of diminished physical security in a remote office, so not replicating sensitive accounts is a good idea!

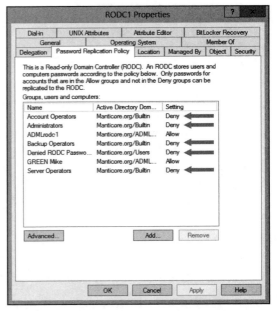

Figure 11.6   RODC Password Replication Policy

Figure 11.6 is displayed by right-clicking the RODC in ADUC and choosing Properties. Click Add to get the wizard that provides the choice of allowing or denying replication, and the standard AD users and groups search dialog will be displayed. Select the users or groups whose passwords will be allowed to replicate and click OK.

You can stop passwords from being replicated for individual users or groups by selecting them in the Password Replication Policy dialog (figure 11.6) and clicking Remove.

If you click the Advanced button

- The Policy Usage tab shows accounts whose passwords are stored on the RODC or accounts that have been authenticated by the RODC. Use the dropdown menu to toggle between the two choices.
- The Resultant Policy tab can be used to determine if a user can be authenticated by the RODC.

Modify the membership of the ADMLrodc1 group (preferred method) using techniques from chapter 4, or manage users individually as described earlier in this chapter.

11.2.3 *Managing the RODC password policy with PowerShell*

If you have multiple RODCs in the same site, allowing password replication by using groups will save you effort and minimize the chances of mistakes.

> **TIP**   Each RODC has an independent password replication policy. If you manage the policy by adding and removing individual accounts, you'll need to

add the account to the policy on both RODCs. If you use the same group for both RODCs, you just have to add the user to the group.

If you allow the user to authenticate against one RODC but not the other, you'll see problems. At best, you may see a slowdown in authentication while the request is relayed to a writable domain controller. At worst, you'll see authentication failures. These issues will be difficult to diagnose because they'll occur intermittently depending on which RODC the user attempts to authenticate against.

The replication policy can be viewed using the GUI, as shown in figure 11.6. You can also view the password replication policy for an individual RODC using Power-Shell; unfortunately you have to perform two passes: one for the accounts allowed to replicate, and one for those denied replication:

```
Get-ADDomainControllerPasswordReplicationPolicy -Identity RODC1 -Allowed
Get-ADDomainControllerPasswordReplicationPolicy -Identity RODC1 -Denied
```

You can also view whether a particular account is allowed to replicate its password to the RODC:

```
PS> Get-ADAccountResultantPasswordReplicationPolicy `
-DomainController RODC1 -Identity dgreen
Allow

 PS> Get-ADAccountResultantPasswordReplicationPolicy `
-DomainController RODC1 -Identity jbloggs
DenyImplicit
```

`DenyImplicit` means replication is denied because it isn't specifically allowed. Other values are `DenyExplicit` (replication is specifically denied for the account) or `Unknown`.

The list of accounts that can replicate their passwords can be managed using the `ADDomainControllerPasswordReplicationPolicy` cmdlets:

```
Add-ADDomainControllerPasswordReplicationPolicy -Identity RODC1 `
-AllowedList 'mgreen'

PS> Get-ADAccountResultantPasswordReplicationPolicy
-DomainController RODC1 -Identity mgreen
Allow
```

> **TIP** You also need to allow the computer account passwords for the machines in the RODC's site to replicate to the RODC.

`Remove-ADDomainControllerPasswordReplicationPolicy` can be used to take an account out of the replication policy. As stated earlier, it's best practice to manage the password replication through group membership, rather than individually.

TRY IT NOW: Discover the RODC password replication policy

Use the GUI tools described in section 11.3.2 to investigate the password replication policy for a RODC in your domain. Repeat using PowerShell cmdlets.

This concludes your lunchtime session on domain controllers. Time to head into the lab.

11.3   *LAB*

This lab covers managing the domain controllers in your domain. Any part of this lab that changes that environment, such as creating a domain controller, shouldn't be performed in a production domain. The activities in this lab should only be performed in a test domain.

11.3.1   *Complete the TRY IT NOW sections*

If you haven't done so already, complete the TRY IT NOW exercises. They're repeated here for your convenience.

DISCOVER THE INSTALLED ROLES

Use Server Manager to discover the installed roles and features on a number of servers in your domain. Repeat using PowerShell cmdlets.

DISCOVER THE RODC PASSWORD REPLICATION POLICY

Use the GUI tools described in section 11.3.2 to investigate the password replication policy for a RODC in your domain. Repeat using PowerShell cmdlets.

11.3.2   *Create a domain controller*

Use the techniques and information in section 11.2.2 to create a domain controller in your test domain.

11.3.3   *Create a RODC*

Use the techniques and information in section 11.3.1 to create an RODC in your test domain.

11.4   *Ideas for on your own*

Domain controllers are fundamental to Active Directory. Do you have enough domain controllers in your environment? Every production domain should have at least two domain controllers, and any location with more than 50 or 60 users or a slow WAN link is a candidate for a domain controller. Review your environment and decide if you need more domain controllers. You should also decide if you need full, writable, domain controllers or if Read-Only Domain Controllers will suffice. Talk to the powers-that-be and convince them to let you build them.

In the next chapter you'll learn about managing your domain controllers.

12
Managing
domain controllers

Domain controllers are the most essential part of your Active Directory. Creating domain controllers was covered in detail in chapter 11, and this chapter shows how to manage them. It starts with discovering the domain controllers in your environment, and then covers testing their availability and the services they offer.

The chapter then moves on to global catalogs—the extra piece of domain controller functionality that enables you to access a subset of the attributes of every object in the forest in every domain. The global catalog is essential for the correct functioning of a multi-domain forest and Exchange email servers. After learning how to find global catalogs, you'll see techniques for promoting domain controllers to be global catalogs (as well as demoting them).

In Active Directory all domain controllers are equal, but some roles (tasks) can only be performed by one domain controller at a time. These are the Flexible Single Master Operations (FSMO) roles. You need to know how to discover the FSMO role holders, what they do, and how to move the role between domain controllers. The chapter also includes a lab section.

First up—how to discover the domain controllers in your environment.

12.1 Discovering domain controllers

Do you know how many domain controllers you have in your domain? Or where they are? In this section you'll learn how to find domain controllers, test that they're available, and discover the services they offer.

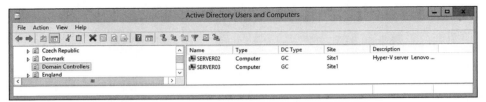

Figure 12.1   Domain Controllers OU showing two domain controllers that are also global catalogs

12.1.1 *Finding domain controllers*

If you have a relatively small environment with only a handful of domain controllers, you can probably keep their names in your head. In larger environments or in an environment that's new to you, you'll need to discover them.

> **TIP** You can only work with one domain at a time when discovering domain controllers because they're domain-specific.

You can discover the domain controllers in your domain in a number of ways.

USING THE GUI TOOLS TO FIND DOMAIN CONTROLLERS

The simplest way is to open ADAC or ADUC and navigate to the Domain Controllers OU. Figure 12.1 illustrates the display in ADUC.

Don't be tempted to move domain controllers out of this default OU. The Default Domain Controllers GPO is automatically applied to this OU, and some tools, such as `dcdiag.exe`, don't work correctly if the domain controller is in another OU.

The display in figure 12.1 shows the name of the domain controller and its type. In this case, both domain controllers are also global catalogs (see section 12.2). It's also possible to use AD Sites and Services to discover domain controllers, as described in section 12.2.1.

USING POWERSHELL TO FIND DOMAIN CONTROLLERS

PowerShell supplies a cmdlet, `Get-ADDomainController`, for finding the domain controllers in your environment. It can display an interesting set of information, including the AD site and IP address:

```
PS> Get-ADDomainController -Filter * |
Format-Table Name, Site, IPv4Address, IsGlobalCatalog, IsReadOnly -AutoSize

Name     Site  IPv4Address   IsGlobalCatalog IsReadOnly
----     ----  -----------   --------------- ----------
SERVER02 Site1 192.168.2.1             True      False
SERVER03 Site1 192.168.2.202           True      False
```

The IPv4 address is shown in the example. The IPv6 address is also available if required. `Get-ADDomainController` looks for domain controllers in the same site as the machine you're using. Use the `-SiteName` parameter to force a search in another site.

You can force the discovery of the domain controller you used to log on to the domain as follows:

```
Get-ADDomainController -Identity ($env:LOGONSERVER).Remove(0,2)
```

TRY IT NOW: Discovering domain controllers

Use the techniques in section 12.1.1 to discover the domain controllers in your domain.

Is there another way using PowerShell? *Hint:* are there computer accounts in a specific OU?

The techniques you've just seen show that the domain controller exists in Active Directory. It doesn't tell you whether the domain controller is online and can accept authentication attempts.

12.1.2 *Testing the availability of a domain controller*

How can you tell if a domain controller is available? The simplest way is to ping the machine name. You could use ping.exe, but the Test-Connection cmdlet is a better proposition:

```
PS> Test-Connection -ComputerName server02 -Quiet -Count 1
True
PS> Test-Connection -ComputerName server03 -Quiet -Count 1
False
```

You also need to test if the services required for users to authenticate are running, as follows:

```
Get-Service -ComputerName server02 -Name ADWS, Netlogon, DFSR, NtFrs, DNS,
    Kdc, W32Time
```

```
Status    Name          DisplayName
------    ----          -----------
Running   ADWS          Active Directory Web Services
Running   DFSR          DFS Replication
Running   DNS           DNS Server
Running   Kdc           Kerberos Key Distribution Center
Running   Netlogon      Netlogon
Running   NtFrs         File Replication
Running   W32Time       Windows Time
```

If any of these services aren't running, your domain controller—and therefore, your users—will have problems.

TRY IT NOW: Testing availability

Use the techniques in section 12.1.2 to test if all of the domain controllers in your domain are available. If you have a very large domain, choose a subset of the domain controllers.

Put together a script that you could run periodically to test your domain controller availability.

12.1.3 Services

Domain controllers can offer a number of services to your environment, as listed in table 12.1. The services are essential to the overall wellbeing of your environment. Some services, such as being the PrimaryDC, can only be provided by one domain controller at a time. Other services, such as GlobalCatalog, can be offered by multiple domain controllers. All domain controllers should offer the KDC, TimeService, and ADWS.

Table 12.1   Domain controller services

Service	Purpose
PrimaryDC	Domain controller holds PDC Emulator role for domain (see section 12.3).
GlobalCatalog	Domain controller holds a copy of the global catalog (see section 12.2).
KDC	Issues authorization access tokens after authentication.
TimeService	The Windows Time Service is running.
ReliableTimeService	The computer time is deemed to be reliable (accurate), usually by synchronizing with an external time source.
ADWS	Active Directory Web Services is running, which is required for the PowerShell cmdlets. ADWS is installed by default on Windows Server 2012 and Windows Server 2008 R2 domain controllers.

You can use `Get-ADDomainController` to discover DCs that offer these services:

```
Get-ADDomainController -Discover -Service PrimaryDC
Get-ADDomainController -Discover -Service GlobalCatalog
Get-ADDomainController -Discover -Service KDC
Get-ADDomainController -Discover -Service TimeService
Get-ADDomainController -Discover -Service ReliableTimeService
Get-ADDomainController -Discover -Service ADWS
```

The output from these queries is of this form:

```
Domain      : Manticore.org
Forest      : Manticore.org
HostName    : {SERVER02.Manticore.org}
IPv4Address : 10.10.54.201
IPv6Address :
Name        : SERVER02
Site        : Site1
```

In theory, you can combine these flags, but my testing has shown issues.

> **TIP** Be careful trying to combine the service flags. Some combinations, such as GlobalCatalog and KDC, don't work together. I recommend either testing all combinations or searching for individual services.

The global catalog is useful in multi-domain environments.

12.2 Global catalog

A domain controller is part of a domain and can only authenticate users in that domain. Multiple domains can't be hosted on a single-domain controller. In a multi-domain forest, there's a need to have a certain amount of information about every object available to domain controllers in all domains. This is the purpose of the global catalog—it hosts a subset of the attributes of every object in the forest.

The global catalog contains a subset of the attributes of an object and is replicated to all domain controllers in all domains in the forest that are configured as global catalog servers.

> **TIP** Remember that global catalogs are domain controllers with enhanced functionality. They're not a separate type of system.

You can modify the subset of attributes contained in the global catalog. By default, the first domain controller in the forest is a global catalog. If other global catalog servers are required, then domain controllers have to be explicitly promoted to fulfill that role.

> **TIP** Exchange servers need a global catalog available in the same AD site. Make sure you have sufficient global catalogs to service your Exchange servers.

If you use Universal groups in your environment, your users will need fast access to a global catalog at logon time to resolve Universal group membership.

You need to be able to find the global catalogs in your environment before you can manage them.

12.2.1 Finding global catalogs

USING GUI

AD Sites and Services is the GUI tool to use to discover the global catalogs in your environment:

1 Open AD Sites and Services (shown in figure 12.2).
2 Open Sites (click the triangle to the left of Sites).
3 Select and open Site name.
4 Select Servers—these are the domain controllers in the site.
5 A display similar to figure 12.2 will be shown.
6 The DC Type will read GC if the domain controller is a global catalog.

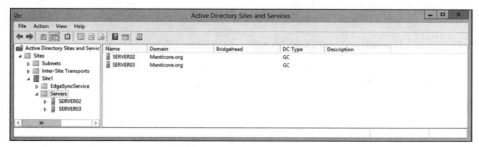

Figure 12.2 Viewing global catalogs in an AD site

The drawback to using the AD Sites and Services tool is that every site has to be checked individually. This is feasible for an AD forest with a handful of sites, but becomes very tedious if you have a large number of sites in your environment.

PowerShell supplies a way to quickly discover all global catalogs.

USING POWERSHELL

You can't discover global catalogs directly by using PowerShell. Global catalogs are forest-level objects and can be found as properties of the forest object:

```
PS> Get-ADForest | select -ExpandProperty GlobalCatalogs
SERVER02.Manticore.org
SERVER03.Manticore.org
```

The `GlobalCatalogs` property retrieved by the `Get-ADForest` cmdlet will supply the name of the global catalogs, but it doesn't show in which site the domain controller can be found. The code can be extended to supply this information:

```
Get-ADForest | select -ExpandProperty GlobalCatalogs |
foreach {
  Get-ADDomainController -Identity $_ |
  select Name, Domain, Site
}
```

Each of the global catalog names produced by the `Get-ADForest` cmdlet is used in `Get-ADDomainController` (the `$_` symbol represents the object coming along the pipeline—in this case the global catalog name). The `select` command restricts the information returned to the domain controller name, domain, and AD site. This is an easy way to check your global catalog coverage.

> **TRY IT NOW: Discovering global catalogs**
>
> Use the techniques in section 12.2.1 to discover your global catalogs. Use the techniques in section 12.1.2 to test whether they're available.
>
> Put together a script that you could run periodically to test your global catalog availability.

After examining your global catalog coverage, you realize you need to create another one, because users in a particular site can't resolve Universal group membership and therefore can't log on. How do you perform that task?

12.2.2 *Creation of a global catalog*

The starting point for creating a global catalog is a domain controller. Ensure that the domain controller has fully replicated (see chapter 16), especially if it's newly created, before you promote it to a global catalog.

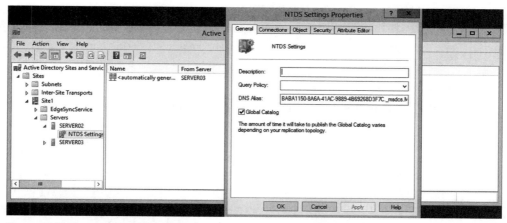

Figure 12.3 Promoting a global catalog

USING GUI

You can use AD Sites and Services to create a global catalog:

1 Open AD Sites and Services.
2 Choose Sites.
3 Select a site name.
4 Choose Servers (these are your domain controllers in the site).
5 Select a server name.
6 Choose and right-click NTDS Settings.
7 Choose Properties (the dialog shown in figure 12.3 will be displayed).
8 Select the Global Catalog checkbox.
9 Click OK.
10 Close the dialog if necessary.
11 Close AD Sites and Services.
12 Wait for the replication to complete.

This is one of the few tasks where it may be easier to use the GUI tool than to use PowerShell.

USING POWERSHELL

Unfortunately, there aren't any cmdlets for working directly with global catalogs, so you have to resort to a script:

```
$dc = "dc02.manticore.org"
$contextType =
➥ [System.DirectoryServices.ActiveDirectory.DirectoryContextType]::
➥ DirectoryServer

$context = New-Object -TypeName
```

```
System.DirectoryServices.ActiveDirectory.DirectoryContext `
-ArgumentList $contextType, $dc

$gc = [System.DirectoryServices.ActiveDirectory.DomainController]::
➥ GetDomainController($context)

$gc.EnableGlobalCatalog()
```

Set the name of the domain controller to promote in the $dc variable. Use the FQDN. Create a `DirectoryContextType` object that's set to `DirectoryServer`. Create a `DirectoryContext` using the `ContextType` and the domain controller name. Create a `DomainController` object using the `DirectoryContext`.

The `EnableGlobalCatalog()` method is used to perform the promotion. Replication will occur and your global catalog will be ready to use once the replication completes. Your domain controller can be used for normal authentication and authorization activities during promotion to a global catalog.

Eventually, you'll need to remove the global catalog from a domain controller, possibly because you're replacing the domain controller.

12.2.3 *Removal*

Removing the global catalog from a domain controller is the reverse of the procedure you followed during the creation described in section 12.2.2. The way to remove the global catalog using ADUC is as follows:

1 Open AD Sites and Services.
2 Choose Sites.
3 Select a site name.
4 Choose Servers (these are your domain controllers in the site).
5 Select a server name.
6 Choose and right-click NTDS Settings.
7 Choose Properties (the dialog shown in figure 12.3 will be displayed).
8 Deselect the Global Catalog checkbox.
9 Click OK.
10 Close the dialog if necessary.
11 Close AD Sites and Services.
12 Wait for the replication to complete.

The PowerShell script to perform the removal is

```
$dc = "dc02.manticore.org"

$contextType =
➥ [System.DirectoryServices.ActiveDirectory.DirectoryContextType]::
➥ DirectoryServer

$context = New-Object -TypeName
```

```
System.DirectoryServices.ActiveDirectory.DirectoryContext `
-ArgumentList $contextType, $dc

$gc =
➥ [System.DirectoryServices.ActiveDirectory.GlobalCatalog]::
➥ GetGlobalCatalog($context)

$gc.DisableGlobalCatalog()
```

This is exactly the same as the creation script, except that the `DisableGlobal-catalog()` method is used in the last line.

All domain controllers in your AD domain are equal, unless they hold one of the FSMO roles.

12.3 *FSMO roles*

There are a number of activities that only one domain controller at a time can be allowed to perform. This is to prevent corruption of the Active Directory and to ensure that requests are managed in a consistent manner. There are five such activities: two at the forest level and three in each domain. These are known as Flexible Single Master Operations, or FSMO. Table 12.2 summarizes these activities. The first domain controller in a forest carries all five roles. When a new domain is created, the three domain-level roles are hosted on the first domain controller in the domain. The roles can be moved between domain controllers.

Table 12.2 FSMO roles, which can only be held by a single-domain controller at a time. The PDC Emulator and RID Master are the most important for day-to-day operations because their absence can stop authentication or the creation of new objects (such as users or computers).

FSMO Role	Level	Activities
Schema Master	Forest	Schema updates are processed on this server.
Domain Naming Master	Forest	Controls changes to the forest, such as addition and removal of domains.
PDC Emulator	Domain	Originally for backward compatibility with Windows NT domain controllers during upgrades. If no Windows NT domain controllers are present, it will have all password changes preferentially replicated so it maintains the latest version. If an authentication attempt fails, another attempt is automatically made against the PDC Emulator in case the password has changed. Acts as a target for Group Policy changes. Acts as a primary time source within the domain. The PDC Emulator in the root domain is the primary time source for the forest.
RID Master	Domain	Relative identifier (RID) Master issues pools of unique identifiers to domain controllers for them to use when new objects are created.
Infrastructure Master	Domain	Maintains references to objects in other domains; for example, users in another domain who are members of a group in the current domain.

The Schema Master and Domain Naming Master roles rarely have any activities to perform. You'll probably only use the Schema Master when extending the AD schema for an Exchange upgrade or when you want to update the version of Windows used by your domain controllers. The Domain Naming Master is only needed when adding or removing domains from your forest.

The PDC Emulator and RID Master are the busiest in a domain because they're involved in day-to-day activities, as detailed in table 12.2. The role of the Infrastructure Master causes a lot of confusion in people's minds because it appears to conflict with the global catalog discussed earlier in this section. The following rules should be adopted:

- In a single-domain forest, the Infrastructure Master is irrelevant and may be hosted on a global catalog.
- In a multi-domain forest where all the domain controllers are also global catalog servers, the Infrastructure Master is irrelevant and may be hosted on a global catalog.
- In a multi-domain forest where only some domain controllers are also global catalog servers, the Infrastructure Master is relevant and must not be hosted on a global catalog.

How can you discover the FSMO role holders in your domain?

12.3.1 *Discovering FSMO role holders*

You can find the domain controllers that hold specific FSMO roles by using PowerShell or the GUI tools.

> **TIP** You can't use ADAC to manage the FSMO roles.

USING THE GUI TOOLS

The three domain-level FSMO roles (discussed in table 12.2) can be discovered using ADUC:

1 Open ADUC.
2 Right-click Domain Name.
3 Choose Operations Masters ....
4 The dialog in Figure 12.4 will open.

Figure 12.4 Domain-level FSMO roles displayed from ADUC

Each FSMO role has its own tab. The RID Master tab is shown in figure 12.4. Select another tab to view the data for the appropriate FSMO role.

The Domain Naming Master is discovered from the AD Domains and Trusts tool:

1 Right-click Active Directory Domains and Trusts (at top of the left pane).
2 Choose Operations Master ....
3 The dialog similar to Figure 12.4 will be displayed.

TIP You need to be a member of the Enterprise Admins group in the root domain to modify the forest by adding or removing domains, and you need to be a member of the Schema Admins group to work with the schema. You'll learn more about these groups in chapter 14.

Discovering the Schema Master involves a bit more work on your part:

1 Register the schema snap-in by running `regsvr32 schmmgmt.dll` from the command line. This only needs to be performed once per server the first time you access the schema snap-in on a particular machine.
2 Open the Run dialog.
3 Type `mmc.exe`.
4 Choose Run as Administrator.
5 Click OK.
6 The Empty MMC console opens.
7 Click File.
8 Click Add/Remove Snap-in ....
9 Choose Active Directory Schema.
10 Click Add.
11 Click OK.
12 Right-click Active Directory Schema.
13 Choose Operations Master ....
14 The dialog similar to Figure 12.4 is displayed.

In all of the GUI tools, the current role holder and an option to change are displayed.

TIP To change any of the FSMO roles, you must run the appropriate GUI tool from a server that isn't the current role holder.

USING POWERSHELL

A simpler, one-step process for discovering your FSMO role holders can be performed with PowerShell. Save the following two lines of PowerShell to a file called `get-fsmo.ps1`:

```
Get-ADForest | Format-Table *master
Get-ADDomain | Format-Table PDCEmulator, *master
```

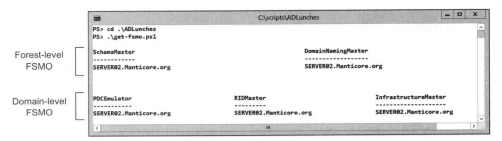

Figure 12.5   Discovering the FSMO roles using the `get-fsmo.ps1` script

The code shows a trick to reduce the amount of typing you need to perform by using wildcards in the property selection of `Format-Table`. This trick works in the other format cmdlets, as well as `Select-Object`.

The script is run as shown in figure 12.5. Note the `.\` before the script name. This is a reference to the current folder. PowerShell doesn't run scripts in the current folder by default. If the script is in another folder, supply the full path to the script.

`Format-Table` is used on each line because the two cmdlets display different properties and the displays will conflict and not display all of your results unless you force the display.

> **WARNING**   Normally you should output objects, not text, as in this example. This is a special case because all you want to see is the name of the individual FSMO role holders.

Figure 12.5 shows the two forest-level FSMO role holders first, and then the domain-level role holders. In this case, the roles are all hosted on the same domain controller, but this isn't a requirement.

TRY IT NOW: Discover the FSMO roles

Use the GUI tools described in section 12.3.1 to discover the FSMO role holders in your environment. Do you have multiple domains? If so, how can you discover all of the FSMO role holders?

Use the `get-fsmo.ps1` script from section 12.3.1 to discover the FSMO roles. Which is easiest? How would you discover all of the FSMO role holders in a multi-domain forest using the `get-fsmo.ps1` script?

12.3.2 *Transferring*

A FSMO role can only be held by one domain controller at a time. You can transfer roles between domain controllers. This is a manual task—there's no way to get this to happen automatically. Many administrators are wary of moving FSMO roles. It's not an action you should perform on a whim, but in my experience it carries minimal risk.

I was working at one customer's site where we transferred FSMO roles between domain controllers on opposite sides of the Atlantic Ocean!

TRANSFERRING A FSMO ROLE USING A GUI TOOL

To change a FSMO role through the GUI tools, you must run from a machine that isn't the current role holder. Open the appropriate GUI tool, as outlined in table 12.3.

Table 12.3 FSMO role and management tools

Role	Tool
Schema Master	AD Schema
Domain Naming Master	AD Domains and Trusts
PDC Emulator	AD Users and Computers
RID Master	AD Users and Computers
Infrastructure Master	AD Users and Computers

The following steps are required to transfer a FSMO role:

1 Point the appropriate tool at another domain controller (if required) by right-clicking on the title of the tool at the top of the left pane, where it'll say something like Active Directory Users and Computers [SERVER02.Manticore.org]. The name in square brackets is the domain controller you're working on.

2 Choose Change Domain Controller… and select the required DC from the list.

3 Open the FSMO dialog as described in section 12.3.1.

4 In the dialog box (see figure 12.4, for example) you should see the name of the selected domain controller in the lower box.

5 Click Change.

6 You'll be asked to confirm the operation. Click Yes to complete the transfer.

TRANSFERRING A FSMO ROLE USING POWERSHELL

Alternatively, you can run the following script:

```
function move-afsmo {
[CmdletBinding()]
param([string]$server,

[ValidateSet("schema", "domain", "rid", "infra", "pdc")]
[string]$fsmo
)
$dom = [System.DirectoryServices.ActiveDirectory.Domain]::GetCurrentDomain()
$sid = ($dom.GetDirectoryEntry()).objectSid
$dc = [ADSI]"LDAP://$server/rootDSE"

switch ($fsmo.ToLower()){
    "schema" {$role = "becomeSchemaMaster"; break}
    "domain" {$role = "becomeDomainMaster"; break}
    "rid"    {$role = "becomeRidMaster"; break}
```

```
    "infra"   {$role = "becomeInfraStructureMaster"; break}
    "pdc"     {$role = "becomePDC"; break}
}

if ($role -eq "becomePDC"){ $dc.Put($role, $sid[0])}
else {$dc.Put($role, 1) }
$dc.SetInfo()
}
```

You use the script like this:

```
Move-afsmo -server server03 -fsmo rid
```

The script finds the domain's SID and creates a directory object for the target domain controller. It then modifies the DC to become the chosen role.

> **TIP** You may see references in the literature or on the web to using the .NET DomainController class to move FSMO roles between domain controllers. My testing has shown that this class doesn't always work. I don't recommend using it.

If the current FSMO role holder is unavailable and won't be brought back online, you'll need to force the transfer of the role, a process known as *seizing the role*.

12.3.3 *Seizing FSMO roles*

Seizing a FSMO role should only be performed if you're 100% certain that the current role holder has failed and can't be brought back online.

> **WARNING** Don't practice this in a production environment because you'll need to remove the old role holder.

Seizing a FSMO role is best performed on the domain controller where you want to move the FSMO role. There isn't a GUI option to perform FSMO role seizure, so the process has to be performed from the command line:

1 Open PowerShell or a command prompt using Run as Administrator.
2 Type `ntdsutil` and press Enter.
3 Type `roles` and press Enter.
4 Type `connection` and press Enter.
5 Type `connect to servername` and press Enter. `Servername` is the name of the domain controller to which the FSMO role will be moved.
6 Type `quit` and press Enter.
7 Type the appropriate command from table 12.4 and press Enter—for instance, if you want to seize the RID Master role, type `Seize rid master` and press Enter.
8 Type `quit` and press Enter.
9 Type `quit` and press Enter.

Table 12.4 `Ntdsutil` **command to seize a FSMO role. Notice that the PDC Emulator doesn't follow the pattern of the other commands. Substitute the appropriate command from the table into step 7 of the instructions in section 12.3.3.**

FSMO Role	Seize Command
Schema Master	`Seize schema master`
Domain Naming Master	`Seize domain naming master`
PDC Emulator	`Seize pdc`
RID Master	`Seize rid master`
Infrastructure Master	`Seize infrastructure master`

The old role holder must be rebuilt (with a different name) before being brought online.

This concludes your lunchtime session on managing domain controllers. Time to head into the lab.

12.4 LAB

This lab covers managing the domain controllers in your domain. Any part of this lab that changes that environment, such as demoting a global catalog, shouldn't be performed in a production domain. The activities in this lab should only be performed in a test domain.

12.4.1 Complete the TRY IT NOW sections

If you haven't done so already, complete the TRY IT NOW exercises. They're repeated here for your convenience.

DISCOVERING DOMAIN CONTROLLERS

Use the techniques in section 12.1.1 to discover the domain controllers in your domain.

Is there another way of using PowerShell? *Hint:* computer accounts in a specific OU?

TESTING AVAILABILITY

Use the techniques in section 12.1.2 to test if all of the domain controllers in your domain are available. If you have a very large domain, choose a subset of the domain controllers.

Put together a script that you could run periodically to test your domain controller availability.

DISCOVERING GLOBAL CATALOGS

Use the techniques in section 12.2.1 to discover your global catalogs. Use the techniques in section 12.1.2 to test whether they're available.

Put together a script that you could run periodically to test your global catalog availability.

DISCOVERING THE FSMO ROLES

Use the GUI tools as described in section 12.3.1 to discover the FSMO role holders in your environment. Do you have multiple domains? If so, how can you discover all of the FSMO role holders?

Use the `get-fsmo.ps1` script from section 12.3.1 to discover the FSMO roles. Which is easiest? How would you discover all of the FSMO role holders in a multi-domain forest using the `get-fsmo.ps1` script?

12.4.2 *Global catalog promotion*

Promote a domain controller to be a global catalog using the GUI tools. Observe the messages you receive. Once replication has changed, reverse the change using Power-Shell.

Try promotion through PowerShell and demotion using the GUI tools.

Hint: you need at least two domain controllers in your domain for this lab to work. If both are global catalogs, perform the demotion first.

12.4.3 *FSMO role transfer*

Transfer the FSMO roles between domain controllers. Be sure to transfer both forest-level roles and at least one domain-level role to gain experience with all of the tools.

Don't seize any of the roles.

12.5 *Ideas for on your own*

Domain controller management is an integral and important part of managing Active Directory. If your domain controllers aren't working, neither are your users. Practice the techniques in this chapter until you're confident in applying them. Use the examples provided to create scripts that you can use to periodically and regularly test your domain controller availability, including the services, global catalogs, and FSMO roles.

In the next chapter you'll learn about protecting the data in your Active Directory, with more information on using protection from accidental deletion and some new techniques to learn: AD snapshots, the AD Recycle Bin, and how to back up and restore Active Directory.

Protecting AD data 13

The data in your Active Directory is precious. If anything happens to it, your users won't be able to log on and perform their work. The organization is in trouble at that point. This chapter shows you how to protect AD data, which, in turn, protects the organization and ultimately protects your job!

> **WARNING** No single scheme of protection is foolproof, which is why I recommend that you implement as many different ways to protect your data as you can.

There are four techniques for protecting your AD data that you'll meet in this chapter. You start with protection from accidental deletion. This technique protects you as an administrator, as well as the data, because it removes the ability to delete objects such as user accounts. It takes away those "oops" moments when you realize you've deleted the wrong account. This protection is a security setting on an object so it can be easily removed when you need to move or delete the object.

Second, snapshots provide a point-in-time copy of the data in your Active Directory. You can take snapshots on a periodic basis and compare the current live object, such as a user account, with a previous version. This provides a method to investigate changes and have the information available so that a change can be reversed if needed.

Next we'll cover the AD Recycle Bin. Introduced with Windows Server 2008 R2, the AD Recycle Bin changes the way deleted AD objects are treated and provides a method of undeleting objects. The object's attributes are preserved so that you have a fully operational user account; for instance, after it's been restored from the AD Recycle Bin.

Finally, backup and restore is the traditional way of protecting data. It still works in a modern AD environment but needs careful consideration. Backing up all of your domain controllers is wasteful and unnecessary, because your AD data is replicated between domain controllers. Determining what to backup and why is covered, as well as the techniques to perform a backup and restore.

You've already seen protection from accidental deletion in action earlier in the book in chapters 2, 3, 6, and 7, so that would be a very good place to start.

13.1 *Protection from accidental deletion*

Several years ago I got a call from my boss. One of our customers had deleted an OU full of user accounts (several hundred) and wanted to know if there was anything we could do to get the data back quickly. They were running an older version on Active Directory, so the short answer was no—they had to perform an authoritative restore (see section 13.2). If they'd been on Windows Server 2008 or later, they could have benefited from using protection from accidental deletion.

You've seen protection from accidental deletion in action a number of times during the early chapters of the book, when creating, moving, and deleting objects, such as user accounts or groups. As a quick refresher, protection from accidental deletion isn't a property of an AD object. It's a security setting that denies the ability to delete to the Everyone group. Everyone is a group that Active Directory automatically creates and maintains. It contains all users, authenticated and unauthenticated, including administrators.

13.1.1 *Using the GUI*

The Protect from Accidental Deletion setting for an AD object can be viewed from the Properties tab. Navigate to the object in ADAC and right-click it. Choose Properties to see the dialog presented in figure 13.1, which shows the ADMLUsers OU. A similar setting is available on all objects, such as users, groups, and computers. You can turn this protection on when you create the object, which is the best way of remembering to do it! One advantage of automating object creation is that setting protection from accidental deletion never gets forgotten.

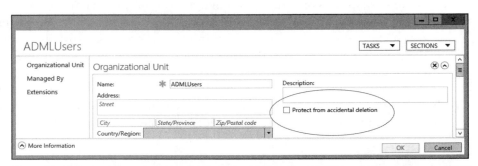

Figure 13.1   Protect from Accidental Deletion setting on the ADMLUsers OU as shown in ADAC

If you're using ADUC, open the properties of the object and view the Object tab. You can toggle the protection on by selecting the checkbox and turn it off by deselecting the box.

13.1.2 Using PowerShell

That's great for a single object, but what if you need to modify the setting for a number of objects—let's say all of the user accounts in the ADMLUsers OU? First, you need to know the current setting:

```
PS> Get-ADUser -Filter * -Properties ProtectedFromAccidentalDeletion `
-SearchBase "OU=ADMLUsers,OU=ADMLunches,DC=manticore,DC=org"  |
Format-Table Name, ProtectedFromAccidentalDeletion -AutoSize

Name             ProtectedFromAccidentalDeletion
----             -------------------------------
GREEN Dave                           False
GREEN Jo                             False
GREEN Mike                           False
GREEN1 Dave                          False
GREEN Dave2                          False
GREAEN Bill                          False
```

For some reason, protection has been turned off on these objects. Even the OU has had the protection removed! At this stage you have a choice. You can click through each object in the GUI, or you can run a little piece of PowerShell as follows:

```
Get-ADObject `
-Identity "OU=ADMLUsers,OU=ADMLunches,DC=manticore,DC=org" `
-Properties ProtectedFromAccidentalDeletion |
Set-ADObject -ProtectedFromAccidentalDeletion:$true
```
❶ Getting an OU

```
Get-ADUser `
-SearchBase "OU=ADMLUsers,OU=ADMLunches,DC=manticore,DC=org" `
-Filter * -Properties ProtectedFromAccidentalDeletion |
Set-ADObject -ProtectedFromAccidentalDeletion:$true
```
❷ Getting a user

Get the object (OU in the first case) ❶ and pipe to `Set-ADobject`. Use the `Protected-FRomAccidentalDeletion` parameter with a value of `$true` to turn it on (use `$false` to turn it off). A similar approach is taken in the second snippet, where the results of `Get-ADUser` ❷ are piped to `Set-ADObject` for the setting to be turned on.

> **TIP** I strongly recommend you enable Protect from Accidental Deletion on all of your data objects. It'll save you grief.

Protection from accidental deletion doesn't protect your environment against mistakes or a rogue administrator. It's possible to turn off the setting and delete the objects. A more likely error is to turn off the setting to move some objects and then forget to turn it back on. I always perform moves using a PowerShell script so that the protection is automatically turned back on. A further layer of protection can be added using AD snapshots.

13.2   Snapshots

An AD snapshot is a copy of your AD database at a point in time. AD snapshots are a useful way to recover from minor changes, such as removing a group by mistake when changing a user's group memberships. You can see what the correct values were and revert to them. They're also a useful troubleshooting tool if you need to determine if changes have been made to an object and what those changes were.

> **Using the snapshot tools**
>
> In the testing on Windows Server 2012 I did for this chapter, I found that
>
> - You can only create snapshots when you're directly accessing the domain controller.
> - The domain controller can only have one network adapter.
> - You need to be running PowerShell and/or cmd.exe with elevated privileges.
> - Ntdsutil.exe will run in a cmd.exe window or a PowerShell window.
> - Dsamain.exe only appears to run in a PowerShell window, even though it's a standard command prompt tool, not a PowerShell command.
>
> I have no explanation for the last point. I haven't seen it referenced elsewhere on the internet and it may be an artifact of my test system. Just be aware that there may be an issue.

13.2.1   Creating a snapshot

Snapshots are created by using the ntdsutil.exe tool, which is installed when you install Active Directory. There isn't a GUI- or PowerShell-based way of performing this task, though ntdsutil can be run from a PowerShell console as shown in figure 13.2. The syntax to create a snapshot is

```
ntdsutil snapshot 'Activate Instance NTDS' Create quit quit
```

The output from the command is shown in figure 13.2. The important part to note is the GUID used to name the snapshot. The GUID is indicated by the arrow in figure 13.2.

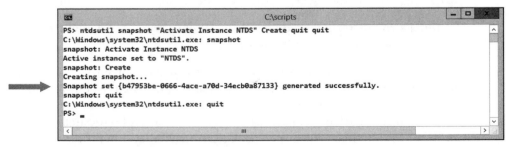

Figure 13.2   Creating an AD snapshot with ntdsutil

The first time you take a snapshot a full copy of your AD database is taken, so the process can take a few minutes depending on the size of your environment. Subsequent snapshots are incremental, so only changes since the last snapshot are captured. This enables the later snapshots to run much more quickly.

> **WARNING** Snapshots are specific to an individual domain controller. They don't replicate between domain controllers. You don't need to take snapshots on every domain controller, but how many domain controllers host snapshots should be determined by your organization's size and needs.

When should you take a snapshot? I'd take them on a periodic basis, maybe weekly or twice a week, depending on the volatility of your environment (this process should be automated using a scheduled task). A sample script to create a scheduled task is provided in the download code for this chapter. I also recommend taking a manual snapshot before commencing any large-scale reorganization or cleanup of your Active Directory.

13.2.2 Viewing existing snapshots

The list of existing snapshots can be viewed using `ntdsutil`. You'll see a display like this:

```
PS> ntdsutil snapshot "List All" quit quit
C:\Windows\system32\ntdsutil.exe: snapshot
snapshot: List All
 1: 2013/03/29:15:38 {bfecad87-0fdd-4ce0-a903-5dcb9801142b}
 2:    C: {f107497f-0386-4447-b002-7532df901b01}
      C:\$SNAP_201303291538_VOLUMEC$\

 3: 2013/03/29:16:48 {b47953be-0666-4ace-a70d-34ecb0a87133}
 4:    C: {425728ad-cdc6-4187-8a36-8039c259ae2e}

snapshot: quit
C:\Windows\system32\ntdsutil.exe: quit
PS>
```

Each snapshot is listed individually with the date and time it was taken, together with its GUID. There are two GUIDs associated with each snapshot. If you compare the preceding output with figure 13.2, you'll see that the first GUID associated with a snapshot (the one on the same line as the date) is shown when the snapshot is created (the second GUID appears to be a unique folder name). The relevant line from figure 13.2 states

```
Snapshot set {b47953be-0666-4ace-a70d-32ecb0a87133} generated successfully.
```

This is also the GUID you need to mount the snapshot, as shown in figure 13.3.

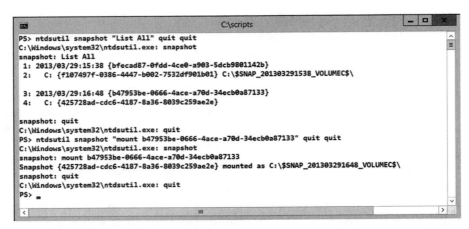

Figure 13.3 Viewing and mounting AD snapshots

13.2.3 *Mounting snapshots*

You mount the snapshot as an instance of AD Lightweight Services (ADLS), which is a cut-down version of Active Directory that's used to provide authentication and authorization for applications. It's used, for instance, when you need a schema modification but don't want to modify your main AD environment. Use ADLS in parallel with your live Active Directory to compare the properties of an object between the snapshot and the live version. A snapshot has to be mounted before you can work with it. The snapshot to be mounted is identified by its GUID (the first GUID displayed for each snapshot):

```
ntdsutil snapshot "mount b47953be-0666-4ace-a70d-34ecb0a87133" quit quit
```

You can mount any of the snapshots to obtain a point-in-time view of your AD data. Once the snapshot has been mounted, you can make it usable using `dsamain.exe`:

```
dsamain -dbpath 'C:\$SNAP_201303291648_VOLUMEC$\Windows\NTDS\ntds.dit'
➥ -ldapport 51389
```

`Dsamain.exe` is installed when you install Active Directory. The `ldapport` parameter defines the TCP port you'll use to connect to the snapshot.

Now that you have the snapshot mounted, you can access the data contained in the snapshot.

> **WARNING** The console in which you run `dsamain.exe` will be locked while the snapshot is being accessed.

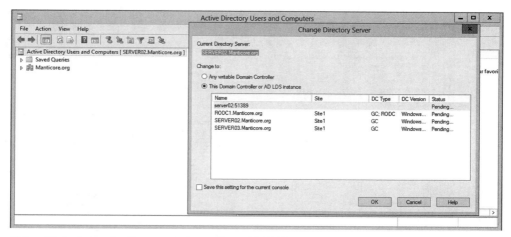

Figure 13.4   Accessing the mounted snapshot with ADUC. Use the local server name and the port number you used when running `dsamain.exe` **to access the snapshot.**

13.2.4   Accessing the data from a snapshot

USING ADUC

You can use AD Users and Computers and change the domain controller to point at the mounted snapshot:

1   Open ADUC.
2   Right-click the Active Users and Computers [server name] line at the top of the right pane.
3   Choose Change Domain Controller… from the context menu.
4   Enter the server name and port number (used in `dsamain.exe`) to create a connection to the snapshot, as shown in figure 13.4.
5   Click OK.
6   There will be a short pause while the tool connects to the snapshot.

TRY IT NOW: Create and mount a snapshot

Create a snapshot of your AD and mount it. Access the mounted snapshot through ADUC.

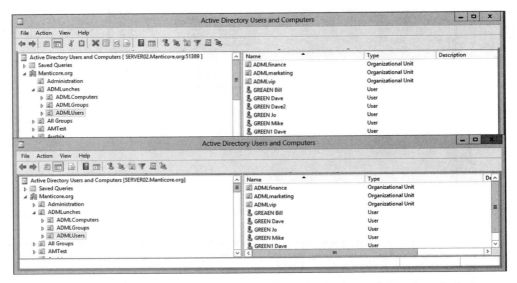

Figure 13.5 Comparing the live version of AD with the snapshot. The snapshot is shown in the top instance of ADUC with the live data underneath.

COMPARING SNAPSHOT DATA WITH LIVE DATA

You can open another instance of ADUC and compare object properties directly. Figure 13.5 shows two instances of ADUC—one connected to the snapshot and one to the live AD.

If you look at a specific user, you can open the properties in each instance of Active Directory and directly compare the properties. Any changes you need to make can be made directly in the live object.

USING POWERSHELL

You can also access the mounted snapshot using PowerShell:

```
PS> Get-ADUser -Identity dgreen -Properties * `
-Server server02.manticore.org:51389 |
select -ExpandProperty memberof

CN=ADMLrodc1,OU=ADMLGroups,OU=ADMLunches,DC=Manticore,DC=org
CN=ADLgroup6,OU=ADMLGroups,OU=ADMLunches,DC=Manticore,DC=org
CN=ADLgroup5,OU=ADMLGroups,OU=ADMLunches,DC=Manticore,DC=org
CN=ADLgroup4,OU=ADMLGroups,OU=ADMLunches,DC=Manticore,DC=org
CN=ADLgroup3,OU=ADMLGroups,OU=ADMLunches,DC=Manticore,DC=org
CN=ADLgroup2,OU=ADMLGroups,OU=ADMLunches,DC=Manticore,DC=org
CN=ADLgroup1,OU=ADMLGroups,OU=ADMLunches,DC=Manticore,DC=org
```

Notice that the port number is appended to the server name to define that you're accessing the snapshot. Compare the results to the live instance:

```
PS> Get-ADUser -Identity dgreen -Properties * `
-Server server02.manticore.org |
select -ExpandProperty memberof
```

```
CN=ADMLrodc1,OU=ADMLGroups,OU=ADMLunches,DC=Manticore,DC=org
CN=ADLgroup5,OU=ADMLGroups,OU=ADMLunches,DC=Manticore,DC=org
CN=ADLgroup4,OU=ADMLGroups,OU=ADMLunches,DC=Manticore,DC=org
CN=ADLgroup3,OU=ADMLGroups,OU=ADMLunches,DC=Manticore,DC=org
CN=ADLgroup2,OU=ADMLGroups,OU=ADMLunches,DC=Manticore,DC=org
CN=ADLgroup1,OU=ADMLGroups,OU=ADMLunches,DC=Manticore,DC=org
```

Comparison of the output shows that the version of the user in the live Active Directory has been removed from ADLgroup6. If this shouldn't have happened, you can easily correct the error.

13.2.5 *Dismounting a snapshot*

Once you've finished with the snapshot, you need to press Ctrl-C in the console where you ran `dsamain.exe`. This will terminate that program. You then run `ntdsutil` to dismount the snapshot:

```
ntdsutil snapshot "unmount *" quit quit
```

Mounting a snapshot in this way provides a way to correct a changed or deleted property, but if the whole object has been deleted, you need to think about restoring the object from the AD Recycle Bin, because you can't restore directly from a snapshot.

13.3 *AD Recycle Bin*

The AD Recycle Bin functions in a similar way to the Windows file system recycle bin in that you can retrieve the complete object that has been deleted. When you delete an object from your Active Directory, it's tombstoned—most of its attributes, including group memberships, are stripped off, and the resultant skeleton object is held in Active Directory for the tombstone period (60 or 180 days, depending on the version of Active Directory you originally installed).

It's possible to restore a tombstoned object, but you need to mount and access an AD snapshot to retrieve the attributes that were removed during the tombstone process. The first step is to install the AD Recycle Bin. Your forest will need to be at the Windows2008R2 functional level for you to install the AD Recycle Bin.

13.3.1 *Installing the AD Recycle Bin*

You won't find the AD Recycle Bin in a default installation of Active Directory. You need to enable it using PowerShell:

```
Enable-ADOptionalFeature 'Recycle Bin Feature' `
-Scope ForestOrConfigurationSet -Target 'manticore.org' `
-Server server02
```

You can use `Get-ADOptionalFeature` to determine if the AD Recycle Bin has been installed.

> **TRY IT NOW: Install the AD Recycle Bin**
>
> Don't do this in a production environment.
>
> In your test environment, check if the AD Recycle Bin has been installed. If it hasn't been installed, install it.

WARNING   Once the AD Recycle Bin has been installed, you can't uninstall it.

I've been asked if there's any good reason not to install the AD Recycle Bin. Apart from the fact that it can't be uninstalled and some organizations don't like that, I can't think of any reason not to install it. It's such a useful tool that I think it should be automatically installed, rather than being an optional feature.

13.3.2 *Searching for and restoring a user account*

The AD Recycle Bin is automatic in its action— once enabled, any deleted objects are automatically moved to the AD Recycle Bin. You need to be able to find the deleted object and then perform a restore. As an example, remove a user:

```
Get-ADUser -Identity dgreen | Remove-ADUser -Confirm:$false
```

Yes, you've left protection from accidental deletion off this account, so it's immediately removed. Oops. Now you have to get the account back. You need to search for the deleted object.

SEARCHING AD RECYCLE BIN ON SPECIFIC PROPERTIES

The `-IncludeDeletedObjects` parameter is required to search the AD Recycle Bin:

```
Get-ADObject -IncludeDeletedObjects -Filter *
```

This shows deleted and live objects, so you need to restrict the returned data to deleted objects only using `Deleted -eq $true` and to user objects using `objectclass -eq 'user'`. The display is truncated to one example to save some trees:

```
PS> Get-ADObject -IncludeDeletedObjects `
-Filter {objectclass -eq 'user' -and Deleted -eq $true} |
select -ExpandProperty Name
Regan1 Jo
DEL:363b5be8-afcb-4089-bbe6-7743e0aff53f
```

FILTERING YOUR SEARCH RESULTS

If your organization has a high turnover of staff—for instance, employment of large numbers of seasonal workers—you may find that there are too many objects in the AD Recycle Bin to easily locate the account you want. You can filter the results based on specific AD properties such as the `samAccountName`:

```
PS> Get-ADObject -IncludeDeletedObjects `
-Filter {samAccountName -eq 'dgreen'}

Deleted           : True
```

```
DistinguishedName : CN=GREEN Dave\0ADEL:28f0c168-d142-417f-a223-
➥ 333488cdaa77,CN=Deleted Objects,DC=Manticore,DC=org
Name              : GREEN Dave
                    DEL:28f0c168-d142-417f-a223-333488cdaa77
ObjectClass       : user
ObjectGUID        : 28f0c168-d142-417f-a223-333488cdaa77
```

Once you have a search filter that produces the desired object, you can pipe the result into `Restore-ADObject`:

```
Get-ADObject -IncludeDeletedObjects -Filter {samaccountname -eq 'dgreen'} |
Restore-ADObject
```

SEARCHING AD RECYCLE BIN BASED ON OU NAME
An alternative is to run your search based on the OU from which the object was deleted. This may be required if you don't know the name. It may be a simpler way to search. Your search is based on the `LastKnownParent` attribute, which stores the OU from which the account was deleted:

```
Get-ADObject -IncludeDeletedObjects -Properties * `
-Filter {Deleted -eq $true } |
where LastKnownParent -like 'OU=ADMLusers*' |
Format-List  Name, objectGUID, LastKnownParent

Name              : GREEN Dave
                    DEL:28f0c168-d142-417f-a223-333488cdaa77
objectGUID        : 28f0c168-d142-417f-a223-333488cdaa77
LastKnownParent   : OU=ADMLUsers,OU=ADMLunches,DC=Manticore,DC=org

Name              : ADML1
                    DEL:acbb7d8c-4dd6-4e6a-8d70-8bef4c3454a7
objectGUID        : acbb7d8c-4dd6-4e6a-8d70-8bef4c3454a7
LastKnownParent   : OU=ADMLUsers,OU=ADMLunches,DC=Manticore,DC=org
```

13.3.3 *Restoring a user account*

Regardless of which search method you used, you can restore your deleted user by using the `objectGUID`:

```
Get-ADObject -IncludeDeletedObjects -Properties * `
-Filter {objectGUID -eq '28f0c168-d142-417f-a223-333488cdaa77'} |
Restore-ADObject
```

> **TRY IT NOW: Delete and restore a user account from the AD Recycle Bin**
>
> Don't do this in a production environment.
>
> Pick a user from the ADMLUsers OU. Check and record some properties of the account, especially the group memberships. If you have AD snapshots enabled, take a snapshot. Delete the account. You can use the GUI tools or PowerShell.
>
> Find the user account in the AD Recycle Bin and restore it. Compare the information you recorded to the restored object.

13.3.4 *Searching for and restoring an OU*

If you're in the scenario outlined at the start of section 13.1 where an OU of accounts has been deleted, the procedure is slightly different. The first step is to search for the OU:

```
Get-ADObject -IncludeDeletedObjects -Properties * `
-Filter {Deleted -eq $true -AND objectclass -eq 'organizationalUnit' } |
    Format-List Name, ObjectGUID, LastKnownParent
```

Modify the filter until you've identified the OU that was deleted. This will look something like

```
Get-ADObject -IncludeDeletedObjects -Properties * `
-Filter {Deleted -eq $true -AND objectclass -eq 'organizationalUnit' `
-AND Name -like 'ADMLusers'}
```

That object is then piped to `Restore-ADObject`:

```
Get-ADObject -IncludeDeletedObjects -Properties * `
-Filter {Deleted -eq $true -AND objectclass -eq 'organizationalUnit' `
-AND Name -like 'ADMLusers'} |
Restore-ADObject
```

This restores the OU for you. You can then identify the accounts (users, groups, and computers) that belong in the OU and restore them, as shown in section 13.3.2. If you have nested OUs, you'll need to restore each of the OUs before restoring the contents. Which object classes would you use to search for deleted groups or computers? *Hint:* display all the properties of an AD object using `Get-ADObject` and you'll be able to identify the class.

You might think that with the AD Recycle Bin enabled you don't need to worry about backing up Active Directory. That's probably a mistake, because backup is still required as the last-chance recovery mechanism, especially in the event of a disaster.

13.4 *Backup and restore*

Backup and restore probably generates as much discussion and argument as any other single topic in IT. Everybody agrees it needs doing, but everyone loves to moan about their backup systems. What often gets missed in the discussion is why you're performing backups.

> **NOTE** Most organizations of any size will have an enterprise-level backup system that's also used to back up their domain controllers. In this section I'm using the native Windows tools as an example that's available to everyone, rather than trying to cover a multitude of backup systems. You'll need to adapt this section to match your backup product.

The only sensible reason for performing backups is to be able to restore your environment in the event of a problem arising. Active Directory, as a system, is dispersed across a number of servers. The loss of a single-domain controller doesn't require a restore—you can always create a new one and let replication repopulate the database. If you're running other services on the domain controller, you may need to restore.

You really need to back up your AD data so that you can restore in the event of data loss. This could happen either through loss of the whole environment or through accidental deletion of a large portion of data—though you've protected your data through the use of protection from accidental deletion, haven't you? The AD Recycle Bin (section 13.3) can help if a small amount of data has been lost, but in the event of a large set of data, you'll probably need to restore.

> **WARNING** Be careful which domain controllers you restore from. The RID Master shouldn't be used, because you may have issued new RIDs since the backup that the restored RID master tries to re-issue, and this will cause problems if objects have the same RID. The safest backup candidates are domain controllers that don't hold FSMO roles.

So how do you back up a domain controller?

13.4.1 Backing up a domain controller

You've all heard of the good old days when everything was much better? In some respects, that's true for native backup tools in Windows Server. It used to be that you could use NTBackup to back up the system state of the domain controller and you automatically got a backup of your Active Directory. Not anymore.

CREATING AN AD HOC BACKUP

The first thing you have to do is install the Windows backup tools, because they aren't part of the default install. Either install from Server Manager (in a similar manner to AD Directory Services in chapter 11), or preferably use PowerShell:

```
Install-WindowsFeature -Name Windows-Server-Backup -IncludeAllSubFeature
```

You can then use the cmdlets to perform a backup:

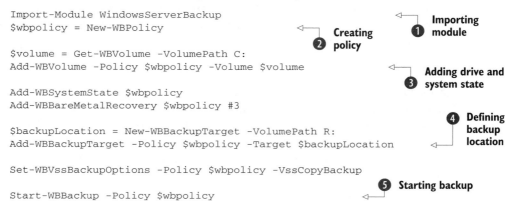

```
Import-Module WindowsServerBackup
$wbpolicy = New-WBPolicy

$volume = Get-WBVolume -VolumePath C:
Add-WBVolume -Policy $wbpolicy -Volume $volume

Add-WBSystemState $wbpolicy
Add-WBBareMetalRecovery $wbpolicy #3

$backupLocation = New-WBBackupTarget -VolumePath R:
Add-WBBackupTarget -Policy $wbpolicy -Target $backupLocation

Set-WBVssBackupOptions -Policy $wbpolicy -VssCopyBackup

Start-WBBackup -Policy $wbpolicy
```

❶ Importing module
❷ Creating policy
❸ Adding drive and system state
❹ Defining backup location
❺ Starting backup

The script starts by importing the module containing the backup cmdlets ❶. It then creates a new backup policy ❷. The C: drive and system state are added to the policy ❸. A backup location of the R: drive is defined ❹ and the backup is started ❺ with Start-WBBackup. You should save code like this into a script so you can reuse it.

The code creates a one-off backup. That's a good idea for a situation where you need an ad hoc backup before you make major changes, but usually you want a backup that looks after itself and runs on a schedule.

CREATING A SCHEDULED BACKUP

You can easily use the listing to create a scheduled backup. Change the last line of the preceding code to this:

```
Set-WBSchedule -Policy $wbpolicy -Schedule 08:00,12:00,16:00,20:00
Set-WBPolicy -Policy $wbpolicy
```

This creates a scheduled backup that runs at 8:00 am, 12:00 pm, 4:00 pm, and 8:00 pm.

That takes care of backing up the data, but how do you perform the most important part—restoring the data?

13.4.2 *Restoring the AD database*

AD restore has two broad strands: nonauthoritative restores and authoritative restores. Nonauthoritative restores allow you to restore the database to a point in time and let the normal AD replication process bring it up to date. This is great if you have a problem with your domain controller—possibly disk related—that causes a problem with the database.

You could also restore the AD database (ntds.dit) file to an alternative location and mount it as described in section 13.2.

> **NOTE** You can't use the backup from one domain controller to restore another. You can only restore from backups that are younger than the tombstone period.

In an authoritative restore, there's either too much for you to recover from the AD Recycle Bin, or you don't (can't?) have the AD Recycle Bin enabled. Imagine that OUs full of accounts have been deleted, for example. You'd use an authoritative restore to retrieve the deleted accounts.

> **WARNING** Don't do this on a production domain controller.

PERFORMING A NONAUTHORITATIVE RESTORE

A nonauthoritative restore is performed when you need to bring the AD database up to date but no data has been lost, so you can allow AD replication to perform the final changes.

Performing a nonauthoritative restore involves starting the domain controller in Directory Services Repair Mode:

1 Restart the domain controller.
2 Press F8 during the boot sequence to display the Advanced Boot Menu options (figure 13.6).
3 Choose Directory Services Repair Mode (DSRM).
4 When you get to the desktop, you'll see Safe Mode in the corners.

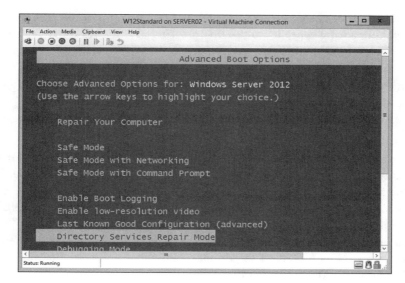

**Figure 13.6
Selecting Directory
Services Repair Mode**

5 Log in as administrator using the DSRM password you set when you created the domain controller and start PowerShell with elevated privileges. Run these commands:

```
$bkup = Get-WBBackupSet | select -Last 1
Start-WBSystemStateRecovery -BackupSet $bkup
```

6 You can add the `-RestartComputer` parameter if you want to automatically force the domain controller to reboot after the restore.

7 The restore will initialize by counting through the files that could be restored and periodically will issue messages of the form `11082 files found for recovery`, as illustrated in figure 13.7.

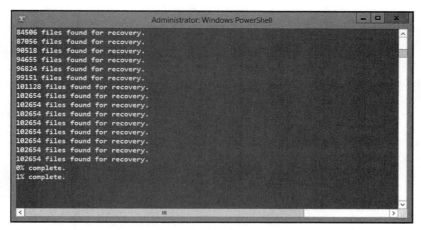

Figure 13.7   Discovering the files that needed to be restored

8   When the system starts counting through the percentage complete, it may seem to be taking a long time. It isn't really restoring all the files it discovered! The system is examining the data in the backup to determine what should be restored.

9   When the restore has finished, reboot the domain controller and allow it to start in the normal manner.

10   AD replication will kick in and bring your database up to date.

PERFORMING AN AUTHORITATIVE RESTORE

In the situation where data has been lost you need to perform an authoritative restore. An authoritative restore is your last best hope of recovering your data. If this fails, it's gone for good.

Let's assume one of your colleagues has accidentally deleted an OU. I'll refer to it as `Test` in this example. Start the domain controller in Directory Services Repair Mode as you learned in the previous section. Log in as administrator using the DSRM password you set when you created the domain controller and start PowerShell with elevated privileges. Run these commands:

```
$bkup = Get-WBBackupSet | select -Last 1
Start-WBSystemStateRecovery -BackupSet $bkup `
-AuthoritativeSysvolRecovery
```

The last line of code—-`AuthortativeSysvolRecovery`—tells the system that you have more work to do after the restore.

In this case you need to use `ntdsutil.exe` to mark the restored OU as authoritative; otherwise replication will delete it again! Open a command prompt with elevated privileges:

1   Type `ntdsutil` and press Enter.

2   Type `activate instance NTDS` and press Enter.

3   Type `authoritative restore` and press Enter.

4   Type `restore subtree "ou=test,dc=manticore,dc=org"` (substitute the distinguished name of your OU) and press Enter.

5   Click Yes in the message box to confirm.

6   You should get a message to confirm the number of objects updated.

7   Type `quit` and press Enter.

8   Type `quit` (again) and press Enter.

Restart the domain controller and AD will replicate the restored data to your other domain controllers.

This concludes your session on the ways to protect your AD data. It's time for a lab to gain more practice with these techniques.

13.5 *LAB*

The techniques in this section are potentially destructive.

> **WARNING** Don't perform this lab in a production environment. It could be severely career-limiting.

You may find it beneficial to discuss this lab with more experienced colleagues before proceeding.

13.5.1 *Complete the TRY IT NOW sections*

If you haven't already done so, complete the TRY IT NOW exercises. They're repeated here for your convenience.

CREATE AND MOUNT A SNAPSHOT

Create a snapshot of your AD and mount it. Access the mounted snapshot through ADUC.

INSTALL THE AD RECYCLE BIN

Don't do this in a production environment.

In your test environment, check whether the AD Recycle Bin has been installed. If it hasn't been installed, install it.

DELETE AND RESTORE A USER ACCOUNT FROM THE AD RECYCLE BIN

Don't do this in a production environment.

Pick a user from the ADMLUsers OU. Check and record some properties of the account, especially the group memberships. If you have AD snapshots enabled, take a snapshot. Delete the account. You can use the GUI tools or PowerShell.

Find the user account in the AD Recycle Bin and restore it. Compare the information you recorded to the restored object.

13.5.2 *Practice adding and removing protection from accidental deletion*

You learned how to add and remove protection from accidental deletion in the earlier chapters on managing user, groups, and computer accounts. Review those chapters if you need to refresh your memory; otherwise, pick an OU and practice adding and removing the protection. Be sure to observe the messages you get when trying to delete a protected object.

13.5.3 *Compare an object in live Active Directory and a snapshot*

One use for snapshots is comparing objects:

1 Create a snapshot of your Active Directory.
2 Change some attributes, including group memberships, of a user account.
3 Mount the snapshot.
4 Compare the user objects in the GUI tools.
5 Can you determine a way to use the information in the snapshot to modify the live object?

13.5.4 *Restore an OU full of accounts from the AD Recycle Bin*

Let's recreate the scenario I told you about at the beginning of section 13.1—restoring an OU full of users:

1 Create a test OU.
2 Create four user accounts.
3 Delete the OU and the accounts.
4 Restore the OU from the AD Recycle Bin.
5 Can you determine a way to modify the live object using the data in the snapshot?

13.5.5 *Restore from backup*

Install the Windows backup feature on your test domain controller. Perform a backup. Delete the test OU from section 13.5.4. Perform an authoritative restore.

13.6 *Ideas for on your own*

You've seen four techniques for protecting the data in your Active Directory: protection from accidental deletion, AD snapshots, the AD Recycle Bin, and backup and restore. These techniques will ensure that your data is as safe as possible.

How is the data in your Active Directory protected? Determine which of the techniques covered in this chapter are in use. Which techniques could you implement to improve the level of protection provided to your AD data? Remember that defense in depth is a proven technique and don't rely on a single protection technique.

In the next chapter you'll see the other side of protecting your AD data when you learn about the AD security model and how to delegate permissions to other users.

Security: Default groups and delegation

In a small organization, you could easily be the only administrator of your Active Directory without being overwhelmed. But imagine an organization with thousands of users—a single administrator will not be sufficient. The simple answer, used by most organizations for historical reasons, is to provide a large number of users domain-administrator-level permissions. This often leads to a situation where no one has overall responsibility for the Active Directory, so it gradually descends into a chaotic state.

> **NOTE** The reason for putting all administrators into the Domain Admins group can be traced back to Windows NT in the mid-1990s. Membership in the Domain Admins group was required to perform any administration tasks.

The better solution is to have a very small, tightly controlled number of domain administrators. Any other user who performs other administration tasks should have the relevant permissions delegated to them. This is the principle of *least privilege*. You provide users the permissions they need to perform their job, and no more.

Active Directory provides a number of default groups that are created at the time it is installed. The default groups are found in either the `Builtin` container or the `Users` container. The first section of this chapter teaches you about the default groups with advice on when to use them and any issues you may encounter in their use.

You can delegate specific permissions, such as the ability to reset passwords, to users or groups of users. The user can then perform this one task, but has no other rights to Active Directory beyond those of a standard user. The second part of the chapter shows how to implement delegation.

Between the default groups and delegated permissions, you can create an administration model for your Active Directory that matches the needs of your organization. The starting point of that model is learning to use AD's default groups.

14.1   *Default groups*

You may think it's odd that there are two containers for default groups. The groups in the `Builtin` container are analogous to those you'd find locally on a server or workstation, such as Administrators or Backup Operators. Those in the `Users` container, such as Enterprise Admins or Group Policy Creator Owners, are unique to Active Directory—you won't find equivalent local groups on any other systems in your environment.

> **TIP** I've seen organizations move the default groups out of the `Builtin` or `Users` container in the mistaken view that it increases security. It doesn't, because these are well-known objects that can be found by name or SID. All that happens is that new administrators become confused.

The default groups are placed in AD containers rather than OUs. Both containers and OUs can have users, groups, and computers as child objects. OUs can have other OUs (but not containers) as child objects, and can have Group Policies applied. Containers can't have other containers or OUs as child objects and can't have Group Policies applied. Figure 14.1 shows the similarities and differences between containers and OUs.

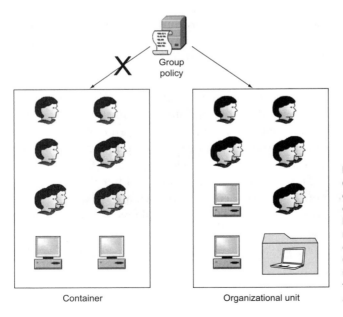

Group policy

Container

Organizational unit

Figure 14.1   The primary difference between OUs and containers is that OUs can contain other OUs and can have Group Policies applied. The icons represent the types of objects that can be created in a container or OU. A single person represents a user, two people represent a group, the monitor represents a computer, and the file represents an OU.

Which groups should you use?

You're the only one who can answer that question for your environment. Many organizations don't give permissions to access domain controllers to anyone but members of the Domain Admins group. Other organizations use a different approach and use some, or most, of the default groups.

The important point to remember is that you only grant permissions to users who actually need them to perform their jobs. Just because the groups are there doesn't mean that you have to put users into them.

Whenever you're thinking about delegation of rights to enable a user or group of users to perform some administration task, always remember the principle of least privilege. Don't give them more than they need.

Let's start by examining the groups in the Builtin container because it occurs first in an alphabetic sort.

14.1.1 *Builtin container*

Remember, the groups in the Builtin container are analogous to those you'd find locally on a server or workstation. When you promote a server to be a domain controller, the local groups become unavailable. They're replaced, for domain controllers, by the groups in the Builtin container.

You can discover the groups in the Builtin container using the GUI tools (the Builtin container is found toward the top of the AD tree view in the GUI tools).

You can alternatively use the PowerShell cmdlet Get-ADGroup to view the Builtin container groups:

```
Get-ADGroup -SearchBase "CN=Builtin,DC=Manticore,DC=org" -Filter * |
select Name
```

TIP DC=Manticore,DC=org is my domain name. Remember to change this for your domain. You can also use Get-ADUser, Get-ADComputer, and Get-ADObject against this container.

Notice that it's CN here, not OU, in the distinguished name, as for the Users container. Utilizing a container rather than an OU is deliberate so that Group Policies will not apply to any user accounts within the container. Since OU stands for organizational unit, you might think that CN stands for container, but it's actually the AD attribute CN that's the object name. The basic rule is that OUs start with OU in the distinguished name, and everything else starts with CN.

Whether you use the GUI tools or PowerShell, you should see a collection of groups, which I've bundled into the following categories for our discussion:

- Operators
- Administrators
- Performance and Event Logs

- Remote Access and Management
- Remote Desktop Services
- Users and Guests
- Miscellaneous

See table 14.1 for all of the possible default `Builtin` container groups.

Table 14.1   Default groups in the `Builtin` container

Operators	Administrators	Performance and Event Logs	Remote Access and Management	Remote Desktop Services	Users and Guests	Miscellaneous
Account Operators	Administrators	Event Log Readers	Remote Desktop Users	RDS Remote-Access Servers	Users	Distributed COM Users
Backup Operators		Performance Log Users	Remote Management Users	RDS Endpoint Servers	Guests	IIS_IUSRS
Cryptographic Operators		Performance Monitor Users	Windows Authorization Access	RDS Management Servers		Certificate Service DCOM Access
Network Configuration Operators			Access Control Assistance Operators	Terminal Server License Servers		Incoming Forest Trust Builders
Print Operators						Pre-Windows 2000 Compatible Access
Server Operators						Replicator

TIP   It's a common mistake to put user accounts into the `Builtin` and `Users` containers. Don't do it, because Group Policies won't apply. The same is true for computer accounts and the `Computers` container (see chapter 6 for details).

Other groups, such as Hyper-V Administrators, may appear, depending on the roles and features you've enabled in your environment. The Hyper-V Administrators will only appear if you have Hyper-V servers in your domain. Some applications, such as the System Center suite of management tools, may also add groups into the `Builtin` container.

TRY IT NOW: Examine the Builtin container

Use ADAC or ADUC to browse the `Builtin` container. Do the groups you see match the list in table 14.1? If not, can you explain the discrepancies?

Let's look at some of these groups in detail, starting with the groups that have "operators" in their name.

OPERATORS

The groups in Operators enable users who aren't members of the Domain Admins group (see Users container in section 14.1.2) to perform administrative tasks on domain controllers. The groups include

- *Account Operators*—Members can administer user, group, and computer accounts. They can't modify the Administrators or Domain Admins, Enterprise Admins, or Schema Admins groups, the Administrator account, or computer accounts in the Domain Controllers OU (another good reason not to move domain controllers out of their default location).
- *Backup Operators*—Members can back up and restore files on domain controllers. They can also restart domain controllers.
- *Cryptographic Operators*—Members can perform cryptographic operations, such as managing the cryptography APIs and components. The group is analogous to the Crypto Officer Role defined in FIPS 140-2 (Federal Information Processing Standard (USA)).
- *Network Configuration Operators*—Members can configure some networking features on domain controllers.
- *Print Operators*—Members can administer printers hosted on domain controllers.
- *Server Operators*—Members can administer the domain controllers, but this doesn't give rights to administer Active Directory.

These groups, apart from Account Operators, are duplicated on servers in the domain. Membership to the AD group doesn't automatically confer membership in the same group on the local machine.

> **TRY IT NOW: Compare the AD and local groups**
>
> Choose one or more machines in your domain and compare the membership of the groups in the Builtin container and the local versions.

ADMINISTRATORS

The Administrators group has unrestricted access to the domain, but those in the group aren't full domain administrators. Members of this group can administer servers and workstations but not domain controllers (that's a job for the Domain Admins group in the Users container; see section 14.1.2).

PERFORMANCE AND EVENT LOGS

The ability to access the data in event logs and performance counters is essential for monitoring and troubleshooting. Groups are available to enable access to this data:

- *Event Log Readers*—Members can read event logs on domain controllers. They can't configure or clear the domain controllers' event logs—that privilege is reserved for the Domain Admins group.
- *Performance Log Users*—Members can log data from performance counters, enable trace providers, and collect event traces on domain controllers.
- *Performance Monitor Users*—Members can view performance counter data on domain controllers.

Users are usually granted membership in both Performance Log Users and Performance Monitor Users, which ensures that they can perform any tasks related to performance monitoring.

REMOTE ACCESS AND MANAGEMENT

In most organizations you'll find that your servers aren't conveniently placed for you to physically access them. They'll be in another room, building, town, or even country. You need to be able to access your servers remotely. You can use the following groups to delegate remote access and management permissions:

- *Remote Desktop Users*—Members are granted the right to log on remotely. Members of the Domain Admins and Administrators groups get this right automatically.
- *Remote Management Users*—Members can access WMI resources over management protocols (such as WS-Management via the Windows Remote Management Service). This applies only to WMI namespaces that grant access to the user.
- *Windows Authorization Access*—Members have access to the computed token-GroupsGlobalAndUniversal attribute on User objects.
- *Access Control Assistance Operators*—Members can remotely query authorization attributes and permissions for resources on this computer.

REMOTE DESKTOP SERVICES

Delivering applications via Remote Desktop Services (RDS, previously known as Terminal Services) is a proven technique for centralizing the administration and delivery of functionality to your users. You'll need to use a number of groups to manage your RDS environment:

- *RDS Remote-Access Servers*—Servers give users of RemoteApp programs and personal virtual desktops access to these resources. In internet-facing deployments, these servers are typically deployed in an edge network. This group needs to be populated on servers running RD Connection Broker. RD Gateway servers and RD Web Access servers used in the deployment need to be in this group.
- *RDS Endpoint Servers*—Servers run virtual machines and host sessions where users' RemoteApp programs and personal virtual desktops run. This group

needs to be populated on servers running RD Connection Broker. RD Session Host servers and RD Virtualization Host servers used in the deployment need to be in this group.

- *RDS Management Servers*—Servers can perform routine administrative actions on servers running RDS. This group needs to be populated on all servers in a RDS deployment. The servers running the RDS Central Management service must be included in this group.
- *Terminal Server License Servers*—Members can update user accounts in Active Directory with information about license issuance, for the purpose of tracking and reporting the terminal server (TS) per user for the Client Access License (CAL) usage, which are the licenses your organization possess to permit access to applications delivered through TS.

USERS AND GUESTS

Standard users aren't forgotten in your delegation model. You can provide a level of access that allows minimum rights to run applications:

- *Users* are prevented from making accidental or intentional system-wide changes and can run most applications.
- *Guests* have the same access as members of the Users group by default. An exception to this is the Guest account, which is further restricted in that it can only access resources available to anonymous access or through the Everyone group. The Guest account is disabled by default and should be left in that state unless your organization has specific need of the account.

MISCELLANEOUS

There are a few groups that don't fit conveniently in any of the categories you've seen so far. They're presented here for completeness:

- *Distributed COM Users*—Members are allowed to launch, activate, and use Distributed COM (DCOM) objects on this machine. DCOM is a method for applications to access remote machines.
- *IIS_IUSRS*—A built-in group used by Internet Information Services (IIS).
- *Certificate Service DCOM Access*—Members are allowed to connect to certification authorities in the enterprise.
- *Incoming Forest Trust Builders*—Members can create incoming, one-way trusts to this forest.
- *Pre-Windows 2000 Compatible Access*—A backward-compatibility group that allows read access on all users and groups in the domain.
- *Replicator*—Supports file replication in a domain.

The other container for default groups is the Users container.

14.1.2 Users container

The Users container is the default container for new user accounts if you don't specify a target OU, and the groups within are unique to Active Directory. A number of default groups can be found in the `Users` container. You can discover the groups in the container by using the GUI tools (ADAC or ADUC) or this PowerShell command:

```
Get-ADGroup -SearchBase "CN=Users,DC=Manticore,DC=org" -Filter * |
select Name
```

Notice that it's `CN` here, not `OU` in the distinguished name, as for the `Builtin` container. Utilizing a container rather than an OU is deliberate so that Group Policies won't apply to any user accounts within the container.

> **WARNING** The `Users` container is the default location for new user accounts. Move them to an OU where Group Policy will apply (following the instructions in chapter 3), or explicitly create them in another location.

Table 14.2 lists the default groups to be found within the Users container. The DHCP-related groups are present because DHCP is running on my domain controller. This isn't a default situation, but it's very common, so I've included it here. For our discussion, I've bundled these groups into five categories:

- Administrators
- Automatically Managed
- DHCP and DNS
- RODC Password Replication
- Miscellaneous

Table 14.2 Default groups in the `Users` container

Administrators	Automatically Managed	DHCP and DNS	RODC Password Replication	Miscellaneous
Enterprise Admins	Domain Computers	DnsAdmins	Allowed RODC Password Replication	RAS and IAS Servers
Schema Admins	Domain Controllers	DnsUpdateProxy	Denied RODC Password Replication	Group Policy Creator Owners
Domain Admins	Domain Guests	DHCP Administrators		Cloneable Domain Controllers
	Domain Users	DHCP Users		Cert Publishers
	Enterprise Read-only Domain Controllers			
	Read-only Domain Controllers			

I've seen a number of organizations move these groups to other OUs in the mistaken belief that it increases security. Leave them alone. It's better practice to ensure your AD administrators are properly trained.

> ### TRY IT NOW: Examine the Users container
>
> Use ADAC or ADUC to browse the `Users` container. Do the groups you can see match the list in table 14.2? If not, can you explain the discrepancies for your environment?

Some of these groups give members full control of the environment. The major groups listed in table 14.2 are outlined in the following sections.

ADMINISTRATORS

Enterprise Admins, Schema Admins, and Domain Admins are the critical groups in your organization. Membership to any of them provides the user with the power to perform a lot of damage in your AD environment. What can you do about it?

The answer is to restrict the membership of these groups. When you consider the permissions that are granted to these groups, it's essential to manage your Active Directory correctly:

- *Enterprise Admins*—Members can administer the entire forest, including all domains. Membership to this group is required to manage AD Sites, Subnets, and Site Links. You must be a member of this group to add or remove domains to or from the forest.
- *Schema Admins*—Members can make changes to the forest schema.
- *Domain Admins*—Members can manage all objects in the domain and all domain controllers and computers joined to the domain. Members of this group are automatically members of the Administrators group on all computers in the domain. You have to be a member of this group to authorize DHCP servers. You must be a member of this group to add or remove domain controllers in an existing domain.

The Enterprise Admins and Schema Admins groups should be empty most of the time. Put accounts in when work is needed and take them out when it's finished. The membership of the Domain Admins group should be tightly controlled, with membership limited to those administrators who really need it. Many tasks can be performed by being a member of other groups or having permissions explicitly delegated.

AUTOMATICALLY MANAGED

Some groups, such as Domain Controllers, Domain Computers, and Domain Users, are populated automatically. You don't need to do anything with these groups—Active Directory will manage them for you. The following groups in the `Users` container fall into this category:

- *Domain Computers*—Contains all workstations and member servers in the domain. Domain controllers aren't members of this group.
- *Domain Controllers*—Contains all domain controllers in the domain.
- *Domain Guests*—Is automatically a member of all local guest groups.
- *Domain Users*—Contains all users in the domain. This group is automatically a member of the local user groups in the domain.

- *Enterprise Read-only Domain Controllers*—Contains all RODCs in the forest. Not populated in a single domain forest.
- *Read-only Domain Controllers*—Contains all RODCs in the domain.

You only need to be aware that these groups exist and where they can be found. Checking the membership of the appropriate group can be a useful part of your troubleshooting process. This was covered in chapter 4 when you learned about AD groups.

DHCP AND DNS

You'll learn more about DNS (Domain Name System) in chapter 15, but for now you need to be aware that using Windows DNS integrated with Active Directory is a very common situation. If your organization is large enough to have separated DNS administration from AD administration, you need to give permissions to the DNS administrators to work with DNS without being able to modify Active Directory.

Similarly, domain controllers often function as DHCP (Dynamic Host Configuration Protocol) servers. It may be a requirement in your organization that DHCP is administered by a separate group. They'll need permissions to do so, because users who aren't members of the Domain Admins group can't make changes to functionality hosted on domain controllers.

> **TIP** DHCP groups will only be present if DHCP is installed on a domain controller.

The requirements just outlined are solved by making users members of these groups:

- *DnsAdmins*—Members can administer DNS objects in the domain. They do not get rights to objects outside the domain.
- *DnsUpdateProxy*—Membership is normally restricted to DHCP servers. It gives the rights to perform dynamic DNS updates on behalf of client machines.
- *DHCP Administrators*—Members can view and modify any settings on the DHCP server. They can create and delete scopes, add reservations, change option values, and create superscopes. They can't authorize or deauthorize DHCP servers.
- *DHCP Users*—Membership provides read-only access to the DHCP servers. You can view objects, but can't add, delete, or modify them.

As with other groups that confer permissions to administer parts of your environment, keep tight control of the membership.

RODC PASSWORD REPLICATION

Two groups exist to control password replication to read-only domain controllers:

- Allowed RODC Password Replication
- Denied RODC Password Replication

Membership dictates whether an account's password is replicated to read-only domain controllers. If an account isn't a member of either group, its account will not replicate. If an account is a member of both groups, then the deny permission takes precedence and the password won't replicate. These groups are domain-wide, so they get automatically applied to new RODCs. Any additional password replication policies you create have to be assigned explicitly to a RODC.

MISCELLANEOUS

As with the `Builtin` container, there are a number of miscellaneous groups that are collected here for completion:

- *RAS and IAS Servers*—Servers can access remote-access properties of users.
- *Group Policy Creator Owners*—Members can modify group policy for the domain.
- *Cloneable Domain Controllers*—Members that are domain controllers may be cloned. Domain controller cloning is a new technique introduced in Windows Server 2012 that enables virtualized domain controllers to be cloned for rapid deployment.
- *Cert Publishers*—Members are permitted to publish certificates to Active Directory.

Default groups in action

Default groups are a great concept, but how do you use them? There are no hard-and-fast rules, as with so much of IT. *You* must decide what's correct for your environment. In a small organization you'll have a couple of people in the Domain Admins group who do everything. In larger organizations you may need to split the tasks of administering the environment across multiple teams. These examples will help you think about when you could and should use the default groups:

Top-level administrators in the organization should be members of the Domain Admins group and the Enterprise Admins and Schema Admins groups as required. In a multi-domain forest your top-level administrators may be permanent members of the Enterprise Admins group. No one needs to be a member of the Schema Admins group on a permanent basis.

Administrators with responsibility for the whole domain should be a member of Domain Admins.

Your Help Desk operators need to manage user accounts and group membership, so make them members of the Account Operators group only. Your second-line support team needs to manage servers and workstations, so make them members of the Administrators group. They can't manage your domain controllers.

If you need people to manage the domain controllers but to not be able to manage Active Directory, make them members of the Server Operators group.

The team members that manage your backups should be members of the Backup Operators group. This group also confers permissions to shut down servers, so be careful with the membership.

Who manages your Group Policies? Make them members of the Group Policy Creator Owners group.

(continued)

Your network team may be made members of DnsAdmins and DHCP Administrators if they're responsible for those aspects of the environment.

Junior administrators may be members of multiple groups, but avoid making them a member of too many groups, because they may end up with more rights than you intended. Always remember the phrase "just because you can doesn't mean you should" and apply it to default groups. Just because a group exists doesn't mean you have to use it—only put users into groups they need to do their job. It's always easier and safer to assign too few rights and slowly add permissions until you get to the correct point, rather than trying to take away rights after the fact.

Don't be afraid not to use a group—for instance, I've never seen the Cryptographic Operators group used.

There are cases where the default groups aren't sufficiently granular or don't do what you need. In those cases you need to think about direct delegation of rights.

14.2 *Delegation*

Using the default groups, can you allocate permissions to perform these individual tasks?

- Reset passwords for all users in an OU.
- Manage the user accounts in a single OU.
- Control the membership of one or more groups.

The correct answer is that you can. However, if I rephrase the question to "Can you allocate permissions to perform the tasks without giving more rights than needed?" the answer is going to be no, because the principle of least privilege would be broken. This is mainly because the user would be able to exercise the permissions across the domain, rather than just the target OU.

You need to delegate permissions to users—or, better still, groups—to perform these tasks and only these tasks. Let's take these three common examples and see how you can delegate permissions in your Active Directory.

> **TIP** Microsoft AD cmdlets don't supply the functionality to perform these tasks, so you have to use ADUC—in particular, the delegation wizard. ADAC can't be used to perform this task.

You'll start by learning how to delegate the management of the user accounts in an OU:

1 Open ADUC.
2 Navigate to OU.
3 Choose OU and right-click.
4 Choose Delegate Control….
5 Delegation of Control Wizard opens.
6 Click Next to move past the opening screen.

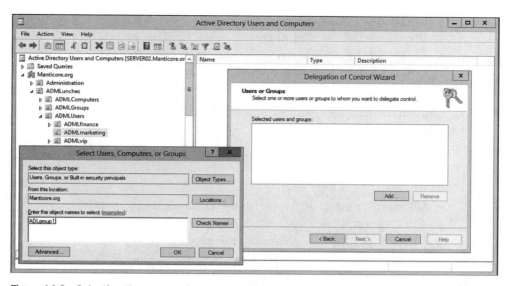

Figure 14.2 Selecting the users and groups to which you'll delegate permission to manage the user accounts

7 Click Add to display Select Users, Computers, or Groups dialog (figure 14.2).

8 Choose Groups (or Users).

9 Click OK.

10 Click Next in the Delegation of Control Wizard.

11 Select Create, Delete, and Manage User Accounts (figure 14.3).

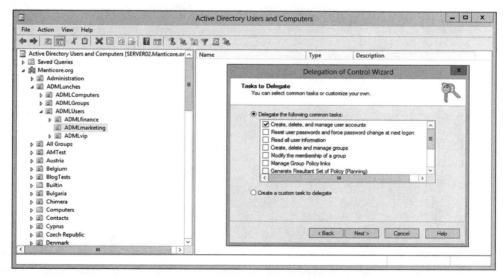

Figure 14.3 Choosing the tasks to delegate for the ADMLmarketing OU

12 Click Next.

13 View the summary information.

14 Click Back to move to previous screens so you can modify delegation if necessary. Click Next to return to the final screen.

15 Click Finish.

You can check the permissions that have been allocated by viewing the security settings on the object:

1 Right-click the OU in ADUC or ADAC.

2 Choose Properties.

3 Choose the Security tab.

4 Choose the ADLgroup1 entry in the group or user names box.

5 Click Advanced.

6 View the permissions granted to the group (figure 14.4).

You can delegate other tasks through the Delegation of Control wizard. The full list of available tasks includes the following:

- Create, delete, and manage user accounts.
- Reset user passwords and force password change at next logon.
- Read all user information.
- Create, delete, and manage groups.
- Modify the membership of a group.
- Manage Group Policy links.

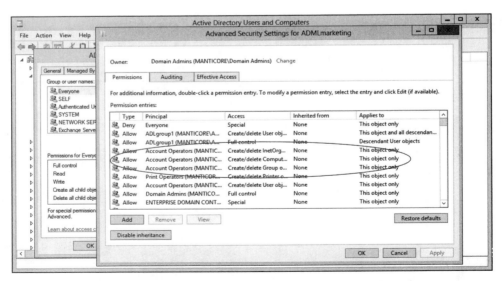

Figure 14.4   Viewing the permissions assigned through the Delegation of Control wizard. The new delegated permissions are circled.

- Generate resultant set of policy (planning).
- Generate resultant set of policy (logging).
- Create, delete, and manage inetOrgPerson accounts (user account built on a different plan).
- Reset inetOrgPerson passwords and force password change at next logon.
- Read all inetOrgPerson information.

NOTE You have to delegate permissions at the OU level. You can't delegate control of a single object, such as a user or group.

Passwords and printer issues between them account for the majority of help desk calls in most organizations. One option is to delegate the permissions to reset passwords into the business units. This removes the burden from your administrators and puts the solution closer to the users. Alternatively, you may delegate the permission to your frontline help desk staff.

TRY IT NOW: Use the Delegation of Control wizard

Use the Delegation of Control wizard in ADUC to delegate the rights to manage the user accounts in the ADMLmarketing OU to ADLgroup1.

The OU and group will exist if you've completed the exercises in the previous chapters. If not, substitute other objects from the test domain.

You now have the required knowledge to manage the default groups and delegate control within your environment. Let's look at practicing those skills in the lab.

14.3 LAB

This lab assumes that you've completed the exercises from the previous chapters. If you haven't performed those exercises, either do them before attempting this lab or substitute OUs, groups, and user accounts from your own test domain. The script buildADMLobjects.ps1 is available in the book's download and can be used to create the OUs, users, groups, and so on.

14.3.1 Complete the TRY IT NOW sections

If you haven't already done so, complete the TRY IT NOW sections from this chapter. The exercises are repeated here for your convenience.

EXAMINE THE BUILTIN CONTAINER
Use ADAC or ADUC to browse the Builtin container. Do the groups you see match the list in table 14.1? If not, can you explain the discrepancies?

COMPARE THE AD AND LOCAL GROUPS
Choose one or more machines in your domain and compare the membership of the built-in operator groups and the local versions.

EXAMINE THE USERS CONTAINER

Use ADAC or ADUC to browse the Users container. Do the groups you see match the list in table 14.2? If not, can you explain the discrepancies for your environment?

USE THE DELEGATION OF CONTROL WIZARD

Use the Delegation of Control wizard in ADUC to delegate the rights to manage the user accounts in the ADMLmarketing OU to ADLgroup1.

The OU and group will exist if you've completed the exercises in the previous chapters. If not, substitute other objects from the test domain.

14.3.2 Default group containers

Why do you think the default groups are in containers rather than OUs? Is there a benefit to having them in OUs?

14.3.3 Add an account to a default group

Add the dgreen account to the Account Operators group. Log on as dgreen and attempt to use the permissions: create, modify, and delete a user account. Are there any restrictions?

Remove the account from the group and repeat the process for the Server Operators and Group Policy Creator Owners groups. What permissions would be granted if a user was a member of all three groups?

14.3.4 Use the Delegation of Control wizard

Use the Delegation of Control wizard to delegate permissions to

- Group ADLgroup2 to reset passwords in the ADMLfinance OU
- Group ADLgroup3 to manage group membership in the ADMLgroups OU

Experiment with the permissions granted to the groups. (*Hint:* add members to the groups.)

14.4 Ideas for on your own

Look at the critical groups (Enterprise Admins, Schema Admins, and Domain Admins) and determine if everyone who is a member should be a member. Remove any accounts that shouldn't be present. Create a plan to check these and other default groups periodically.

Is the membership of those groups under change control? If not, work with the owner of the change control system in your organization to get them under change control.

Managing DNS

DNS (Domain Name System) can be thought of as the telephone book for your network. When you need to communicate with a remote machine, you usually do so by typing the machine name into the client software or command. DNS is then interrogated by your system to discover the IP address of the remote system. Once that address has been obtained, your system can initiate communication through automatic and standard networking techniques.

DNS extends beyond your organization, because it's normal for your DNS servers to be configured to communicate with DNS on the internet and hand off the resolution of queries they can't handle.

> **NOTE** This chapter assumes that you're familiar with the concept of DNS and understand how it works in your environment.

The chapter starts with an overview showing how DNS works with Active Directory and explaining what's required for a non-Microsoft DNS to work with Active Directory. Next, we'll look at a DNS server configuration and see how to work with DNS zones and records. From there, we'll move on to testing whether your systems are working correctly with DNS, and we'll conclude with a lab.

First, though, how does DNS work with Active Directory?

15.1 *Overview of DNS and Active Directory*

Active Directory relies on DNS for a number of services. When a machine starts on the network, it queries DNS to discover the nearest domain controller via the SRV (service) records. Without this information, your machine won't connect to the domain and you won't be able to log on.

Many, if not most, organizations use Microsoft DNS because it integrates with Active Directory. This has a number of benefits:

- *Single replication topology*—AD replication controls DNS replication, instead of requiring the configuration of a separate topology.
- *Multimaster DNS servers*—Records can be written to any DNS server, instead of just the primary DNS server.
- *Dynamic updates*—The client machines can update their own records.
- *Secure updates*—Enables controlling which users and computers can update DNS records.

It's possible to use a non-Microsoft DNS, but this requires more work on your part.

15.1.1 *Using Microsoft DNS*

Microsoft DNS has the advantage that it's designed to integrate with Active Directory and it comes in the box. It also uses GUI tools that follow the pattern you're used to and can be administered from PowerShell.

INSTALLING DNS

When installing Active Directory, one of the options is to install DNS at the same time. If you're using Microsoft DNS, this is the recommended approach. You saw how to configure the domain controller creation process to install DNS in chapter 11.

Once DNS is installed on your domain controller, the standard AD replication process will copy the data onto the new DNS server. You'll learn more about replication in chapter 17.

DNS MANAGEMENT TOOLS

You have a number of options for managing DNS. You can manage Windows DNS using the DNS GUI console or you can use PowerShell. The DNS GUI is relatively unchanged across the current versions of Windows Server.

Windows Server 2012 introduced a PowerShell module for administering DNS; it also works against Windows Server 2008 R2 servers (I haven't tested it against Windows Server 2008 but I expect it to work). If you don't have access to the Windows Server 2012 module, you can administer Windows Server 2008 and 2008 R2 DNS servers using WMI.

> **NOTE** The Windows Server 2012 DNS module can't be installed on down-level versions of Windows because it relies on WMI classes that don't exist on these earlier versions of Windows. You can use it from a Windows Server 2012 or Windows Server 2012 R2 machine to administer DNS on down-level machines.

The Windows Server 2008 WMI classes are installed on DNS servers when DNS is installed. The classes are well documented at http://msdn.microsoft.com/en-us/library/windows/desktop/ms682123(v=vs.85).aspx. This chapter provides the information required to administer DNS to meet your needs as an AD administrator. If you'd like to dig further into DNS, reading chapter 9 of my book *PowerShell in Practice* (Manning, 2010) is highly recommended.

You don't have to use Microsoft DNS with your Active Directory. You can use a non-Microsoft DNS if you already have a DNS infrastructure in place. There are a few issues you need to be aware of if you follow that route.

15.1.2 Using non-Microsoft DNS

It's possible to use a non-Microsoft DNS such as BIND (https://www.isc.org/downloads /bind/), Cisco Network Registrar (http://www.cisco.com/en/US/products/sw/ netmgtsw/ps1982/), or the Nominum products (http://www.nominum.com/ solutions/). Other free and commercial offerings are available, which can be discovered through an internet search.

A non-Microsoft implementation of DNS has to meet the following requirements to support DNS:

- Must support SRV records
- Should support dynamic updates
- Should ideally support incremental zone transfers

The latest versions of BIND support all of these. You must check compliance on any other DNS in use in your organization.

If you use a non-Microsoft DNS, you'll need to utilize the management tools that are applicable to your DNS implementation. The rest of the chapter assumes you're using Microsoft DNS. You'll need to amend the techniques to use the appropriate management tools for your environment. The tasks will be the same irrespective of the type of DNS you use.

15.2 DNS server administration

DNS is a system that tends to look after itself. If you've implemented a dynamic DNS (recommended), your systems will register themselves in DNS when they start. This saves you a lot of work! Unfortunately, this doesn't mean that everything is done for you. There are still a number of tasks you need to perform, including viewing and changing the server level settings, managing DNS zones, and managing forwarders. Let's examine the server configuration.

15.2.1 Viewing DNS server settings

Once the DNS server is installed, you probably won't need to do much to it in the way of administration. Your time will be spent working with the zones and records. You may need to check DNS server settings.

You can view the settings as follows:

1 Open the DNS Manager console.
2 Right-click the DNS server.
3 Choose Properties.

You can control

- The IP addresses on which DNS listens for requests
- Servers to which your DNS server will forward requests it can't resolve—usually the internet
- Root hints—the top-level DNS servers on the internet
- Logging and monitoring
- Security
- Record scavenging

A full listing of the DNS server settings, including the zones on the server, can be obtained using the Windows Server 2012 PowerShell cmdlet:

```
Get-DnsServer -ComputerName server02
```

TRY IT NOW: Examine DNS server settings

Find the DNS server in your environment—preferably your test environment—and examine the settings using the GUI tools and PowerShell. Is there any information available in one that isn't available in the other?

Once your DNS server is configured to your satisfaction, it's time to look at DNS zones.

15.2.2 *Creating zones*

A DNS zone is a partition in the DNS namespace. One DNS zone will match the name of your AD domain. This is the forward lookup zone used to discover IP addresses from machine names. A reverse lookup zone is used to supply a machine name when an IP address is given. You can think of DNS zones as analogous to OUs in AD—they're containers for DNS records.

If you install DNS as part of your initial Active Directory installation, you'll find two zones are created:

1 A forward lookup zone that matches the AD domain name—for example, `manticore.org` in figure 15.1.
2 A forward lookup zone whose name starts with _msdcs—for example, `_msdcs.manticore.org` in figure 15.1. This is used by Active Directory to store the SRV DNS records that are used to advertise AD services through DNS.

You may need to create additional zones because

- You introduce additional domains into the environment.
- You need to create a reverse lookup zone.
- You segregate part of the environment.

You can create a zone using the DNS GUI tool or PowerShell.

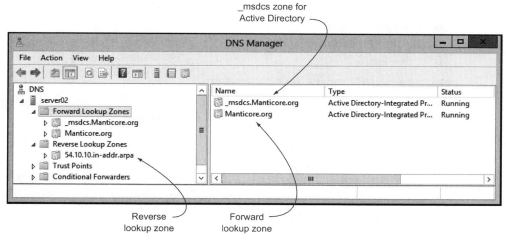

Figure 15.1 AD-integrated zones

CREATING A FORWARD LOOKUP ZONE WITH THE GUI

Creating a zone using the GUI tools involves running a wizard:

1 Open the DNS Manager console (figure 15.1).
2 Right-click Forward Lookup Zones.
3 Choose New Zone.
4 Click Next to bypass the wizard's start page.
5 On the Zone Type page, choose Primary Zone and ensure the checkbox is selected to store the zone in Active Directory.
6 Click Next.
7 On the Zone Replication Scope page, choose To All DNS Servers Running on Domain Controllers in This Domain: <domain name>. The other choices are to replicate to all DNS servers running on domain controllers in the forest or an option that mimics the replication method in Windows 2000. The latter isn't recommended.
8 Click Next.
9 Type the zone name (figure 15.2).
10 Click Next.

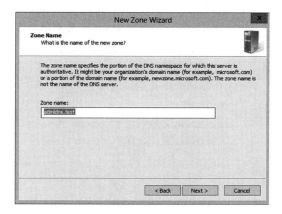

Figure 15.2 Creating a DNS zone

11 On the Dynamic Update page, choose Allow Only Secure Dynamic Updates.

12 Click next.

13 Review the summary.

14 Click Finish.

CREATING A REVERSE LOOKUP ZONE WITH THE GUI

Creating a reverse lookup zone is very similar, except that after step 8 in creating a forward lookup zone, a page is displayed to choose an IPv4 or IPv6 reverse lookup zone. Choose IPv4 and click Next. The dialog in figure 15.3 is displayed. Supply a network and the reverse lookup zone name will be populated for you. Click Next.

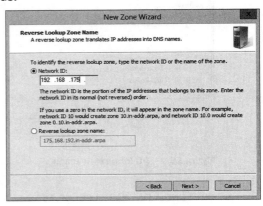

Figure 15.3 Creating a reverse lookup zone using the GUI

Complete the wizard following steps 11–14 of the forward lookup zone creation process.

Alternatively, you can create zones using PowerShell.

CREATING A FORWARD LOOKUP ZONE WITH POWERSHELL

If you're using Windows Server 2012 (as recommended) you have access to a Power-Shell module for working with DNS if you've installed DNS on the server or if the RSAT tools are available. The module is called `DnsServer`. The module will be automatically loaded for you when you open PowerShell.

> **TIP** Be careful, because there's also a module called `DnsClient` that's used for managing the client side of DNS, such as the DNS server names and the client cache.

You can create a zone using this syntax:

```
Add-DnsServerPrimaryZone -Name "admldns.test" `
-ComputerName server02  -ReplicationScope "Domain" -PassThru
```

Provide the zone name and the replication scope of the `Domain` or `Forest`. The default is to create an AD-integrated zone.

CREATING A REVERSE LOOKUP ZONE USING POWERSHELL

Creating a reverse lookup zone is just as easy:

```
Add-DnsServerPrimaryZone -NetworkID "192.168.175.0/24" `
-ComputerName server02  -ReplicationScope "Domain"
```

The full network address, including the subnet mask, is supplied along with the replication scope.

NOTE The observant reader will notice that –Passthru was used for creating the forward zone, but not the reverse. This parameter has no bearing on the zone creation but displays output to the screen when present. Without it, you just get the prompt returned.

CREATING A FORWARD LOOKUP ZONE USING WINDOWS SERVER 2008

Creating zones directly with the Windows Server 2008 WMI classes is nearly as straight-forward:

```
Invoke-WmiMethod –ComputerName server02 `
-Namespace root\MicrosoftDNS `
–Class MicrosoftDNS_Zone –Name CreateZone `
-ArgumentList $null, $null, $true, $null, 'admldns.test', 0
```

The first two arguments are AdminEmailName and DataFileName, which are both optional. In this case they've been set to null values, so they're ignored. The $true argument indicates you're creating an AD-integrated zone. The next $null represents an IP address that you don't need. This is followed by the domain name, and the final value of 0 indicates that you're creating a primary zone.

CREATING A REVERSE LOOKUP ZONE USING WINDOWS SERVER 2008

Creating a reverse lookup zone is almost the same:

```
Invoke-WmiMethod –ComputerName server02 `
-Namespace root\MicrosoftDNS `
–Class MicrosoftDNS_Zone –Name CreateZone `
-ArgumentList $null, $null, $true, $null, '175.168.192.in-addr.arpa', 0
```

The main difference is the name. A reverse lookup zone is always of the form C.B.A.in-addr.arpa where C, B, and A are the first three octets of the subnet reversed. A network of 192.168.175.0 becomes 175.168.192.in-addr.arpa.

TRY IT NOW: Create a DNS zone

Using the instructions in section 15.2.2, create two DNS zones:

Create a forward lookup zone called admldns.test.

Create a reverse lookup zone using the network address 192.168.175.0/24.

Create the zones with either the GUI tools or PowerShell. Delete the zones and repeat with the other technique.

Your network doesn't exist in isolation. You'll need to create links to other domains. The links are known as forwarders.

15.2.3 *Creating forwarders*

Conditional forwarders are created to enable your DNS servers to forward requests to a specific domain. A normal forwarder will forward all requests to one or more DNS

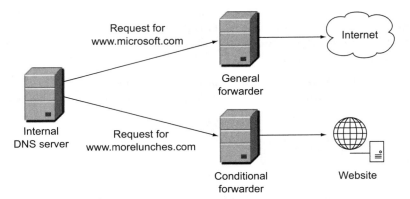

Figure 15.4   General and conditional forwarders. The general forwarder leads to the internet (top branch), while the conditional forwarder (bottom branch) leads to a specific website.

servers; a conditional forwarder will only forward requests for the one domain. Figure 15.4 illustrates this concept.

Imagine, for a moment, that you've created a conditional forwarder to more-lunches.com. If a request to resolve www.morelunches.com is received by your internal DNS server, it'll forward it to the DNS server indicated by the conditional forwarder. Any other request, such as www.microsoft.com, will be forwarded through your general forwarder for resolution by the internet DNS servers.

General forwarders are normally created in your perimeter network (also referred to as a DMZ, or demilitarized zone, though only the abbreviation is used) and usually remain unchanging. You can create conditional forwarders on your internal DNS server.

CREATING CONDITIONAL FORWARDERS USING THE GUI

The DNS console provides a simple mechanism for creating conditional forwarders:

1   Open the DNS Manager console.
2   Right-click Conditional Forwarders.
3   Choose New Conditional Forwarder....
4   Complete the dialog shown in figure 15.5.
5   Type the domain name, such as morelunches.com.

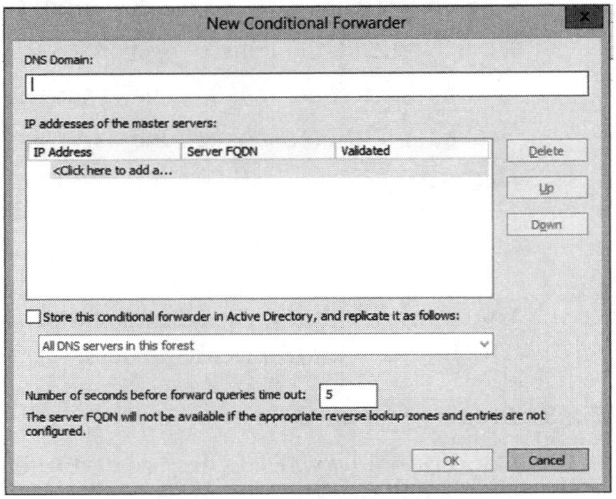

Figure 15.5   Creating a conditional forwarder

6 Type an IP address of the DNS server you're forwarding to for this domain. Multiple machines can be added for redundancy.

7 The address will be validated. If validation fails because your machine can't communicate with the proposed forwarder, the creation will fail.

8 Choose Store This Conditional Forwarder in Active Directory.

9 Choose All "DNS Servers in This Forest".

10 Click OK.

PowerShell supplies a command-line alternative.

CREATING CONDITIONAL FORWARDERS USING POWERSHELL

The `Add-DnsServerConditionalForwarderZone` PowerShell cmdlet is used to create conditional forwarders:

```
Add-DnsServerConditionalForwarderZone -Name "morelunches.com" `
-ReplicationScope "Forest" `
-MasterServers 172.23.90.124, 172.23.90.125
```

The same information is required as in the GUI setup: the name of the domain, the IP addresses of the servers to which requests should be forwarded, and how the conditional forwarder data should be replicated. Creation will fail if your DNS server can't communicate with the servers to which you're forwarding.

> **TRY IT NOW: Create a conditional forwarder**
>
> Using the instructions in section 15.2.3, create a conditional forwarder.
>
> Use PowerShell or the GUI tools to create a conditional forwarder to another DNS domain in your environment. Use another test domain for preference.

CREATING A GENERAL FORWARDER USING THE GUI

You'll rarely need to do this, but just in case you do need to add a general forwarder to your DNS server, you can perform these steps:

1 Open the DNS Manager console.

2 Choose the DNS server to configure.

3 Right-click the server name.

4 Choose Properties.

5 Choose Forwarders.

6 Type the IP address.

CREATING A GENERAL FORWARDER USING POWERSHELL

You can also use this PowerShell command:

```
Add-DnsServerForwarder -IPAddress 54.65.76.87 -PassThru
```

Once you have some zones created, it's time to create some DNS records.

15.3   DNS records

DNS zones contain records for individual machines in your environment. The minimum is a record in the forward lookup zone known as an *A record*. A records are for IPv4 addresses. If you're actively using IPv6 addresses, you'll need to create AAAA records. A (and AAAA) records are used to supply an IP address when you submit the machine name to the DNS.

There are occasions when you know the IP address but need the machine name. This involves using a pointer record (PTR) in a reverse lookup zone. The abbreviation PTR is always used when discussing reverse lookup records.

The lifecycle of a DNS record is very simple, because it's created and eventually destroyed when the machine to which it refers is no longer required. The other important action you need to perform is viewing the DNS records.

15.3.1   Viewing records

A useful troubleshooting technique, in the case of machine connectivity problems, is to check if a system is correctly registered with DNS. You can use the DNS console or check using PowerShell. You'll learn how to test if a system can find the DNS server and resolve a machine name in the next section. For now, let's browse DNS.

USING THE GUI TOOL TO FIND RECORDS

Finding a record in the DNS console is simply a matter of opening the DNS console and browsing the required zone as shown in figure 15.6.

PowerShell supplies a way to perform much more granular searches.

USING POWERSHELL TO FIND RECORDS AND FILTER RESULTS

With the Windows Server 2012 cmdlets, you can easily view all of the records in the zone or just the records for a single machine.

The -ZoneName parameter is used to restrict the query to a particular zone. Querying a forward lookup zone requires the full zone name:

```
Get-DnsServerResourceRecord -ZoneName 'admldns.test'  `
-ComputerName server02
```

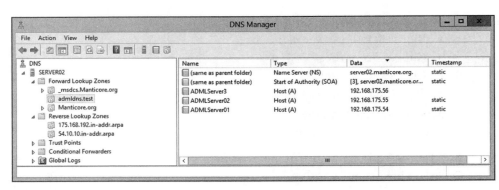

Figure 15.6   Viewing DNS records in a forward lookup zone

The `-ComputerName` parameter in all of the examples in this section refers to the DNS server. When you query a reverse lookup zone, you have to type a bit more because of the structure of the zone name:

```
Get-DnsServerResourceRecord -ZoneName '175.168.192.in-addr.arpa' `
-ComputerName server02
```

Alternatively, you can restrict your query to the DNS records for a single machine:

```
Get-DnsServerResourceRecord -Name "ADMLServer01" -ZoneName 'admldns.test'
-ComputerName server02
```

A similar syntax is used for PTR records, except that the name is the last part of the IP address:

```
Get-DnsServerResourceRecord -Name '54' `
-ZoneName '175.168.192.in-addr.arpa' `
-ComputerName server02
```

USING WMI CLASSES TO FIND RECORDS

Using the old-style WMI classes, you can view DNS records by record type. All of the records hosted on the DNS server will be returned unless you use a filter. In this case the filter restricts the returned-to data to a single zone. The point to note is that `ContainerName` is used for the zone:

```
Get-WmiObject -NameSpace 'root\MicrosoftDNS' -Class Microsoft_Atype `
-ComputerName server02 -Filter "ContainerName = 'admldns.test'" |
Select OwnerName, IPAddress
```

You can do the same for the reverse lookup zone:

```
Get-WmiObject -Namespace root\MicrosoftDNS -Class MicrosoftDNS_PTRType `
-Filter "ContainerName = '175.168.192.in-addr.arpa'" |
select OwnerName, RecordData
```

Viewing records is useful for troubleshooting, but the other aspect of administering DNS records is managing their lifecycles.

15.3.2 Adding records

If you're using an AD-integrated DNS, the records in your forward lookup zones will, for the most part, be maintained automatically. Servers will refresh their records when they restart and workstations will have their records refreshed by DHCP.

Occasionally you may need to create records—for instance, if you've assigned another IP address to a machine or you need to create an entry for a website. The DNS GUI tool is one way to create new records.

USING THE GUI TOOL TO CREATE NEW RECORDS

The DNS console supplies a number of wizards for creating a new DNS entry. The commonest record is an A (or AAAA for IPv6) record. You can create a new record as follows:

1 Open the DNS Manager console.
2 Navigate to the correct forward lookup zone.

3   Right-click the zone name.
4   Choose New Host (A or AAAA)....
5   The dialog in figure 15.7 is displayed.
6   Complete the dialog.
7   Click Add Host.
8   Click OK on the confirmation message box.
9   Add another host or click Cancel to close the dialog.

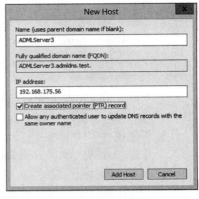

In the dialog the checkbox was selected that forced creation of a new PTR record. This is one good reason for using the GUI: you can create the forward and reverse lookup records in one pass.

Figure 15.7   Creating a DNS A record

USING THE GUI TOOL TO CREATE A NEW PTR

If you need to create a PTR record on its own, the process is very similar:

1   Open the DNS Manager console.
2   Navigate to the correct forward lookup zone.
3   Right-click the zone name.
4   Choose New Pointer (PTR)....
5   Complete the dialog in figure 15.8.
6   Click OK.
7   The record is created and the dialog is closed.

When you open the dialog, part of the IP address (taken from the reverse lookup zone name) is already filled in for you, which reduces the typing. You can also browse the forward lookup zones to find the machine, rather than typing the name.

Figure 15.8   Creating a PTR record

You can also create DNS records using PowerShell.

USING POWERSHELL TO CREATE A RECORD

If you use PowerShell to create DNS records, you have to create the forward and reverse records separately. In Windows Server 2012 you have cmdlets from the Dns-Server module to simplify the process.

Creating an A record uses this syntax:

```
Add-DnsServerResourceRecordA -Name "ADMLServer01" `
-ZoneName 'admldns.test'  -IPv4Address '192.168.175.54' `
-ComputerName server02
```

The –Name parameter refers to the name of the system for which you're creating the record. The –ComputerName parameter refers to the DNS server.

You can also create a PTR record:

```
Add-DnsServerResourceRecordPtr –Name '54' `
-ZoneName "175.168.192.in-addr.arpa" `
-PtrDomainName  'ADMLServer01.admldns.test'  `
-ComputerName server02
```

The trick here is that the –Name refers to the last part of the IP address, in this case 54, and the –PtrDomainName needs the full FQDN of the server. Cmdlets for other common record types are given in table 15.1.

Table 15.1 Cmdlets for creating other common DNS records

Cmdlet	Creates
Add-DnsServerResourceRecordAAAA	IPv6 forward lookup record
Add-DnsServerResourceRecordCName	Alias record
Add-DnsServerResourceRecordMX	Mail server record

USING OLDER VERSIONS OF WINDOWS TO CREATE RECORDS
Older versions of Windows (Windows Server 2008 R2 and older) aren't forgotten; you can create records using the old WMI classes.

An A record is created with the MicrosoftDNS_AType class:

```
Invoke-WmiMethod -Namespace root\MicrosoftDNS -Class MicrosoftDNS_AType `
-Name CreateInstanceFromPropertyData -ArgumentList "admldns.test", server02,
    "192.168.175.55", "ADMLServer02.admldns.test"
```

The arguments are the zone name, DNS server, IP address, and FQDN of the machine for which a record is being created.

A PTR record is created using similar syntax but based on the Microsoft-DNS_PTRType class:

```
Invoke-WmiMethod -Namespace root\MicrosoftDNS -Class MicrosoftDNS_PTRType `
-Name CreateInstanceFromPropertyData `
-ArgumentList "175.168.192.in-addr.arpa", 'server02',
'55.175.168.192.in-addr.arpa', "ADMLServer02.admldns.test"
```

In this case the arguments are the zone, DNS server name, full reverse lookup IP address (including the zone name), and FQDN of the machine.

TRY IT NOW: Create DNS records

Using the instructions in section 15.3.2, create two DNS records: one using the GUI and one using PowerShell.

Create an A record for server01.admldns.test with an IP address of 192.168.175.54, and for server02.admldns.test with an IP address of 192.168.175.55.

There isn't a way to create the A record and the PTR record simultaneously with PowerShell, though you could create a script to handle the work for you. If you don't feel comfortable creating scripts, try these books: *Learn Windows PowerShell 3 in a Month of Lunches* and *Learn PowerShell Toolmaking in a Month of Lunches*, both by Don Jones and Jeffrey Hicks (Manning, 2012).

15.3.3 *Deleting records*

Deleting DNS records is a relatively infrequent operation, usually only performed when a resource such as a server or web site is decommissioned. In the GUI, too, navigate to the record you wish to delete, right-click it, and choose delete.

With PowerShell you can use the `Remove-DnsServerResourceRecord` cmdlet:

```
Remove-DnsServerResourceRecord -ZoneName admldns.test `
-Name ADMLserver01 -RRType A

Remove-DnsServerResourceRecord -ZoneName 175.168.192.in-addr.arpa `
-Name 54 -RRType PTR
```

The zone name, name of the machine, and record type have to be supplied.

Using the older WMI classes, you should get the record and then pipe it to `Remove-WmiObject`:

```
Get-WmiObject -Namespace root\MicrosoftDNS -Class MicrosoftDNS_AType `
-Filter "OwnerName  = 'ADMLServer01.admldns.test'" |
Remove-WmiObject

Get-WmiObject -Namespace root\MicrosoftDNS -Class MicrosoftDNS_PTRType `
-Filter "OwnerName  = '54.175.168.192.in-addr.arpa'" |
Remove-WmiObject
```

> **TRY IT NOW: Delete DNS records**
>
> Using the instructions in section 15.3.3, delete the two DNS records you created in section 15.3.2: one using the UI and one using PowerShell.

Having a full set of DNS records is great, but how do you know your machines can find the DNS server?

15.4 *Testing DNS servers*

You know that computers in a Windows environment use DNS to discover IP address information when they need to communicate with other systems. Usually everything works, but sometimes problems arise and you're in the hot seat trying to discover why something isn't working. Testing a DNS is a common troubleshooting step in these cases. You need to test that your system can find a DNS server and that the DNS server is responding to your system. In the case of an AD-related problem, you also need to test that the SRV records can be found.

15.4.1 *Testing systems can find a DNS server*

If your machines can't find a DNS server, they won't be able to communicate with Active Directory and your users won't be able to logon and work. The tests in this section are all performed using PowerShell.

The first step is to ensure that the machine is configured with the address of one or more DNS servers:

```
Get-WmiObject -Class Win32_NetworkAdapterConfiguration `
-Filter "IPenabled=$true" |
select DNSDomain, DNSHostName, DNSServerSearchOrder
```

You'll see something like this, probably with multiple IP addresses, listed under the `DNSServerSearchOrder` property:

```
DNSDomain       DNSHostName DNSServerSearchOrder
---------       ----------- --------------------
manticore.org W12SUS        {10.10.54.201}
```

The next step is to determine if your system can contact the DNS server:

```
PS> Test-Connection -ComputerName 10.10.54.201 -Quiet
True
```

If a connection is made, you'll see a reply of `True`. A reply of `False` indicates that the test failed and the machine couldn't be contacted. If you want to see more detail, leave the `-Quiet` parameter off the command.

The last test is to ensure that the machine you're contacting really is a DNS server:

```
PS> Resolve-DnsName -Name $env:COMPUTERNAME -Server 10.10.54.201

Name                  Type TTL  Section  IPAddress
----                  ---- ---  -------  ---------
W12SUS.Manticore.org AAAA 1200 Question fe80::64bb:f110:306e:b700
W12SUS.Manticore.org AAAA 1200 Question fe80::d9c4:87b9:ec29:1d18
W12SUS.Manticore.org A    1200 Question 192.168.2.170
W12SUS.Manticore.org A    1200 Question 10.10.54.170
```

The `-Name` is the name of the local machine and the `-Server` is the DNS server (in this case the IP address is used). `$env:COMPUTERNAME` is the environmental variable holding the computer name.

You can also test the DNS server itself:

```
PS> Resolve-DnsName -Name 10.10.54.201 -Server 10.10.54.201

Name                     Type TTL  Section NameHost
----                     ---- ---  ------- --------
201.54.10.10.in-addr.arpa PTR  1200 Answer  server02.manticore.org
```

This uses the reverse lookup zone to resolve the name of the DNS server.

Now that you know the DNS server, you need to test whether it has the records for DNS to function correctly with your Active Directory.

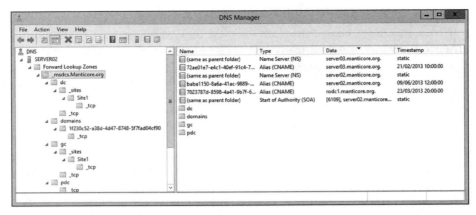

Figure 15.9   Structure of the _msdcs zone

15.4.2 *Testing SRV records*

The SRV records stored in a DNS are used to advertise specific services used in Active Directory. The SRV records are stored in the _msdcs forward lookup zone, as shown in figure 15.9.

The _msdcs zone contains the following subzones:

- dc provides SRV records for the domain controllers in the domain. There's a folder called Sites that has a subfolder per site in your Active Directory. (Sites are explained in chapter 16.)
- domains shows the different domains in your forest—in this case there's only one.
- gc has records for the global catalogs.
- pdc (primary domain controller, but refers to the PDC emulator FSMO role; see section 12.3) stores the records for the global catalogs in your forest.

Figure 15.10 illustrates the SRV records in my test domain.

```
PS> Get-WmiObject -Namespace 'root\MicrosoftDNS' -Class MicrosoftDNS_SRVType -ComputerName server02 -Filter "ContainerNa
me = '_msdcs.manticore.org'" | select OwnerName, RecordData | ft -a

OwnerName                                                                      RecordData
---------                                                                      ----------
_kerberos._tcp.Site1._sites.dc._msdcs.manticore.org                            0 100 88 server03.manticore.org.
_kerberos._tcp.Site1._sites.dc._msdcs.manticore.org                            0 100 88 rodc1.manticore.org.
_kerberos._tcp.Site1._sites.dc._msdcs.manticore.org                            0 100 88 server02.manticore.org.
_ldap._tcp.Site1._sites.dc._msdcs.manticore.org                                0 100 389 server03.manticore.org.
_ldap._tcp.Site1._sites.dc._msdcs.manticore.org                                0 100 389 rodc1.manticore.org.
_ldap._tcp.Site1._sites.dc._msdcs.manticore.org                                0 100 389 server02.manticore.org.
_kerberos._tcp.dc._msdcs.manticore.org                                         0 100 88 server03.manticore.org.
_kerberos._tcp.dc._msdcs.manticore.org                                         0 100 88 server02.manticore.org.
_ldap._tcp.dc._msdcs.manticore.org                                             0 100 389 server03.manticore.org.
_ldap._tcp.dc._msdcs.manticore.org                                             0 100 389 server02.manticore.org.
_ldap._tcp.1f230c52-a38d-4d47-8748-5f7fad04cf90.domains._msdcs.manticore.org   0 100 389 server03.manticore.org.
_ldap._tcp.1f230c52-a38d-4d47-8748-5f7fad04cf90.domains._msdcs.manticore.org   0 100 389 server02.manticore.org.
_ldap._tcp.Site1._sites.gc._msdcs.manticore.org                                0 100 3268 rodc1.manticore.org.
_ldap._tcp.Site1._sites.gc._msdcs.manticore.org                                0 100 3268 server02.manticore.org.
_ldap._tcp.Site1._sites.gc._msdcs.manticore.org                                0 100 3268 server03.manticore.org.
_ldap._tcp.gc._msdcs.manticore.org                                             0 100 3268 server02.manticore.org.
_ldap._tcp.gc._msdcs.manticore.org                                             0 100 3268 server03.manticore.org.
_ldap._tcp.pdc._msdcs.manticore.org                                            0 100 389 server02.manticore.org.
```

Figure 15.10   SRV records

The OwnerName property indicates where the record sits in the _msdcs zone and the RecordData indicates the domain controller that offers those services. In Site1 I have three domain controllers—server03, rodc1, and server02—all offering Kerberos and LDAP services. Only server02 and server03 show in the global catalog (gc) list.

The numbers under the RecordData property indicate priority, weight, and port, respectively.

If you know the AD site your machine sits in, you can discover whether AD services are available to it through the SRV records. You'll learn how to discover the AD site of a system in chapter 16.

This concludes your work with DNS. It's time to head into the lab to put it into practice.

15.5 LAB

This lab is designed to provide practice working with the techniques described in this chapter. As always, please don't experiment in your production environment.

15.5.1 *Complete the TRY IT NOW sections*

If you haven't already done so, complete the TRY IT NOW sections from this chapter. The exercises are repeated here for your convenience.

EXAMINE DNS SERVER SETTINGS

Find the DNS server in your environment—preferably your test environment—and examine the settings using the GUI tools and PowerShell. Is there any information available in one that isn't available in the other?

CREATE A DNS ZONE

Using the instructions in section 15.2.2, create two DNS zones:

- Create a forward lookup zone called admldns.test.
- Create a reverse lookup zone using the network address 192.168.175.0/24.

Create the zones with the either the GUI tools or PowerShell. Delete the zones and repeat with the other technique

CREATE A CONDITIONAL FORWARDER

Using the instructions in section 15.2.3, create a conditional forwarder. Use PowerShell or the GUI tools to create a conditional forwarder to another DNS domain in your environment. Use another test domain for preference.

CREATE DNS RECORDS

Using the instructions in section 15.3.2, create two DNS records. Create one A record for server01.admldns.test with an IP address of 192.168.175.54, and another for server02.admldns.test with an IP address of 192.168.175.55.

DELETE DNS RECORDS

Using the instructions in section 15.3.3, delete the two DNS records you created in section 15.3.2: one using the UI and one using PowerShell.

15.5.2 *Create another DNS zone*

Create a second DNS zone on one of your DNS servers and create a number of DNS records. Can you make it non-AD integrated?

Next, create the associated PTR records in a reverse lookup zone:

- Forward lookup zone name: `admllab.test`
- Computer names:
  - LabServer01
  - LabServer02
  - LabServer03
- Network: 172.16.1.0/24

Finally, create a conditional forwarder to that zone on another DNS server.

15.5.3 *Examine zone contents*

Use the PowerShell techniques presented in this chapter to examine the zones on your DNS servers and to examine the records in your zones.

15.6 *Ideas for on your own*

DNS is fundamental to the correct functioning of your AD. Instigate a policy of examining the DNS servers on a periodic basis to ensure their configuration doesn't deviate from your standards. Can you automate that process? An example will be provided through morelunches.com.

Are there any redundant records in your DNS zones? Examine the zones and remove any old records that are no longer required. Can you automate this?

In the next chapter you'll investigate the AD physical topology: sites, subnets, and site links.

16
Managing sites and subnets

Active Directory, like all IT systems, is ultimately dependent on the underlying network. It needs to store some network information so that client machines can identify their physical locations in AD terms. For example, this information is required for identifying the nearest domain controller.

NOTE   You must be a member of the Enterprise Admins group to manage the AD topology components.

The AD components—sites, subnets, and site links—are referred to as the AD physical topology. This chapter starts with a quick review of the AD site and subnet concepts you need to understand. You then jump straight into managing AD sites—how to view the site information and how to create them. This will involve the use of PowerShell cmdlets introduced in Windows Server 2012 and the venerable AD Sites and Services GUI tool. The lifecycle of AD subnets is next, following the pattern of viewing, creation, and management. The last major section deals with AD site links, which are the replication traffic pathways through your environment. The chapter concludes with a lab, giving you a chance to practice working with these aspects of your Active Directory.

First, though, a quick bit of theory.

16.1   AD site and subnet concepts

The AD physical topology is made up of three components:

- Sites
- Subnets
- Site links

The components are outlined in table 16.1. The correct configuration of these components is essential for a number of activities, including logon and replication between domain controllers, which you'll learn about in chapter 17.

Table 16.1 AD's physical topology components

Item	Definition and Purpose
Site	A site is a collection of machines connected at LAN speed. This usually translates to a building (or group of buildings). Sites are used for a number of purposes: to control replication between domain controllers, to determine the domain controller a user will authenticate against, for the instance of a site-aware application (such as DFS) that will be accessed, and also to apply group policy.
Subnet	A subnet is equivalent to a networking subnet. It defines a set of IP addresses. Subnets are linked to a site and define the IP addresses available in that site. This aids machines in finding a domain controller. The subnet information is stored in Active Directory for reference purposes. It's not used to control the network or IP addresses assigned to client machines.
Site Link (a.k.a. intersite transports)	A site link is a logical link in Active Directory between two sites. Replication between domain controllers follows the site link topology. The replication traffic will follow, but real, physical, network site links control the routing (in AD) of that traffic. If a domain controller isn't available in the user's site, the site links are used to find an available DC.
Site Link Bridge	A site link bridge consists of a set of site links that are transitive—all of the sites in the bridge can communicate directly with each other. By default, all site links are bridged. This should only be changed if there are underlying network routing issues that prevent all sites from communicating directly with each other.

The AD physical topology has a low volatility. You'll rarely need to make changes to your sites and subnets, but you need to understand how they work because they can have a big impact on replication, authentication, and general AD health. As an example, I've seen problems where organizations have created new network subnets but not defined them in Active Directory. This has caused machines located on those subnets to fail when authenticating because they can't find a domain controller.

> **TIP** Build a friendly relationship with your network team. You'll be working very closely with them, especially when you're troubleshooting AD replication problems.

The AD site topology maps directly onto your physical network topology. This is implicit in the definition of a site, but it needs to be emphasized.

TRY IT NOW: Investigate your sites and subnets

Think of the major locations in your organization. Are they defined as sites in Active Directory? Are the subnets correctly defined for those sites?

You may need to talk to your organization's network team to get the information you need.

An AD site doesn't have to contain a domain controller. You can have a site defined that doesn't have a domain controller. Site links are used to define which domain controller users in that site should authenticate against. Some applications, such as Distributed File System and SharePoint, are aware of AD sites and use the site information to discover the nearest server supplying the required service.

You have a few options for managing the physical topology components in your Active Directory:

- *AD Sites and Services*—This GUI tool has been available since Active Directory was introduced with Windows 2000 and has barely changed in that time.
- *PowerShell cmdlets*—These were introduced with Windows Server 2012. You can now manage all aspects of AD's physical topology with these cmdlets.
- *PowerShell scripts*—These are your only PowerShell option if you don't have a Windows Server 2012 system in your environment. The scripts are a bit complicated. Examples are provided in the download code.

TIP It's worth introducing a Windows Server 2012 system into your environment just for the extra management capabilities.

16.1.1 *Best practices for managing AD topology*

These best practices are exhaustive but are something to keep in mind when working with your AD topology:

- Add descriptions to AD site and subnet objects.
- Add location information to AD site and subnet objects.
- Only put two sites in a site link.
- Standardize the costs you use on your links and ensure they aren't multiples of each other.
- Don't disable site link bridging.

That's the end of the background information. It's time to learn how to manage this aspect of your Active Directory starting with AD sites.

16.2 *AD sites*

Active Directory has to have at least one site defined. When you create the first domain controller in your forest, a site is created. It's called `Default-First-Site-Name`. If you create your domain controller from the command line as recommended in chapter 11, you can assign another name to the first site. Alternatively, you can rename the site post-creation of your Active Directory.

You'll need to view the current topology and create new sites. Deleting sites is a much rarer occurrence in most organizations and can be accomplished using the GUI tools. First, though, how do you discover the sites in your organization?

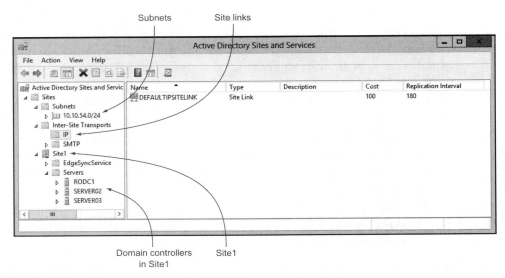

Figure 16.1   Viewing sites and subnets in ADSS

16.2.1 *Viewing current sites*

As an administrator, you'll spend a lot of your time viewing various data types in Active Directory. This may be prompted as part of a troubleshooting exercise, in answer to a query, or as a way to confirm some particular aspect of the data.

You can investigate your AD site information using AD Sites and Services (GUI).

USING GUI

You can open AD Sites and Services (ADSS) from the Tools menu on the Server Manager console or by searching. You'll see something similar to figure 16.1, which illustrates the state of the AD topology in my test environment before I started the development of this chapter. In a production environment you'd expect to see more data.

Subnets and site links (listed as Inter-Site Transports in figure 16.1) are explained in later sections of this chapter. I have a single site: Site1. This has three domain controllers under the Servers folder.

> **NOTE**   The servers shown in ADSS are domain controllers. You won't see member servers in this tool. You can't administer the domain controllers through ADSS, because it'll only allow modification of the replication links, not the base machine.

You can also find the same data with PowerShell.

USING POWERSHELL

The new cmdlets in the AD module that work with the AD topology all have nouns that start ADReplication. The cmdlet to retrieve information about your AD sites is Get-ADReplicationSite.

NOTE The AD topology is used for more than replication between domain controllers, as explained in section 16.1. The naming convention that the AD team has adopted makes it easy to discover the cmdlets you use for working with the AD topology.

You use the `Get-ADReplicationSite` cmdlet to find out about your AD sites:

```
PS> Get-ADReplicationSite

Description                     :
DistinguishedName               : CN=Site1,CN=Sites,CN=Configuration,
                                  DC=Manticore,DC=org
InterSiteTopologyGenerator      : CN=NTDS Settings,CN=SERVER02,CN=Servers,
                                  CN=Site1,CN=Sites,CN=Configuration,
                                  DC=Manticore,DC=org
ManagedBy                       :
Name                            : Site1
ObjectClass                     : site
ObjectGUID                      : fc2ec937-4ed2-44f7-882b-ce581a9dffc2
ReplicationSchedule             :
UniversalGroupCachingRefreshSite :
```

The default display is to show information, as above, for all sites. You can filter the results to the required sites if needed by using the `-Filter` parameter:

```
Get-ADReplicationSite -Filter {Name -eq 'Site1'}
```

You could also use a wildcard search:

```
Get-ADReplicationSite -Filter {Name -like 'Lon*'}
```

> **TRY IT NOW: View your sites**
>
> Open AD Sites and Services and browse your AD sites.
>
> Use the PowerShell cmdlet `Get-ADReplicationSite` to compare the information available.

Creating new AD sites is unlikely to be a frequent job, but you need to know how to perform this task.

16.2.2 *Creating an AD site*

You may need to create a new AD site for a number of reasons, usually connected to a change in the physical locations occupied by your organization, such as

- A new office has been opened.
- Your company has acquired another company and you're bringing them into your Active Directory.

The site can be created using ADSS (GUI) or PowerShell.

USING GUI

One of the good things about the AD GUI tools is that they're consistent. You can use what you've learned using ADUC when starting to work with ADSS. The following instructions for creating a new AD site will seem familiar when compared to creating a group or OU that you've learned about in earlier chapters.

To create a new AD site

1 Open AD Sites and Services.
2 Right-click Sites.
3 Choose New Site....
4 The dialog in figure 16.2 opens.
5 Complete the dialog by entering a name for the new site and choosing an existing link.
6 Click OK.
7 You'll see a message box stating you need to
   - Ensure the new site is linked to existing sites.
   - Add subnets to the site.
   - Install a domain controller or move one into the site.
8 Click OK to close the message box.

Figure 16.2   Creating a new site

TIP   When using the GUI, you have to select a site link, even if it's one you don't want to use (step 5 above). Don't worry—you can change it later, as you'll see in section 16.4.

Congratulations! You now have a new AD site. Unfortunately, the GUI doesn't let you set a number of properties, such as description and location, during creation. You can set the additional properties on the site post-creation as follows:

1 Open AD Sites and Services.
2 Choose Sites.
3 Right-click the required site.
4 Choose Properties.
5 Type the description on the General tab.
6 The location can be added on the Location tab.
7 Protection from accidental deletion can be turned on using the checkbox on the Object tab.
8 Click OK to save the changes and close the Properties dialog.

If you're creating the site as part of a larger process, you may want to use PowerShell to reduce the work you need to perform.

USING POWERSHELL

You've already met the `Get-ADReplicationSite` cmdlet for viewing site data. When thinking about the PowerShell naming conventions, it shouldn't come as a surprise that you use `New-ADReplicationSite` to create a new site. The cmdlet is used like this:

```
New-ADReplicationSite -Name ADMLsite2 -Description "ADML test site 2" `
-ProtectedFromAccidentalDeletion $true `
-OtherAttributes @{Location = "Dallas"}
```

Do you notice the differences between creating a site in the GUI and using Power-Shell? The GUI doesn't allow you to set a description or location, and you can't enable protection from accidental deletion. You can do this in one pass when using Power-Shell. Also, the GUI forces you to select a site link at the time you create a new site; PowerShell lets you specify the site link later on.

> ### TRY IT NOW: Create AD sites
>
> Use the management tools to create two AD sites with the following data:
>
> Site 1:
> Name: ADMLsite1
> Description: ADML test site 1
> Location: Toronto
> Protect from Accidental Deletion: Enabled
>
> Site 2:
> Name: ADMLsite2
> Description: ADML test site 2
> Location: Dallas
> Protect from Accidental Deletion: Enabled
>
> Use the GUI to create one site and PowerShell to create the other. When using the GUI, select any appropriate site link.

Once you've created a new site, the information will need to replicate to your other domain controllers. All of the topology data is stored at the AD forest level, so replication could take some time in a large environment.

> **TIP** If you need to delete an AD site, the easiest way is to open AD Sites and Services; select the site and click the red cross on the icon bar to perform the deletion.

AD sites need to have subnets associated with them so that machines can identify their site.

16.3   Subnets

AD subnets are used so that a machine can work out which AD site they should be in. If you have a subnet that hasn't been defined to Active Directory, any machines will have difficulty identifying which AD site they should be in. This can easily lead to them authenticating against a domain controller that's inappropriate from a network standpoint, which will cause a poor logon experience for those users. They'll complain!

The first thing you need to learn is how to discover the subnets defined to your Active Directory.

16.3.1   Viewing subnets

You have the usual choices of using ADSS or PowerShell to view subnet data. In some ways, the information provided in the GUI is more useful when browsing.

USING GUI

The subnet information is stored under the Subnets folder of ADSS, as shown in figure 16.3.

The Subnet name is always given in network and prefix notation; for instance, 10.10.54.0/24. ADSS shows the location and description, which can be very useful if you put the associated AD site into the description.

PowerShell provides an easy-to-use alternative.

USING POWERSHELL

You can use the `Get-ADReplicationSubnet` cmdlet to view subnet data. The syntax is as follows:

```
PS> Get-ADReplicationSubnet -Filter *

DistinguishedName : CN=10.10.54.0/24,CN=Subnets,CN=Sites,
                    CN=Configuration,DC=Manticore,DC=org
Location          :
Name              : 10.10.54.0/24
ObjectClass       : subnet
ObjectGUID        : ecb6a176-304f-487c-96ed-005f17d35796
Site              : CN=Site1,CN=Sites,CN=Configuration,DC=Manticore,DC=org
```

Figure 16.3   Viewing subnet information in Active Directory

The site information is included, which is useful, but it needs to be extracted from the site's distinguished name. The location is displayed by default, but the description isn't.

Creating subnets may happen periodically in your environment if your network keeps growing or the network team decides to reorganize the IP addressing scheme.

16.3.2 *Creating subnets*

You get the usual two options for creating subnets. ADSS follows the pattern for other creation actions.

USING GUI

ADSS is the GUI tool for creating subnets. You should have a good guess at how the process works. The following steps will enable you to create a new subnet:

1 Open AD Sites and Services.
2 Right-click Subnets.
3 Choose New Subnet.
4 The dialog in figure 16.4 opens.
5 Type the subnet name in the Prefix box.
6 The name will be echoed in the lower box.
7 Select an AD site to which the subnet will be associated.
8 Click OK.

As with AD sites, you can't add a description or location when creating a subnet. You can configure these other properties post-creation:

1 Open AD Sites and Services.
2 Choose Subnets.
3 Right-click the required subnet.
4 Choose Properties.
5 Type the description on the General tab.
6 The location can be added on the Location tab.
7 Protection from accidental deletion can be turned on using the checkbox on the Object tab.
8 Click OK to save the changes and close the Properties dialog.

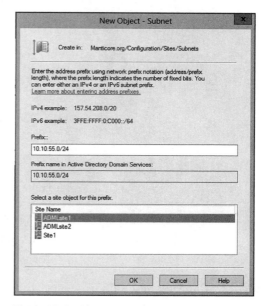

Figure 16.4   Creating an AD subnet

Alternatively, you can do most of this in one pass using PowerShell.

USING POWERSHELL

The `New-ADReplicationSubnet` cmdlet is used to create an AD subnet:

```
New-ADReplicationSubnet -Name '10.10.56.0/24' -Location 'Dallas' `
-Description 'ADML site 2 subnet' -Site ADMLsite2
```

Oddly, the cmdlet doesn't allow you to enable protection from accidental deletion during the creation process. Either use the GUI as described above, or use this Power-Shell syntax:

```
Get-ADReplicationSubnet -Identity '10.10.56.0/24'  |
Set-ADObject -ProtectedFromAccidentalDeletion $true
```

> **TRY IT NOW: Create AD subnets**
>
> Use the management tools to create two AD subnets with the following data:
>
> Subnet 1:
> Name: 10.10.55/24
> Site: ADMLsite1
> Description: ADML site 1 subnet
> Location: Toronto
> Protect from Accidental Deletion: Enabled
>
> Subnet 2:
> Name: 10.10.56/24
> Site: ADMLsite2
> Description: ADML site 2 subnet
> Location: Dallas
> Protect from Accidental Deletion: Enabled
>
> Use the GUI to create one site and PowerShell to create the other.

16.3.3   *Deleting subnets*

If you need to delete a subnet—for instance, if your network team decides to reorganize the network—you can select the subnet in the GUI tool and click the Delete button (red cross), or use this PowerShell code:

```
Get-ADReplicationSubnet -Identity '10.10.56.0/24'   |
Remove-ADReplicationSubnet
```

> **TIP**   Remember that you can use `-Whatif` to test the deletion process without actually deleting the object.

Now that you've created some sites and associated subnets with them, it's time you discovered how AD sites are linked for replication.

16.4   Site links

Unless you work in a small organization that exists in only a single location, you'll have multiple sites defined in your Active Directory. Those sites will probably, but not definitely, have domain controllers. AD site links are required between your sites. Site links serve a couple of purposes:

- They control AD replication between domain controllers in different sites.
- They provide a mechanism for clients to discover a domain controller if one isn't available in the local site.

Before you learn how to manage the lifecycle of AD site links, you should know how to discover the existing site links in your environment.

16.4.1   Viewing site links

You'll find it useful to view the existing site links when you're troubleshooting replication issues (this is explained in chapter 17). Site links, as part of the AD topology, are defined at the forest level, so you need to be a member of the Enterprise Admins group to manage them.

ADSS is used to view site links.

USING GUI

Figure 16.5 should look familiar. This time, notice the site links in my test environment before I started developing this chapter.

You can view the site links following these steps:

1 Open ADSS.
2 Navigate to Inter-Site Transports.
3 Choose IP or SMTP as appropriate to view your site links.

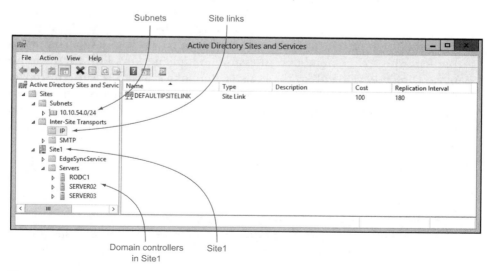

Figure 16.5   Viewing site links

That's not bad—you've met two oddities in a three-step process! First, the GUI refers to AD site links as "Inter-Site Transports." That's really just a terminology issue and you'll find that common usage is "AD Site Links."

Second, you have two options: IP and SMTP. These refer to the transport mechanism used to move the data over the link. The two options are described in table 16.2.

WARNING Be aware of the difference between the transport mechanisms. Selecting the wrong one will have an adverse impact on your AD replication.

Figure 16.5 illustrates a site link called DEFAULTIPSITELINK. This is created by default when Active Directory is first installed. You're not given the option to change it during installation. The data shows two of the properties of the site link: Cost and Replication Interval. These two properties cause a lot of confusion between them.

Table 16.2   AD site link transport mechanisms

Mechanism	Transport Medium	Comments
SMTP	SMTP (email)	Replication messages converted to email messages Replication is asynchronous Need certificate to encrypt and sign messages Doesn't replicate data such as users and groups; only replicates configuration data
IP	RPC over IP	Requires reliable, dedicated network links Replication is synchronous Replication is between pairs of domain controllers at a time

SMTP-based transport should only be used for replicating configuration data to an isolated domain at the end of a slow and unreliable network link. I expect that the links in your environment are configured to use IP as their transport mechanism.

Cost is a relative and arbitrary value assigned by you to provide Active Directory with a tool to work out the best way to replicate data if you have a complicated environment with a large number of sites and multiple network links between those sites. Active Directory will add up the costs of the links it has to traverse to replicate data between sites. If multiple routes are available, Active Directory will select the route with the lowest cost. If you search the internet, you'll find many suggestions for assigning costs based on network speed and reliability. I've found that these simple rules will usually suffice:

- Standardize the costs you use.
- Assign a low cost such as 100 (default) to the fastest, most reliable link between two locations.
- Assign a higher cost to other links.
- Don't use a multiple of your default cost for the higher cost (I suggest something like 330) to ensure that you can't arrive at identical costs for multiple routes.

The second property—Replication Interval—is the frequency at which replication is started in minutes. For example, in figure 16.6, the Replication Interval is 180 minutes.

Figure 16.6 shows the properties of the site link. This dialog is opened by right-clicking the appropriate site link and choosing Properties.

The Cost and Replication Interval properties are shown at the bottom-center of the dialog. The sites contained in the site link are shown in the right-hand box, and the sites that aren't part of the link are shown in the left-hand box.

PowerShell supplies a mechanism for discovering the same data.

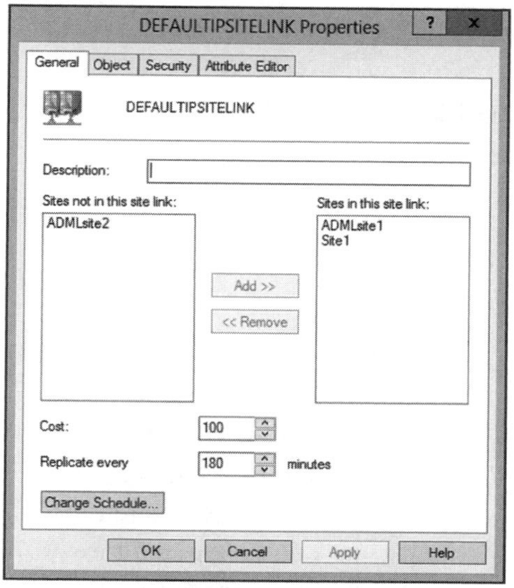

Figure 16.6   Viewing site link properties

USING POWERSHELL

The `Get-ADReplicationSiteLink` cmdlet can be used to view your site links:

```
PS> Get-ADReplicationSiteLink -Filter *
```

```
Cost                          : 100
DistinguishedName             : CN=DEFAULTIPSITELINK,CN=IP,
                                CN=Inter-Site Transports,CN=Sites,
                                CN=Configuration,DC=Manticore,DC=org
Name                          : DEFAULTIPSITELINK
ObjectClass                   : siteLink
ObjectGUID                    : ceb4fbc5-4df3-42db-8078-41ce47460354
ReplicationFrequencyInMinutes : 180
SitesIncluded                 : {CN=ADMLsite1,CN=Sites,
                                  CN=Configuration,DC=Manticore,DC=org,
                                  CN=Site1,CN=Sites,
                                  CN=Configuration,DC=Manticore,DC=org}
```

Most of the data from figure 16.6 is shown, except the sites that aren't a member of the site link.

> ### TRY IT NOW: View site links
>
> View the existing site links in your environment. Use ADSS and PowerShell. Compare the results.
>
> Are there any site links that contain more than two sites? Do all site links have a description?

Now you have a feel for the data needed for a site link. Next, let's look at creating them.

16.4.2 *Creating site links*

You should only have two AD sites in a site link. This means that every time you add a new site, you should be creating a new site link. These are separate actions in the GUI, but you could create a single PowerShell script to perform both actions.

First, you need to learn how to create a new site link.

USING GUI

This is another task that you perform in ADSS:

1 Open ADSS.
2 Choose Inter-Site Transports.
3 Right-click IP.
4 Choose New Site Link….
5 The dialog in figure 16.7 opens.
6 Complete the dialog.
7 Type a name for the link.
8 Select sites to be part of the link from the right column.
9 Click Add>>.
10 Click OK.

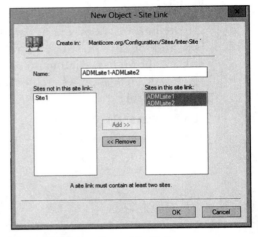

The Cost defaults to 100 and the Replication Interval defaults to 180 minutes. These properties can be modified later.

Figure 16.7   Creating a Site Link

> **TIP** Instead of using the site names, you could use the locations. This is useful in a large, dispersed environment with differing network speeds to the various locations. In this example, the site link name would become Toronto-Dallas, which gives more meaning to the name.

When you create a site link with PowerShell, you get more options.

USING POWERSHELL

If you create a site link with the `New-ADReplicationSiteLink` cmdlet, you can configure the cost and the replication frequency (configured in minutes) using the `-Cost` and `-ReplicationFrequencyInMinutes` parameters, respectively:

```
PS> New-ADReplicationSiteLink -InterSiteTransportProtocol IP `
    -Name 'ADMLsite1-ADMLsite2' `
    -SitesIncluded ADMLsite1, ADMLsite2 -Cost 100 `
    -ReplicationFrequencyInMinutes 180 `
    -Description "Primary site link between ADMLsite1 and ADMLsite2" `
    -PassThru
```

```
Cost                          : 100
DistinguishedName             : CN=ADMLsite1-ADMLsite2,CN=IP,
                                CN=Inter-Site Transports,CN=Sites,
                                CN=Configuration,DC=Manticore,DC=org
Name                          : ADMLsite1-ADMLsite2
ObjectClass                   : siteLink
ObjectGUID                    : 559f76cf-66d8-4ce7-8720-8587f8d21041
ReplicationFrequencyInMinutes : 180
SitesIncluded                 : {CN=ADMLsite1,CN=Sites,
                                  CN=Configuration,DC=Manticore,DC=org,
                                  CN=ADMLsite2,CN=Sites,
                                  CN=Configuration,DC=Manticore,DC=org}
```

The -Passthru parameter is required to produce a display when the site link is created. If you don't use it, you won't see any output.

16.4.3 *Removing sites from site links*

At this stage, assuming that you created it in the TRY IT NOW exercise, you'll see that ADMLsite2 is a member of both your new site link and the default site link. This isn't ideal, so you want to remove ADMLsite2 from the default site link.

You can view the sites in a site link as follows:

```
PS> Get-ADReplicationSiteLink -Identity DEFAULTIPSITELINK |
select -ExpandProperty SitesIncluded

CN=ADMLsite1,CN=Sites,CN=Configuration,DC=Manticore,DC=org
CN=Site1,CN=Sites,CN=Configuration,DC=Manticore,DC=org
```

You can remove a site from a site link like this:

```
Set-ADReplicationSiteLink -Identity DEFAULTIPSITELINK `
-SitesIncluded @{Remove='ADMLsite1'}
```

Use -SitesIncluded @{Add='<site name>'} to add a site into a link. The Add and Remove actions can be performed simultaneously in one hash table if required.

When you create a site link through the GUI, the Cost and Replication Interval properties are automatically set to the default values. You probably want to modify these properties.

16.4.4 *Modifying site links*

Site links have three properties that control replication:

- Cost
- Replication Interval
- Schedule

You've already met the Cost and Replication Interval properties. The Schedule property defines the times during which replication can start.

> **NOTE** Once replication has been initiated between two domain controllers, it'll continue until it's finished, even if that extends beyond the scheduled period.

Site link modification can be performed through the Properties dialog.

USING GUI

You haven't seen ADSS before this chapter, but you're going to be very familiar with it by the end of the chapter. You can modify an AD site link by following this process:

1 Open ADSS.
2 Navigate to Inter-Site Transports.
3 Choose IP.
4 Right-click a site link.
5 Choose Properties.
6 The dialog in figure 16.8 opens.

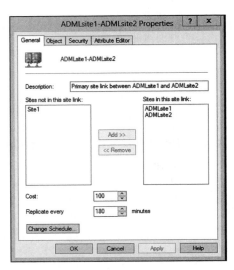

From this dialog you can

1 Modify the sites in a site link. Select the site and click Add or Remove as appropriate.
2 Modify the cost by overtyping or using the control to change the value.
3 Modify the Replication Interval by overtyping or using the control to change the value. The lowest value to which you can set this is 15 minutes.
4 Click OK or Apply to save the changes.

Figure 16.8   Properties for the ADMLsite1–ADMLSite2 link

You can modify the replication schedule by clicking Change Schedule…, shown in figure 16.8. This will display the dialog in 16.9.

The dialog shows 24 blocks, each representing a one-hour time interval, for each day of the week. Time blocks in which replication is enabled are colored blue; white blocks indicate that replication can't occur.

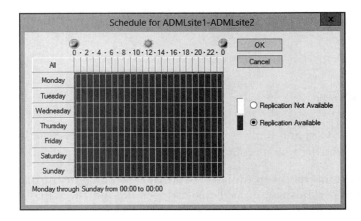

Figure 16.9   AD site link replication schedule

NOTE The GUI only allows you to set the schedule in blocks of one hour. PowerShell enables you to set the schedule in blocks of 15 minutes.

The replication schedule is set to 24/7 as a default. You can change the schedule by selecting one or more time blocks and selecting the appropriate radio button to enable or disable replication. Click OK to save the change.

PowerShell offers the option of changing the properties in one pass.

USING POWERSHELL

The PowerShell verb for cmdlets that change properties is Set. You can use the Set-ADReplicationSiteLink to change your site links.

You can change the cost, in this case to 150:

```
Set-ADReplicationSiteLink -Identity 'ADMLsite1-ADMLsite2' -Cost 150
```

You can change the replication interval; the value is always in minutes:

```
Set-ADReplicationSiteLink -Identity 'ADMLsite1-ADMLsite2' `
-ReplicationFrequencyInMinutes 30
```

Changing the schedule is a little more complicated:

```
$schedule = New-Object -TypeName
➥ System.DirectoryServices.ActiveDirectory.ActiveDirectorySchedule
$schedule.ResetSchedule()
$schedule.SetDailySchedule("Nineteen","Zero","TwentyThree","FortyFive")
Set-ADReplicationSiteLink -Identity 'ADMLsite1-ADMLsite2' `
-ReplicationSchedule $schedule
```

Create an object for the new schedule. Use the ResetSchedule() method to ensure the schedule is empty. Set a daily schedule. This is defined as having a start time and end time. The hour (24-hour clock) and minutes in 15-minute blocks (zero, fifteen, thirty, or forty-five) are supplied for the times. The Set-ADReplicationSiteLink cmdlet is used to apply the schedule.

If you need to set a split replication schedule—for instance, outside out-of-business hours—you need to configure a block of time at the start of the day and another block at the end of the day. This is accomplished by defining and applying two separate schedules as shown in the following code:

```
$schedule = New-Object -TypeName
➥ System.DirectoryServices.ActiveDirectory.ActiveDirectorySchedule
$schedule.ResetSchedule()
$schedule.SetDailySchedule("Zero","Zero","Six","Fifteen")
Set-ADReplicationSiteLink -Identity 'ADMLsite1-ADMLsite2' `
-ReplicationSchedule $schedule

$schedule.SetDailySchedule("Nineteen","Zero","TwentyThree","FortyFive")
Set-ADReplicationSiteLink -Identity 'ADMLsite1-ADMLsite2' `
-ReplicationSchedule $schedule
```

> **TRY IT NOW: Create and modify a site link**
>
> Create a new site link using ADMLsite1 and ADMLsite2.
>
> The site should be called Toronto-Dallas. Set the Cost to 100 and the Replication Interval to 180 minutes.
>
> Modify the Cost to be 330 and the Replication Interval to 30 minutes.
>
> Modify the replication schedule so that the link is only used outside of business hours. Set the Schedule property to
>
> - All day Saturday and Sunday
> - 8 p.m. to 5 a.m. Monday to Friday

The last piece of the puzzle for the AD topology is a quick look at site link bridges.

16.4.5 *Site link bridges*

By default, all site links are bridged. This means that if Site A can talk to Site B and Site B can talk to Site C, then Site A can talk to Site C. This is also known as being transitive. In rare cases (such as a large environment with poor network links) you may need to disable this so that you can control replication manually.

To disable site link bridging

1 Open ADSS.
2 Navigate to Inter-Site Transports.
3 Right-click the IP folder.
4 Choose Properties.
5 Uncheck Bridge All Site Links.
6 Click OK.

If you disable site link bridging, you must then create your own bridges:

1 Open ADSS.
2 Navigate to Inter-Site Transports.
3 Right-click the IP folder.
4 Choose New Site Link Bridge.
5 Highlight the sites you want to bridge in the left box.
6 Click Add.
7 Click OK.

I'll repeat myself by stating that you shouldn't do this without very good reason, and I don't expect you to need to do it in a Windows Server 2008 or Windows Server 2012 environment.

That concludes your look at the AD topology. Let's round off this lunchtime with a trip to the lab.

16.5 LAB

This lab is designed to provide an opportunity for you to practice managing your AD topology. As always, please don't experiment in your production environment.

16.5.1 Complete the TRY IT NOW exercises

If you haven't already done so, complete the TRY IT NOW exercises. The information is repeated here for your convenience.

INVESTIGATE YOUR SITES AND SUBNETS

Think of the major locations in your organization. Are they defined as sites in Active Directory? Are the subnets correctly defined for those sites?

You may need to talk to your organization's network team to get the information you need.

VIEW YOUR SITES

Open AD Sites and Services and browse your AD sites. Use the PowerShell cmdlet `Get-ADReplicationSite` to compare the information available.

CREATE AD SITES

Use the management tools to create two AD sites with the following data:

Site 1:

- Name: ADMLsite1
- Description: ADML test site 1
- Location: Toronto
- Protect from Accidental Deletion: Enabled

Site 2:

- Name: ADMLsite2
- Description: ADML test site 2
- Location: Dallas
- Protect from Accidental Deletion: Enabled

Use the GUI to create one site and PowerShell to create the other. When using the GUI, select any appropriate site link.

CREATE AD SUBNETS

Use the management tools to create two AD subnets with the following data:

Subnet 1:

- Name: 10.10.55/24
- Site: ADMLsite1
- Description: ADML site 1 subnet
- Location: Toronto
- Protect from Accidental Deletion: Enabled

Subnet 2:

- Name: 10.10.56/24
- Site: ADMLsite2
- Description: ADML site 2 subnet
- Location: Dallas
- Protect from Accidental Deletion: Enabled

Use the GUI to create one site and PowerShell to create the other.

VIEW SITE LINKS

View the existing site links in your environment. Use ADSS and PowerShell. Compare the results.

Are there any site links that contain more than two sites? Do all site links have a description?

CREATE AND MODIFY A SITE LINK

Create a new site link using ADMLsite1 and ADMLsite2.

The site should be called Toronto-Dallas. Set the Cost to 100 and the Replication Interval to 180 minutes.

Modify the Cost to be 330 and the Replication Interval to 30 minutes.

Modify the replication schedule so that the link is only used outside of business hours. Set the Schedule property to

- All day Saturday and Sunday
- 8 p.m. to 5 a.m. Monday to Friday

16.5.2 *Map your AD topology*

Create a map of your AD topology. An example is provided in the book's download. On the map show

- AD sites
- AD site links
- Site link costs
- Domain controller location
- IP subnets if you have space

Create a process to keep this up to date.

16.5.3 *Bring a new location into your environment*

Your organization has opened an office in another town and you have to create the AD topology to accommodate the office.

- Create a new AD site:

  1 Name: San Diego
  2 Description: San Diego new office
  3 Protect from Accidental Deletion: Enabled

- Create a new subnet and assign to the new site:
  1. Name: 10.10.60/24
  2. Site: San Diego
  3. Description: San Diego subnet 1
  4. Location: San Diego
  5. Protect from Accidental Deletion: Enabled

- Create another subnet and assign to the new site:
  1. Name: 10.10.61/24
  2. Site: San Diego
  3. Description: San Diego subnet 2
  4. Location: San Diego
  5. Protect from Accidental Deletion: Enabled

- Create a site link:
  1. Sites: ADMLsite1 and San Diego
  2. Cost: 150
  3. Replication frequency: 30 minutes
  4. Replication schedule: 24/7

- Create a second site link:
  1. Sites: ADMLsite2 and San Diego
  2. Cost: 530
  3. Replication frequency: 120 minutes
  4. Replication schedule: 7 p.m. to 4 a.m.

What is the preferred route for replication?

- From Toronto to San Diego?
- From Dallas to San Diego?

16.6 *Ideas for on your own*

Your AD topology isn't very volatile, but errors can have a huge impact. I've seen an organization's Active Directory brought to its knees because the site links were incorrectly configured. Spend some time examining your topology and determining if it's optimum for your organization. Check any sites that have multiple site links to ensure that replication traffic is flowing in the way that you think it is.

Using the techniques presented in this chapter, come up with a plan for adding new locations into your Active Directory. Concentrate on the information you need to gather. Can you create a script that creates and configures all of the topology objects in one pass?

In the next chapter you'll learn how the AD topology is used for replication of AD data between domain controllers.

AD replication 17

You've seen that AD domain controllers work in a multi-master fashion. This means that you can make changes, like modifying a user account or changing group membership on any domain controller. If that's all that happens, you'll be left with multiple versions of the same user account or groups that "think" that they have different membership lists depending on which domain controller you're looking at. This is a recipe for chaos.

> **TRY IT NOW: Test data is identical across domain controllers**
>
> Check the same user account on different domain controllers. Is the information identical? Can you see anything different between the two versions? Make the same check for the membership list of a group.

Hopefully you've found that the data associated with users, groups, and other objects is the same across domain controllers. You'll find some minor differences in the information held for an individual object on each domain controller, but this has to do with keeping track of the object, such as the Update Sequence Number (USN).

Active Directory needs a process to ensure that when an object is changed on one domain controller, that change is communicated to all other relevant domain controllers. This process is called replication.

In this chapter we'll look at how replication works, configuring replication, testing that it's working correctly using Repadmin and PowerShell, and forcing replication using Repadmin and ADSS. Finally, we'll conclude the chapter with a lab.

Let's begin by covering the basics of how replication between domain controllers works.

17.1 How replication works

When you think about replication, you need to consider two scenarios. The first scenario is where all of the domain controllers are in the same AD site—this is referred to as intrasite replication. The second scenario is a bit more complicated because there are multiple AD sites to consider. This is referred to as intersite replication. The replication process is identical for intrasite and intersite replication. There are a few complications around intersite replication we won't discuss until you've got intrasite replication down solid.

> **NOTE** For completeness, there's a third scenario that covers what happens when a new domain controller is created. This was explained in chapter 11.

Staying with our motto, we'll start out easy and look at replication within a site.

17.1.1 Intrasite replication

When we discuss active replication within a site, we normally refer to it as intrasite replication. Think about a site with three domain controllers, as shown in figure 17.1.

The replication explanation will be based on making a change to one domain controller and discovering how that change is replicated to the other domain controllers in the site. When you make a change, such as creating a new user account, the domain controller to which you're attached—let's say DC1—will save that change in its database. That change is allocated a USN by the domain controller.

> **NOTE** USNs are allocated sequentially to each change (also referred to as a transaction). USNs are unique to the domain controller. There's no correlation between USNs on different domain controllers.

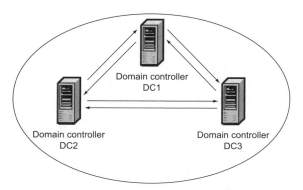

Figure 17.1 Intrasite replication among three domain controllers. The arrows indicate that replication occurs as two one-way replication processes to create bidirectional replication between pairs of domain controllers.

Replication only occurs between pairs of domain controllers. In figure 17.1 this means the following replication pairs exist:

- DC1–DC2
- DC1–DC3
- DC2–DC3

Each pair of domain controllers maintains its own replication conversation, which draws information from two tables of values: the high-watermark vector and the up-to-dateness vector.

The high-watermark vector is the highest USN that a domain controller has received from a direct replication partner. Each domain controller maintains a table of these values.

The up-to-dateness vector is the highest USN that a domain controller has received from another domain controller. Each domain controller maintains a table of up-to-dateness vectors from every domain controller that has ever existed in the forest. This table also contains a timestamp of the last time the domain controller successfully replicated with each remote domain controller.

TRANSACTION 1

As an example, we'll look at the replication of a change from DC1 to DC2. At a point in time (at hourly intervals if no other replication occurs), DC2 automatically requests any new updates from DC1. If a change occurs before then, DC1 notifies DC2 of any changes so that DC2 can initiate replication. The request from DC2 includes

- USN for DC1 taken from DC2's high-watermark vector table
- USN for DC1 taken from DC2's up-to-dateness vector table
- Maximum number of objects and values DC2 can receive, which is used to limit the network bandwidth used by replication (if required)

DC1 will now decide which objects need to be replicated to DC2. It does this by comparing its own highest USN with the high-watermark vector received from DC2. Any object with a USN greater than the high-watermark vector needs to be replicated. These changes are replicated to DC2 and given a USN on DC2. The high-watermark vector on DC2 for DC1 is updated to reflect the highest DC1 USN that's been received.

NOTE If five user objects are created on DC1 and replicated to DC2, the USN on DC2 only increments by one because the updates occur in one transaction.

At some time in the future, DC1 will request updates from DC2. Remember, replication is only one-way. It has to be triggered separately at each end. DC2 will send all the objects that have a USN higher than the high-watermark vector that DC1 holds for it.

NOTE Within a site, a domain controller will hold a change for approximately 15 seconds before replicating that change. This allows any other rapidly occurring changes to be bundled into the same replication transaction. For most practical purposes, it's safe to assume that replication within a site occurs immediately after the change is committed to Active Directory.

Okay—everything's good and the domain controllers are happily replicating away.

Actually, no, it's not all good, because the new user object that you replicated from DC1 was given a new USN on DC2. That means it'll be above the high-watermark vector of DC1 and will be replicated back to DC1, where it'll be given a new USN, which means it gets replicated back to DC2 and so on.

If this really happened, Active Directory would be paralyzed. What stops this continuous replication and re-replication is the up-to-dateness vector. It's sent along with the high-watermark vector. When a domain controller is deciding what to send, it looks at the up-to-dateness vector and filters out any object that has a USN below the up-to-dateness vector it's been sent.

How does it do that? The originating domain controller and the original USN are preserved on the object, which means they can be compared with the up-to-dateness vector table and filtered out of the replication process, because the requesting domain controller already has them.

By now you're probably feeling a bit dazed. Don't worry, this is a complicated subject and many IT pros don't understand it properly. Let's look at this process again considering the values of the various counters, which should make it clearer.

TRANSACTION 2

Your starting point is the two domain controllers, as shown in table 17.1. An object will be created on DC1 and replicated to DC2.

Table 17.1   Replication starting point

	DC1	DC2
USN	1000	2000
High-watermark vector	2000	1000
Up-to-dateness vector	2000	1000

You now create the user object on DC1, and it gets a USN of 1001 (table 17.2).

Table 17.2   New object created

	DC1	DC2
USN	1001	2000
High-watermark vector	2000	1000
Up-to-dateness vector	2000	1000

Replication occurs and the USN on DC2 is increased. The high-watermark and up-to-dateness vectors are reset (table 17.3).

Table 17.3   Postreplication of object

	DC1	DC2
USN	1001	2001
High-watermark vector	2000	1001
Up-to-dateness vector	2000	1001

If you create a group on DC2, it'll be given the USN of 2002 (table 17.4).

Table 17.4   Object created on DC2

	DC1	DC2
USN	1001	2002
High-watermark vector	2000	1001
Up-to-dateness vector	2000	1001

DC1 requests replication. It has a high-watermark vector of 2000 for DC2, so the updates associated with USN 2001 (user) and 2002 (group) should be sent. But because DC2 has an up-to-dateness vector of 1001 for DC1, it doesn't send the user update because it had an originating USN of 1001. Only the group update is sent.

> **TRY IT NOW: Replication exercise on paper**
>
> Work through a couple of examples like this to boost your understanding of the process and the interaction between the USN and the high-watermark and up-to-dateness vectors.

To make things a bit more complicated, if you consider the three domain controllers in figure 17.1, you can create a user object on DC1 as before. It'll replicate to DC2 and DC3 directly from DC1. When DC2 tries to replicate with DC3, the object would be resent, but DC2 already has it as shown by the up-to-dateness vector, so it isn't included in the replicated data.

17.1.2   *Naming contexts*

Unfortunately, life and Active Directory are a little bit more complicated than the picture painted in the previous section. This complication arises because Active Directory isn't treated or organized as a single massive block. It's divided into a number of sections known as *naming contexts* (NCs). NCs are a way to segment the data in Active

Directory so that replication can occur in a more granular fashion. You don't need to worry about creating NCs—Active Directory does it for you. All of the data you've worked with is in the configuration NC (sites, subnets, and site links) or the domain NC (users, groups, and computers).

The reason for this little side trip into the AD structure is that replication is actually managed at the naming context/application partition level (application partitions will be explained shortly). This means that the process we stepped through in section 17.1.1, where we examined how data is replicated, is repeated for every NC or application partition that a domain controller stores. Nothing changes in the way replication occurs—the USN together with the high-watermark and up-to-dateness vectors are still involved. The complication arises in that separate high-watermark and up-to-dateness vectors are maintained for each individual NC or application partition on each domain controller.

There are three default naming contexts, as shown in table 17.5.

Table 17.5   Default naming contexts

Naming Context	Forest or Domain	Data Stored
Configuration	Forest	Forest configuration; for example, sites and subnets, exchange
Schema	Forest	Schema object class and attribute definitions
Domain	Domain	Domain-specific data; for example, users, groups, and computers

Just so we don't think this is too easy, Microsoft introduced the ability to create your own sections of Active Directory known as *application partitions*. Application partitions function like NCs except

- They can't contain security principals like users, groups, computers, and so on.
- You can control the domain controllers to which they replicate.
- No objects in an application partition are replicated as part of the global catalog.
- Objects in an application partition can't be moved outside that partition.

In chapter 15 we saw that DNS can be integrated with Active Directory. If this option is used, then DNS uses application partitions to store its data. Two application partitions are created when installing a new forest:

- DomainDnsZones: Replicates to domain controllers in the domain that are also DNS servers
- ForestDnsZones: Replicates to all domain controllers in the forest that are also DNS servers

This gives more granularity and control compared to the original Windows 2000 situation, where DNS data was replicated to all domain controllers in the domain. You can also create your own application partitions to control DNS replication if required. This ability isn't needed in a small organization, but could be useful in a large, multidomain, multisite, AD environment where you need more granular control of DNS replication.

> **TRY IT NOW: View DNS partitions**
>
> Check your DNS configuration to see which partitions your DNS zones use for replication.
>
> *Hint:* check the properties of the zone.

If you've ever wondered why DNS data seemed to replicate at a different rate from user information, it's because the two data sets are in different naming contexts/application partitions.

The great thing about NCs is that you don't need to configure anything. Active Directory takes care of it for you.

17.1.3 *Intersite replication*

Sites and site links were covered in chapter 16. Please review that chapter if you haven't worked through it.

Replication between sites is handled in a similar manner to replication within a site. Figure 17.2 shows an example with two sites, each of which has three domain controllers.

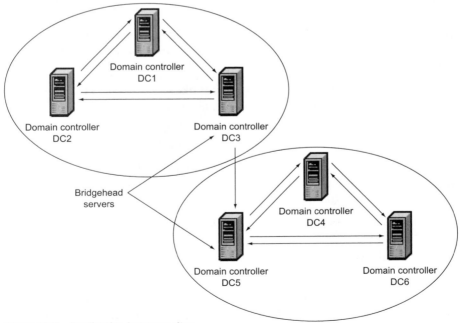

Figure 17.2   Replication between sites

Replication within a site occurs as described in section 17.1.1. This gives you two sets of replication partners:

- DC1–DC2; DC1–DC3; DC2–DC3
- DC4–DC5; DC4–DC6; DC5–DC6

Somehow these two sets of domain controllers need to replicate with each other. One possible way would be for each domain controller in each site to replicate directly with every domain controller in the other site. I'll leave that as an exercise for you to work out the replication partners if you want! This would theoretically work, but would be very wasteful in terms of network bandwidth, because data would be transferred multiple times between sites. It'd also cause the domain controllers to perform extra, unnecessary work.

To streamline the replication process, a bridgehead server is automatically selected for each site by Active Directory. These replicate across the site link using the replication frequency and schedule defined on the link. The replication occurs between these bridgehead servers exactly as described earlier, meaning that each NC and application partition is replicated individually. The bridgehead servers then replicate the data to the domain controllers within their site.

> **TIP** You can manually designate bridgehead servers, but I don't recommend doing this if you can avoid it. If they fail, AD won't designate new ones for you. If AD selects a bridgehead server which subsequently fails, AD will automatically select another domain controller to act as the bridgehead server.

For example, if you make a change on DC1 in figure 17.2, that change will replicate to DC2 and DC3 almost immediately. DC3 will replicate the change to DC5 in the other site. DC5 will then replicate the change to DC4 and DC6 within its site.

TRY IT NOW: Discover bridgehead servers

Work through the sites and site links with the AD Sites and Services GUI tool to determine the way data replicates between sites. Draw a diagram similar to figure 17.2 if it helps your visualization. Does the same domain controller function as a bridgehead server for multiple site links?

17.1.4 *Global catalog replication*

You'll remember learning about global catalogs in chapter 12. The global catalog is a subset of the data from all domains in the forest. This means that a domain controller that's configured as a global catalog server will hold a partial copy of the domain NC for each domain in the forest. Replication for these NCs is managed by Active Directory as part of the standard replication process. There's no separate replication process for the global catalog.

Table 17.6 summarizes the NCs that would be expected on domain controllers in a multidomain forest. The table shows the major NCs and how they're replicated to domain controllers and global catalogs across multiple domains.

Table 17.6 **Replication of naming contexts in a multidomain forest**

NC/Partition	Domain Controller Domain A	Global Catlog Domain A	Domain Controller Domain B	Global Catalog Domain B
Schema	Yes	Yes	Yes	Yes
Configuration	Yes	Yes	Yes	Yes
Domain A NC	Yes	Yes	No	Partial
Domain B NC	No	Partial	Yes	Yes
ForestDNSZones	Yes if DNS server	Yes if DNS server	Yes if DNS server	Yes if DNS server
DomainDnsZones— Domain A	Yes if DNS server	Yes if DNS server		
DomainDnsZones— Domain B			Yes if DNS server	Yes if DNS server

17.2 *Configuring replication*

Active Directory has a process known as the Knowledge Consistency Checker (KCC). The KCC runs inside Active Directory and can't be accessed directly. Its job is to generate and maintain the connections that are used to perform replication between domain controllers. The KCC isn't involved in the replication of data. Its responsibility is to create and maintain the replication connections in response to changes in the AD topology (sites and site links).

Figure 17.1 shows that within a site, replication occurs between pairs of domain controllers. As domain controllers are added to a site, the change on one domain controller has to pass through more replication "hops" to reach all the other domain controllers. There's a practical limit to the number of hops; otherwise, replication within a site would take too long and the domain controllers would have different versions of the data.

Within a site, replication connections between domain controllers are configured so that there are no more than three hops between any pair of domain controllers. If domain controllers are added or removed from a site, the KCC automatically modifies the replication pairings to ensure that the three-hop rule is maintained.

The KCC uses the Intersite Topology Generator (ISTG) to create connection objects between domain controllers in different sites. The connections are based on the site links you've defined between your sites. The costs you defined for those links are taken into account. Bridgehead servers will be defined automatically for you as part of this process. If a bridgehead server should fail, the KCC will regenerate the replication connections and designate a new bridgehead server.

Define your own replication topology

You may look at the replication topology defined by the KCC, using ADSS or PowerShell, and decide you don't like it. At this point, you may be tempted to manually create connection objects to force replication to work the way you think it should.

I have one word of advice: *DON'T*.

I've seen some awful replication problems because administrators decided they would create replication objects to force replication down the route they wanted. In one of the worst cases, a domain controller was receiving replicated data from two sources and couldn't determine which was correct, and so it rejected all replications.

If the replication connections don't appear to be correct, then check the site link definitions. Most likely you need to modify them as shown in chapter 16.

Let the KCC do its job and Active Directory will be much happier. Your life will be easier as well.

17.3   *Testing and forcing replication*

Ideally your environment will have a monitoring system, such as System Center Operations Manager, that will actively monitor AD replication and tell you if something isn't working. If you don't have such a tool, then you need to do it the hard way.

There are a number of ways to test if replication is working, but they all involve the command line. There isn't a good GUI tool for replication administration and testing.

17.3.1 *Testing replication using Repadmin*

Repadmin is a command-line tool supplied with Windows Server that can be used from a domain controller to test and administer replication:

```
PS> repadmin /replsummary
Replication Summary Start Time: 2012-06-30 18:07:18

Beginning data collection for replication summary, this may take awhile:
  .....


Source DSA           largest delta    fails/total %%    error
   DC02                     :16s      0 /   5       0
   SERVER02                 :08s      0 /   5       0


Destination DSA      largest delta    fails/total %%    error
   DC02                     :08s      0 /   5       0
   SERVER02                 :16s      0 /   5       0
```

The output shows the source and destination domain controllers (server02 and server03, respectively) and any failure or errors in replication.

17.3.2 *Testing replication using PowerShell*

Windows Server 2012 introduced PowerShell cmdlets for working with AD replication. You'll start with those cmdlets and then discover a script-based technique that you can use with earlier versions of Windows.

IF YOU HAVE WINDOWS SERVER 2012

Windows Server 2012 introduces a number of cmdlets for working with AD replication. These new cmdlets provide a simple way to investigate replication in your environment.

You can start by discovering the replication partners of a domain controller:

```
PS> Get-ADReplicationConnection


AutoGenerated                        : True
DistinguishedName                    : CN=5c3fe559-f743-4179-8920-065267ad9f3,
                                       CN=NTDS Settings,CN=SERVER02,
                                       CN=Servers,CN=Site1,CN=Sites,
                                       CN=Configuration,DC=Manticore,DC=org
InterSiteTransportProtocol           :
Name                                 : 5c3fe559-f743-4179-8920-5065267ad9f3
ObjectClass                          : nTDSConnection
ObjectGUID                           : fdf94db0-fa2b-473e-b4f7-66f0ad41ea8d
PartiallyReplicatedNamingContexts    : {}
ReplicatedNamingContexts             : {DC=DomainDnsZones,DC=Manticore,DC=org,
                                         DC=ForestDnsZones,DC=Manticore,DC=org,
                                         CN=Schema,CN=Configuration,
                                         DC=Manticore,DC=org,
                                         CN=Configuration,
                                         DC=Manticore,DC=org...}
ReplicateFromDirectoryServer         : CN=NTDS Settings,CN=SERVER03,
                                         CN=Servers,CN=Site1,CN=Sites,
                                         CN=Configuration,DC=Manticore,DC=org
ReplicateToDirectoryServer           : CN=SERVER02,CN=Servers,CN=Site1,
                                         CN=Sites,CN=Configuration,
                                         DC=Manticore,DC=org
ReplicationSchedule                  :
    System.DirectoryServices.ActiveDirectory.ActiveDirectorySchedule
```

You can pick an individual server to test:

```
Get-ADReplicationConnection `
-Filter {ReplicateFromDirectoryServer -like "*server03*"}
```

> **WARNING** The documentation for this cmdlet states that the server name should be used in the filter. It doesn't work! The filter expects to use the full information as shown in the previous example. Use –like to shortcut the data you need to enter.

You can view the up-to-dateness vector tables on your domain controller:

```
Get-ADReplicationUpToDatenessVectorTable -Target server02
```

The cmdlet outputs data like this for every partition that's being replicated:

```
LastReplicationSuccess : 21/06/2013 21:42:38
Partition              : DC=Manticore,DC=org
PartitionGuid          : 1f230c52-a38d-4d47-8748-5f7fad04cf90
Partner                : CN=NTDS Settings,CN=SERVER03,
                         CN=Servers,CN=Site1,CN=Sites,
                         CN=Configuration,DC=Manticore,DC=org
PartnerInvocationId    : 0fd132b3-3983-4f3c-8f8e-4c5bf0170d9f
Server                 : SERVER02.Manticore.org
UsnFilter              : 258264
```

Interestingly, this will show the up-to-dateness vector table for domain controllers that no longer exist in the environment. Domain controllers never forget a replication partner.

A quick test of the replication state can be performed like this:

```
Get-ADReplicationPartnerMetadata -Target server02, server03 `
-PartnerType both
```

The code displays the replication metadata for replication partners. You can show inbound replication or both inbound and outbound. There's a lot of output, but the most useful parts are

```
LastChangeUsn              : 258172
LastReplicationAttempt     : 23/06/2013 10:48:01
LastReplicationResult      : 1722
LastReplicationSuccess     : 21/06/2013 21:42:40
Partition                  : DC=Manticore,DC=org
UsnFilter                  : 258172
```

The dates of the last replication attempt and success can show you immediately if you have replication problems.

You can also test directly for replication failures:

```
Get-ADReplicationFailure -Target server02

FailureCount    : 12
FailureType     : Link
FirstFailureTime : 21/06/2013 21:42:40
LastError       : 1256
Partner         : CN=NTDS Settings,CN=SERVER03,
                  CN=Servers,CN=Site1,CN=Sites,
                  CN=Configuration,DC=Manticore,DC=org
PartnerGuid     : 72ae01e7-e4c1-40ef-91c4-7d85cc94f62f
Server          : SERVER02.Manticore.org
```

The first failure time is useful because you can link that to other activities in the environment.

TRY IT NOW: Test your replication

Use the PowerShell cmdlets to test the replication status between a pair of domain controllers.

IF YOU DON'T HAVE WINDOWS SERVER 2012

Alternatively, if you don't have access to the Windows Server 2012 AD cmdlets, a simple PowerShell script can be used to test replication:

```
$dom = [System.DirectoryServices.ActiveDirectory.Domain]
➥ ::GetCurrentDomain()                                          ❶ Get domain

$dom.FindAllDomainControllers() |                    Discover domain
foreach {                                          ❷ controllers
 $_.Name
 $contextType = [System.DirectoryServices.ActiveDirectory.
 ➥ DirectoryContextType]::DirectoryServer          ❸ Create
                                                      context type
$context = New-Object -TypeName
 ➥  System.DirectoryServices.ActiveDirectory.DirectoryContext
 ➥  -ArgumentList $contextType, $($_.Name)          ❹ Create context

$dc = [System.DirectoryServices.ActiveDirectory.
 ➥  DomainController]::GetDomainController($context)   Get domain
                                                      ❺ controller

$dc.GetAllReplicationNeighbors() |
 select PartitionName, SourceServer, UsnLastObjectChangeSynced,   Discover
 LastSuccessfulSync, LastAttemptedSync, LastSyncMessage,          replication
 ConsecutiveFailureCount                                        ❻ data
}
```

The script starts ❶ by discovering the current domain (it's always easier to run these scripts inside the domain). The domain controllers are discovered, ❷ and a context type ❸ and context ❹ are created for each of them. These parameters are used to get an object representing the domain controller ❺ that uses the `GetAllReplication-Neighbors()` method to discover the replication data ❻. The script produces output of this form for each naming context on each domain controller:

```
PartitionName              : CN=Schema,CN=Configuration,DC=Manticore,DC=org
SourceServer               : SERVER02.Manticore.org
UsnLastObjectChangeSynced  : 1106353
LastSuccessfulSync         : 30/06/2012 18:07:11
LastAttemptedSync          : 30/06/2012 18:07:11
LastSyncMessage            : The operation completed successfully.
ConsecutiveFailureCount    : 0
```

This can produce a lot of output and can take a long time to run if you have a large number of domain controllers. The domain controllers to be tested can be restricted by specifying their names to the script rather than discovering them.

17.3.3 Forcing replication using Repadmin

Repadmin can also be used to force replication using this syntax to synchronize all domain controllers:

```
PS> repadmin /syncall /d:
CALLBACK MESSAGE: The following replication is in progress:
    From: CN=NTDS Settings,CN=DC02,CN=Servers,CN=Site1,CN=Sites,
CN=Configuration,DC=Manticore,DC=org
    To  : CN=NTDS Settings,CN=SERVER02,CN=Servers,CN=Site1,CN=Sites,
CN=Configuration,DC=Manticore,DC=org
CALLBACK MESSAGE: The following replication completed successfully:
    From: CN=NTDS Settings,CN=DC02,CN=Servers,CN=Site1,CN=Sites,
CN=Configuration,DC=Manticore,DC=org
    To  : CN=NTDS Settings,CN=SERVER02,CN=Servers,CN=Site1,CN=Sites,
CN=Configuration,DC=Manticore,DC=org
CALLBACK MESSAGE: SyncAll Finished.
SyncAll terminated with no errors.
```

The messages indicate the start of replication for an individual domain controller and that replication has successfully completed. Any errors or failures in replication would be reported.

17.3.4 Forcing replication with AD Sites and Services

The AD Sites and Services GUI tool can be used to force replication between domain controllers as follows:

1. Open the tool and navigate to Sites > Site name > Servers > Server > NTDS Settings.
2. Right-click the connection object.
3. Choose Replicate Now as shown in figure 17.3.

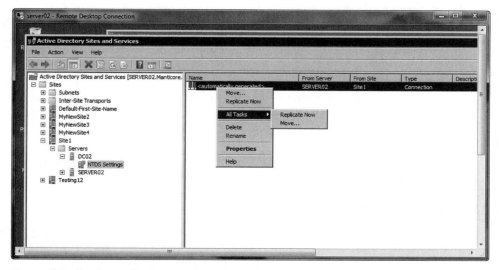

Figure 17.3 Forcing replication to a domain controller

This process has to be repeated for the other Domain Controller in the replication pair.

This concludes your introduction to replication. It's time to practice these techniques in the lab.

17.4 LAB

These tasks can be quite involved if you have a large domain. Just work with a portion of the domain if that helps. The important point is to understand how replication works, not to spend a lot of time on the exercises.

17.4.1 Complete the TRY IT NOW sections

If you haven't already done so, complete the TRY IT NOW exercises. The information is repeated here for your convenience.

TEST DATA IS IDENTICAL

Check the same user account on different domain controllers. Is the information identical? Can you see anything different between the two versions? Make the same check for the membership list of a group.

REPLICATION EXERCISE ON PAPER

Work through a couple of examples, as shown in section 17.1.1, to fix your understanding of the replication process and the interaction between the USN and the high-watermark and up-to-dateness vectors.

VIEW DNS PARTITIONS

Check your DNS configuration to see which partitions your DNS zones use for replication. *Hint:* check the properties of the zone.

DISCOVER BRIDGEHEAD SERVERS

Work through the sites and site links with the AD Sites and Services GUI tool to determine the way data replicates between sites. Draw a diagram similar to figure 17.2 if it helps your visualization. Does the same domain controller function as a bridgehead server for multiple sites links?

TEST YOUR REPLICATION

Use the PowerShell cmdlets to test the replication status between a pair of domain controllers.

17.4.2 Paper replication exercise

Perform a paper replication of an object among three domain controllers based on the example in section 17.1.1.

17.4.3 Application partitions

Determine the application partitions used for your AD-integrated DNS. Use this information to determine the domain controllers to which DNS data is replicated.

17.4.4 Replication times

Using the site link information in your Active Directory, work out how long it takes a change to replicate completely—that is, for the changed data to be on all domain controllers. For the sake of this exercise, assume that intrasite replication is instantaneous.

17.4.5 Partitions

The NCs and partitions available on a domain controller can be viewed at CN = Partitions, CN = Configuration, DC = *your_domain_name* in ADSIEdit. Check the partitions on your domain controllers.

17.4.6 PowerShell cmdlets

Read the help files on the PowerShell replication cmdlets. Test using the cmdlets' other parameters and using the examples as a guideline. *Hint:* use Get-Help and the cmdlet name.

17.5 Ideas for on your own

If you get the chance, fully investigate the replication topology of your domain. Use the lab exercises to help build up that picture. It's also a very good idea to investigate the Directory Service log on the domain controllers. Any replication-related issues or problems will show up in the event logs, giving you some ideas for investigations. In particular, look for events 1388, 1925, 1988, 2042, 2087, 2088, and 2095 from the NTDS KCC and NTDS replication sources. Create a process to regularly check for replication issues.

Your favorite technical forum is also a good place to investigate the sorts of replication problems other people are seeing and may give you some ideas for things to look out for.

In the next chapter we'll investigate trusts between AD domains.

Managing AD trusts 18

Your AD forest is a security boundary that you can use to stop unauthorized access to your environment. If your organization could exist in isolation and not have any interaction with other organizations, security would be simple. Unfortunately, that's not the case in most organizations—potentially there are customers, suppliers, partner organizations, other parts of your organization, and companies that your organization is acquiring or with which they're merging, all requiring access to resources in your AD environment.

The method you'll use to control, manage, and secure this external access is creating AD trusts between your environment and the external environment. You can then control who can gain access to your environment and what they can do once they have that access.

Just as you'd only give someone a key to your front door if you trusted them, you should only allow access to your Active Directory if you trust those accessing it.

> **NOTE** Trust management is an activity that you have to perform in conjunction with the administrator of the other domain. You can create, modify, and delete trusts at your end of the link, but you need the other administrator to perform the same tasks at their end as well.

We haven't discussed trusts yet, so we'll spend a little time covering the concepts behind them. Then we'll move into the trust lifecycle, which starts with creation. Trusts don't require a lot of management once they're created, but you'll need to occasionally verify that they still work and reset them if they have issues. You have the option of using a GUI tool or PowerShell to manage trusts—you'll learn both in this chapter.

> **TIP** Do you know the trusts that have been enabled in your environment? If you don't, use the techniques in this chapter to discover the trusts, document them, and check that they're all still needed.

Trusts eventually come to the end of their useful lives, and you should remove them once that point has been reached. A trust gives external users access to your environment, so leaving redundant trusts in place is a security risk. Finally, a lab to practice the techniques for managing trusts completes the chapter.

18.1 Trust concepts

Before you get to the practical, you need to learn a little theory. We'll cover administering trusts, the three main types of trusts you'll run into, and key terms.

18.1.1 Administering trusts

The first thing you need to know is which tools can be used to administer trusts. Your repertoire gains another GUI tool: AD Domains and Trusts (ADDT). This is the only way to administer trusts.

AD DOMAINS AND TRUSTS

The important part of ADDT is the domain properties dialog, as shown in figure 18.1. You can reach the properties dialog as follows:

1 Open ADDT.
2 Right-click the domain of interest.
3 Choose Properties.

The important tab is the Trusts tab, as shown in figure 18.1.

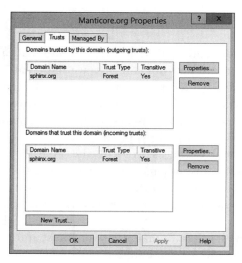

Figure 18.1 Viewing the trust relationships for a domain. The figure shows that a transitive forest trust exists between the manticore.org domain and the sphinx.org domain.

The Trusts tab is the easiest way to view the trusts that exist in your domain. The General tab enables you to set a description for the domain, and the Managed By tab enables you to supply information on who manages the domain, but not to grant them any privileges to do so.

> **TRY IT NOW: AD Domains and Trusts**
>
> Open ADDT and view the information available. If you have multiple domains in your forest, compare the information available.

You'll learn how to use ADDT in the remaining sections of this chapter.

POWERSHELL

Unfortunately, you don't get much in the way of PowerShell cmdlets for administering trusts. There's one cmdlet—`Get-ADTrust`—that you can use to view the trusts connecting to your domain.

   If you want to manage trusts, you need to use the GUI.

> **NOTE** It's possible to write a PowerShell script that uses .NET classes to manage trusts. Working with trusts is an infrequent activity, so it's probably not worth the effort for most organizations.

Just to complicate matters, there are a number of different trust types of which you need to be aware:

- Shortcut trusts
- External trusts
- Forest trusts

We'll cover each one of these in this chapter.

18.1.2 *Shortcut trusts*

When you create another domain in your forest, a two-way trust is automatically created between your original domain and the new domain. If you then create a third domain, it's also trusted. Figure 18.2 shows a forest with a number of domains. The dotted lines between the domains represent the automatically created trusts. These are nicely behaved because you don't have to create them—it's done automatically—and they look after themselves, so there's no work for you.

   The automatically created trusts use the Kerberos protocol (the same protocol you use to log on to the domain) and are transitive, meaning that if domain A trusts domain B (figure 18.2), and domain B trusts domain D, then domain A trusts domain D. The trusts are all two-way, so the relationship among A, B, and D is also true in the reverse direction.

   The practical benefit of this is that all of the domains in your forest automatically trust each other without any effort by you to make it happen.

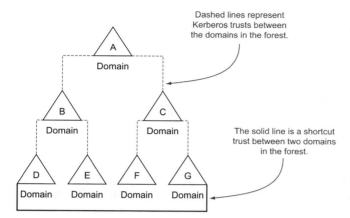

Dashed lines represent Kerberos trusts between the domains in the forest.

The solid line is a shortcut trust between two domains in the forest.

Figure 18.2 A shortcut trust enables direct communication between domains in a forest.

One drawback to a multi-domain forest is that if the domains at the extreme edges of the forest need to communicate, it can take a long time. Consider a user in domain D attempting to access a resource in domain G. The following steps occur:

1 The domain controller (DC) in domain G contacts the DC in domain C...
2 which contacts the DC in domain A...
3 which contacts the DC in domain B...
4 which contacts the DC in domain D to validate the user.

If a significant number of users in domain D need to access resources in domain G, this will generate a lot of traffic and access will be slow. The answer is to create a shortcut trust (the thick, dark, line in figure 18.2), which enables the domain controllers in domain G to communicate directly with those in domain D.

> **TIP**   Creating a trust of any type doesn't automatically confer access privileges to users in the other domain. Those permissions have to be explicitly granted.

Besides speeding up authentication, a shortcut trust also has the lowest security risk of any of the trust types because both ends of the trust are in your forest.

> **TIP**   You should create this type of trust when you have many domains and users are complaining about the time taken to access resources in domains at the other end of the forest. Only create shortcut trusts as you need them, not as a matter of routine.

You only need to worry about shortcut trusts in a forest with a significant number of domains. Creating a trust to a domain outside your forest—called an external trust—is much more common.

18.1.3   *External trusts*

Your organization is unlikely to exist in a vacuum. It's becoming a frequent requirement for administrators to create trusts between their AD environments and other

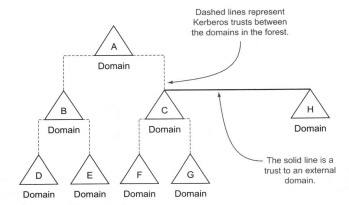

Dashed lines represent Kerberos trusts between the domains in the forest.

The solid line is a trust to an external domain.

Figure 18.3   A trust to an external domain

domains. A common reason for doing this is that your email system is hosted in a separate domain, possibly at a supplier or cloud provider, and you create a trust to that domain. Figure 18.3 illustrates a common situation for external trusts.

The domains in your AD environment are linked by automatically created trusts represented by the dotted lines. You need to enable the users in domain C to access resources in the external domain (H) and vice versa—this is achieved through the external trust. The users in the external domain won't get access to resources in any other domain in your forest. There's no automatic right of access from the remote domain to any other domain including child domains (in this case F and G).

If you have a situation where you need to grant access to multiple domains on one or both sides of the trust, you need to use a forest trust.

18.1.4   Forest trusts

Figure 18.4 shows the situation with two separate forests. You need to grant access to resources in multiple domains on both sides of the trust. You could, in theory, create a large number of external trusts to manage this, but a forest trust is much easier to manage.

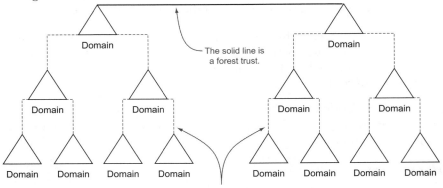

The solid line is a forest trust.

Dashed lines represent Kerberos trusts between the domains in the forest.

Figure 18.4   A forest trust links the root domains of two forests.

The forest trust is created between the root domains of the forest. This one single trust enables you to grant access to resources across the two forests. A common scenario for using this type of trust is in mergers and acquisitions where you have to manage two sets of IT during transition activity.

As with everything in IT, there's some terminology surrounding trusts that needs to be mastered.

18.1.5 Terminology

Trusts have their own set of terminology that you need to be aware of, because it's used extensively in the documentation and can be confusing.

> **TIP** Spend time mastering this terminology. Come back and re-read as required.

TRANSITIVE

In an AD forest, as shown in figure 18.4, the automatically created trusts are *transitive*. This means that if

1 Domain A trusts domain B,
2 and domain B trusts domain C,
3 then domain A trusts domain C.

You can make trusts non-transitive during the creation process, but it'll involve more work on your part in future administration. Be aware of the transitive nature of trusts in your environment so that your security isn't compromised. Check your trusts regularly using ADDT.

ONE-WAY TRUST

A *one-way trust* is created so that domain A trusts domain B but domain B doesn't trust domain A. This is often seen when creating trusts to external domains. A common scenario for using a one-way trust is when your Exchange server is hosted in an external forest. You only need the domain containing your Exchange server to trust the domain with your user accounts. The trust relationship doesn't have to be extended in the other direction.

TWO-WAY TRUST

A *two-way trust* is created so that domain A trusts domain B and domain B simultaneously trusts domain A. This enables users in either domain to be granted access to resources in either domain.

A two-way trust is actually created as two one-way trusts, so it's possible to remove the trust relationship in one direction if required.

TRUST DIRECTION

The way trust directions are described in the documentation and ADDT can be confusing. The two terms that cause the most confusion are *incoming* and *outgoing*. The definitions of these terms are supplied in table 18.1. The table should be used in conjunction with figure 18.1.

Table 18.1   One-way trust directions

Direction	Meaning
Incoming trust	The trust is created in your domain (the trusted domain) and you can access resources in the domain that trusts you (the trusting domain). They can't access resources in your domain.
Outgoing trust	The trust is created in your domain (the trusting domain). Members of the other domain (the trusted domain) can access resources in your domain but you can't access resources in their domain.

These terms apply to external trusts and to forest trusts.

Now that you know how to view the existing trusts and understand the theory behind trusts, let's look at creating trusts.

18.2   Creating trusts

Before you can create a trust between two domains, there are some prerequisites you must meet:

- There must be network connectivity between the domains.
- There must be DNS forwarding in place so that each domain can perform DNS lookups on the other domain. (You learned how to create a conditional forwarder in section 15.2.3.)
- Both forests need to be at Windows Server 2003 forest-functional level or above to create a forest trust.
- Accounts with administrative privileges must be available. Either you have an account in both domains, or you're in contact with the administrator of the remote domain.

Creating a trust is a two-stage process. First you create the trust in your domain, and then create it in the other domain.

18.2.1   Create a trust in your domain

Creating the trust in your domain can be accomplished by following these steps:

1 Open AD Domains and Trusts.
2 Right-click the domain name.
3 Choose Properties.
4 Choose the Trusts tab as shown in figure 18.5.

Figure 18.5   Trusts tab from the domain properties in ADDT

TIP Ensure that exactly the same options are selected at each stage, as when creating your side of the trust. Sending screenshots to the remote administrator may help.

1 Click New Trust….
2 Click Next to skip the New Trust Wizard Welcome page.
3 Type the name of the forest or domain to which you're creating a trust, as shown in figure 18.6. You can use a NetBIOS or DNS name for domains but only a DNS name for a forest trust. I recommend standardizing on DNS names.
4 Click Next.
5 Choose to create an External Trust or a Forest Trust as shown in figure 18.7.
6 Click Next.

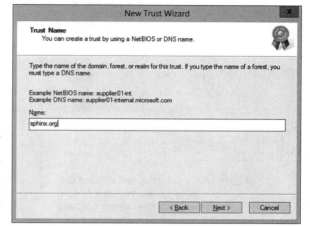

Figure 18.6 Supplying a name for the external domain or forest. Standardize on DNS names rather than NetBIOS names. A realm is similar to a Windows domain but is a set of Unix/Linux computers that use Kerberos for authentication.

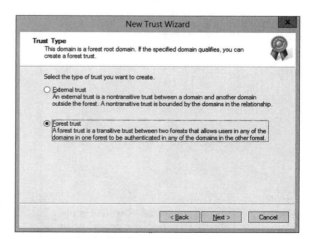

Figure 18.7 Selecting the trust type. In this case, a forest trust is selected.

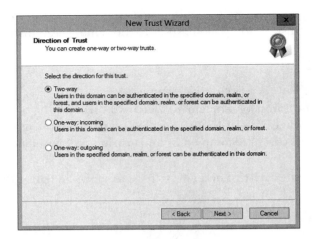

Figure 18.8   Select the trust direction. A two-way trust is the default.

7   Choose the trust direction as shown in figure 18.8.

8   Click Next.

9   Choose the side of the trust to create as shown in figure 18.9. Usually, it'll be your domain only.

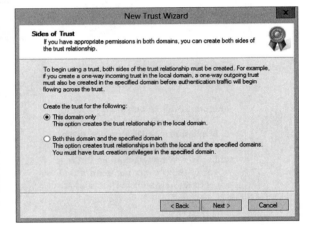

Figure 18.9   Selecting the sides of the trust. In this case, the trust is only created in the current domain. You need appropriate credentials in the other domain if you want to create both sides simultaneously.

10   Click Next.

11   Choose the trust authentication level as shown in figure 18.10.

12   Click Next.

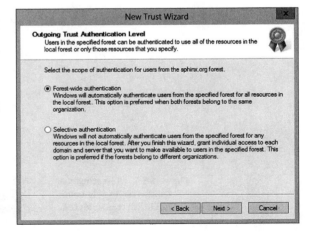

Figure 18.10   Controlling the authentication level. Be careful when granting forest-wide authentication.

13 If you're only creating one side of the trust, you'll be asked for a password. Supply and confirm the trust password. Make sure you remember this because it'll be needed when the other side of the trust is created. I recommend making this a strong password.

14 If you're creating both sides of the trust, you'll need to supply credentials for the remote domain.

15 Click Next.

16 Review the settings.

17 Click Next.

18 You'll see a message that the trust relationship was successfully created.

19 Click Next to configure the trust.

20 You'll be asked to confirm the outgoing trust. You can only do this if the other side of the trust has been created.

21 Click Next.

22 You'll be asked to confirm the incoming trust. You can only do this if the other side of the trust has been created.

23 Click Next.

24 Click Finish to close the wizard.

TRY IT NOW: Create a trust

Use the procedure in section 18.2.1 to create a trust.

Now it's time to create the other side of the trust.

18.2.2 *Create a trust in a remote domain*

Creating the trust in the remote domain follows exactly the same procedure listed in the previous section, except for the name of the forest or domain that's supplied. The remote administrator has to use your domain or forest name.

There are a couple of points to note:

- Remember to send the correct information, preferably screenshots, to the administrator in the remote domain.
- The same password must be used on both sides of the trust.

At this stage, the remote administrator can confirm the outgoing trust. The incoming trust can only be confirmed if the remote administrator has access to an account with administrative privileges in your domain.

TRY IT NOW: Create the remote side of the trust

Use the procedure in section 18.2.2 to finish creating the trust.

18.3   Managing trusts

Trusts usually require very little in the way of management once they're functioning. If you suspect that a trust is showing problems, you should perform a validation. If the validation shows any problems, you can reset the trust password. If that doesn't work, you'll need to remove the trust and recreate it.

18.3.1 Verifying trusts

You can verify your trusts using ADDT:

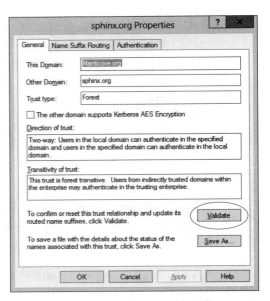

1 Open ADDT.
2 Right-click your domain.
3 Choose Properties.
4 Choose the Trusts tab.
5 Choose the trust to test.
6 Click Properties as shown in figure 18.11.
7 Click Validate (circled in figure 18.11).
8 You'll be asked if you wish to validate the incoming trust. If so, you need to supply credentials for the remote domain.
9 If you only validate the outgoing trust, you get a message: "The outgoing trust has been validated. It's in place and active."
10 If you also validate the incoming trust, the message reads, "The trust has been validated. It's in place and active."

Figure 18.11   Trust properties. The General tab supplies information on the trust direction and the nature of its transitivity and also enables you to validate the trust.

In both cases, you're asked if you need to update the name suffix routing information. This is only required if you've added new child domains to your forest. So answer no.

> **TRY IT NOW: Validate the trust**
>
> Use the procedure in section 18.3.1 to validate the trust.

18.3.2 Resetting trusts

Follow the instructions in the previous section to validate the trust. If you have problems validating the trust—usually an error message stating the remote domain controller can't be contacted—you'll be prompted to change the password on the trust.

You'll need to change the password at both ends of the trust for it to work. The easiest way to do this is to perform the validation at both ends and reset the password (to the same value) when prompted.

NOTE You can only reset the trust if the validation attempt fails.

The last step in the trust lifecycle is removing the trust.

18.3.3 Removing trusts

All objects in Active Directory have a lifecycle, and trusts are no exception. There are many possible reasons for needing to remove a trust including

- The external domain or forest is no longer trusted due to changing business requirements.
- Reorganization or migration of Active Directory reduces the number of domains, making the shortcut trust superfluous.
- Application changes remove the need for a trust; for example, the application is now accessed as a web service.

TIP Keeping the number of forests and domains in your organization to a minimum will reduce the need for trusts.

Removing trusts is also performed through ADDT:

1 Open ADDT.
2 Right-click your domain.
3 Choose Properties.
4 Choose the Trusts tab.
5 Choose the trust to remove.
6 Click Remove.
7 You'll be asked if you want to remove the trust from the local domain only or from both domains.
8 If you select both domains, you'll need to supply credentials for the remote domain.
9 Click OK.
10 You'll be asked to confirm—click Yes.
11 The trust will be removed.

> **TRY IT NOW: Remove the trust you've created**
>
> Use the procedure in section 18.3.3 to remove the trust. Ensure you've removed the trust from both domains.

You've completed this lesson on trusts. It's time for a quick lab.

18.4   LAB

This lab gives you an opportunity to practice working with trusts.

18.4.1   *Complete the TRY IT NOW exercises*

If you haven't done so already, please complete the TRY IT NOW exercises from this chapter.

AD DOMAINS AND TRUSTS

Open ADDT and view the information available. If you have multiple domains in your forest, compare the information available.

CREATE A TRUST

Use the procedure in section 18.2.1 to create a trust.

CREATE THE REMOTE SIDE OF THE TRUST

Use the procedure in section 18.2.2 to finish creating the trust.

VALIDATE THE TRUST

Use the procedure in section 18.3.1 to validate the trust.

REMOVE THE TRUST YOU'VE CREATED

Use the procedure in section 18.3.3 to remove the trust. Ensure you've removed the trust from both domains.

18.4.2   *Repeat the exercises*

Repeat the TRY IT NOW exercises, working through the different trust types. Try creating both sides of the trust simultaneously.

18.5   *Ideas for on your own*

Once your trust is working, there isn't much to do, though you need to consider trusts in your AD maintenance plans. I recommend creating a process to periodically review the trusts in your environment, validate if they're still required, and remove any unnecessary trusts. Perform the review on a monthly basis unless your organization needs a more frequent review.

Unfortunately, Active Directory won't report a problem with a trust in a direct manner. The first inkling of problems will be help desk calls. Frequent checking should help you catch the problem first.

In the next chapter we'll look at extending your troubleshooting skills.

Part 4

Maintenance and Troubleshooting

This final section of the book is concerned with keeping your Active Directory working. It's a fact of life that things go wrong, and when they do you need to be able to find the cause and put it right. Chapter 19 provides a set of troubleshooting techniques to help diagnose the causes of problems.

You saw some user-related troubleshooting in chapter 5. Chapter 19 builds on those techniques and supplies tests you can perform based on what you leaned in parts 2 and 3 of this book.

Ideally, you want to spot trouble before it affects the users. This is the concept of monitoring and maintenance. Chapter 20 shows how to apply what you've learned so that you can proactively test your AD. This will enable you to spot and fix problems before they reach your users.

Chapter 21 provides a brief overview of technologies that are related to Active Directory. You'll meet these technologies in your career as an AD administrator and having a starting point will be useful when you need to investigate them in depth. Chapter 21 also contains your final exam.

The book ends with chapter 22 looking ahead to cloud computing.

Troubleshooting your AD

Wouldn't life be wonderful if you could set things up and they just ran without problems? In reality, things go wrong and you have to fix them. And troubleshooting, unfortunately, is a never-ending part of the administrator's role. Even after 25 years in IT, I still spend part of every week troubleshooting. Sometimes they're my problems, and sometimes I'm helping someone else troubleshoot their problems. Troubleshooting, like the tides, will always be with us.

This is your second round of troubleshooting in this book. The reason for leaving it until nearly the end is that you needed to learn the facets of Active Directory covered in parts 2 and 3. This chapter will cover a number of troubleshooting situations: user problems, computer-related problems, and replication problems. In some cases, the answer is contained in one of the earlier chapters; therefore, you'll be referred to the relevant chapter rather than repeating the information here.

TIP It can sometimes be difficult to categorize problems. The divisions I've used in this chapter give a sensible structure to the chapter. You'll notice there's significant overlap in the use of the techniques—for instance, a computer-related test can also be used in troubleshooting what is apparently a user-related problem. Your troubleshooting techniques need to span all scenarios.

If you cast your mind back to chapter 5, you learned about troubleshooting some of the common problems associated with users and groups, including

- Expired passwords
- Resetting passwords
- Locked accounts
- Incorrect group membership

These issues are directly related to the state of the user account. Unfortunately, this isn't the full list of things that can go wrong for your users. The first section of this chapter deals with some of the other problems that you'll come across, including

- Logon problems
- Logon scripts
- User rights

WARNING It's not possible to cover all potential scenarios in this book. I recommend you make notes on new troubleshooting scenarios as you come across them so that you can refer to them in future troubleshooting situations.

Computer-related problems tend to be fewer in number, but can have an equally large impact. Section 19.2 deals with this type of problem.

Active Directory itself doesn't demonstrate many problems, but you may come across replication-related problems. You've already seen some of the techniques for investigating replication in chapter 17. The final section of this chapter builds on those techniques.

A lab section rounds out the chapter, so you get the opportunity to practice the troubleshooting techniques.

WARNING In some of the cases, you'll only be able to see how things look when everything is functioning normally. It can be very difficult, if not impossible, to intentionally trigger some of the situations. If you know what things should look like, it'll aid you in spotting when something is wrong.

Let's get started with those troublesome users.

19.1   *User problems*

User problems that are due to Active Directory are usually related to logon issues or permission issues of one form or another. You already learned in chapter 5 how to investigate and deal with problems that are related to the user account. In this section you'll expand on that knowledge and look at logon-related problems, problems caused by logon scripts, and rights-related problems.

19.1.1   *Logon problems: Many users*

In terms of scale, logon problems break down into two main groups:

- Large numbers of users can't log on.
- One or a few users can't log on.

Your approach will be different depending on the apparent scale of the problem. Sometimes what seems like a problem affecting a small group of users escalates because you picked up the problem reported by the people getting into work early.

If you get reports of large numbers of users not being able to log on, the possible causes could include

1 Network problems are preventing users from connecting to a domain controller.
2 A domain controller has failed. This could be a hardware failure, or one of the required services may not be running.
3 A global catalog isn't available for similar reasons to the second cause.

NETWORK PROBLEMS

If you suspect a network problem, you need to involve your network folks to resolve the problem. Giving them as much information as possible will aid their troubleshooting process. This information could include

- Numbers of users and departments affected
- Location of users: building, floor, and area within floor
- Timeframe of problem developing

A FAILING DOMAIN CONTROLLER OR GLOBAL CATALOG

Determining if a domain controller or global catalog has failed can involve a number of tests. While I refer just to domain controllers here for simplicity, these tests apply equally to domain controllers or global catalogs. One thing to note, however, is that if you're using Universal groups (all Exchange distribution lists are Universal groups) and a global catalog isn't available, your users won't be able to log on.

FIRST TEST: PING THE DOMAIN CONTROLLER

The obvious test is to ping the domain controller. Open a PowerShell prompt and type this command:

```
Test-Connection -ComputerName server02
```

The system should return four ping tests by default. Check to see that the IPv4 and IPv6 address information is available. Turning off IPv6 on the later Windows server operating systems can have unpredictable consequences.

SECOND TEST: MAKE SURE THE REQUIRED SERVICES ARE RUNNING

Assuming you can ping the domain controller, test whether the required services are running.

> **TIP** Testing the required services is covered in depth in section 20.2 in chapter 20. Many of the tests in that chapter can also be used for troubleshooting.

A good simple test is to ensure that the AD Domain Services service is running:

```
Get-Service -Name NTDS -ComputerName server02
```

AD Domain Services is the display name of the service and NTDS is the actual service name. A status of Running is good. Anything else indicates a problem.

Alternately, you may prefer to use the `Get-Service` cmdlet to return data for all services and inspect the results for anomalies.

THIRD TEST: PERFORM AN AD LOOKUP

You can test performing an AD lookup as follows:

```
Get-ADUser –Identity "richard" –Server server02
```

If things are working correctly, you'll get the required results; this test determines that not only is your domain controller working, but it's returning the correct data when queried. If the domain controller can't be reached, you'll receive an error message indicating the server doesn't exist, is currently down, or doesn't have Active Directory installed.

A similar test can be performed by attempting to connect to a specific domain controller using ADUC (see section 12.3.2 for instructions on changing domain controllers if you can't remember how to do it).

FOURTH TEST: CHECK SRV RECORDS IN DNS

If the domain controller is available but the users can't find it because the correct SRV records in DNS aren't available, you'll need to test and correct that issue as shown in section 19.2.2.

FIFTH TEST: RDP TO DOMAIN CONTROLLER

One final test would be to attempt to create a remote desktop connection (RDP) to the domain controller. You can then investigate the system directly.

TRY IT NOW: Test domain controller

Perform the tests in this section against one or more domain controllers in your environment. Take careful notice of the results and record if necessary. If you know what to expect, you can spot the problems much more easily.

Repeat the tests against a global catalog. Are there any differences?

The other end of the spectrum is when one, or only a few, users can't log on.

19.1.2 *One user can't log on*

If a single user can't log on, your immediate response should be to perform the tests in chapter 5:

- Expired account
- Expired password
- Disable account
- Locked out

TIP   If you have a process to automatically disable inactive accounts, you may occasionally inadvertently disable a required account. This could happen in the case of a user who has been absent due to a long-term illness.

Assuming those tests are passed, what else could cause the problem?

One possibility is that the user's computer isn't connecting to the network correctly. Does it have the correct IP address? You could ask the user to run `ipconfig` for you, but you'd most likely have to talk them through the process. You can find the computer's IP address from the comfort of your own desk using a little bit of PowerShell:

```
Get-WmiObject -Class Win32_NetworkAdapterConfiguration `
 -Filter "IPEnabled=$true" -ComputerName testpc27 |
select IPAddress, IPSubnet, DefaultIPGateway,
DNSServerSearchOrder, DHCPEnabled
```

If you don't get the expected results, you'll need to investigate and remediate the networking configuration on the PC.

Other tests include

- Checking if the PC is a member of the domain and that the computer account is valid. The tests in section 19.2.1 can be used to perform these checks.
- Checking that the PC can find a domain controller. Does the IP address match with a site in Active Directory? Is the domain controller advertising the correct SRV records?

> **TRY IT NOW: Test PC**
>
> Perform the tests in this section against one or more PCs in your environment. Take careful notice of the results and record if necessary. If you know what to expect, you can spot the problems much more easily.

In this section you've discovered how to investigate user-related logon issues. When a user logs on to the domain, a script known as a logon script will often be configured to run. Logon scripts are a known cause of problems.

19.1.3 *Logon scripts*

Logon scripts have traditionally been used to supply configuration data to a user, such as printer mappings and drive mappings. Most, if not all, of the functions of logon scripts can be performed by using the Preference options in GPOs, as you learned in chapters 8 and 9. Many organizations still use logon scripts for historical reasons, so knowing how to troubleshoot them is beneficial.

Users can experience problems due to logon scripts. For instance

- The user doesn't have a logon script configured.
- The user has the wrong logon script configured. (This is especially prevalent in organizations with departmental-level logon scripts where users move departments.)
- There's an error in the logon script.

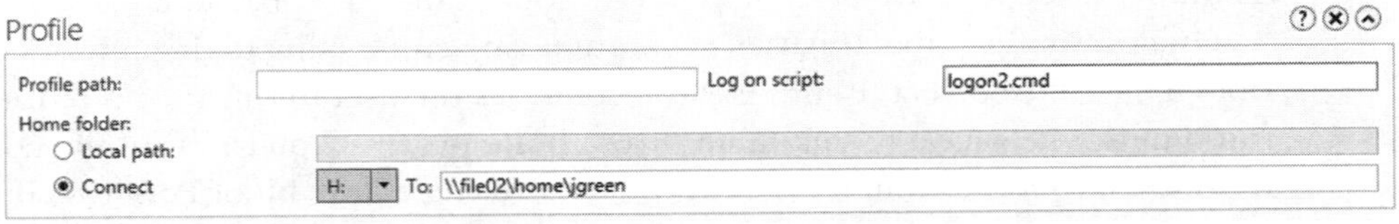

Figure 19.1   User Profile properties showing logon script and home drive

If you suspect that the user isn't getting the correct logon script, check what Active Directory thinks it should be, and then check the contents of the logon script file on the domain controller to which the user is authenticating.

FIRST TEST: CHECK LOGON SCRIPT SETTINGS IN ACTIVE DIRECTORY

The first step is to investigate the logon script settings for the user. Logon scripts can be allocated to users via the Profile tab of the user properties in ADUC or the Profile section of the user properties in ADAC (figure 19.1).

You can view the logon script allocated to a user through ADUC, ADAC, or this PowerShell code:

```
Get-ADUser -Identity "jgreen" -Properties scriptpath
```

The name of the logon script will be shown in the `scriptpath` property.

> **TIP** `scriptpath` isn't one of the standard properties returned by `Get-ADUser`. If you're returning multiple nonstandard properties or just investigating a user's configuration, use `-Properties *` to return all properties.

You can also allocate logon scripts through a GPO. You need to check which is used in your environment.

> **TIP** It's possible to allocate logoff scripts through a GPO, but in my experience, this is rarely done.

If a logon script is set, the next step is to check that it exists.

SECOND TEST: CHECK LOGON SCRIPT EXISTS

Logon scripts are stored in the SYSVOL share on domain controllers, which by default is located at C:\Windows\SYSVOL\sysvol (the case change is correct).

If there's any doubt about the SYSVOL location, use

```
Get-WmiObject -Class Win32_Share -ComputerName server02
```

This code will enumerate the shares on the domain controller supplying the name, description, and file system path. In the C:\Windows\SYSVOL\sysvol folder, you'll find a folder with the same name as your domain, which contains two additional folders as shown in figure 19.2.

Check the scripts folder to determine whether the logon script exists.

The SYSVOL share is replicated between domain controllers. If the logon script isn't on the domain controller, investigate AD replication to determine if there's a

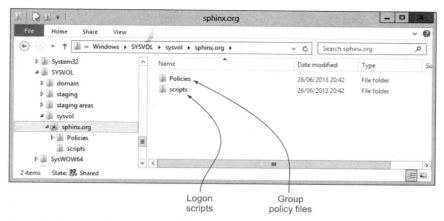

Figure 19.2   Contents of the sysvol folder on a domain controller. The domain name in this example is sphinx.org.

problem preventing the logon script from being replicated. If the logon script is present, the third step is to determine if it's correct.

THIRD STEP: CHECK LOGON SCRIPT CONTENTS

You'd usually write logon scripts as batch files, or occasionally as VBScript files. It's possible to write logon scripts in PowerShell, but it requires more work. I recommend using GPO preferences instead.

Open the script in Notepad and check that the script is correct. Especially check that the network drive and printer mappings are correct.

> **TRY IT NOW: Logon scripts**
>
> Find the SYSVOL share on your domain controllers. It's set when the domain controller is created.
>
> Investigate the logon script allocated to a user in your environment. Use ADAC, ADUC, and PowerShell to find the script name. Open the script on a domain controller to view the contents.

Rights and permissions can have an adverse impact on your users if they aren't configured correctly.

19.1.4   User rights

You saw in chapter 5 that user rights to resources are granted through groups. You give the group the rights and permissions and add the user to the group. If a user can't access a file share, application, or device (such as a printer), your first check should be making sure that the user is in the correct group.

If the user is in the right group, the next step is to check out the group's policies. GPOs can also grant or deny rights that affect users directly or indirectly. In the

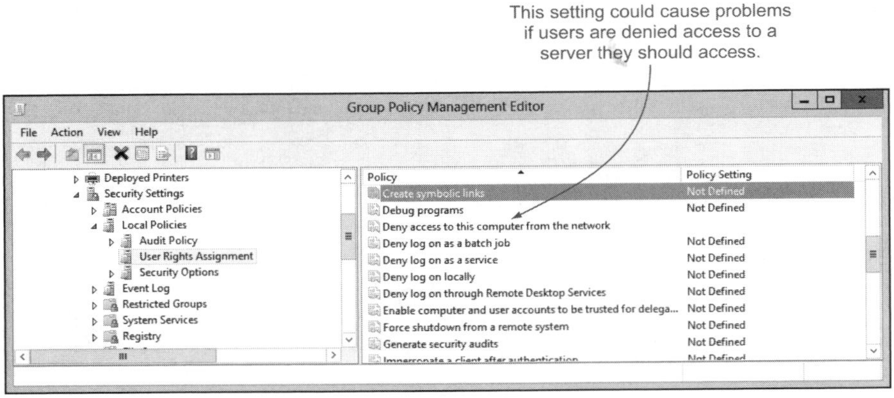

This setting could cause problems
if users are denied access to a
server they should access.

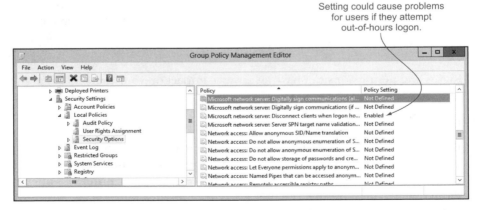

Figure 19.3   Checking the User Rights Assignment. If the Policy Setting says anything but "Not Defined," you should check what has been set.

Computer Configuration > Policies > Windows Settings > Security Settings > Local Policies > User Rights Assignment section, you'll find a number of settings that control what users can do or access, as shown in figure 19.3.

These settings will usually be used in the GPOs applied to servers. Some examples are

- Deny access to this computer from the network. If your user is a member of a group denied access, they won't be able to connect to the computer. This setting is shown in figure 19.3.
- Take ownership of files and other objects. If a user is granted this permission and changes the permissions on a file or folder, other users may be locked out of the file.

The Computer Configuration > Policies > Security Settings > Security Options section can also cause issues if misconfigured, as shown in figure 19.4.

Setting could cause problems
for users if they attempt
out-of-hours logon.

Figure 19.4   Checking the Security Options. If users are disconnected when logon hours have expired, they won't be able to log on outside of the defined hours.

For instance

- *Microsoft network server*—Disconnect clients when logon hours expire. If you set the hours in which users can log on and then set this on the server, their sessions will be disconnected at the end of their logon hours and they may lose work. This setting is explicitly shown in figure 19.4.
- *System settings: optional subsystems*—Defines the subsystems that are needed to support your applications. If a required subsystem isn't allowed, it'll stop your application from working.

These may seem not to be user-related issues, but the problem will be reported by your users as an inability to connect to the particular server or application.

Your troubleshooting for this type of problem consists of running the Resultant Set of Policies wizard on the Group Policy Management Console (see section 9.3) for the user and computer. You may need to run the wizard in two batches—one for the user and one for the computer—to discover the full suite of settings.

> **TRY IT NOW: User rights**
>
> Use the Resultant Set of Policies wizard to determine the settings for one or more users against one or more servers. If you see any problems, investigate further and try applying a filter to the GPOs so they don't affect users. Work through the GPOs removing the filter from each in turn until the GPO causing the problem is discovered. Check each setting in the GPO by reading the explanation until you find the setting causing the problem.

TIP Don't run the wizard against a domain controller, because ordinary users aren't allowed direct access to domain controllers.

After user settings, computers are the next biggest area likely to cause problems.

19.2 *Computer-related problems*

One of the most common computer problems related to Active Directory that you'll see is a user not being able to log on. In chapter 6 you saw that there's a secure channel between a domain controller and a computer. The password on the secure channel is reset automatically every 30 days. If the password gets out of step on the machine and the domain controller, your user won't be able to log on. Reset the computer account using the techniques in chapter 6.

Other computer-related problems include

- Logon workstation restrictions, which are restrictions on the computers a user can use
- Failure to discover a domain controller

We'll cover both of these issues in more detail next because they're a bit more involved.

19.2.1 *Logon workstation restrictions*

Creating restrictions on who can use a machine and for how long is a response to potential security issues. Implementing these restrictions can cause you a headache when troubleshooting logon issues if you forget to check them. Everything will seem fine, but users won't be able to log on.

LIMITING THE WORKSTATIONS USERS CAN LOG ON TO

The default is that users can log on to any workstation in the domain. There are scenarios where you might want to restrict the machines that a group of users can use. Some examples include

- A lab where you want people to only log on to machines in the lab
- A training area to which people are restricted until they've mastered your organization's procedures
- A confidential project where you want to ensure that the data is only accessed from specific machines

Unfortunately, you have to set the restrictions directly on the user account. You can restrict users to one or several machines. You can enter this information via the Log On To link on the Account section of the user properties in ADAC as shown in figure 19.5.

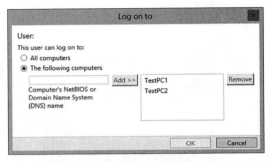

Figure 19.5   Setting workstation logon restrictions. A similar dialog is available through the Log On To button on the Account tab in ADUC.

If you have to perform this action for a number of users, use the PowerShell cmdlet:

```
Set-ADUser -Identity jgreen -LogonWorkstations "Test01,Test02,Test03"
```

The workstations are presented as a string, with the individual names separated by a comma. If you think a problem may be related to workstation restrictions, you can perform this test:

```
Get-ADUser -Identity jgreen -Properties userWorkstations
```

LIMITING THE AMOUNT OF TIME USERS CAN BE LOGGED IN FOR

A similar restriction is available for the hours users can log on. You may want to restrict certain users; for instance, temporary staff who should only be able to log on during business hours.

> **NOTE**   A script for setting logon hours is available in the download code for this chapter. It's called `set-logonhours.ps1`.

You can test for logon hour restrictions like this:

```
Get-ADUser -Identity jgreen -Properties logonHours
```

If the property is set, you should either view the data in the GUI tools as shown in figure 19.6, or run the `get-logonhours.ps1` script from the download code.

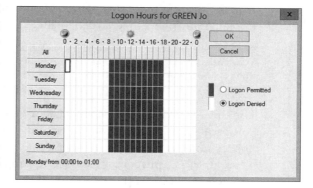

Figure 19.6   A user with restricted logon hours. This user can only log on between 08:00 and 18:00.

A very security-conscious organization may prohibit weekend logons as well.

> **TRY IT NOW: Logon restrictions**
>
> Examine your user population to determine if any restrictions have been set. If you find any restrictions, are they really needed?
>
> *Hint:* use `Get-ADUser` with `-Filter*` instead of an identity.
>
> Is there a way to show just the users who have the restrictions?

Before your users can logon, your computers have to contact the domain and authenticate themselves with a domain controller. If this fails, your users will experience problems.

19.2.2 *Failure to discover a domain controller*

Domain controllers provide authentication and authorization services to your users. If a user's computer can't contact a domain controller, those services won't be available. There are a couple of ways to deal with a computer that can't discover its domain controller: you can confirm that the IP is correct, and you can test the SRV records.

CONFIRM THE IP ADDRESS

If the IP address of your machine isn't on the correct subnet, it won't find the domain controller and your users will have problems. In section 19.1.1 you learned how to find the IP address of a machine. Put that knowledge to use by testing the machine's IP address and comparing it to the AD Subnets defined for the AD Site the machine should be in.

TEST THE SRV RECORDS

Your workstations use SRV records in DNS to discover their domain controller. Section 15.4.2 explained and demonstrated the SRV records for a domain. If you're having trouble locating the domain controller, you want to first view the SRV records for the domain controllers in a particular site:

```
Get-DnsServerResourceRecord -ZoneName _msdcs.Manticore.org `          ← Get resource
-ComputerName server02 -RRType SRV |            ← Supply DNS        ❶ record
where HostName -like "*Site1*" |  ←┐            ❷ server name
Format-Table -AutoSize -Wrap      ❸ Filter on AD Site
```

Use the `Get-DnsServerResourceRecord` cmdlet ❶ from Windows Server 2012. When you create the domain controller and install DNS during the creation process, the _msdcs zone is automatically created for you. This zone hosts the SRV records. The `-ComputerName` property ❷ is used to supply the DNS server to test. Filter the records on the `HostName` property ❸. Use `-like` because you're performing a partial match on the site name. The data is formatted to make it readable on your screen.

Each domain controller should have records with a `HostName` of this form:

```
_kerberos._tcp.Site1._sites.dc
_ldap._tcp.Site1._sites.dc
```

In addition, a global catalog should have a record with a `HostName` like this:

```
_ldap._tcp.Site1._sites.gc
```

If the correct SRV records aren't present for a domain controller, you could try a number of things:

1   Restart the domain controller—the SRV records should be regenerated. A standard Windows restart is all that's required. Just make sure your users are aware it's happening.
2   Delete any existing SRV records for the domain controller, allow replication to remove the records from the other domain controllers, and restart the domain controller to force SRV record regeneration (see section 15.3.3).
3   Manually add the SRV records to DNS (see section 15.3.2, but use the Create Other Records option).

> **TRY IT NOW: SRV records**
>
> Use the code in section 19.2.2 to test the SRV records in one of your AD sites.
>
> Compare the results from multiple DNS servers. Do they match? What could be the problem if they don't match?

If the domain controllers are available and contactable, the replication has probably failed.

19.3   *Replication*

Replication between domain controllers should take care of itself once it has been properly configured. However, other issues—for instance, networking problems or configuration changes made in error—may prevent replication from working properly. Your users will experience problems if replication doesn't happen. This could be due to password changes, account modifications, group membership changes, and even GPOs not replicating correctly.

There are two strands to investigating replication: the data itself and the event logs on the domain controllers.

> **TIP** You can simulate replication problems in your test environment by taking a domain controller offline. Don't do this in a production environment.

You saw how to investigate replication in chapter 17, so we'll start by building on those techniques.

19.3.1 *Replication data*

Active Directory can supply information on replication success or failure at a domain controller level. There are third-party tools, such as those from Quest, that will monitor your whole Active Directory and determine if you have problems, but they're beyond the price range of many organizations. The information in this section will enable you to discover replication problems.

Chapter 17 showed you some techniques for testing replication. Those techniques can be extended to give a troubleshooting process that you can use repeatedly. You need to start by identifying the domain controllers in the AD site to which the users or computers having problems belong.

GET DOMAIN CONTROLLERS IN AN AD SITE

Unfortunately, relating a domain controller to an AD site isn't as straightforward as you might hope. You can work around the limitations of the cmdlets like this:

```
Get-ADComputer -SearchBase "OU=Domain Controllers,DC=Manticore,DC=org" `       Get computer
-Filter * |                                                                    objects ❶
foreach {
  Get-ADDomainController -Identity $_.DNSHostName                              Get domain
  } |                                                                          controller ❸
  where Site -eq 'Site1'        ❹ Filter by AD site
```

Pipe into foreach ❷

Get the AD computer objects in the OU named Domain Controllers ❶. Pipe the results into `foreach` ❷ and get the corresponding AD domain controller object ❸ using the `DNSHostName` property of the computer object to identify the particular domain controller you want. You can perform a final filter on the AD site name (using `where`) ❹ to restrict the results to the site you want.

Now that you know the domain controllers in your site, you can test to see if they have replication problems.

TEST REPLICATION

One of the great strengths of PowerShell is that you can easily build up a complicated processing sequence in stages. Building on the code you used to find the domain controllers in an AD site, you'll extend the script to also test for replication failures, as shown in the following listing.

Listing 19.1   Testing replication failure

```
Get-ADComputer -SearchBase "OU=Domain Controllers,DC=Manticore,DC=org" `
 -Filter * |                                          ◁─┐   Get AD computer
foreach {                                               ❶   objects
  Get-ADDomainController -Identity $_.DNSHostName       ◁─┐  Get domain
 } |                                                      ❷  controllers
 where Site -eq 'Site1' |          ◁──❸ Filter of AD site
 foreach {
    if (Test-Connection -ComputerName $psitem.Name -Quiet -Count 1){
      Get-ADReplicationFailure -Target server02        ◁─┐  Test for replication
    }                                                    ❹  failure
    else {
      Write-Warning -Message "Cannot contact $($psitem.Name)"  ◁─┐  Warn if can't
    }                                                            ❺  connect
 }
```

Technically, this listing is a single line of PowerShell! As you read through the listing, notice that the individual commands are all linked into a single pipeline. Start by retrieving the list on domain controllers from the OU named Domain Controllers ❶. It's possible to put domain controllers into other OUs, but this isn't recommended, because it means that you have to apply domain controller-related GPOs multiple times, and some of the utilities only work if the domain controller is in the default location.

The DNSHostName property of each domain controller is used in Get-ADDomain-Controller ❷. A filter ❸ is applied to restrict the domain controllers passed for further processing to only those in the AD site you're testing.

Each domain controller in the site is tested to see if it can be contacted using Test-Connection. If the connection attempt succeeds, Get-ADReplicationFailure is used to test the domain controller for any failures ❹. If the connection attempt fails, a warning message ❺ is displayed on the screen.

> **TRY IT NOW: Replication testing**
>
> Use listing 19.1 to test for replication failures on domain controllers in an AD site in your organization.
>
> What data is returned if there are no failures associated with a particular domain controller?

The last source of troubleshooting information is the event logs on your domain controllers.

19.3.2 *Event logs*

All Windows machines have a set of event logs that are installed with the operating system. When you add roles to a server, extra event logs are created. On a Windows Server 2012 domain controller, these extra logs can include

- AD web services
- DFS replication
- Directory service
- DNS server
- File replication service
- Key management service

NOTE You don't access the log files directly (they're found in the C:\Windows\System32\Winevt\Logs folder). Use the PowerShell cmdlets discussed below to interrogate the event logs.

The log name is indicative of the aspect of the system on which the log is reporting. In addition, the Security log will record the logon, logoff, and privilege assignments, together with any auditing records you've configured the system to collect.

TIP The Security log will contain thousands of records—just starting and logging onto my test domain controller generated 737 records! Think about how you want to filter the data before querying the log so that you reduce the time the system takes to respond.

These logs are the original Windows-style logs. There's a whole suite of additional logs in the format introduced with Windows Server 2008, but they won't give you any additional information.

TYPES OF EVENT LOGS

Event log entries can be for an error, a warning, or information. There's a hierarchy of seriousness regarding these, as follows:

1. *Error messages*—The system has noticed that something has gone wrong. Investigate these messages.
2. *Warning messages*—The system is giving you a warning that something is happening that may not be beneficial or that may impact your system.
3. *Informational messages*—The system is telling you that something is happening. It probably isn't anything to worry about, but I recommend becoming familiar with the informational messages your domain controllers produce so you know what's normal.

`FailureAudit` and `SuccessAudit` entries are also possible, but they're unlikely to be as useful in troubleshooting as the other three types.

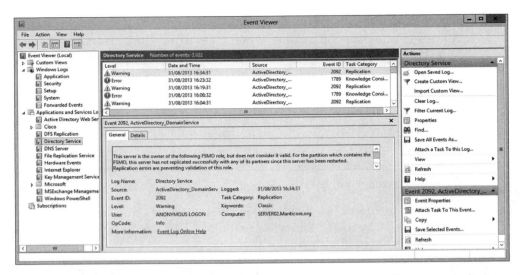

Figure 19.7   Using the Event Viewer GUI tool. The top of the center pane supplies an opportunity to visibly inspect the entries for problems. Each entry has to be selected individually to read the message.

The `Get-Eventlog` PowerShell cmdlet is your key to investigating the event logs. You could also use the Event Viewer GUI tool as shown in figure 19.7, but you'll be stepping through individual records and the filtering isn't as easy.

The `Get-EventLog` cmdlet also has a `-ComputerName` parameter, so you can easily interrogate the logs on a remote machine.

FILTERING EVENT LOG RESULTS

There are so many possible error conditions (and Microsoft changes the event information with new Windows versions) that it's almost impossible to give a definitive set of tests, but here are a number of timeless test filtering techniques you can adapt to suit your circumstances.

FILTER BY DATE

Event logs can accumulate data over a number of days, weeks, or even months, depending on the log configuration and frequency of event generation. When you're troubleshooting, you're usually only interested in the most recent data. For instance, to return the data from the Directory Service log for the last three days, use this PowerShell code:

```
Get-EventLog –LogName 'Directory Service' `          ←❶ Log name
-After (Get-Date).AddDays(-3) `                       ←❷ Time period
-ComputerName server02
```

This code illustrates the general method of interrogating an event log. The log name is required ❶. You can discover the list of available logs like this:

```
Get-EventLog –List –ComputerName server02
```

A filter is useful to reduce the data to manageable proportions. In this case, you're taking all events after a certain date. The date is generated using the `Get-Date` Power-Shell cmdlet to retrieve today's date ❷ and the `AddDays()` method is used to subtract three days.

On my test domain controller, this test generated the following:

- 47 warnings
- 34 errors
- 27 informational messages

You need a process to filter through the event log messages to find the important ones.

FILTER BY EVENT TYPE

When you're troubleshooting, the error messages are a good place to start. If you adapt the code in the previous section, you can just return the error messages (or warnings, if you're performing a more general investigation):

```
Get-EventLog -LogName 'Directory Service' `
-After (Get-Date).AddDays(-3) -EntryType Error `
-ComputerName server02
```

The `-EntryType` parameter is used to filter the event types you want to see. On my test machine, I received data from two sources:

- NTDS replication
- NTDS general

You can also filter on the source of the log entry.

FILTER ON DATA SOURCE

You can extend the filtering to include the data source:

```
Get-EventLog -LogName 'Directory Service' `
-After (Get-Date).AddDays(-3) -EntryType Error `
-Source 'NTDS Replication' `
-ComputerName server02
```

The `-Source` parameter is used to filter on the event log source. An event log source is an identifying label indicating from which part of the system the event originated. The returned data includes a message supplying information about the error. Unfortunately, this is usually truncated in the default display because of the number of fields returned. You can also format the returned data:

```
 Get-EventLog -LogName 'Directory Service' `
-After (Get-Date).AddDays(-3) -EntryType Error `
-Source 'NTDS Replication' `
-ComputerName server02 |
Format-Table Index, Message -Autosize -Wrap
```

Cutting down the display in this way will enable you to view the whole message, which hopefully will point you in the correct direction to solve the problem.

TIP   You can use these filter techniques in any order or combination. They've been presented in this manner to show you one way to focus on the records that will solve your problem.

These techniques can be used with all of the event logs discussed at the start of this section.

TRY IT NOW: Event logs

Choose one of the event logs and investigate as detailed in section 19.3.2. Did you find any errors? Did you find any useful information that denotes normal operations?

Repeat with another log to practice the techniques.

That concludes your lesson on troubleshooting techniques. You can practice further in the lab.

19.4   LAB

This lab is designed to allow you to practice the troubleshooting techniques from this chapter. Remember that in many cases you'll see the normal state when running the tests, because it's difficult to force errors to occur.

19.4.1   Complete the TRY IT NOW exercises

If you haven't already done so, complete the TRY IT NOW exercises from the chapter. The exercises are repeated here for your convenience.

TEST DOMAIN CONTROLLER
Perform the tests in section 19.1.1 against one or more domain controllers in your environment. Take careful notice of the results and record if necessary. If you know what to expect you can spot the problems much more easily.

Repeat the tests against a global catalog. Are there any differences?

TEST PC
Perform the tests in section 19.1.1 against one or more PCs in your environment. Take careful notice of the results and record if necessary. If you know what to expect you can spot the problems much more easily.

LOGON SCRIPTS
Find the SYSVOL share on your domain controllers. It's set when the domain controller is created.

Investigate the logon script allocated to a user in your environment. Use ADAC, ADUC, and PowerShell to find the script name. Open the script on a domain controller to view the contents.

USER RIGHTS

Use the Resultant Set of Policies wizard to determine the settings for one or more users against one or more servers. If you see any problems, investigate further and try applying a filter to the GPOs so they don't affect users. Work through the GPOs, removing the filter from each in turn until the GPO causing the problem is discovered. Check each setting in the GPO by reading the explanation until you find the setting causing the problem.

LOGON RESTRICTIONS

Examine your user population to determine if any restrictions have been set. If you find any restrictions, are they really needed?

    Hint: use `Get-ADUser` with `-Filter*` instead of an identity.

Is there a way to show just the users who have the restrictions set?

SRV RECORDS

Use the code in section 19.2.2 to test the SRV records in one of your AD sites. Compare the results from multiple DNS servers. Do they match? What could be the problem if they don't match?

REPLICATION TESTING

Use listing 19.1 to test for replication failures on domain controllers in an AD site in your organization.

    What data is returned if there are no failures associated with a particular domain controller?

EVENT LOGS

Choose one of the event logs and investigate as detailed in section 19.3.2. Did you find any errors? Did you find any useful information that denotes normal operations?

    Repeat with another log to practice the techniques.

19.4.2 Automation

Combine the scripts you've seen in this chapter to perform the tests with minimal input. Try to get as many tests as possible into a single script to reduce you work. Should you put all of the tests in one big script or have several smaller ones? Why?

19.5 Ideas for on your own

Learning how to troubleshoot AD-related problems is an ongoing task. You're very unlikely to meet all of the possible problems, but you'll meet a lot of them over the course of your AD administration career. There are some things you can do to help increase your knowledge and therefore increase your troubleshooting skills:

- *Create a troubleshooting toolkit.* Take the code from the book and create a set of scripts you can use to perform the various tests discussed in this and other chapters.
- *Keep a record of AD-related troubleshooting incidents.* Record the symptoms, the cause, and what you did to fix the issue. This will build into a valuable reference

over time, as well as possibly highlight areas in your Active Directory for remedial work.

- *Read around the topic.* There's a wealth of material on the Microsoft TechNet site to start with. Investigate the content and set some goals regarding your reading efforts.

- *Look at the AD-related forums and think about the questions that come up.* You don't have to post answers, but trying to solve the problem in your own mind and then checking with the posted answers can be a valuable learning experience. Don't be surprised if you find yourself disagreeing with some of the posted answers. There are a lot of opinionated people on some of the forums who aren't necessarily correct!

You're on the last lap now; the next chapter is the last full learning chapter of the book and deals with maintaining and monitoring Active Directory.

Maintaining and monitoring Active Directory

20

You might think from earlier chapters that Active Directory looks after itself and that you don't need to do much to keep it healthy. To a certain degree that's true, but like any complex mechanism, a little bit of care and attention goes a long way. You get your car checked and serviced regularly, and Active Directory is no different in its requirements for regular health checks.

You can accomplish those checks with a little bit of monitoring and maintenance. Monitoring means keeping an eye on the system so you can spot trouble before it develops—like taking your car to the garage when the engine makes noises you don't recognize as being normal. Maintenance is like keeping your engine's oil levels topped up—it helps to keep things running normally and prevents bigger problems from developing.

This chapter starts by introducing you to the Microsoft Operations Framework (MOF) reliability workbooks. MOF is Microsoft's implementation of the Information Technology Infrastructure Library (ITIL), found at http://www.itil-officialsite.com/. ITIL, now in version 3, is a set of documents describing best practices in IT service management. Originally a U.K. standard, it now has worldwide adoption. The MOF reliability workbooks provide a set of recommendations for things to monitor and maintenance tasks across a number of Microsoft technologies.

Monitoring, if you're lucky, will be easy in your organization. You'll have an Enterprise class monitoring system with a dedicated team to take all that hassle off your shoulders. No? Oh well, in that case the second section of this chapter is just for you. It describes a number of things you can monitor, and shows you how to perform the monitoring. The examples are pulled from the MOF reliability workbook for Active Directory.

The final section of the chapter is concerned with maintenance—the proactive activities you perform to keep your Active Directory healthy. You'll probably never be thanked for performing these activities, but you'll definitely hear about if you don't and problems arise.

> **TIP** Be sure that you check maintenance routines against your organization's IT and business policies—you won't be looked on favorably if you delete old accounts after 60 days and the business wants them kept for 90 days.

Let's start by having a quick look at the MOF reliability workbooks.

20.1 *Microsoft Operations Framework reliability workbooks*

The core MOF documentation is highly recommended as a starting point for managing your Windows environment. You can find it online at http://technet.microsoft.com/en-us/library/cc506049.aspx.

> **TIP** Remember that all best practice is generic in nature. There are times it won't fit your needs. Be prepared to step outside the recommendations, but document why you're doing so. Documenting the exceptions will make you think about whether it's a real exception or it just seems too hard to implement the suggestion.

The MOF reliability workbooks are available as part of the MOF Technology Library at http://technet.microsoft.com/en-us/library/ee923724.aspx. They cover a number of technologies, including

- Active Directory
- Exchange 2010
- Hyper-V
- Internet Information Server (IIS)
- SQL Server

The reliability workbooks are delivered as Excel spreadsheets and are updated on a periodic basis, so it's worth checking every so often to see if you have the latest version.

> **TRY IT NOW: Download the AD MOF reliability workbook**
>
> Download the AD reliability workbook from http://technet.microsoft.com/en-us/library/ee923724.aspx. You'll get a zip file containing
>
> - Administrator's Guide to Reliability Workbooks (Word document)
> - Reliability Workbook for Active Directory Domain Services (Excel spreadsheet)
>
> Examine the contents of the workbook.

The AD reliability workbook contains a number of worksheets:

- An Overview sheet that provides a set of definitions.
- A Monitoring Activities sheet that details approximately 80 items that Microsoft recommends you monitor.
- A Maintenance Activities sheet that details approximately 65 activities that you may need to perform to maintain your AD environment.
- A list of approximately 15 Health Risks that details AD-related risks to your environment and actions you can perform to mitigate those risks.
- A set of 15 standard changes that should become part of your change control process.
- A sheet acknowledging the authors, reviewers, and editors of the reliability workbook.

WARNING Don't try and implement all of the activities described in the workbook in one "big-bang" approach. Select those activities that make the most sense for your environment and implement those first. The items in this chapter were chosen to be a good starting point.

The workbook details the items you should be considering together with

- The area of Active Directory under consideration—for instance, domain controllers or user accounts.
- The requirements you need to meet.
- Frequency of examination; some of the suggested frequencies seem a bit on the high side, so don't be afraid to change them to suit your environment.
- Techniques for manual performance of the task or suggestions for automating the task. The assumption is that the System Center Operations Manager will be used for monitoring automation, but the supplied information can be transposed to other monitoring systems or you can create PowerShell scripts to perform the monitoring.

There are more activities than we can cover in this book. In the chapter you'll see some examples of how to take the suggestions in the workbook and turn them into a monitoring and maintenance system you can implement to suit your needs.

20.2 *Monitoring*

If you have an Enterprise monitoring solution, such as System Center Operations Manager, you should use that to monitor your Active Directory. Organizations that don't possess such a tool can create their own monitoring solution using a number of PowerShell scripts. The 80 items Microsoft suggests you monitor can be grouped—for instance, a number of checks on services are suggested, and by combining those checks into one script you can achieve multiple goals.

In this section you'll see suggestions for

- Testing availability
- Checking services
- Viewing permissions
- Testing user passwords

These have been chosen to give you a cross-section of examples you can extend.

20.2.1 *Testing availability*

Availability can mean a number of things. You can assume that for the purposes of this section, availability means that

- You can connect to the domain controller over the network.
- Your DNS server has the correct SRV records for the domain controller.

A simple ping test proves that you have network connectivity.

If you use the domain controller's name, you also test DNS resolution for the domain controller. There are a few options you can employ when testing the network connectivity. The first option is presented in listing 20.1 and shows how to test network connectivity to the FSMO role holders. Testing each individual role ensures that you receive the correct response even if the roles move. If you hard-code the role holder names, you're assuming the roles haven't moved.

Listing 20.1 Testing FSMO role holder availability

```
$for = [System.DirectoryServices.ActiveDirectory.Forest]
➥ ::GetCurrentForest()                                        ◁——❶ Get forest

Test-Connection -ComputerName $for.SchemaRoleOwner -Count 2       ❷ Ping forest
Test-Connection -ComputerName $for.NamingRoleOwner -Count 2          FSMO

$dom = [System.DirectoryServices.ActiveDirectory.Domain]
➥ ::GetCurrentDomain()                                        ◁——❸ Get domain

Test-Connection -ComputerName $dom.PdcRoleOwner -Count 2          ❹ Ping
Test-Connection -ComputerName $dom.InfrastructureRoleOwner -Count 2   domain
Test-Connection -ComputerName $dom.RidRoleOwner -Count 2             FSMO
```

You start by creating an object representing the forest ❶. This contains the names of the schema master and the domain naming master. A ping test for each is performed ❷ using the PowerShell `Test-Connection` cmdlet.

A second object representing the domain ❸ supplies the name of the PDC emulator, the infrastructure master, and the RID master. `Test-Connection` ❹ is again used to test network connectivity.

A second option is to test each domain controller, as shown in the next listing.

Listing 20.2 Testing domain controller availability

```
$dom =
➥ [System.DirectoryServices.ActiveDirectory.Domain]::GetCurrentDomain()
foreach ($dc in $dom.DomainControllers){
Test-Connection -ComputerName $dc -Count 2
}
```

The domain object has a list of domain controllers. Iterate through that list and use `Test-Connection` to perform the ping test.

The final option is to test global catalog availability, as shown in the following listing.

Listing 20.3 Testing global catalog availability

```
$for =
➥ [System.DirectoryServices.ActiveDirectory.Forest]::GetCurrentForest()
foreach ($gc in $for.GlobalCatalogs){
Test-Connection -ComputerName $gc -Count 2
}
```

This time the forest object is used because it carries the list of global catalogs.

If you have a very large AD environment, you may not want to test all of the domain controllers or global catalogs in a single test. In that case, use the individual names in a series of tests, though you may want to run a full test periodically.

DNS hosts a number of SRV records that advertise the services offered by an individual domain controller. The following listing illustrates how to test your SRV records.

Listing 20.4 Testing domain controller SRV records

```
$dom = [System.DirectoryServices.ActiveDirectory.Domain]::GetCurrentDomain()
foreach ($dc in $dom.DomainControllers){          ←── ❶ Iterate
  Get-DnsServerResourceRecord -RRType SRV -ComputerName server02 `      domain
  -ZoneName manticore.org |                                            controllers
  where {$_.RecordData.DomainName -eq "$dc."} |
  sort hostname |
  Format-Table -AutoSize
}
```

Get SRV records ❷

Iterate over the list of domain controllers ❶. For each domain controller, get the SRV records ❷ using `Get-DnsServerResourceRecord`.

> **NOTE** The `Get-DnsServerResourceRecord` cmdlet is only available on Windows Server 2012 and later.

The domain and DNS server are supplied as parameters to the cmdlet. You'll need to filter on the individual domain controller's fully qualified domain name (FQDN) to separate out the results for each domain controller. You do need the "." at the end of the FQN.

> **TRY IT NOW: Test the availability of your domain controllers**
>
> Use the scripts in listings 20.1 through 20.4 to test the availability of your domain controllers.
>
> What results do you get if a domain controller can't be reached by `Test-Connection`?

The availability tests prove your domain controllers are contactable across the network, but that's only part of the overall test. You also need to test that the services critical to your Active Directory are running.

20.2.2 *Checking services*

The MOF reliability workbook suggests that you monitor a number of services (the service name is given in parentheses), including

- Replication service (DFSR and NtFrs)
- Kerberos Key Distribution Center service (Kdc)
- Windows Time Service (W32Time)

In addition, I recommend that you also test whether the following services are running:

- AD Web Services (ADWS)
- DNS server (DNS)
- Windows event log (EventLog)
- Group Policy client (gpsvc)
- Netlogon (Netlogon)
- AD Domain Services (NTDS)
- Windows update (wuauserv)

Other services can be added if you desire. You can, obviously, log on to each domain controller and manually inspect that the required services are running, but that's a tedious activity, and you could be performing much more interesting tasks. Automate the test by using a script like the following listing.

Listing 20.5   Testing running services on domain controllers

```
$session = New-PSSession -ComputerName 'server02', 'server03'      ◁ ─┐  Create PowerShell
                                                                       │  remoting session ❶
'DFSR', 'NtFrs', 'Kdc', 'W32Time', 'ADWS', 'DNS',
'EventLog', 'gpsvc', 'Netlogon', 'NTDS', 'wuauserv' |
foreach -BEGIN {
 $sb = {                                              ◁ ── Create script
  param($service)                                        ❸ block
  Get-Service -Name $service
 }
} -PROCESS {                                                            ❹ Run
Invoke-Command -Session $session -ScriptBlock $sb -ArgumentList $psitem    command
}                                                                      ❺ Delete remoting
                                                         ◁ ──             session
$session | Remove-PSSession
```

Define service list ❷ → points to the `'DFSR', 'NtFrs', ...` block

Create a PowerShell remoting session ❶ to the required domain controllers. If you don't know how to use PowerShell remoting, I recommend *Learn PowerShell 3 in a Month of Lunches* by Don Jones (Manning, 2012). The remoting session enables you to run commands on the remote machine and get the results back on your workstation.

A list of services ❷ is placed on the PowerShell pipeline. The `foreach` command creates a script block ❸. This is only performed once because it's in the `BEGIN` block. Each service name is processed by the `PROCESS` block ❹. The service name is sent as an argument to the script block and `Invoke-Command` is used to send the command to the remote machines. The final act of the script ❺ is to delete the remote sessions.

The results from the script look like this:

```
Status   Name    DisplayName              PSComputerName
------   ----    -----------              --------------
Running  DFSR    DFS Replication          server02
Running  DFSR    DFS Replication          server03
Running  NtFrs   File Replication         server02
Running  NtFrs   File Replication Service server03

<display truncated for brevity>
```

Using `Invoke-Command` and a remote session facilitates the display of the remote computer name as part of your results without any processing on your part.

> **TRY IT NOW: Test the services on your domain controllers**
>
> Modify the script in listing 20.5 to test the services on your domain controllers.
> Do you need to add any more services to the list?

Over time the number of people with extra privileges in your domain will grow. You should monitor who has these privileges.

20.2.3 *Viewing permissions*

There are a number of very sensitive groups in your Active Directory, such as the Enterprise Admins group, the Domain Admins group, and groups that give access to sensitive data. Keep tight control of these groups, because one of the biggest causes of a misconfigured Active Directory is too many uncontrolled administrators. You don't want to give Domain Admin membership to someone who will misuse those privileges either deliberately or through ignorance.

You learned about default security groups in chapter 14. These are the groups you need to test, and preferably have under change control. You can use Group Policy to restrict the membership of these groups. Alternatively, audit their membership on a regular basis and remove users who shouldn't be in the groups.

Auditing group membership doesn't have to be an arduous task. You can create a report using the following listing.

Listing 20.6   Testing default group membership

```
$ous = @()                                              ◄──❶ Get domain
$dom = Get-ADDomain

$ous += "CN=Builtin,$($dom.DistinguishedName)"          ◄──❷ Create OU list
$ous += "CN=Users,$($dom.DistinguishedName)"

foreach ($ou in $ous){
     $groups = Get-ADGroup -SearchBase $ou -Filter * |
     where {$_.Name -ne 'Domain Users' -and $_.Name -ne 'Domain Computers'}

  foreach ($group in $groups){
    Get-ADGroupMember -Identity $group.DistinguishedName |       ◄──┐
    select @{Name='OU'; Expression={$ou}},                          ❹ Get group
    @{Name='Group'; Expression={$group.Name}},                        membership
    @{Name='Member'; Expression={$psitem.Name}}
  }

}
```

Get groups ❸ (margin annotation)

This script may appear a bit complicated, but it's just two loops, one inside the other. You start by creating an array to hold the list of OUs you want to examine ❶. The domain name and associated data is retrieved using the Get-ADDomain cmdlet.

> **TIP** This approach isn't direct, but it has the advantage of being portable, so you don't need to worry about which domain you're working in. Always try to access data in a portable manner rather than hard-coding the domain details.

A list of OU distinguished names is added to the array ❷. The listing only uses the Builtin and Users containers, but you can add other OUs if you wish. The groups in each OU are retrieved in turn ❸. The Domain Users and Domain Computers groups are excluded because they're maintained automatically by Active Directory and will contain all users and computers, respectively.

Each group has its membership checked ❹. An object is created and output, with the OU distinguished name, the name of the group, and the name of the group member. You can then use the data to create your report. There's no output generated for groups that don't have any members.

Another important part of monitoring your environment is to make sure that the settings applied to your users, such as password policies, are configured correctly.

20.2.4   *Testing user passwords*

There are many settings and configuration items in Active Directory that affect users. If you automate your user creation and change processes, together with using GPOs, the settings and configuration will be handled for you, and, more importantly, will be consistent. In terms of monitoring, the most important aspects are checking the password policies applied to your users.

FINDING PASSWORDS THAT DON'T HAVE AN EXPIRATION DATE

The first check is to determine if any user accounts are configured so that their password never expires. This may seem like a good idea at first, because password resets form a large part of the administrator's workload. But in reality, setting all passwords to never expire will weaken your security and leave your organization vulnerable to attack.

You can test for accounts that have their password set to never expire using the `Search-ADAccount` cmdlet:

```
Search-ADAccount -PasswordNeverExpires -UsersOnly |
select Name, DistinguishedName
```

This command will search the whole of your domain for accounts where the password is set to never expire. The `Name` and `DistinguishedName` of the account will be displayed. If you wish, you can use the `-Searchbase` parameter to restrict the check to a single OU tree.

CHECKING PASSWORD POLICIES IN A DOMAIN

The other item that should be checked is the password policy or policies enforced in your domain. As a minimum, you'll have a default policy that can be viewed like this:

```
Get-ADDefaultDomainPasswordPolicy |
select *Password*
```

Sample results are as follows:

```
MaxPasswordAge        : 42.00:00:00
MinPasswordAge        : 00:00:00
MinPasswordLength     : 7
PasswordHistoryCount  : 24
```

The minimum and maximum password ages are shown as timespans (days.hours:minutes:seconds).

If you've used fine-grained password policies, you can easily check their settings:

```
Get-ADFineGrainedPasswordPolicy -Filter * |
Select Name, *Password*
```

This will display the same set of information as the default policy, plus the name of the policy.

> **TRY IT NOW: Test password settings**
>
> Use the code in section 20.2.4 to test your password settings.
> Do you need to change any of them?

Monitoring your Active Directory and its settings is good practice. Performing some routine maintenance as well takes things to another level.

20.3   *Maintenance*

Back in the days of the mainframe, the phrase *preventative maintenance* was frequently used. It means you're spending some time and effort to ensure that things keep running smoothly. If you do this right and automate the tasks, it won't take much of your working time and you solve at least some problems before they arise.

So, what sort of things should you do as part of your maintenance routine? Possibly the single most effective task you can perform is to clean up old accounts in your Active Directory, which you'll learn to do here with PowerShell. If this doesn't happen, the old accounts accumulate and you end up with a big mess of accounts that take weeks of effort to unravel. Cleaning out old accounts also stops them from being an attack vector for hostile access.

The AD database is critical to the health of your environment. If the disk on which it's hosted runs out of disk space, the database could be corrupted. It'll certainly stop working. The SYSVOL share (containing logon scripts and GPO settings data) is hosted on the same drive as the database, if the installation defaults are adopted, and can also be badly affected by disk space issues. Monitoring disk space will enable you to spot impending issues.

Time is very important in an AD environment. If the time shown by the system clock on your workstation is more than five minutes different from the domain controller, you won't be able to log on. A simple script can be used to compare the times of multiple machines and report differences.

Your first maintenance task is to spring-clean your Active Directory and remove the old, unused accounts.

20.3.1   *Clean up old accounts*

People join your organization and others leave. Desktop refresh projects add new computer accounts as they roll out people's new machines, but they usually don't remove the old accounts. Projects add new servers—possibly for new applications or to replace applications—but somehow there's always a server or two left behind. After a relatively short while, you end up with hundreds, or even thousands, of unused accounts that clutter up your Active Directory and make it inefficient. I've seen many organizations where the old, unused accounts were two, three, or even five times more numerous than the live accounts.

> **TIP** One of the first things I look at when investigating a new Active Directory is how many old, unused accounts are present. It's usually a lot. The fact that they exist is indicative of an environment that hasn't been properly maintained. It's also a consultant's delight because it's a quick-win activity that's easy to spot, and the fix is easy to implement.

Before jumping into showing you how to discover and remove old accounts, there are a few things you should think about. The first one being, what's your organization's definition of an old account?

It's fairly easy to identify old computer accounts. The password for the secure channel is updated every 30 days. If a machine hasn't updated its password for more than 30 days, it's not on the network and should be considered an old account.

Users are a bit more difficult because they can have extended periods of absence due to illness, maternity leave, and sabbaticals. You need to understand your organization's policy on these subjects to achieve a sensible balance. Most organizations adopt a multiple of the maximum password age to test against. For instance, if a user hasn't logged on for three months, there's a good chance they've left the organization.

A quick way to test accounts that haven't been active for 90 days is to use `Search-ADAccount`:

```
Search-ADAccount -AccountInactive -TimeSpan 90.00:00:00 |
select Name, DistinguishedName, LastLogonDate
```

The `LastLogonDate` property was introduced in Windows Server 2008 R2 and is a readable form of the `LastLogonTimeStamp` property.

Logon times

There are three different times related to logon available on an AD user account:

`LastLogon` is specific to the individual domain controller to which the user authenticated. This attribute isn't replicated between domain controllers.

`LastLogonTimeStamp` is replicated between domain controllers, but may be up to 14 days out of date because it's only updated periodically.

`LastLogonDate` is a human-friendly version of LastLogonTimestamp and follows the same replication rules.

You can view the three properties relating to logon times:

```
Get-ADUser -Identity richard -Properties * | select *logon*

BadLogonCount          : 0
lastLogon              : 130308150075222788
LastLogonDate          : 06/12/2013 14:49:44
```

```
lastLogonTimestamp    : 130308149849641986
logonCount            : 3595
LogonWorkstations     :
MNSLogonAccount       : False
SmartcardLogonRequired : False
```

The `LastLogonDate` is readable, but the `LastLogon` and `LastLogonTimeStamp` are stored using the `FileTime` structure, which represents the number of 100-nanosecond intervals since January 1, 1601. You need to do a little work to make them readable. The code to make the properties readable is annotated in the following code:

```
Get-ADUser -Identity richard -Properties * |
select Name, LastLogonDate,
@{N='LastLogonTimeStamp';
    E={[DateTime]::FromFileTime([int64]::Parse($_.LastLogonTimeStamp))}},
@{N='LastLogon'; E={[DateTime]::FromFileTime([int64]::Parse($_.LastLogon))}}
```

Make LastLogon readable ┈┈▷

Make LastLogonTimeStamp readable

```
Name              : Richard
LastLogonDate     : 06/12/2013 14:49:44
LastLogonTimeStamp : 06/12/2013 14:49:44
LastLogon         : 06/12/2013 14:50:07
```

The minor difference in times is because `LastLogonTimeStamp` is updated immediately, but `LastLogon` isn't updated until the logon process has finished. One last thing to consider with logon times is that the `Search-ADAccount` syntax used earlier will return accounts that haven't logged on yet. You don't want to remove brand-new accounts that haven't been used, so change the syntax to

```
Search-ADAccount -AccountInactive -UsersOnly -TimeSpan 90.00:00:00 |
where LastLogonDate |
select Name, DistinguishedName, LastLogonDate
```

The difference is using `where LastLogonDate` to filter out accounts that don't have a value for `LastLogonDate`. Active Directory supplies a null value for properties that aren't set, which PowerShell treats as false, so the filter doesn't pass that account.

> **TRY IT NOW: Test for inactive accounts**
>
> Use the code in section 20.3.1 to test for inactive user accounts.
>
> How would you test for inactive computer accounts?

Once you've identified accounts that haven't logged on in your test period, you need to decide what to do with them. The first thing to do is either delete or disable the accounts, as you learned in chapter 3. This prevents them from being used. If you disable the accounts, copy them to an OU just for disabled accounts and delete them after a further period of three months (or whatever fits your organization).

Another common maintenance task is testing the disk space available for your AD database.

20.3.2 *Disk space monitoring*

I was once called into an organization that was having problems with their Active Directory. There were numerous issues, but one of the worst appeared to be a replication problem. Once I dug into it a little more, it became apparent that the problems were caused by the disk hosting the AD database running out of space.

You can monitor disk space by regularly running a script that measures the available space and records the results. First, you need the data, which you can obtain through the following listing.

Get domain objects ❶
Get disk space ❸

Listing 20.7   Monitoring disk space

```
$dom = [System.DirectoryServices.ActiveDirectory.Domain]::GetCurrentDomain()

foreach ($dc in $dom.DomainControllers){
 Get-WmiObject -Class Win32_Volume -ComputerName $dc `
-Filter "Name='C:\\'" |
 select Name,
@{N='Size(GB)'; E={[Math]::Round(($_.Capacity / 1GB),2)}},
@{N='Free(GB)'; E={[Math]::Round(($_.FreeSpace / 1GB), 2)}},
@{N='PercFree';
   E={[Math]::Round((($_.FreeSpace / $_.Capacity) * 100) ,2 )}},
   PSComputerName
}
```

❷ **Iterate domain controllers**
❹ **Convert to GB**
❺ **Calculate percentage free**

The domain object is created ❶ and then the script iterates over the set of domain controllers ❷. The Win32_Volume WMI class is used to obtain the disk information ❸ for the C:\ drive of each domain controller.

> **NOTE** If you've put the database on another drive, you'll need to change the script to gather data from the correct drive.

WMI returns the disk capacity and free space in bytes, so you need to perform a calculation on each property to obtain the data as gigabytes, which is more usable ❹. A final calculation ❺ provides the percentage of free space.

For each domain controller your results will look like this:

```
Name            : C:\
Size(GB)        : 180.46
Free(GB)        : 18.03
PercFree        : 9.99
PSComputerName  : SERVER02
```

Save the data in a spreadsheet or database. A graph of those results will show you the trend of disk space usage over time. Test the disk space on your domain controllers at least monthly.

TRY IT NOW: Test domain controller disk space

Use the code in listing 20.7 to check your domain controller disk space.

The final maintenance task in this section is testing the time on your domain controllers.

20.3.3   *Test domain time synchronization*

Time is very important to Active Directory. If the time between a domain controller and the machine from which you're trying to authenticate is off by more than five minutes, your authentication attempts will fail. The next listing shows how to test the current system time on your domain controllers.

Listing 20.8   Testing domain controller time

```
$dom = [System.DirectoryServices.ActiveDirectory.Domain]::GetCurrentDomain()
$dom.DomainControllers | select Name, CurrentTime
```

The domain object has a property called `DomainControllers`. This is a collection of objects representing domain controllers. Each domain controller object has a number of properties, including the `CurrentTime`. The script uses the collection of domain controllers, and for each object the script selects the name and current system time.

> **WARNING**   The time that's reported is Greenwich Mean Time (GMT), not your local time, but as long as the results are the same (allowing for processing time), you have a successful test.

If you want to see the current local time on the domain controllers, you could use the code in the following listing.

Listing 20.9   Testing domain controller local time

```
                    $dom = [System.DirectoryServices.ActiveDirectory.Domain]::GetCurrentDomain()
Get
domain ❶
                    foreach ($dc in $dom.DomainControllers){         ◁── ❷ Iterate domain
                                                                             controllers
Get
OS data ❸          Get-WmiObject -Class Win32_OperatingSystem -ComputerName $dc |
                    Select PSComputerName,
                    @{Name='LocalTime';
                       Expression={$_.ConvertToDateTime($_.LocalDateTime)} }    ◁── ❹ Convert time
                    }
```

Get the domain controllers ❶ as before. This time, use a `foreach` loop to iterate through the domain controller names ❷. Each domain controller is used in a call ❸ to the `Win32_OperatingSystem` WMI class.

> **NOTE**   I've used `Get-WmiObject` to retrieve the information. If you have PowerShell 3.0 installed on all of your domain controllers, you could use `Get-CimInstance` instead.

The `PSComputername` property is selected, and a calculation is performed on the `LocalDateTime` property using the `ConvertToDateTime()` ❹ method to make the date readable.

> ### TRY IT NOW: Test time synchronization
>
> Use the code in listings 20.8 and 20.9 to test your domain controller time.
> When would it be a good idea to only use the time reported as GMT?

You now have a good grounding in monitoring and maintaining your AD environment. In reality, the two sets of tasks overlap, and you should view them both as protecting your environment and your users. It's time to round out the chapter by heading into the lab.

20.4 LAB

This lab will provide practice in the monitoring and maintenance techniques you've learned in this chapter.

20.4.1 Complete the TRY IT NOW sections

If you haven't already done so, complete the TRY IT NOW sections. They're repeated here for your convenience.

DOWNLOAD THE AD MOF RELIABILITY WORKBOOK

Download the AD reliability workbook from http://technet.microsoft.com/en-us/library/ee923724.aspx. You'll get a zip file containing

- Administrator's Guide to Reliability Workbooks (Word document)
- Reliability Workbook for Active Directory Domain Services (Excel spreadsheet)

Examine the contents of the workbook.

TEST THE AVAILABILITY OF YOUR DOMAIN CONTROLLERS

Use the scripts in listings 20.1 through 20.4 to test the availability of your domain controllers.

What results do you get if a domain controller can't be reached by `Test-Connection`?

TEST THE SERVICES ON YOUR DOMAIN CONTROLLERS

Modify the script in listing 20.5 to test the services on your domain controllers.

Do you need to add any more services to the list?

TEST GROUP MEMBERSHIP

Use the script in listing 20.6 to test the membership of your default domain groups.

Do you need to add other OUs to the list?

Hint: you may want to consider adding OUs containing groups that access sensitive data, such as finance and HR information. You could move those groups to one OU for ease of administration and reporting.

TEST PASSWORD SETTINGS

Use the code in section 20.2.4 to test your password settings.

Do you need to change any of them?

TEST FOR INACTIVE ACCOUNTS
Use the code in section 20.3.1 to test for inactive user accounts.

How would you test for inactive computer accounts?

TEST DOMAIN CONTROLLER DISK SPACE
Use the code in listing 20.7 to check your domain controller disk space.

TEST TIME SYNCHRONIZATION
Use the code in listings 20.8 and 20.9 to test your domain controller time.

When would it be a good idea to only use the time reported as GMT?

20.4.2 *Old accounts*

Determine what you'll do with old user and computer accounts once you've identified them. Initiate a regular clean-up exercise.

20.4.3 *Review the workbook*

Examine the workbook in terms of what's been covered in earlier chapters. What tests can you perform using the information from those chapters?

20.5 *Ideas for on your own*

The most important thing you can take away from this chapter is the commitment to yourself to work through the MOF reliability workbook for Active Directory and to implement the other tasks that haven't been covered in this chapter. You'll find that many of the maintenance tasks can be performed using scripts you create by modifying the examples in earlier chapters. If you get stuck, you can always ask questions on the PowerShell forums.

Some possible maintenance activities include the following:

- Identify and remove groups with no members
- Test backups using the techniques in chapter 13
- Check account lockout policy
- Check that the domain controllers are in the correct OU and site
- Check the server manager for any reported issues, especially if using server groups

The next chapter is the one you've been eagerly anticipating—the final exam! It also presents an overview of some technologies that are related to or interact with Active Directory.

Future work and final exam 21

Congratulations! You're very near to the finishing line.

You'll find that this chapter is a little different. In the first section, you'll be introduced to some extension topics—technologies that are heavily integrated with Active Directory, but that aren't part of the core of Active Directory:

- AD Certificate Services (ADCS)
- AD Rights Management Service (ADRMS)
- AD Federation Services (ADFS)
- AD Lightweight Services (ADLS)

By the end of this section, you'll know where to start when it's time to bring these technologies into your organization.

> **TIP** Microsoft rebranded a number of technologies during the Windows 2008 release cycle by adding Active Directory to their name. The technologies integrate with Active Directory but aren't part of it.

There isn't a lab section in this chapter; instead, in the second section you'll have a final exam. Consider this your graduation exercise. When you complete the exercise, it means you've mastered the topics presented in the book, and, more importantly, you have the skills and knowledge to safely administer your AD environment.

21.1   Extension topics

There are a number of technologies affiliated with Active Directory of which you need to be aware:

- *AD Certificate Services*—Used to provide certificates that can be used for things like authentication and encryption.
- *AD Rights Management Service*—Used to control access to documents and what can be done with those documents.
- *AD Federation Services*—Used to grant access to one or more web-based applications to people outside your organization.
- *AD Lightweight Services*—Used to supply directory services in isolated situations, such as applications in the perimeter network.

Let's jump into AD Certificate Services.

21.1.1   AD Certificate Services

You use certificates all the time, even if your organization doesn't have its own certificate handling infrastructure. Every time you use a secure website (where you see the padlock symbol in the browser), you're using certificates to encrypt the traffic to that website. The website's certificate has been purchased from a commercial certificate authority. This can get expensive if you need a lot of certificates for internal use. That's when you use ADCS to create your own certificate authority. ADCS is Microsoft's implementation of a Public Key Infrastructure (PKI).

ADCS installs as a Windows role.

> **WARNING** Don't install ADCS on the domain controllers in your production environment. Create dedicated infrastructure (virtual or physical) for these servers. ADCS should be on dedicated servers to enable maximum protection for domain controllers and certificate servers. Upgrades become very complicated when ADCS is installed on domain controllers, because you often can't perform a simple in-place upgrade, which means migrating the ADCS on to another server.

Installing ADCS isn't just a simple matter of installing the software and diving straight in. There are a number of issues you need to consider, such as

- Certificate servers
- Lifetimes
- Types
- Enrollment

Let's start with the certificate servers.

CERTIFICATE SERVERS

How many layers of certificate servers, also known as certificate authorities (CAs), will you need? Figure 21.1 illustrates a common deployment pattern using three tiers of certificate servers.

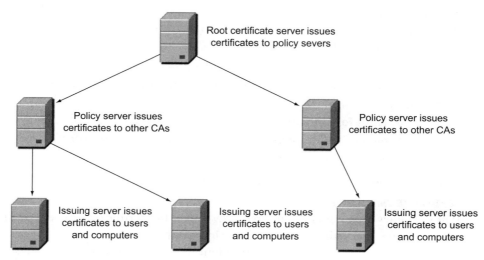

Figure 21.1 Three-tier deployment of certificate servers

Here's a breakdown of the three main types of certificate servers you might need:

1   A root CA that issues certificates to other certificate servers in the hierarchy so that they're authorized to issue certificates. This server will create and issue to itself a self-signed certificate that's the root of all certificates issued by your CA hierarchy. Your root CA must be kept secure to ensure that your whole environment isn't compromised.

2   One or more policy servers that issue certificates to your issuing servers and define the rules—for instance, the types of certificate that can be issued and who can approve certificates.

3   One or more issuing servers that issue certificates to your users and computes, control the revocation of certificates, and store the certificate database.

You may need all three layers, but in many organizations the layers can be reduced by combining the policy servers with the issuing servers.

CERTIFICATE LIFETIMES

The lifetime of certificates issued to your users and computers needs to be wholly contained within the lifetime of your root and policy CA certificates. An example of the lifetime hierarchy is

- Root certificate: 10 years
- Policy CA certificate: 5 years
- End user and computer certificates: 1 year

The various certificates are commonly renewed after half their lifetime has expired.

CERTIFICATE TYPES

What type, or types, of certificates will your CAs issue? Windows CAs can issue a wide variety of certificates; for instance

- User and computer identification and authentication
- Email encryption (users outside of the organization will need a certificate)
- File encryption (EFS)
- Smart cards for authentication
- Securing internal websites with Secure Socket Layer (SSL) certificates
- Domain controller certificates

You should configure your CAs to only issue the certificates you need.

CERTIFICATE ENROLLMENT

Will you allow your users to automatically enroll for certificates, or will you require them to request a certificate from an administrator?

Some certificates, such as computer identification and EFS, can sensibly be configured for automatic enrollment. Other certificates, such as those used in smart cards and for SSL, should require administrator involvement.

Be prepared to spend the necessary time designing your certificate polices and infrastructure to ensure you get it right. It's much easier to make changes at the design phase than post-implementation.

21.1.2 *AD Rights Management Service*

Most organizations have sensitive data that must be protected. This could range from financial data, to information about future plans, to customer-related data. Exposure of this data could damage your organization commercially or in a reputational manner. In the worst case, regulatory authorities could become involved.

You can use standard file and share permissions to control who can access the data in terms of reading and modifying it, but how do you prevent someone from copying the data onto portable media and walking out of the building, or emailing the data to a competitor?

ADRMS provides a solution to this problem. It integrates with client applications such as Microsoft Office and server applications such as Microsoft Exchange and Microsoft SharePoint to enable you to set and enforce usage policies on documents. In addition to the usual access permissions, you can control what actions the user can perform on the data. For instance, you can prevent the following as appropriate:

- Copying and pasting
- Save or save as
- Forwarding through email
- Printing
- Editing
- Exporting email messages

You'll need to implement a number of components in your ADRMS infrastructure.

ADRMS ROOT CLUSTER

The Root Cluster manages all certification and licensing requests for clients. You can have a number of servers in the cluster for redundancy. The cluster must have internet connectivity to Microsoft during installation so that the Microsoft Enrollment service can sign the cluster's server licensor certificate.

WEB SERVICES

The ADRMS web services are provided to clients through a website hosted in IIS. Other required features include

- Windows Process Activation Service
- Message queuing

Client connectivity can be unencrypted or use SSL for further protection.

LICENSING-ONLY CLUSTERS

Licensing-only clusters are optional. They're used to provide publishing licenses and user licenses. You'd normally use a licensing-only cluster to provide ADRMS to a specific part of the organization.

If you don't implement any licensing-only clusters, the Root Cluster will provide the required licenses to the end users.

ACTIVE DIRECTORY

Active Directory provides a number of services in an ADRMS environment:

- Hosts the pointers to the ADRMS URL
- Hosts the groups used to control ADRMS

DATABASE SERVICES

SQL Server is used to store configuration settings and keys (both server and client). A cache of expanded group memberships (obtained from Active Directory) is also stored in SQL Server.

ADRMS CLIENT

New content is created through an ADRMS-aware client application such as Microsoft Office. The user can apply a precreated policy template to the document when it's saved that dictates which other users can access the document and what they can do with it. If, for example, a user attempts to email a copy of the document to an external organization, Exchange will read the policy applied to the document and prevent the email from leaving your organization.

21.1.3 AD Federation Services

Many businesses need to give external organizations access to a particular internal application, and as your organization's business expands, so too will the number of organizations needing such access. One way to solve this problem is to use trusts between your organization and the external organizations (see chapter 18), but you'll

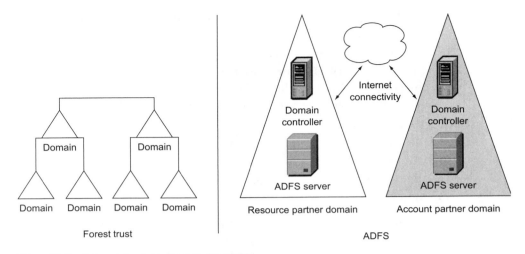

Figure 21.2   A forest trust compared with ADFS

need to create a new trust for each new organization and the users will have to reauthenticate as they access the application. A forest trust is shown on the left side of figure 21.2.

An alternative to using trusts is to federate your AD with the external AD to provide access to the specific web-based applications. This approach enables single sign-on (SSO) access to the application from the external users' domains so that they don't need to reauthenticate. The best part of using ADFS, from your vantage point, is that the administrators in the external domains are responsible for granting access to the application, which moves the workload off of you.

ADFS requires a number of components to be configured. The right side of figure 21.2 illustrates an ADFS configuration. The major components of ADFS are

- *Federation trust*—Configuration enabling ADFS to work
- *Account partner*—Domain containing accounts
- *Resource partner*—Domain containing application or other resource
- *Federation service*—Hosted on ADFS servers

Let's start with federation trusts.

FEDERATION TRUST

A federation trust is created between your organization and one or more external organizations to allow those organizations access to specific applications. Federation trusts are created between federation servers running ADFS. The federation trust is created in the configuration in the account partner and the resource partner—there isn't a physical trust as with a forest trust.

NOTE Federation trusts aren't related to the AD trusts you learned about in chapter 18.

ACCOUNT PARTNER

An account partner is the external organization that hosts and manages the user accounts. AD or ADLS accounts can be used to provide access to the application. The federation server in the account partner organization issues security tokens that make assertions about the users—for instance, the user can perform certain actions. The tokens are presented across the federation trust to the resource partner.

RESOURCE PARTNER

The resource partner organization hosts one or more web applications. Resource partners trust the account partners to authenticate the users and provide them with security tokens.

FEDERATION SERVICE

The federation service is installed when you install the ADFS role on a Windows server, shown as the ADFS server in figure 21.2. An instance of the federation service is required in both the account partner and the resource partner.

In the account partner, the federation service is responsible for

- Verifying user credentials against Active Directory.
- Populating organization claims—for example, group membership—from data stored in Active Directory.
- Mapping organization claims to federation claims—for instance, members of a particular group may be granted access to more functionality in the application.
- Packaging the claims in a digitally signed security token so it can be sent to the resource partner.

The federation service in the resource partner will

- Verify that incoming security tokens come from a trusted organization.
- Map incoming claims to resource organization claims—for instance, mapping the required access to the correct group in the resource domain's Active Directory.
- Package the resource organization claims into a new digitally signed token that's presented back to the client. The client then presents the new token to the application.

The last topic you need to cover in this area is ADLS.

21.1.4 *AD Lightweight Services*

ADLS is a way to provide authentication to applications without using a full Active Directory. It used to be known as AD Application Mode (ADAM). You might use ADLS in these types of scenarios:

- You need to provide a directory service for developers so they can test their applications.
- An application requires a schema extension, but you can't perform that schema extension in your main Active Directory.

- An application exists in your perimeter network (DMZ) that requires authentication. It's not safe to put a full domain controller into the perimeter network. Install ADLS and replicate data from your Active Directory to the ADLS sever. Microsoft uses this scenario for Edge servers in Exchange 2007 and 2010.

You can administer ADLS using the techniques you've learned in the earlier chapters of the book. With ADLS, you'll concentrate on the data (users, groups, and computers), because the topology concepts (sites, subnets, and so on) don't exist in this cutdown version of Active Directory.

ADLS is installed as a Windows feature. Multiple instances of ADLS can be hosted on the same server.

Data can be replicated between instances of ADLS. You can also replicate your main AD data out to an ADLS instance—for example, Exchange 2007 and 2010 do this for the Edge server role.

This concludes the book as far as on-premises Active Directory is concerned (chapter 22 looks at Active Directory in the cloud), though in reality your learning never finishes. I'm still learning new things about Active Directory, and I've been working with it since 2000. One thing that does help is practicing the techniques. This is the purpose of the final exam.

21.2   *Final exam*

This isn't so much of an exam as a final lab that pulls together many of the topics and skills you've learned while reading this book. There's no pass or fail. Use the exercise to ensure you've mastered the skills from earlier chapters. If you're unsure of anything, refer back to the appropriate chapter and refresh your memory.

> **TIP** Don't worry about looking things up if you're unsure of how to proceed. There are things that I do so infrequently that I always double-check with the documentation before proceeding. PowerShell syntax is a classic example. The help files are there for you to check your coding. Use them—don't guess.

You've already performed all of the tasks in this exercise. There are no trick questions. Your mission—should you choose to accept it—is to perform the AD administration tasks required to bring a new office online in your organization. As with all of the exercises in this book, sample answers will be provided in the download from the book's website.

21.2.1   *Scenario*

Your company in Seattle has been very successful over the last few years and has decided to open an office in London. The new office requires the following modifications to your Active Directory:

- New AD site and subnet
- Create domain controller in new office

- New OUs, users, and groups
- New compute accounts
- New GPOs for user and computer configuration
- New PSOs for finance group and HR group located at new site
- Delegate password management to groups at new site
- Configure AD replication to the new site
- Create monitoring processes

Each of these steps will be covered in detail in the next section. Feel free to add further activities to extend your practice if you desire. It's your test lab.

21.2.2 Activities

Perform the following activities to complete the scenario presented in the previous section. If you can't complete any part of the exercise due to the limitations of your test environment (for instance, you can't route between multiple subnets), modify the lab to suit your environment.

AD SITE AND SUBNET
Create an AD site:

- Name: London.
- Location: London.
- Description: AD site for new London office.
- Subnet: `10.14.06.0/16` (you can use any suitable subnet); set the subnet description and location to match the site.

DOMAIN CONTROLLER
Create a new domain controller for the London site:

- Name: LondonDC.
- Type: Writable domain controller.
- Install DNS as part of the process.
- Check that the correct SRV records have been created.

OUS
Create the OUs listed in table 21.1.

Table 21.1   OUs for the London site

Name	Description	Location
London	Top-level OU for London	Root of domain
Users	London users	London OU
Computers	London workstations	London OU
Groups	London groups	London OU

Remember to enable Protect from Accidental Deletion!

USER ACCOUNTS AND GROUPS

Create the user accounts listed in table 21.2. Create the groups in the table and add the users to the appropriate groups. Create the users and groups in the appropriate OU.

Table 21.2   Users and groups for the London site

First Name	Last Name	samAccountName	Group Membership
Aimee	Jones	ajones	LondonManagers, Londonfinance
Alex	Smith	asmith	Londonapp1, London HR
Ann	Green	agreen	Londonfinance, LondonConfidential
Clare	Brown	cbrown	Londonapp1, Londonapp2
Harry	Black	hblack	Londoncomms, LondonSales
June	Sherman	jsherman	LondonConfidential, Londonapp2
Pat	Lee	plee	Londoncomms, LondonSales
Robert	Grant	rgrant	Londonapp1, London HR
Ron	Stuart	rstuart	Londoncomms, LondonSales
Sarah	Salisbury	ssalisbury	LondonManagers, ,Londonfinance
Tom	Lincoln	tlincoln	Londonapp1, Londonapp2
William	Churchill	wchurchill	Londonapp1, Londonapp2, Londonfinance

COMPUTER ACCOUNTS

Create accounts for the new computers in the correct OU. Create the computer names as `LondonPC01` to `LondonPC12`.

GPOS

Create a GPO for user configuration with the following settings:

- Set the wallpaper (use a picture of your own devising or one of the pictures available in a default Windows installation).
- Set the idle time before the screensaver starts. Configure the machine to lock when the screensaver starts.

Create a GPO for computer configuration with the following settings:

- Configure a printer (Hint: Preferences).
- Ensure a system restore can be performed (Hint: Administrative Templates > System).

Link the GPOs to the appropriate new OU you created.

PSOS

Create two new PSOs for the finance group and HR group in the London site. Use the following information for the finance group's PSO:

- Name: LondonfinancePSO
- Password length: 12 characters
- Maximum password age: 20 days

The PSO for the HR group should be created with these settings:

- Name: LondonHRPSO
- Password length: 11 characters
- Maximum password age: 25 days

Apply the PSO to the appropriate group.

DELEGATE PASSWORD MANAGEMENT

Delegate password management for the London users' OU to the LondonHR group.

CONFIGURE AD REPLICATION

Create and configure an AD site link between the new London site and the Seattle site:

- Name: Seattle–London
- Replication cost: 50
- Replication frequency: 30 minutes
- Replication schedule: 8:00 p.m. to 6:00 a.m.

MONITORING

Configure processes to monitor

- AD replication between the Seattle and London sites
- Disk space on the new domain controller
- Domain controller availability and services

One final action would be to create one or more PowerShell scripts to automate these tasks. If your company continues to be successful, you'll be called on to perform these actions on a frequent basis. Automate it now and save time in the future.

21.3 *Ideas for on your own*

This isn't the end of your AD learning process. You're able to manage your Active Directory on a day-to-day basis and have been exposed to the common troubleshooting scenarios. A book of this size can't cover every eventuality and you should expect, occasionally, to meet new problems. When you do and you find the solution, make sure that you document it so you can refer to it in the future. Better still: share it with the community of IT administrators.

AD changes and evolves as new versions of Windows are released. For instance, Windows Server 2012 R2 was released during the writing of this book. Everything you've learned in this book is applicable to Windows 2012 R2. Make sure you keep up to date with what's new so that you can advise your organization on the adoption of the new features. Even better, you'll be prepared to administer the new features when they go live in your organization.

Your organization will evolve in parallel with AD technologies. Are there changes in your organization that introduce the need to consider a branch office scenario? Do any of the applications being introduced into your organization need their own authentication mechanism that would mean using AD Lightweight Services?

The premise of this book is to provide you with the skills and knowledge you need to administer you organization's Active Directory. The underlying theory has been covered in sufficient depth for your day-to-day work. There's more information available that will extend your AD knowledge—the Microsoft website is a great place to start. Investigate and learn so that you become the go-to guy in your organization for Active Directory.

A running theme throughout the book has been automating your AD administration. Embrace automation and automate as much as you can. This won't put you out of a job; it'll make time for you to learn and experiment as described earlier in the section.

Above all else, enjoy what you do!

Into the cloud 22

If you look up into the sky, you'll see clouds. They can be dark and forbidding, white and fluffy, or extremely wispy and nebulous. Cloud computing is a bit like that. It seems to be all things to all vendors, and can vary from a nebulous concept to something that appears to be very threatening and will cause you lots of problems. As usual, with any big change in the IT landscape, the truth is somewhere in between.

The *cloud* is viewed as the "next big thing" in computing. You can't read anything from the computer press or any of the major vendors without tripping over the term. So what is it, and what does it mean to you as an AD administrator?

This chapter starts by examining the phenomenon that's cloud computing and explains the types and service models. You'll then learn how your Active Directory can migrate into the cloud—either totally or partially—and how you can integrate with a cloud-based Active Directory. If you do migrate your organization's infrastructure into the cloud, you can simplify your AD topology by reducing the number of AD sites. Windows Azure Active Directory is a directory service based in the cloud to which you can integrate your on-premises Active Directory. After learning what Azure is, you'll learn how to administer the major data types—users and groups.

The nature of the material in this chapter means you don't have to do a lab. TRY IT NOWs can't be provided either, unless you have a Windows Azure AD instance to work with. You can get a free trial at http://office.microsoft.com/en-us/try, which will allow you to experiment based on the examples later in the chapter.

Before you can understand how Active Directory can work in a cloud computing scenario, you need to know a bit more about cloud computing in general.

22.1   *What is a cloud?*

Cloud computing doesn't have a standard definition. If you ask 100 IT administrators to define cloud computing, you'll probably get at least 101 answers. One definition that I like is from the U.S. National Institute of Standards and Technology (NIST; http://csrc.nist.gov/publications/nistpubs/800-145/SP800-145.pdf). Their definition states that the following five characteristics define a cloud computing solution:

1 *On-demand self-service*—The customer can provision computing resources at their convenience.
2 *Broad network access*—Resources are available remotely and are accessible from a variety of devices.
3 *Resource pooling*—The provider operates their resources in a multitenant model.
4 *Rapid elasticity*—Resources can be provisioned and de-provisioned to meet rapid changes in demand.
5 *Measured service*—Resource usage is monitored and reported so that the customer and provider have full information on resource consumption.

A cloud solution will be created from a number of infrastructure components:

Virtualization platform
Storage
Network

There are a number of ways that cloud computing can be delivered. We'll cover some of the basic ones next.

22.1.1   *Cloud types*

Rather than being discrete items, these definitions should be viewed as possible ends of the spectrum. In reality, the definitions are blurred due to the rapidly evolving nature of the subject and the integration of managed services into the mix.

Many organizations don't migrate all of their computing resources to a cloud. A split of cloud and traditional data center operations is common.

PUBLIC

A public cloud is available for any consumer—individual or organization—to purchase resources. Windows Azure (http://www.windowsazure.com/en-us/) and Amazon Web Services (http://aws.amazon.com/) are two examples of public clouds.

Public clouds are hosted by the provider and made available to the consumer over the internet, or, possibly, through dedicated connections.

PRIVATE

In a private cloud, the underlying infrastructure is dedicated to a single customer. This could be hosted by a cloud provider (off premises) or by the organization itself (on premises).

On-premises private clouds can be constructed from scratch by the organization purchasing the required components and performing the integration to produce the cloud. The software that controls the cloud and provides automation functionality must be purchased or written to meet the organization's requirements. Major vendors, such as HP, IBM, and Dell, offer a one-stop "cloud in a box" that delivers all of the components required to create your private cloud.

HYBRID

A hybrid cloud can be viewed as the best (or possibly worst, depending on your point of view) of public and private clouds. In the hybrid model, the organization uses two or more cloud infrastructures that are linked to enable data and application portability.

One such scenario would involve an organization maintaining most of its computing on a private cloud and utilizing a public cloud for peak-demand periods—for example, an online retailer that needed to increase capacity in the time up to the Christmas holiday period.

In addition to the types of cloud available, you also need to be aware of the various models for delivering services through cloud computing.

22.1.2 *Service models*

The way services are delivered in cloud computing is usually referred to as "X as a Service," where X could be infrastructure, software, backup, storage, or any other computing service. Anything as a *Service* is one of the latest terms to be coined and is taken to mean any service that the provider (internal or external) can deliver through their cloud infrastructure. Some of the more common service offerings are infrastructure, platform, and software as services.

INFRASTRUCTURE AS A SERVICE

With the Infrastructure as a Service (IaaS) model, the cloud provider supplies the storage, hardware, networking, and virtualization platform. The customer typically pays on a per-use—often per virtual server—pattern.

Examples of IaaS providers include Amazon Web Services, Rackspace, and Windows Azure.

PLATFORM AS A SERVICE

Platform as a Service (PaaS) provides a computing platform and solution stack as a service. The customer creates, configures, and deploys their applications using the tools provided by the vendor. The applications are hosted on the infrastructure provided by the vendor, such as Amazon or Microsoft.

SOFTWARE AS A SERVICE

Software as a Service (SaaS) involves the provider hosting the application and data for the customer. Common types of software delivered in this manner include Microsoft Office productivity suites and email (for example, Office365), customer relationship management (CRM; for example, Salesforce), and databases (for example, SQL Azure).

22.2 *Active Directory in the cloud*

By now you may be thinking that cloud computing is going to negate the skills you've learned while working through this book. In fact, your AD knowledge will stand you in good stead if and when your organization moves into a cloud computing scenario.

If you think about the options for using cloud computing within your organization, you end up with a number of broad-brush pictures for IaaS:

- Not using the cloud at all
- All infrastructure in the cloud
- Infrastructure in multiple clouds
- Mixture of cloud (private or public) and traditional data center

In these scenarios, the data in your Active Directory (users, groups, and computers) remains exactly as it was before the migration to a cloud-based infrastructure. The impact will be on the topology of your Active Directory, and in most cases will simplify your Active Directory.

If your organization isn't using cloud computing, nothing has changed in your Active Directory and you can carry on administering it using the techniques you've learned in chapters 1 through 21. On the other hand, if you've moved all of your infrastructure to the cloud, nothing much changes either.

22.2.1 *All infrastructure in the cloud*

In this scenario, your organization has moved completely into the cloud. This could be for a number of reasons, including

- Avoiding the cost of hardware replacement
- Data center lease has expired
- Data center consolidation initiative deems a cloud solution is most cost-effective

You might not be consulted about this decision, but you'll need to administer the results. Your organization's infrastructure will be something like that shown in figure 22.1.

In this scenario your servers and domain controllers are virtual machines in a cloud environment. It could be an on-premises private cloud or a cloud (public or private) hosted at your suppliers. You use the tools you've seen throughout the book to connect to the domain controller and perform your administration.

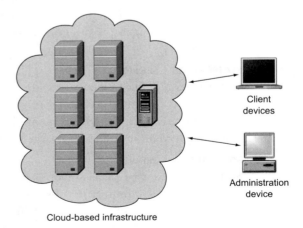

Figure 22.1 **All infrastructure is in the cloud**

Apart from possibly the location of the infrastructure, nothing has changed in your environment. This is no different in concept from having a single data center with your domain controllers centralized in that one location. Your organization just needs to ensure that you have sufficient bandwidth between the supplier and your users, but that's not an AD problem.

You can really simplify your Active Directory in this type of situation:

- Define one AD site and ensure that all subnets are correctly defined and allocated to that site.
- Replication is intrasite, which removes replication time lags and reduces bandwidth requirements.
- Reduce the number of domain controllers (you always need at least two in a production domain—don't be tempted to drop below that number).

How does this picture change if you're using multiple clouds?

22.2.2 Infrastructure on multiple clouds

If you use multiple clouds, which could be any mixture of private and public and on- or off-premise, you have the situation illustrated in figure 22.2.

Figure 22.2 shows two clouds in use, but there's no reason you can't have more. Each cloud has one or more domain controllers plus a set of servers. The way you manage this depends on the purpose of the clouds. A number of scenarios are possible.

BOTH CLOUDS ARE USED FOR PRODUCTION

In this case you may be splitting the production servers between the clouds, or one may be production and the other is treated as a disaster recovery site. In Active Directory you simply treat each cloud as an AD site.

Your domain controllers need to be configured to replicate between the sites, but this is no different from a situation with multiple physical locations being treated as

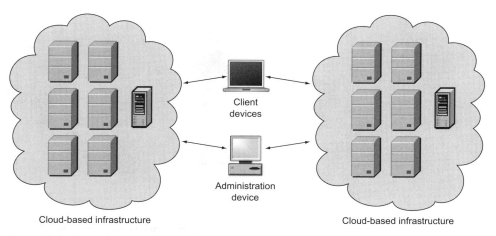

Client
devices

Administration
device

Cloud-based infrastructure   Cloud-based infrastructure

Figure 22.2   An environment with multiple clouds

different AD sites. You'll need to define the locations with the client (and administration) devices as AD sites (even though they don't have domain controllers).

CLOUDS HAVE DIFFERENT PURPOSES

In this scenario your clouds have different purposes. They could be, for example

- *Two domains in a single forest*—Administer as one forest with multiple AD sites. A trust will automatically exist between the domains.
- *Two parts of the organization that need to be in separate forest*—Keep two separate AD instances.
- *Multiple account forests and a resource forest (hosting Exchange)*—Create appropriate trusts between the forests.
- *A production domain and a test domain*—No direct contact between the domains, so keep as two separate AD instances.

Other combinations are possible. Whatever your exact situation, you'll be administering one or more AD forests in exactly the same way you would if they were hosted in traditional data centers.

The final option to consider in this section is a mixture of a traditional data center and the cloud.

22.2.3 *Infrastructure in data center and cloud*

Hosting Active Directory with a combination of a traditional data center plus the cloud is illustrated in figure 22.3.

In this scenario you could have multiple clouds and/or multiple data centers, depending on the size of your organization. This scenario is an extension of the one in section 22.2.2, with the addition of physical data centers as AD sites. The same set of options applies for managing your AD instances.

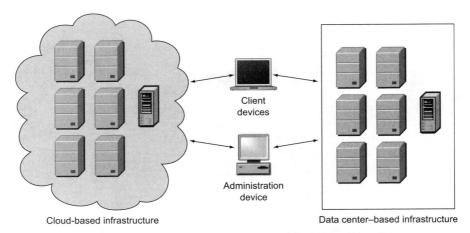

Cloud-based infrastructure   Data center–based infrastructure

Figure 22.3   A heterogeneous environment with cloud-based and data center-based infrastructure

Using the cloud to host your infrastructure doesn't have a great impact on your Active Directory because you can treat the cloud instances as AD sites and manage them as you would physical sites. If your organization starts to use SaaS, you may need to think about using Windows Azure Active Directory.

22.3 *Windows Azure Active Directory*

Many applications—for instance, SQL Server and Exchange—require you to authenticate before allowing access to the application and, more importantly, the underlying data. If you're lucky, those applications will allow you to use Active Directory to perform that authentication. The authentication is performed by Active Directory, and permissions to access the application, and therefore the data, are granted to the user account, or in many cases a group of which the user is a member.

This is great because it saves you tons of work. But what happens when you start to migrate some of these applications to SAAS instances? Your Active Directory won't work in this situation because there's no way for the application to perform the required authentication steps.

This is where you need to consider Windows Azure Active Directory (WAAD; http://www.windowsazure.com/en-us/services/active-directory/).

22.3.1 *What is WAAD?*

WAAD is a cloud-based identity management system designed to provide an identity service across Windows Azure, Office 365, and other cloud services (including third parties). It can act in a standalone manner or can be integrated to extend your organization's Active Directory into the cloud, enabling you to solve a number of problems:

- Enables your users to continue to use their corporate credentials to access the SaaS applications, giving your users a single sign-on (SSO) capability across their corporate and SAAS applications.
- Enables Windows Azure multifactor authentication, which enhances your security when accessing cloud-based applications.
- Enables your Active Directory to integrate with other web identity providers, such as Microsoft Account (formerly Windows Live ID amongst other names), Yahoo!, and Facebook.
- Provides a mechanism for developers to query directory data to manage users and groups.

NOTE You're responsible for your AD service and the data it contains. With WAAD, you're only responsible for maintaining the data. It's Microsoft's responsibility to ensure the service is available.

So how do you use WAAD?

22.3.2 *Using WAAD*

You have two options when using WAAD, depending on what the users need to do:

- WAAD can be the only directory service for individuals who only use SaaS applications.
- WAAD can be integrated with your Active Directory to provide SSO capabilities across your enterprise's whole application portfolio.

> **WARNING**   WAAD is a multitenant service, meaning that your organization's directory data is stored alongside that of numerous other organizations. This may not fit with your organization's security requirements.

If you need to offer your users an SSO experience, it means that their user account information needs to appear in your Active Directory and in WAAD. You can spend a lot of time and effort retyping the data or you can synchronize the data from your Active Directory to WAAD, as illustrated in figure 22.4.

In figure 22.4 the user logs on to the domain. The Active Directory is federated with WAAD using Active Directory Federation Services (ADFS). When the user attempts to access the SaaS application (which is configured to use WAAD for authentication), a token is issued to the user by WAAD that the user can then present to the application (represented by the dashed line in figure 22.4). This all happens automatically in the background without any need for intervention by the user. The connections run through the user's device, which is why the token issuing appears to involve the user.

The SaaS application then uses the token to determine the user's level of access to the application during the time the user is connected to the application. During this session, the SaaS application may be configured to query WAAD for further information about the user (represented by the curved, dotted line in figure 22.4).

Please note the direction of synchronization—it's from your Active Directory into the cloud. That way you and your organization retain control of the data at all times.

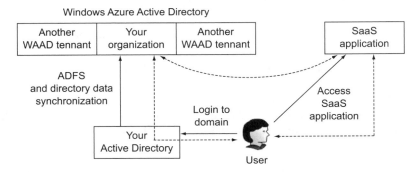

Figure 22.4   Using WAAD to authenticate against a SaaS application

22.3.3 WAAD compared to Active Directory

At the time of writing, WAAD can't be considered a complete replacement for your on-premises Active Directory. When compared to the Active Directory based on Windows Server domain controllers, WAAD currently has a number of differences including

- A simpler schema
- A nonextendable schema—it's a multitenant offering, so the schema has to be fixed
- No Group Policy
- Not capable of storing computer objects
- Doesn't support LDAP
- Won't authenticate computers, so you can't use it to log on to machines that only use WAAD for authentication

It may be that WAAD will eventually replace Active Directory, or will have all of the functionality so that it could replace your organization's Active Directory. I don't expect this to happen any time soon, so your AD skills are still going to be needed.

Having examined cloud computing and how it interacts with your Active Directory, lets close this chapter by looking at how you, as an administrator, work with WAAD.

22.4 Working with WAAD

You have two main options for managing Windows Azure Active Directory. You can use one of a number of portals or you can use the Windows Azure Active Directory PowerShell module. Remember, you're only administering the data—users, groups, and so on. You don't get to manage the underlying service (this is the way most cloud-based products work).

The AD-related tasks you can perform include

- Create, modify, and delete user accounts.
- Manage passwords.
- Migrate from existing environments to the cloud.

TIP   Remember that if you're synchronizing your organization's Active Directory with WAAD, you can perform the administration locally and the changes will be uploaded to WAAD.

Let's have a quick look at the portals before jumping into using PowerShell.

22.4.1 Portals for WAAD

You're spoiled for choices with regards to portals. Your options will depend on the services for which you're using WAAD, but they can include

- Windows Azure Management portal
- Windows Azure AD portal
- Windows Intune portal
- Office 365 account portal

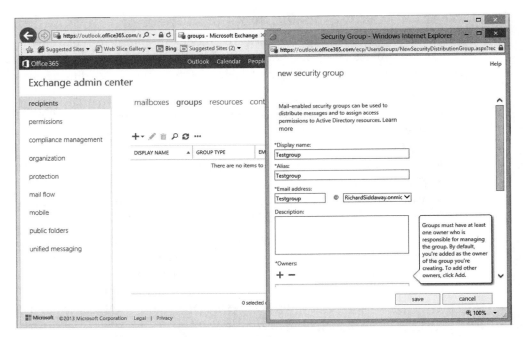

Figure 22.5   Creating a security group in the Office 365 portal

In all cases you have a web-based GUI interface for managing user accounts. As an example of using one of the portals, consider figure 22.5, which shows a security group being created in the Office 365 portal.

The portal illustrates a number of task-based options along the left edge of the diagram. Choose Recipients and then Groups from the horizontal list. Click the plus sign under mailboxes to display the new security group dialog. A limited amount of information, which should be familiar to you from chapter 4, is required:

- Group display name—Same as name in Active Directory
- An alias for the group—Compare to samAccountName in Active Directory
- An email address

Optionally you can add a description and another owner. The creator is automatically an owner.

This interface, and the other portals, provides a minimalist approach to administrative functionality that should be intuitive to you after using the AD tools you've learned about throughout the book. The advantage of portal-based administration is that it's web-based, so you can perform the tasks from anywhere you have internet connectivity.

Your alternative to using a portal is to use Windows PowerShell.

22.4.2 *PowerShell for WAAD*

The Windows Azure Active Directory PowerShell module can be downloaded from http://technet.microsoft.com/en-us/library/jj151815.aspx. This page also serves as a gateway into the online help for the WAAD PowerShell cmdlets. The cmdlets in this module have similar names to those in the Active Directory you've already seen. Table 22.1 lists some of the more common cmdlets you'll need and compares them with their AD equivalents.

Table 22.1   Representative WAAD and AD cmdlets

Item	WAAD	Active Directory

User	`Get-MsolUser`
	`New-MsolUser`
	`Set-MsolUser`
	`Remove-MsolUser`
		`Get-ADUser`
		`New-ADUser`
		`Set-ADUser`
		`Remove-ADUser`

Group	`Get-MsolGroup`
	`New-MsolGroup`
	`Set-MsolGroup`
	`Remove-MsolGroup`
		`Get-ADGroup`
		`New-ADGroup`
		`Set-ADGroup`
		`Remove-ADGroup`

The biggest difference is in the prefix applied to the noun: Active Directory uses `AD` and WAAD uses `Msol` (Microsoft online; in fact, the module is called MSOnline).

Once you've downloaded and installed the WAAD module, you need to connect to your WAAD instance.

CONNECTING TO WAAD

Connecting to your WAAD instance is achieved by using the `Connect-MsolService` cmdlet:

```
$cred = Get-Credential
Connect-MsolService –Credential $cred
```

The `Get-Credential` will prompt you for the username and password to create the credential. Alternatively, you can use `Connect-MsolService` without the credential and you'll be automatically prompted for the logon information. `Connect-MsolService`, like all of the WAAD cmdlets, assumes that you have a connection to the internet. You can't connect without one!

> **TIP**   When you've finished administering WAAD, you can disconnect by closing your owerShell session.

Now you're connected. How about administering some users?

ADMINISTERING WAAD USERS

You normally want to do four things to users—okay, there are some users you probably want to do more to, but that's another story—create, view, modify, and delete. This is the CRUD lifecycle you've seen throughout the book.

TIP Make sure you read the help files for any WAAD cmdlets you're using because there are some subtle (and not so subtle) differences compared to the AD cmdlets.

Creating a user can be performed using `New-MsolUser`. You can use it in much the same way as `New-ADUser` from chapter 2:

```
New-MsolUser -UserPrincipalName alex@manticore.org `
-DisplayName 'Alex Skipton'  -FirstName 'Alex'  -LastName 'Skipton' `
-UsageLocation 'GB' -LicenseAssignment 'Manticore:Standard'
```

There are two parameters you haven't seen before: `UsageLocation` defines the country where the service is consumed, and `LicenseAssignment` assigns a license to the user. Cloud services are paid for on a resource basis and in this case it's per user, so you have to grant the user a license; otherwise they can't use WAAD to authenticate. Notice that you don't need a `samAccountName`. You either need to set a password using the `-Password` parameter during creation or you can use `Set-MsolUserPassword`, which you'll also need when the user forgets their password.

Viewing user information is the province of `Get-MsolUser`:

```
Get-MsolUser -All
```

This will return all users in your WAAD.

A single user can be viewed by giving an identifier such as `UserPrincipalName`:

```
Get-MsolUser -UserPrincipalName robert@manticore.org
```

If you want to filter the users for whom you're retrieving information, you can use one of several filters. Enabled or disabled accounts can be discovered:

```
Get-MsolUser -EnabledFilter 'EnabledOnly'
Get-MsolUser -EnabledFilter 'DisabledOnly'
```

You can filter by city, state, or country:

```
Get-MsolUser -City 'London'
Get-MsolUser -State 'Washington'
Get-MsolUser -Country 'US'
```

Finally, you could filter by partial name:

```
Get-MsolUser -SearchString 'Richard'
```

All users with "Richard" somewhere in their display name or email address will be returned.

You have fewer options in terms of attributes that you can modify with WAAD compared to Active Directory:

```
Set-MsolUser -UserPrincipalName ann@manticore.org `
-Title "Manager" -Department "Headquarters"
```

To delete a user you can modify this code:

```
Remove-MsolUser -UserPrincipalName jo@manticore.org -Force
```

The `-Force` parameter suppresses the message from asking for interactive confirmation.

The other major data area to manage is groups.

ADMINISTERING WAAD GROUPS

It shouldn't come as a surprise that you create a group in this manner:

```
New-MsolGroup -DisplayName 'Baston' `
-Description 'Users based in Baston'
```

Adding a group member is a bit more complicated than with Active Directory:

```
$user = Get-MsolUser -UserPrincipalName ann@manticore.org
$group = Get-MsolGroup | where {$_.DisplayName -eq "Baston"}

Add-MsolGroupMember -GroupObjectId $group.ObjectId `
-GroupMemberType 'User' -GroupMemberObjectId $user.ObjectId
```

Start by getting the user based on the user principal name (or any other search criteria). The `$group` variable is used to hold the group information—again discovered by searching. Finally, the `Add-MsolGroupMember` cmdlet is used to add the user into the group.

> **TIP** I recommend creating scripts that take a user and group name as parameters and using those to perform group membership additions and removals.

Removing a member from a group is the opposite of adding:

```
$user = Get-MsolUser -UserPrincipalName ann@manticore.org
$group = Get-MSolGroup | where {$_.DisplayName -eq "Baston"}

Remove-MsolGroupMember -GroupObjectId $group.ObjectId `
-GroupMemberType 'User' -GroupMemberObjectId $user.ObjectId
```

I can't cover all of the possible actions you could perform when administering WAAD, but the information presented here will cover at least 90% of your activity.

22.5 *Afterword*

Congratulations on getting to the end of the book. You now have a solid understanding of Active Directory and how to administer it. Whether your organization's Active Directory is on site, in the cloud, managed through WAAD, or a mixture of two or more of these, you have the skills you need to manage that Active Directory.

Cloud computing seems to be the way forward, but next year something completely different may come along that turns all of our thinking upside down again. Whatever happens, there will still be a need for Active Directory and skilled people to look after it. By reading this book, you've made a big commitment to your future and to building a skill set that will be usable and wanted.

Enjoy your future in AD administration and remember to keep on learning—there's always something new.

appendix A
Searching Active Directory

You've seen many examples of searching Active Directory throughout the book. Unless you work in a very small organization where you know every member of the staff, you'll need to search Active Directory to find the user, group, or computer you need to work with. This appendix pulls together the examples you've seen already and a new set of search filters that you can use directly or with a little bit of modification. The searches are shown in PowerShell, but remember that the LDAP filters can be used in ADUC.

The Microsoft AD cmdlets can be used in a number of ways:

- Supply a value to the `Identity` parameter.
- Supply an LDAP filter.
- Supply a PowerShell filter.

You'll see how the different filters work. There are two ways to filter your search in the AD cmdlets: using PowerShell syntax, which you already know, and using LDAP query syntax. The main objects you'll search for are users, groups, and computers. Examples of the filters (PowerShell and LDAP) are provided for the main searches you're likely to conduct. The appendix closes with a look at searching in the GUI tools.

A.1 PowerShell Identity parameter

The `Identity` parameter takes one of several types of values:

- Account name
- Distinguished name
- GUID
- Security identifier

Let's look at these in order. The examples in the following sections all return the same user account.

A.1.1 Account name

The account name is commonly used for searching. This is the logon ID or samAccountName:

```
Get-ADUser -Identity dgreen
```

If your organization has a consistent method of producing samAccountNames (as recommended in chapter 2), you'll probably be able to guess the required value and use it. I've worked in places where the samAccountNames are assigned in sequence and follow a pattern, such as two letters and three numbers. Life becomes difficult at that point because you can't easily work out the required value.

A.1.2 Distinguished name

Searching for a user based on the distinguished name is performed like this:

```
Get-ADUser -Identity "CN=GREEN Dave, `
OU=ADMLUsers,OU=ADMLunches,DC=Manticore,DC=org"
```

The distinguished name supplies the full path to the object. You can break down the distinguished name like this:

- *Object name*—For instance, CN=GREEN Dave.
- *OU path*—For instance, OU=ADMLUsers,OU=ADMLunches. The OU path starts with the OU containing the object and adds on parent OUs.
- *Domain*—For instance, DC=Manticore,DC=org.

To create a distinguished name, you need to know the name of the object, the full OU path, and the domain. This makes the distinguished name a difficult choice for searching.

A.1.3 GUID

The GUID is a unique identifier for the object. As such, it's an ideal candidate for searching. You can use the GUID to search for a user in this manner:

```
Get-ADUser -Identity '28f0c168-d142-417f-a223-333488cdaa77'
```

Now, I'll bet you're looking at that and thinking "I'm not going to use that because I'll never remember the GUID for one user, never mind however many thousands of users there are in the environment." You're probably right. I can't remember ever using it, but it's included for completeness.

A.1.4 Security identifier

The security identifier (SID) looks similar to the GUID:

```
Get-ADUser -Identity 'S-1-5-21-3881460461-1879668979-35955009-6270'
```

I doubt it'll ever be your primary search criterion, but it does come in handy when checking users against permissions. The SID is the item that's recoded on the object.

When you check the security permissions on an object using the GUI tools, the names are normally resolved. If name resolution can't occur, you'll see the SID. Try searching on the SID to identify the user. Search both live and deleted accounts.

Using Get-ADObject

One question I'm frequently asked is if it's better to use `Get-ADObject` as a generic search tool or to use the object type-specific cmdlets such as `Get-ADUser`, `Get-ADComputer`, and `Get-ADGroup`.

I always use the object-specific cmdlets because they're simpler. If I use `Get-ADObject -LDAPFilter "(Name=*test*)"` in my test environment, I get 11 users, 6 OUs, 17 groups, and a partridge in a pear tree.

I have to add another element to the filter to restrict the return to specific types:

```
Get-ADObject -LDAPFilter "(&(objectcategory=user)(Name=*test*))"
Get-ADObject -LDAPFilter
➥  "(&(objectcategory=organizationalUnit)(Name=*test*))"
Get-ADObject -LDAPFilter "(&(objectcategory=group)(Name=*test*))"
```

This is extra work that you don't need. Stick with the object-specific cmdlets. Similar filters can be constructed if you use the `-Filter` parameter.

When searching for an object in Active Directory, you usually have the object's name. This means that you have to resort to one of the two filter parameters: `-LDAPFilter` or `-Filter`. The LDAP filter requires you to use LDAP query syntax.

A.2   *LDAP query syntax*

The GUI tools ADAC and ADUC can use LDAP filters to query Active Directory, or they can use a more normal language-based approach. PowerShell can also use LDAP filters. You can go a long way without learning how to use the LDAP query syntax, but you need to understand it for a number of reasons:

- It explains what's happening under the covers in the more normal language-based searches.
- It enables you to understand scripts that have been written to perform AD searches (from before the cmdlets were available) and to use and understand the filters you find in those scripts.

A.2.1 *Basic filters*

Your starting point for any search is an LDAP filter. A common filter looks something like this:

```
"(&(|(sn=Jones)(sn=Smith))(givenname=Jo))"
```

No, you may not run away—it's not really complicated once you break it down. You need to treat this in the same way you used to treat algebra at school—use the parentheses, start in the middle, and work out. Your starting point is the two statements:

```
(sn=Jones)
(sn=Smith)
```

The first means "surname (AD attribute name `sn`) is equal to Jones", and the second means "surname is equal to Smith". You now need to move out a level:

```
(|(sn=Jones)(sn=Smith))
```

If I tell you that the | symbol means "or," your filter now reads "surname equals Jones or Smith." There's another statement at the same level:

```
(givenname=Jo)
```

This means "first name (AD attribute name `givenname`) equals Jo". These two statements are bracketed together as

```
(&(|(sn=Jones)(sn=Smith))(givenname=Jo))
```

You need to be aware of a quirk in the syntax of these filters. Don't leave a space between the attribute name and the operator like this:

```
"(&(|(sn=Jones)(sn=Smith))(givenname =Jo))"
```

Your query will fail if you do, and you'll most likely not get any results.

Now what does the filter `(&(|(sn=Jones)(sn=Smith))(givenname=Jo))` mean? It translates as "all objects where surname equals Jones or Smith and first name equals Jo". That's not so bad, is it?

> **TIP** When you're creating your own filters, build them up like this. Start with one attribute, and once you're sure that it's returning the correct results, add others and the required logical operators.

A.2.2 Filter operators

At its simplest, an LDAP filter breaks down to three things: an attribute, an operator, and a value to test against, as shown in table A.1.

Table A.1   Anatomy of an LDAP filter

Item	Example
Attribute	sn
Operator	=
Value	Jones

You can use other simple operators as listed in table A.2.

Table A.2   Simple LDAP filter operators

Operator	Meaning	Example
=	Equals	`(sn=Jones)`
>=	Greater than or equals	`lockouttime>=1`
<=	Less than or equals	`uSNCreated<=14000`
=*	Presence	`sn=*`
=X*Y	Substring	`sn=CH*HILL`

At some stage, you'll try to perform a query of the form `lockouttime>1` or X < Y and it will fail. Don't worry about it—just remember that you need to use >= or <= as your operator. You may need to alter the values you're using to compensate for the use of the >= or <= operators.

The presence operator, =*, tests if an attribute has a value. It doesn't care what that value is. Be careful not to confuse the presence and substring operators because they both use the * symbol.

TIP You'll find references online and elsewhere that refer to an approximately equal operator symbolized by ~=. This gives unpredictable results and should be avoided.

A.2.3 Logical filter operators

You've seen that logical operations can be performed in LDAP filters. The three logical operators are summarized in table A.3.

Table A.3   LDAP filter logical operators

Operator	Meaning	Example
&	And	`(&(sn=Jones)(givenname=Samuel)`
|	Or	`(|(sn=Jones)(sn=Smith)`
!	Not	`(&(givenname=Samuel)(!(sn=Jones)))`

The examples in this section explain how to use these logical operators.

If you look at scripts that have been written to search Active Directory, you'll find that they use one of these filters:

```
(objectclass=user)
(objectclass=user)(objectcategory=user)
(objectclass=computer)
(objectclass=group)
```

They're used to restrict the type of object returned by the search. The first one returns users and computers. Yes—that's right. Computer objects are derived from user objects. If I run a query in my test domain based solely on (objectclass=user), I get 942 users and 20 computers returned!

If you want to only deal with users, extend the query slightly as (object-class=user)(objectcategory=user). This will only return users. You'll need to use the & (and) logical operator. Computers can be found using (objectclass=computer). The final filter, (objectclass=group), is used to restrict the search to groups.

> **TIP** If you're sure that you don't have users, groups, or computers with the same name, you can ignore these filters. They may prove useful when you're searching on other attributes.

A.2.4 Filters on bitwise flags

Some AD attributes, such as UserAccountControl, are a collection of bitwise flags—each bit carries an individual meaning. In the case of the UserAccountControl attribute, bit 2 (value 2) indicates the account is disabled and bit 9 (value 512) indicates a normal account. Using these attributes is messy but these examples will make things clearer.

One of the most common queries using the UserAccountControl attribute is to find disabled accounts. This can be accomplished with the following filter:

```
(useraccountcontrol:1.2.840.113556.1.4.803:=2)
```

The important parts of the filter are the attribute (useraccountcontrol) and the value (2). The odd-looking bit in the middle (:1.2.840.113556.1.4.803:) tells LDAP to perform a bitwise "or" that tests if the bit of which the value is 2 is set. There's an easier way to find disabled user accounts, as you discovered in section 4.2.

A.2.5 Controlling the size of results

Depending on the size of your Active Director, you may need to control the amount of data returned. This can be accomplished by using the -ResultPageSize (number of objects to return in one page; the default is 256) and -ResultSetSize (number of objects to return; the default is $null, which returns all objects) parameters in Power-Shell. In the GUI tools you control this by setting the filter options in ADUC (View menu) or the Management List Options from the Manage drop-down menu.

LDAP versus PowerShell filters

When you search Active Directory with PowerShell, you can use an LDAP filter or a more natural language filter.

```
Get-ADUser -LDAPFilter "(sn=Smith)" | select Name, DistinguishedName
Get-ADUser -Filter {sn -eq 'Smith'} | select Name, DistinguishedName
```

These two queries give exactly the same results. So which should you use?

> **(continued)**
>
> I recommend using the LDAP filters for two reasons:
>
> The same filter can be used in PowerShell and the GUI tools.
>
> It's less confusing.
>
> When you're more confident with PowerShell, I encourage you to experiment with the
> `-Filter` parameter. One immediate use is to display all of the objects in an organizational unit.
>
> The `-Filter` parameter is also easier to use for wildcard searches.

A.2.6 Filter on an OU

It's easy to see all of the users or computers in a single OU using the GUI tools—you just browse. Using PowerShell, you achieve it like this:

```
Get-ADObject -Filter * -SearchBase "OU=England,DC=Manticore,DC=org"
➥ -SearchScope subtree
```

The filter parameter with a value of `*` in the preceding code indicates all objects should be returned. The `-SearchScope` parameter can be used to restrict the search to a number of levels of child OUs, the given OU, or the whole OU tree below the search base (default).

You now know how to construct an LDAP filter to search your Active Directory. It's time for you to put that knowledge to work and discover how to search for user accounts. Before that, though, you need to be aware of the "fuzzy" logic that you can get Active Directory to apply when searching.

A.3   Ambiguous name resolution

If you know part of the user's name, you might think about trying a wildcard search in Active Directory:

```
£> Get-ADUser -Identity Smith*
Get-ADUser : Cannot find an object with identity: 'Smith*' under:
    'DC=Manticore,DC=org'.
At line:1 char:1
+ Get-ADUser -Identity Smith*
+ ~~~~~~~~~~~~~~~~~~~~~~~~~~~
    + CategoryInfo          : ObjectNotFound: (Smith*:ADUser) [Get-ADUser],
    ADIdentityNotFoundException
    + FullyQualifiedErrorId :
    ActiveDirectoryCmdlet:Microsoft.ActiveDirectory.Management.ADIdentityNot
    FoundException,Microsoft.ActiveDirectory.Management.Commands.GetADUser
```

The search fails because you have to give an exact name when using the `Identity` parameter. There are two ways to perform a wildcard search using the AD cmdlets. The first way is to use the `-Filter` parameter:

```
Get-ADUser -Filter {Name -like "Smith*"}
```

You can then refine the filter to give the exact user you need to work with.

The alternative is to use the `-LDAPFilter` parameter:

```
Get-ADObject -LDAPFilter "(anr=Smith)"
```

Ambiguous name resolution (ANR) enables you to find objects in Active Directory when you only have a fragment of the name. A number of attributes are searched when using ANR; for example, the search on Smith in the previous code will expand to include the following:

- Displayname
- Givenname (first name)
- Name (cn)
- samAccountName (login id)
- sn (last name)

An ANR search is treated as a wildcard search, so the real search will be `(cn=Smith*)`, and so on.

ANR is generally a good thing because it helps you find objects much more easily, but if you create a complicated search query that expands to multiple ANR searches, there can be an adverse impact on performance.

A.4   *Searching for specific users*

In this section you'll meet a lot of filters. They're presented in forms suitable for the `-Filter` and `-LDAPFilter` parameters. This dual format helps you learn LDAP filters by presenting a "normal language" alternative. You'll start by searching by name.

In chapters 5 and 19 you saw how to use `Search-ADAccount` to discover users with

- Disabled accounts
- Expired accounts
- Inactive accounts
- Expired passwords
- Locked-out accounts

`Search-ADAccount` is the easiest method of discovering this information and is the recommended approach to solving those search tasks. You can search for accounts for other reasons. The starting point is often the name.

A.4.1 Searching by username

Users have multiple names. Some are even repeatable. The names in which we're interested are

- First name
- Last name
- Full name

- samAccountName
- Display name

TIP Remember that the samAccountName can be used in the -Identity parameter.

To save space, I'll present the filters with the occasional full example in table A.4 to demonstrate any issues.

Table A.4 Filters for searching by name

Search Requirement	PowerShell Filter	LDAP Filter
Full name	`{Name -eq 'SMITH Samuel'}`	`"(cn=SMITH Samuel)"`
First name	`{GivenName -eq 'Samuel'}`	`"(givenname=Samuel)"`
Last name	`{Surname -eq 'Smith'}` `{Sn -eq 'Smith'}`	`"(sn=SMITH)"`
samAccountName	`{samAccountName -eq 'ssmith'}`	`"(samAccountName=ssmith)"`
Partial samAccountName	`{samAccountName -like '*smith*'}`	`"(samAccountName=*smith*)"`
Partial Displayname	`Displayname -like '*smith*'`	`"(DisplayName=*smith*)"`
Description	`{description -like "*President*"}`	`"(description=*President*)"`

If you use a wildcard search, these three filters will give different results:

```
Get-ADUser -Filter {Name -like "*Smith"}
Get-ADUser -Filter {Name -like "Smith*"}
Get-ADUser -Filter {Name -like "*Smith*"}
```

Select the wildcard pattern you need. It's often necessary to use a more open search (for example, `"*Smith*"`) and refine after you see the initial results.

You'll have to use the -Properties parameter if you want to see the Displayname in the results:

```
Get-ADUser -Filter {Displayname -like '*Smith*'} -Properties displayname
```

Searching on elements of the address information can be useful.

A.4.2 Searching by organization information

In your environment, can you determine which users are based in London? Assuming you populate the address information, you can use a query like this:

```
Get-ADUser -LDAPFilter "(l=London)"
```

One of the joys of working with Active Directory is the quirky property names. You have to use l (L works in PowerShell, ADAC, and ADUC). Table A.5 details some common organizational-based searches.

Table A.5   Filters for searching by organization information

Search Requirement	PowerShell Filter	LDAP Filter
Country	`{c -eq 'GB'}` `{country -eq 'GB'}`	`"(c=GB)"`
City	`{l -eq 'London'}` `{City -eq 'London'}`	`"(l=London)"`
State/Province	`{st -eq 'England'}` `{state -eq 'England'}`	`"(st=England)"`
Street	`{streetaddress -like "*Downing*"}`	`"(streetAddress=*Downing*)"`
PO Box	`{postOfficeBox -like "*10*"}`	`"(postOfficeBox=*10*)"`
Postal Code (zip code)	`{postalcode -like "L10*"}`	`"(postalCode=L10*)"`
Office	`{physicalDeliveryOfficeName -like "Downing*"}`	`"(physicalDeliveryOfficeName=Downing*)"`
Company	`{company -eq 'International Rescue'}`	`"(company=International Rescue)"`
Department	`{department -like "*Downing*"}`	`"(department=Downing*)"`
Job title	`{Title -eq 'Prime Minister'}`	`"(Title=Prime Minister)"`

You might want to combine these filters if you have multiple locations—for instance, to filter on city and state, use the following:

```
Get-ADUser -Filter {st -eq 'England' -and l -eq 'York'}
Get-ADUser -LDAPFilter "(&(st=England)(l=York))"
```

> **TIP** If you're not sure of the property name, use a GUI tool to set the value and then use the Attribute Editor to find it.

Searching for the direct reports of a manager is an interesting task. Active Directory stores the DistinguishedName of the manager in the manager attribute. You have to first find the manager:

```
$managerdn = (Get-ADUser -Identity awelles).DistinguishedName
```

The manager's DistinguishedName is then used in the search:

```
Get-ADUser -Filter {manager -eq $managerdn}
Get-ADUser -LDAPFilter "(manager=$managerdn)"
```

There are a few other attributes on which you may need to search for users.

A.4.3 Miscellaneous search attributes

In theory, you can search on any attribute in Active Directory, but the value of a search lies in the results that help you solve your immediate problem. Logon scripts and when a user account was modified are the two most common examples.

LOGON SCRIPTS

Logon scripts sometimes cause problems. Can you discover which users are using a particular logon script?

```
Get-ADUser -LDAPFilter "(scriptPath=mylogon.vbs)"
Get-ADUser -Filter {scriptPath -eq 'mylogon.vbs'}
```

Either search will give a list of users who have `mylogon.vbs` set as a logon script. This search is useful if you need to change logon scripts for a set of users (you can pipe the search results into `Set-ADUser`), or if you're tracking down logon problems as described in chapter 19.

USER ACCOUNT MODIFIED DATE

The modification date for an account can tell you if a recent change could be at the root of a problem. Assume that you want the changes after the following:

```
$date = ([datetime]"12 September 2013")
Get-ADUser -Filter {whenchanged -gt $date}
```

Using an LDAP filter is a bit more complicated because you have to present the time as generalized UTC. This means changing 12 September 2013 into 20130912000000.0Z:

```
$test = ([datetime]"12 September 2013").ToString("yyyyMMddHHmmss")+ ".0Z"
Get-ADUser -LDAPFilter "(whenchanged>=$test)"
```

> ### Generalized UTC
> There are a number of ways you can represent a date and time; for example
> 10 October 2013 5:30 p.m.
> 10/10/13 5:30 p.m.
> 10/10/2013 17:30
> Generalized UTC is just another way of representing a date and time that takes this form:
> ```
> YYYYMMDDHHmm[. |, fraction][SS][(+ | -)HHMM)|Z]
> ```
> YY = four-digit year
> MM = two-digit month
> DD = two-digit day
> HH = two-digit hours
> mm = two-digit minutes
> SS = two-digits seconds
> [. |, fraction] = fraction of a second

(continued)

+ | – = plus or negative offset for time zone given in hours and minutes (two digits each)

z = coordinated UTC (GMT)

So our earlier example would become `20131010173000.0Z` if GMT, or `20131010173000.0-5000` if you wanted the same time in EST.

That concludes your tour of the options for searching for users. Searching for groups is much simpler.

A.5   Searching for groups

The only searches for groups that you're likely to perform will be by name. The filters are shown in table A.6. Use these filters with `Get-ADGroup`.

Table A.6   Filters for searching for groups by name

Search Requirement	PowerShell Filter	LDAP Filter
Full name	`{Name -eq 'ADLgroup6'}`	`"(Name=ADLgroup6)"`
samAccountName	`{samAccountName -eq 'ADLgroup6'}`	`"(samAccountName=ADLgroup6)"`
Partial samAccountName	`{samAccountName -like 'ADLgroup*'}`	`"(samAccountName=ADLgroup*)"`
Description	`{Description -like 'ADL*'}`	`"(Description=*ADL*)"`

The other important aspect of groups is their membership. The members of a group can be displayed as follows:

```
Get-ADGroup -LDAPFilter "(samAccountName=ADLgroup6)" | Get-ADGroupMember
```

Computers are the final type of object for which you'd commonly search.

A.6   Searching for computers

Computer searches are also simple compared to those for users. The common search types and the related filters are shown in table A.7. Use these filters with `Get-ADComputer`.

Table A.7   Filters for searching for computers

Search Requirement	PowerShell Filter	LDAP Filter
Full name	`{Name -eq 'Win8'}`	`"(Name=Win8)"`
Partial name	`{Name -like 'Win*'}`	`"(Name=Win*)"`

Table A.7 **Filters for searching for computers** *(continued)*

Search Requirement	PowerShell Filter	LDAP Filter
samAccountName	`{samAccountName -eq 'Win8$'}`	`"(samAccountName=Win8$)"`
Description	`{Description -like '*AD Lunches*'}`	`"(Description=*AD Lunches*)"`
Operating system	`{OperatingSystem -like '*Windows*2012*'}`	`"(OperatingSystem=*Windows*2012*)"`

A.7 Other miscellaneous searches

I don't think there's anything else of interest in the AD computer object for searching purposes. IP addresses are held, but you have to know the exact address to search for. It's easier to perform a DNS search as shown in chapter 15.

It's possible to use LDAP-style filters in searches performed using the GUI tools.

A.8 Searching with the GUI tools

You can use the GUI tools for searching Active Directory, but I don't think it's as efficient as other approaches, which is why I've left this section to the end of the appendix. Both ADAC and ADUC can be used to search Active Directory.

USING ACTIVE DIRECTORY ADMINISTRATIVE CENTER

A search in ADAC is initiated by clicking the `Global Search` option in the List view pane, which opens the dialog shown in figure A.1.

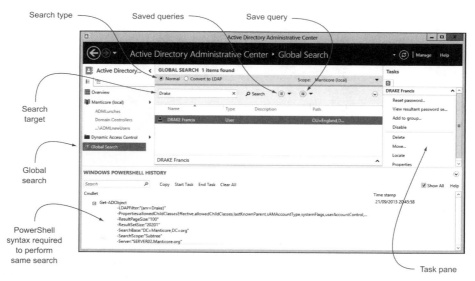

Figure A.1 **Searching in ADAC. The target can be expressed as a name or LDAP filter. Searches can be saved and reused. The search scope can span the whole domain or specified OUs.**

The search-type buttons can be used to search on a name as shown in figure A.1, or the `Convert to LDAP` button can be used to change to using LDAP query syntax. If you type a name into the dialog before converting, the entry is converted to an LDAP query. Queries can be saved using the `Save` button. Saved queries can be accessed for reuse or modification.

TIP   If you create a complex LDAP query, make sure you save it before closing down ADAC.

Click Search to interrogate Active Directory when you've finalized your query. The results are shown in the pane below your query (highlighted in figure A.1). The tasks you can perform on the object are shown in the Task pane.

One of the most useful features of ADAC in Windows Server 2012 is that it exposes the PowerShell commands that ADAC uses in the background. These are shown in the Windows PowerShell History pane at the bottom of ADAC. The syntax can be copied to the clipboard for pasting into your scripts.

USING ACTIVE DIRECTORY USERS AND COMPUTERS

The ADUC tool also has a search facility that's accessed by right-clicking the domain name and choosing Find. The search dialog is shown in figure A.2.

You enter the name you want to search for and click the Find Now button. The results are shown in the Search Results pane at the bottom of the dialog. Notice the Find and In drop-drown menus. The default search is for users or groups across the whole domain. These options can be changed by using the drop-down menus.

LDAP queries are also available. Choose Custom Search in the Find drop-down menu. Click the Advanced tab and you'll discover a box to enter an LDAP query.

Figure A.2 Searching in ADUC by partial name. Use the Find drop-down menu to switch to Custom Search and use the Advanced tab to switch to an LDAP filter. The search scope can be domain or specific OUs.

appendix B
Migrations and upgrades

The fact that AD objects have a finite lifecycle has been a recurring theme throughout the book. It shouldn't come as a surprise to you that your Active Directory has a lifecycle. When an Active Directory doesn't meet your requirements, there are two things you can do:

- Migrate to a new AD structure
- Upgrade the existing AD

These topics could fill a book in their own right. This appendix is designed to give you an overview of the issues involved in migrations and upgrades.

> **TIP** Any migration or upgrade activity should be taken as an opportunity to clean up your Active Directory. Get rid of the old accounts, empty groups, and anything else you don't need. It takes time upfront, but your job will be easier in the long run.

Let's look at migrations first.

B.1 Migrations

There are a number of reasons why an Active Directory may no longer be required, including

- Your company has merged with or been acquired by another company. Your Active Directory needs to be migrated into the other company's Active Directory.
- The existing Active Directory was designed a number of years ago and doesn't meet the business needs. You may migrate to a new structure in the existing forest or you may migrate into a completely new forest.
- The Active Directory has been so badly managed that it has unrepairable problems. In this case the best thing to do is to migrate to a new Active

Directory that's designed and administered according to best practice. I've seen this in practice and it's not a nice project.

In any migration project involving cross-domain migration, you'll need a trust in place between the two domains—usually a two-way trust. If you can't get permission to set up the trust between the domains, the migration techniques discussed below won't work and you'll have to create new accounts for all of the users and other objects.

There's the separate but closely related scenario where the fabric of your Active Directory is good but the OU structure no longer meets your needs. You need to reorganize the OUs and their contents. This is the easiest scenario to deal with, so let's start there.

B.1.1 Modifying the OU structure

In this scenario you keep your domains, forests, and AD topology. You're moving AD data objects (users, groups, and computers) between OUs. This has the lowest risk and lowest impact of any of the migration scenarios. You saw how to move individual objects between OUs in chapter 7.

Moving the whole contents of an OU to another OU can be accomplished as shown in the following listing.

Listing B.1   Moving the contents of an OU

```
Get-ADObject -Filter {objectclass -eq 'user'}  `
-SearchBase "ou=ADMLusers,ou=ADMLunches,dc=manticore,dc=org" |      ❶ Get objects
foreach {
Set-ADObject -Identity $($_.distinguishedname) `
-ProtectedFromAccidentalDeletion:$false
                                                                    ❷ Unprotect objects
Move-ADObject -Identity $($_.distinguishedname) `
-TargetPath "ou=ADMLnewUsers,ou=ADMLunches,dc=manticore,dc=org" `
-Verbose
}                                                                   ❸ Move objects

Get-ADObject -Filter {objectclass -eq 'user'} `
-SearchBase "ou=ADMLnewUsers,ou=ADMLunches,dc=manticore,dc=org" |
Set-ADObject  -ProtectedFromAccidentalDeletion:$true
                                                                    ❹ Protect objects
```

Start by getting the objects contained in the OU ❶. I've assumed you want all users, so a simple filter is used. You can modify the filter using the information in appendix A. A very strong recommendation throughout the book has been to use protection from accidental deletion. Assuming you've followed that recommendation, the next step is to remove that protection—temporarily ❷. If you don't remove the protection, you won't be able to complete the move, so it's wise to include that step if you're not sure of the settings on your objects.

The object can now be moved to the target OU ❸. I've used the -Verbose parameter so that you get some feedback on the move.

The final step is to reapply the protection so that your objects can't be accidentally deleted ❹. In my experience, this setting more than pays for the time you spend modifying. You only need one "oops" moment when you've realized you've just deleted the wrong object to understand.

You can move objects between OUs as quickly or as slowly as you need. The moves can happen during business hours, but I recommend doing them out of hours so that there are no complications due to clashing GPOs applied to the source and target OUs. You did remember to rework the GPOs, didn't you?

The other migration scenarios can be grouped together under the scenario of moving to a new domain.

B.1.2 Moving users to a new domain

You have two choices when a user has to move between domains:

- Create a new account for the user
- Move the user account

The same two choices exist for other objects like groups and computers. The choice is often out of your control; for instance, I've been involved in a number of migrations where I was responsible for the target domain but wasn't allowed any access to the source domain. This meant I couldn't perform a migration and the users got brand-new accounts and groups.

NOTE You can migrate groups in exactly the same manner. Section B.1.2 applies equally well to both groups and users.

In some respects, creating new accounts is the easier option.

CREATING NEW ACCOUNTS

Chapter 2 showed you how to create user accounts. You can use that information to create new accounts in bulk before your users are active in the new domain. You need information from the source domain administrators:

- Name—Full name including first and last name.
- Group membership—Presumably you'll recreate a similar set of groups for the users.

You'll have to bring together a set of information for each user:

- Specific membership requirements in existing groups
- Logon scripts
- Phone and address information
- Organization information like job title and manager
- Whether the password needs to be replicated to one or more RODCs
- GPOs to be applied

Once you have this information, you can create the new accounts.

TIP Leave the accounts disabled until the users actually need them.

In this and any other migration activity, expect the list of users being migrated to change frequently. Deleting accounts for users who suddenly won't be migrating is a quick operation. Using the automation skills you've learned will enable you to deal with the sudden influx of new users who were discovered toward the end of a project. It always happens. Believe me, and be prepared.

MOVING ACCOUNTS

Moving accounts between domains is more complicated. The main issue you need to consider is whether the old identity of the account needs to be preserved. Under the covers, a lot of AD functionality is based on the security identifier (SID) of the object. If the user or group needs access to data or applications in the old domain, you need to preserve the SID. Luckily, AD objects have an attribute called SIDHistory that can be used to store the previous SIDs applied to the object.

When you migrate an object between domains, you are in reality creating a new object in the target domain. This will have a new SID assigned by the domain controller that creates the object. Your migration technique must append the SID the object carries in the source domain to the SID history attribute of the new object. Active Directory will check both the SID and the SID history when determining if an object is authorized to access a resource.

If the user accounts are in the same forest, you could use Move-ADObject to move the object to the new domain. In addition to the data seen earlier, you need to supply a domain controller in the new domain and a credential that has permissions to create objects in the new domain.

The alternative is to use a migration tool—either a commercial tool, or the free but less-featured AD Migration Tool (ADMT) from Microsoft. This tool will migrate the accounts for you and perform other actions such as applying permissions for the new forest to data held on computers.

As of the time of writing, ADMT doesn't support Windows Server 2012. Details of a work-around using Windows Server 2008 R2 can be found at http://support.microsoft .com/kb/2753560/en-us?wa=wsignin1.0.

Users and groups aren't the only objects involved in a migration. You have to consider the computers.

B.1.3 Moving computers between domains

In the ideal case, the users moving into your domain get brand-new machines and you don't have to worry about migrating their workstation computers. Unfortunately, many migration projects don't have the budget to follow this route, which means you have to migrate the machines.

You could remove the computer from the old domain and add it into the new domain, but your user will lose their settings on the machine and permissions to access any data on that machine. You need to follow this process:

1 Migrate the users and groups.
2 Modify network settings on the workstation, especially the DNS servers, so the machine can find the new domain.

3 Use ADMT or another tool to reapply permissions to the machine.

4 Remove the machine from the old domain.

5 Add the machine to the new domain.

ADMT (or your migration tool of choice) will examine all of the files on the machine and determine who has permissions to those files. It'll look for the matching user or group in the new domain based on the SID history. Assuming it can track down the new user account, it'll apply the same permissions to the new account that the old account had.

The tools will then take the machine out of the old domain and add it into the new domain. A restart is involved at each stage.

> **TIP** I've seen frequent failures when migration tools attempt to add the computer into the new domain. Be prepared for the failure and the need to perform the action manually. Remember that the `Add-Computer` cmdlet in PowerShell 2.0 and later can be used to join a computer to the domain.

Many configuration settings are applied to workstations via GPOs. It's possible to clone GPOs into the new domain as part of your migration process.

B.1.4 Moving GPOs between domains

You don't migrate the GPOs directly. The process involves these steps:

1 Back up the GPO in the source domain.

2 Restore the GPO in the target domain.

3 Link the restored GPO to the appropriate OUs.

4 Test.

This process enables you to migrate GPO settings, but in most cases I think you're better off recreating the necessary GPOs and settings rather than attempting a migration. If you recreate, it's easier to understand what settings are being applied and how they interact with preexisting GPOs.

The final piece in the migration jigsaw is your data.

B.1.5 Moving data between domains

The number one responsibility of all IT administrators is protecting your organization's data. This is even more important in a migration scenario because you have to ensure that

- The data is migrated and nothing is lost.
- The users who should access the data can continue to do so.
- The users who shouldn't access the data can't suddenly gain access to it .

Data can be broken down into two main groups: unstructured and structured.

UNSTRUCTURED DATA

Unstructured data is held on your file servers. It's the Word documents and Excel spreadsheets that your users create and store. Access to this type of data is based on share and file permissions. These need to be modified to enable the users to continue accessing the data post-migration.

The same technique you applied when moving the user's computers (see section B.1.3) can be applied to your file servers. Be prepared for this process to take a long time. I recommend running the re-permissioning overnight or over a weekend. You may need to break the file system into chunks to make the process more manageable. The file server and data is moved into the new domain and your users can access their data.

If you can't apply this technique, you'll need to copy the data to a new server in your domain and then manually apply permissions. This process is much more error-prone, so expect a period with lots of calls along the lines of "I can't access …."

STRUCTURED DATA

Structured data is the data held in your applications:

- Databases
- Email systems
- Collaboration systems

Migrating this data can be very difficult if you don't have a migration tool to perform the task. The time saved on migrating this type of data often justifies the cost of the tool.

In the worst-case scenario you'll need to unload the data from the application in the source domain, copy it to the new domain, and load it into a new instance of the application. This is a time-consuming process that your users will find frustrating because a period of settling in will be required before everything is working to everyone's satisfaction.

A related topic is performing an AD upgrade. This has less impact on your users but still involves a lot of work for you.

B.2   Upgrades

Upgrading your Active Directory refers to changing the version of Windows on your domain controllers. New AD functionality is only introduced with new Windows versions; for instance, the AD Recycle Bin was introduced in Windows Server 2008 R2. It isn't available in early versions of Windows but is still available in later versions such as Windows Server 2012 R2.

Why would you want to upgrade? There are two main reasons for upgrading your Active Directory:

- The version of Windows you're using on your domain controllers won't be supported by Microsoft much longer. Windows versions have an approximate 10-year lifecycle. I strongly recommend that you don't wait until the last minute to upgrade.
- Your organization wants to use the new functionality in Active Directory and needs to upgrade the domain controllers to access the functionality. Applications that interact with Active Directory, such as Exchange, may also drive the need for an upgrade.

TIP Performing a number of test upgrades in a lab environment is strongly recommended before making changes to your production Active Directory.

An AD upgrade consists of these high-level steps:

- Upgrade the AD schema.
- Upgrade first domain controller.
- Upgrade subsequent domain controllers.
- Decommission old domain controllers.
- Raise forest and domain levels.
- Install new AD functionality.

This raises a frequently asked question: do you actually upgrade a domain controller, or do you rebuild the domain controller with the new version of Windows?

My preference is to rebuild. If you upgrade an existing domain controller, you keep the accumulated baggage on the server including any misconfigurations, old files that have been dumped on the machine, and old software information. In a virtualized environment it's very easy to create a new machine, so the rebuild option becomes even more attractive.

At the time of writing, Windows Server 2003 is approaching the end of its support lifecycle. Many organizations will need to upgrade their Active Directories in the next few years.

The first step is upgrading the schema.

B.2.1 Upgrade the AD schema

Upgrading or modifying the AD schema fills a lot of administrators with dread. The reason for this is that it's a one-way street. Once you've upgraded, you can't go back. There are a number of actions you can take to minimize the risk. Please notice I said "minimize" the risk. Any change in a production environment carries a risk of issues arising that adversely impact the environment. It's your job to minimize that risk.

Windows Server 2012 R2 schema issue

If you introduce a Windows Server 2012 R2 server into your domain and install the Active Directory, you'll receive an error when you attempt to retrieve all properties of a user:

```
Get-Aduser -Identity richard -Properties *
This option appears to be broken in Windows 2012 R2 / PowerShell 4
PS C:\Windows\system32> Get-ADUser -Identity richard -Properties *
Get-ADUser : One or more properties are invalid.
Parameter name: msDS-AssignedAuthNPolicy
At line:1 char:1
+ Get-ADUser -Identity richard -Properties *
+ ~~~~~~~~~~~~~~~~~~~~~~~~~~~~~~~~~~~~~~~~~~~~
```

(continued)

```
    + CategoryInfo : InvalidArgument: (richard:ADUser) [Get-ADUser],
ArgumentException
    + FullyQualifiedErrorId :
ActiveDirectoryCmdlet:System.ArgumentException,Microsoft.ActiveDirectory
.Management.Commands.GetADUser
```

The problem is that the cmdlets are looking for specific attributes that are introduced in the Windows Server 2012 R2 schema. If they aren't found, an error is generated. The short-term workaround is to adopt this approach:

```
Get-ADUser -Identity richard| Get-ADObject -Properties *
```

The long-term fix is to upgrade the schema to Windows Server 2012 R2-level. You can do this without changing the domain controllers.

Alternatively, keep performing your administration on Windows Server 2012 machines.

PERFORM TESTS

Have you upgraded a schema before? When was the last time you performed this action? Have you performed an upgrade to the version you propose to use?

Most administrators don't perform a schema upgrade very often. The most effective thing you can do is perform test migrations in a lab environment. Create a test domain and upgrade the schema. Perform the action several times to ensure you're comfortable with the action. Use virtual machines so that you can destroy them at the end of the testing cycle.

MANUAL SCHEMA UPGRADE

Windows Server 2012 changed the way schema upgrades are performed. In previous versions you had to manually upgrade the schema before creating the first domain controller with the new Windows version. Now the schema upgrade is part of the domain controller promotion—unless, of course, you prefer to do it manually or you want to test the process:

1 Make sure the account you're using is a member of the Enterprise Admins and Schema Admins groups.
2 Mount the media containing the new version of Windows.
3 Navigate to D:\support\adprep (assuming the media is available on the D: drive).
4 Run `adprep/forestprep`. This needs to be run once in the forest. It must be run on the schema operations master for the forest.
5 When that has completed, run `adprep/domainprep`. This needs to be run once in each domain on the infrastructure master for the domain.
6 Run `adprep/domainprep/gpprep` (this modifies GPO permissions to support Resultant Set of Policies modelling) on the infrastructure master in each domain. This isn't required if you ran this for an early version of Windows.

7 Run `adprep/rodcprep` on any computer in the domain if you want RODCs in that domain. You don't need to run this if you ran it for earlier versions of Windows.

You can use the code in the following listing to test the version of your schema before and after an upgrade.

Listing B.2   Testing the schema version

```
$sch =
➥ [System.DirectoryServices.ActiveDirectory.ActiveDirectorySchema]
➥ ::GetCurrentSchema()                                          ← Get schema
$de = $sch.GetDirectoryEntry()                                    ❶ version
switch ($de.ObjectVersion)        ←❷ Test schema version
{
  13{"{0,25} " -f "Schema Version $($de.ObjectVersion) = Windows 2000"
     break}
  30{"{0,25} " -f "Schema Version $($de.ObjectVersion) = Windows 2003"
     break}
  31{"{0,25} " -f "Schema Version $($de.ObjectVersion) = Windows 2003 R2"
     break}
  44{"{0,25} " -f "Schema Version $($de.ObjectVersion) = Windows 2008"
     break}
  47{"{0,25} " -f "Schema Version $($de.ObjectVersion) = Windows 2008 R2"
     break}
  56{"{0,25} " -f "Schema Version $($de.ObjectVersion) = Windows 2012"
     break}
  69{"{0,25} " -f "Schema Version $($de.ObjectVersion) = Windows 2012 R2"
     break}
  default{"{0,25} {1,2} " -f "Unknown Schema Version",         ←
     $($de.ObjectVersion)                                       ❸ Report error
     break}
}
```

Use the .NET class to get the current schema ❶. Use the `ObjectVersion` property in a `switch` statement to test the possible values ❷. When a match is found, the correct Windows version is returned. If you don't match with any of the options, you drop through to the default option that prints the version it found ❸.

TIP If you get a version number returned that lies between two of the options, it probably means you're running a beta or preview version. This isn't a good place to be, and I recommend you upgrade to a supported version.

UPGRADE FIRST DOMAIN CONTROLLER
You've upgraded the schema, so you need to install the first domain controller with the new version of Windows. My recommendation is that you create a new domain controller on the principle that if something goes wrong, you still have your original domain controllers and your users won't be adversely affected.

The steps needed here were covered in chapter 11, so I'm only giving you a quick recap:

1 Create a virtual machine or prepare hardware if using a physical server.
2 Install Windows.

3   Configure the server including server name and networking.

4   Join to the domain.

5   Install AD Directory Services.

6   Promote to the domain controller.

Once the promotion has occurred, you need to wait for replication to complete before your new domain controller is completely ready for use. Once you have the first domain controller built, I recommend leaving a little time (a day or so) before upgrading the subsequent domain controllers.

UPGRADE SUBSEQUENT DOMAIN CONTROLLERS

This is the tedious part of the process—working through your domain controllers to replace them with machines running the new operating system. There are a few things to remember at this stage:

- Don't take a domain controller down during the day when users are authenticated and logged on. Either perform the work out of hours, or take the machine down overnight so it won't authenticate users.
- Ensure there's always at least one domain controller in every AD site that should have a domain controller.
- Ensure that users can always access a global catalog server because their email will stop working if you don't! That will definitely make the help-desk phones ring.
- Transfer the FSMO roles before working on a domain controller that holds any of the roles.

My preference is always to create new domain controllers and decommission the old ones. In my experience, it minimizes the disruption to the users and means the bulk of the work can be performed during normal business hours.

DECOMMISSION OLD DOMAIN CONTROLLERS

Once you have your new domain controllers built, it's time to decommission the old ones. The cleanest way to decommission a domain controller is to

- Demote the domain controller
- Remove the machine from the domain
- Destroy the virtual machine or dispose of (or possibly reuse) the hardware if it's a physical machine

Remember to ensure that the FSMO roles have been transferred before decommissioning a domain controller that holds one—you'll be prompted otherwise. Also, ensure you're not trying to remove the last global catalog. You'll be prompted about that as well.

If something goes wrong with the demotion, you can delete the computer account for the domain controller, which will also delete the domain controller-specific data from the Active Directory. You had to perform a special cleanup in older versions of Windows—progress is a wonderful thing.

With the old domain controllers gone, you're ready to raise the forest and domain levels.

RAISE FOREST AND DOMAIN LEVELS

The forest and domain levels cause a lot of confusion. These levels control two things:

- The version of Windows you can use on domain controllers
- The functionality available in Active Directory

Raising the forest and domain levels is another action that's one-way—it can't be reversed. For instance, once you've raised the domain level to Windows Server 2012, you can't have any domain controllers that are built with Windows Server 2008.

> **TIP** You can roll back from Windows Server 2012 or Windows Server 2008 R2 to Windows Server 2008 R2 or Windows Server 2008. No other rollbacks are possible.

The extra functionality available with your new version of Windows is ready to install.

INSTALL NEW AD FUNCTIONALITY

Some new AD functionality comes preinstalled. The AD Administrative Center was installed as part of the promotion process. Fine-grained password policies automatically became available when you raised the domain level.

The AD Recycle Bin is the first of a new wave of functionality that has to be installed. The installation process was covered in chapter 13, but to quickly recap you use

```
Enable-ADOptionalFeature 'Recycle Bin Feature' `
-Scope ForestOrConfigurationSet                 `
-Target 'manticore.org' -Server server02
```

The `Target` is your domain. Once you've installed the AD Recycle Bin, you can't uninstall it because it changes the way deletions work, as detailed in chapter 13.

At this stage, you've completed the upgrade and you can sit back and enjoy playing with the new features—until it's time for the next upgrade.

index